D1527651

THE HUMAN ANIMAL

THE HUMAN ANIMAL

by Weston La Barre

THE UNIVERSITY OF CHICAGO PRESS

CHICAGO AND LONDON

THE UNIVERSITY OF CHICAGO PRESS, CHICAGO 60637

The University of Chicago Press, Ltd., London W.C. 1

To MY WIFE, MY SONS, and MY DAUGHTER,
who taught me these things

Harrow the house of the dead; look shining at

New styles of architecture, a change of heart.   w. h. AUDEN

The present edition has changed a few minor wordings in the text, but no major argument. In two important matters (race as adaptive and the old Anaxagoras-Aristotle argument) on which my views have somewhat shifted focus, I have left the text unchanged, and in readily identifiable paragraphs in the appendix I have criticized my own earlier opinions from the viewpoint of new evidence. I think no one who values scientific reasoning either makes or expects an apology for such a change of mind.

Introduction

Western culture is a strange paradox. For thousands of years we have proclaimed our primary or even exclusive allegiance to the spiritual world. But somehow, in the meantime, in spite of this protested loyalty —whether backsliding, offhanded, unwitting, absent-minded, or perverse—we have historically created the most unusual and complex material culture the world has ever seen! This result is hardly to be expected from our pretensions and suggests that we have had some confusion about our nature and our motivations, for we have surely shown less confusion about the nature of the physical world. At the same time, we have not been very clear about the nature of the realities we call "spiritual."

A good deal of this confusion comes from the use of traditional concepts, which, when we look at them more critically, we can now see are inadequate. Modern man is coming to realize that there is only one integrated, unified *kind* of world, not two. But this is not all. We are sometimes deeply *motivated* to be confused about our human nature.

That is, there are some aspects of man's nature which we have reasons for choosing not to know. In the current and chronic human predicament, man has as many psychological blind spots and wilful misapprehensions about himself as does any patient of a psychiatrist. And for much the same reason: we, like the patient, are afraid of what we are. We wish to maintain other pretenses and to preserve certain delusions about ourselves, not to look at unwelcome facts; and we have our own peculiarly human reasons for all this, as we will see later.

But almost in spite of ourselves the facts about man have been steadily accumulating. Paleontology—the study of ancient life from its fossil remains—has given us a clear picture not only of the biological history behind man but also of the main outlines of his immediate ancestry. Physical anthropology, which used to be a dreary and sterile bone-measuring science, too often used to argue the "superiority" of one race over another, has now become a genuine "human biology." And biology itself, transformed by a century of growing insights into organic evolution, has given us a better sense of man's basic nature and of his place in the larger natural order.

The social sciences have also grown in knowledge. Sociology, soundly based on the essentially social nature of man, has learned so much as to be a large group of specialties in itself. Cultural anthropology—the study of the socially inherited behavior patterns of men in different societies—has collected such a mass of information about the various ways in which man can be human that the professional student can barely specialize in one continent alone. Archeology, the main tool in the study of prehistory, now tells us not only the relative sequences of stratification but also, with the Carbon 14 technique, even something like absolute dating in time. Comparative linguistics has advanced its claim to being the most exact of the social sciences; and anyone who knows recent work will admit that it has made a good case. Psychology, and especially clinical psychology, has sharpened our understanding of man's behavior; while the more one learns of modern dynamic psychiatry, the more respect for it increases as one of the most subtle, precise, and profound disciplines of the human mind. Indeed—and I think rightly so—few of the newer generation of social anthropologists consider themselves fully equipped to get the best out of field work unless they have some knowledge of clinical psychology and analytic psychiatry. This is only one of the many signs that students of the social sciences are increasingly aware that they have much to learn from one another.

Both in theory and in practice the social sciences are moving steadily in the direction of co-operation and integration. For example, sociologists and anthropologists now borrow each other's insights and techniques with the same abandon as college roommates borrow each other's shirts and neckties. In fact it is hard to tell the difference between them to an interested person, beyond stating weakly, and not at all accurately, that anthropologists study primitive peoples and sociologists civilized ones. Cultural anthropologists are admittedly partly historians, and modern historians are intentionally students of cultural history. Applied anthropology and political science merge skills in administering our Pacific island dependencies. Government cannot get along without the economist. Jurisprudence and the law look into analytic psychiatry for insights, only to discover that the social caseworker has preceded them there. In fact, the modern child-guidance clinic is a team made up of the social worker, the psychiatrist, and the psychologist. The projective techniques of the clinical psychologist are among the best diagnostic tools of modern psychiatry, and of course the field anthropologist has long since borrowed them for research purposes. It is as if we had cut up the subject of man like a meat pie. But as all the specialists start from a common center, when each of them learns more of his own terrain, then all the social scientists begin to realize that the whole is a large circle and not a small triangular wedge—and that there are solid meat, hot potatoes, and gravy in all the slices.

The whole trend of twentieth-century science is plainly toward integration, a fact indicated in the very names of new disciplines: psychosomatic medicine, biochemistry, psychobiology, and the like. The integrative movement in the social sciences derives further significance from this state of affairs. Our knowledge of the parts has now reached a stage when we can begin to seek a "holistic" understanding of larger wholes. Possessing now an anatomy of our various subjects, so to speak, we can begin to see the functioning physiology and relationships of these structures. Science, too, is discovering that there is only "one world."

Probably the best example of this holistic naturalism is found in mathematical physics. By looking at the nature both of stars and of atoms and by an effort of superb intellectual synthesizing, Einstein has sought to encompass them both within one consistent system, expressed in a mere handful of equations. In philosophy—partly derived from modern mathematics but almost equally inspired by the biological concept of the organism—we have Whitehead's impressive and deep-rooted holism, which sees all reality as a system of functional relationships. In psychiatry the commonest criticism of Freud has been that he was far too biological in his psychology. In psychology itself, the older elementistic behaviorism (which, in ignoring consciousness, left out the central fact of psychology) is gone, and modern learning theory is in fact highly concerned with psychic motivation; Gestalt psychology, a sophisticated and contemporary system philosophically, is thoroughly holistic in its very essence. In biology the interest in the ecological approach is giving us a larger sense of the complex relationships of organisms and environments. Perhaps because of the nature of their subject matter, biologists are inescapably driven to a larger organismic view of life; and among biologists, none is more holistic *ab ovo*, so to speak, than Edwin Grant Conklin. W. B. Cannon's pan-systemic physiology and Sir Charles Sherrington's integrative neurology make sense to both psychologists and psychiatrists—and, indeed, the psychosomatic physician applies these same total-organism views to the practice of medicine.

Anthropology, too, is working in this direction. Curiously enough, however, it is one of its greatest scientific successes which has heretofore impeded its progress: the discovery that the physical "racial" differences among men have nothing to do with the specific cultural differences among them. Racial traits are genetically inherited; cultural traits are socially inherited. Since these vary independently, physical anthropologists can study this intricate animal biologically—but they do it mostly without any reference to its most significant and conspicuous animal adaptation, culture! Likewise, some anthropologists (I think mistakenly) believe that their subject matter is solely that *abstraction from human behavior,* culture, and not properly the study of man in all his aspects; and some of them, the "culturologists," have even seriously suggested that we ought to study culture as if human beings had never existed! Nevertheless, as we will see, it is impossible for the biology and the sociology of man to remain forever isolated from each other.

In thus maintaining the unnatural dichotomy between the physical and the "spiritual" attributes of man, anthropology seems largely to have escaped the widespread integrative trend of modern science. It is in an unusual and atypical position in thus housing the ghost of the old body-mind "problem," an animism not yet exorcised from our science. Nevertheless, it is quite plain that physical anthropologists and cultural anthropologists have much of crucial significance to say to each other. Part of the problem is the sheer bulk of the specialized knowledge that keeps them apart. But another part of the problem is that we have been operating with ancient concepts, deeply though often imperceptibly imbedded in our thinking, that we would judge archaic if we were fully aware of them. We still suffer from the old definition of man as half reprobate ape and half apprentice angel, made up partly of opprobrious and regrettable material body and partly of intrinsically perfect "spirit." This definition sees pretty well to it that never the twain shall meet, even conceptually, much less socially.

Many thoughtful anthropologists are beginning to see that it is a mistake to proceed as if the works of the mind had nothing to do with the needs of the body, and as if the structure of man's body had nothing to do with the way his mind works culturally to secure his satisfactions. Anthropologists now see that we have been so successful in establishing the relativity of cultures as to risk throwing out the baby with the bath: the universal similarities of all mankind. Understandably, then, there is now a strong movement back to the search for essential human nature. It is here that the necessary collaboration of the physical and the cultural anthropologist is most significant and fruitful. For man is an animal *with peculiar biological traits as a species* which make him human. Man's *significantly human traits* are possessed indifferently by all the races of men. Of course it remains true that whatever is universally possessed physically by man can never be used to explain cultural variations. But all human beings have a culture of some sort, and cultures are possessed by human beings alone. The possession of cultures uniquely and universally by *Homo sapiens* must therefore be understandable in terms of those biological traits which all groups of mankind jointly share. This does not mean, of course, that any culture can be "reduced" to biology—the more especially since racial differences have nothing to do with cultural differences—but it does mean that the generic fact of culture ultimately rests upon biological traits of the species *Homo sapiens*. *Man's "human nature" derives from the kind of body he has.* This can be discussed in terms of matter-of-fact, concrete, verifiable, and tough-minded propositions, without special pleading, and without abandoning a consistent naturalism.

Some of these concepts are unfamiliar to most people, and a few of them are a bit technical—but there is hardly any subject matter that is more rewarding to understand than man himself. We have tried to translate the specialists' discoveries into something that makes integrated sense to the thoughtful reader. If he is sometimes surprised about what he discovers concerning this strange and wonderful animal, well, that is the risk that every explorer must take. In any case, this book is an attempt to relate for the intelligent reader what we now know about these matters. It views man, quite simply, as a biological species, with the essential characteristics of his behavior, including social behavior, as growing out of his biological uniqueness. It views man genetically, as the contemporary result of a very long and complex chain of multiple and diverse evolutionary changes. This evolutionary process can be seen as one requiring an enormous and wasteful variety of experiments in order to develop increasingly successful adaptations to the changing evironment—the environment in the case of man including his social and political, as well as biological, adaptations. The view of man's animal past, therefore, carries profound implications for *culture as man's ecology*, that is, the adaptations to his peculiar total environment which significantly includes his fellow-man.

This book tries to take a consistently naturalistic view of man, uniting the biological discoveries of physical anthropology with the ethnological discoveries of cultural anthropology. I shall attempt to do this, in addition, in terms consistent with the findings of the most sophisticated and practical psychology available in contemporary times, the psychoanalytical psychology of Freud. The peculiar availability of analytic psychology for this purpose is based on the fact that, alone among psychologies, it has taken seriously the human body as a place to live in, as it has been alone in taking seriously the symbolic *content* and *purpose* of thought. Psychoanalysis is also peculiar among psychologies in rigorously keeping its attention, despite alarmed and apprehensive outcries, on the proper data of psychology: whole, functioning human beings in real contexts. It has neither statistically dismembered the human person, created artificial "experimental" milieus, nor regressed defeated and dismayed to a frankly animal psychology or disguised neurophysiology. It is true that the classical theory of Freud is in some ways "culture-bound"; but this conveniently correct criticism has too often been exploited to rationalize turning our backs on a psychology that has sometimes disenchanting things to say about man.

In order to give a proper biological background for the understanding of man, the first chapter is devoted to a rapid survey of the evolutionary facts pertinent to man's basic organic prehistory. Next, attention is focused on the group of animals, the Primates, to which man belongs, after which, still more sharply, on the man-like apes, the anthropoids. The physical uniquenesses and specializations of man are then discussed, in particular his fateful two-footedness and the biologically unprecedented consequences of human handedness. Primate and human physiological and social peculiarities and the origins of fatherhood are next discussed—necessarily in connection with specialized human motherhood and the biological "infantilization" of human infants. A comparative study of sexual and marital arrangements shows next how widely tribal customs can vary culturally within the limits of the same human biology; and immediately following this the physical variations in man, and their significance, are similarly shown as they operate within the same biological limits that are universal to man. With these racial variations now described, we next see them in the biological context of man's odd kind of evolution "backwards." An investigation of speech—the fundamental symbolic system and uniquely human cultural trait—then introduces a description of human psychosexuality, the consequences of this sexuality in various cultural institutions, and its other consequences in the possibility and the fact of mental illness among humans. The next chapter is an illustrative object lesson taken from man's basic ethnography—that is, culture traits so ancient as to have diffused universally, or nearly so, among all groups of men, those traits that have arisen so immediately from his human situation as to constitute universally human ways of perceiving the world. This chapter on man's earliest cultural beliefs also shows how and why and to what an extravagant degree this symbol-using animal can make disastrously wrong analyses of reality and of himself. The final chapter seeks to point out the significance for man's future of the many inferences we can draw from his biology and history.

To experts my scientific obligations will be plain: to Edward Sapir, linguist, ethnologist, and founder of the modern psychologically oriented studies of culture; to Franz Weidenreich, human paleontologist and physical anthropologist; to Julian Huxley, biologist and humanist; to the Yerkes, husband and wife, primatologists; and to Géza Róheim, psychoanalyst and ethnologist, from whose polemic and provocative writings I have learned a great deal. But the greatest debt I know by far is to the work and to the writings of Sigmund Freud, Karl Abraham, Ernest Jones, and Sandor Ferenczi.

Each of the specialists—biologist, primatologist, physical anthropologist, linguist, and psychiatrist—whose scientific territory a cultural anthropologist has ventured to invade, may feel that at some points I have given less than the irreducible minimum of attention to facts in their sciences to give any proper picture of man. But perhaps they will indulge me when they see that my aim has been to be selective of the significant rather than exhaustive, and synthesizing rather than minutely analytical—precisely so I might be able to show that no proper picture of man is possible without including *at least these data* from each of these scientists' special fields.

More personal debts I owe to generous colleagues who read the manuscript, often without agreeing with interpretations, though helping me to avoid errors in fact: Melville and Frances Herskovits, Carl and Erminie Voegelin, Sherwood Washburn, George Devereux, and Géza Róheim. In many instances all these persons have earnestly sought to correct my errors. If errors remain, the fault is not theirs but mine, that I have persisted in them.

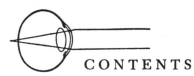

CONTENTS

1. From Amoebas to Mammals

Living organisms are different from machines. The difference, however, is not easy to puzzle out—mainly because there is so much of the
orderly machine in the very living organisms we study. Also, the careful
biologist tries to avoid any mystical or wishful imputation to organisms
of qualities which cannot be demonstrated or observed. For the biologist is himself an organism, and as an objective scientist he does not
want his preferences or his hopes to become mixed up with his data.
Every investigator must look into the possibility of error inherent in the
instruments he uses to assess reality; here the instrument introducing
possible bias is the investigator himself.

And yet, ultimately, the difference between organisms and machines
can be stated only in terms of that which organisms alone manifest in
themselves: living organisms have *purposes*. Immediately it will perhaps be objected that machines have "purposes" too: a machine is for
typewriting, for printing a book, for conveying a writer out to a cabin
in the woods where he hopes to write a book. But the "purposes" of

machines are purposes in a different sense: they are really the purposes *of the organisms* (men) that built the machines and that built *their* purposes into the machines. Machines are incomplete images or copies of men, not men of machines. "Man" is the larger system and includes machines.

A machine is thus only a pseudo-organism in terms of purposes, a mere thing that so far as we know is always the product of the organism man. Man's purposes are merely imported into and translated into the machine, which otherwise has no purposes *for itself*. Furthermore, if breakdown in any way deflects the machine from its purpose, the machine is powerless to repair itself or to reconstitute its functioning again. But within wide limits the organism can so reconstitute itself and can, moreover, create or reproduce others of its own kind. An organism, then, once established as an organism, has its own internal economy which it proposes stubbornly to preserve and which indeed it is largely able to preserve. Thus we can say that only an organism has its own internal purposes which belong to it intrinsically and that a machine, so far as we know, is merely an extension of the specific pur-pose of organisms, men.

As organisms we know immediately that we have purposes, will, motivations, and wants. But this is not the whole picture: an organism is not the whole of reality. There is something outside the organism, something non-organic with respect to the organism's purposes—offer-ing, to be sure, the basis for the gratification of its needs, but evidently indifferent or obdurate, outside the organism, and not automatically yielding to its will. Thus we have in our basic biological picture two things. There is some kind of "outside" reality, with its own rules and laws which are not necessarily the organism's choices in the matter. And there are organisms, which are part of this reality and which must therefore obey all its rules and laws but which, as organisms, differ from inorganic reality in having purposes—purposes that so far as we can discern end with the boundaries of the organisms. (Put in another way: it was the first organism which first brought the concepts of "inside" and "outside" into the universe.) So stated, these two prin-ciples may be unsatisfying to some people, who seek to find the pur-poses inside organisms somehow comfortably duplicated outside them as well. But the biologist's purpose is not to cosset but to understand organisms; his principles are at least minimal and tough-minded.

Certainly the biologist can never deal with organisms alone, but only with organisms in environments. An organism without an environment is not merely inconceivable, it is impossible. There can be no "inside" unless there is also an "outside": an organism not in its special dynamic relationship with the rest of reality would not be living, but dead—hence not an organism and hence part of the inorganic universe. For though organisms are "insides," they remain nevertheless within the universe. Organisms are not self-sufficient, closed systems: they can maintain their functioning only as open systems within a larger reality, the energies of which they appropriate and exploit for their purposes.

Matter can evidently exist without manifest purpose. But purpose or will or "spirit" does not exist to our knowledge without matter. Therefore, matter is logically prior to life and is the more all-inclusive concept or system. Likewise, the only wills or purposes we know are those of material organisms; and we must therefore assume, if we are not to make fantasies contrary to the evidence, that purpose first entered the material universe with the first organism. Whether the whole of reality is an organism or a machine (or neither) is a larger metaphysical question into which the biologist need not enter, focusing his attention as he does on organisms and on environments—which are only *part*-aspects, as we shall see, of total reality.

The biologist, then, has two concepts: matter and life (which is a special phase or state of matter). He studies both living organism and material environment, environment being particular aspects of total material reality but both, organism and environment, being wholly material entities. All scientists assume that there is an external reality: a reality to be known and a reality that may be known, but the existence of which does not depend upon the scientist's or any other organism's knowing of it. An organism knows reality only to the extent that it can effectively respond to reality and achieve its purposes through it; but the whole of reality is obviously more than any organism's knowledge of it. An organism's "knowledge" is its environment. An organism, so to speak, only knows what it needs to know, or perhaps more correctly only needs what it knows to need—needs being purposes. In this sense, evolution is life learning about matter (or, what amounts to the same thing, matter learning purposes). And in so far as an organism is a "machine," it is a self-constituted machine or one constituted by another or others of its kind. But it is a machine with its own internal purposes and knowledge of the external world added, since purposes are feckless and meaningless without knowledge. This means that an organism can manifest and exemplify mechanical principles in itself, at the same time that it is more than a machine. These are really quite simple concepts—inside and outside, purpose and matter—but much follows from them.

Consequently, we may view evolution as the gradual unfoldment and increase of organisms' purposes. The evolution of species is a series of successive plant or animal inventions for new purposes, or living matter's progressive discoveries of the physical and chemical properties of matter. An organism is a machine for living purposes, "living" being defined for each kind of organism as the collection of specific things it can do (or knows what to do) with matter. Thus plants illustrate the chemical discovery of chlorophyll and the organic invention of means to achieve the "photosynthesis" of carbohydrates by the use of chlorophyll, water, air, and sunlight. By these means, plants achieve the appropriation into an organism of energies that are nonorganic in origin (the atomic transformation of the sun's substance)—the first and perhaps the greatest invention of living matter.

At this stage, plants now have an environment, but their own existence already further modifies this. The new organic aspect of reality, plant life, is soon "discovered" by emergent animals, which learn to appropriate for themselves these energies already organically prepared for them by other living beings: animals are predatory upon plants, and soon indeed upon other animals. It is possible that animals are ultimately life's response to the astronomical fact of night and day on the earth. Plants are primarily anabolic (energy-synthesizing) by day and catabolic (energy-expending) by night. The animal gives up the plant's daytime anabolism and adopts its night-time catabolism all around the clock; it is no very great step for the erstwhile "plant" to change from living on its own photosynthetic capital to stealing that of other individual plants. The "plant" that eats the food created by, stored up in—and constituted by!—another plant is already (with one exception to be mentioned presently) a full-blown animal. Such an organism does not change its food but only the economics of obtaining it: it stops making it and begins taking it. In fact, there still exist some organisms that are ambiguously plant-animals, both photosynthetic (food-making) and predatory (food-taking) by turns.

But single-celled organisms are limited by inexorable physical laws. They may never grow beyond a very small size. The reason for this is a matter of geometry: the cytoplasm or cell contents and their physiological necessities increase as the *cube*, whereas the food-obtaining and waste-discharging surface of the cell increases only as the square of the diameter of the organism. Hence the enlarging cell would starve itself to death, so to speak, or poison itself with its own waste products. Of course the cell could stop obtaining food and diet its way back to its earlier small size—but then, throughout eons, our single cell would surely fall victim to some vicissitude of its environment, die without progeny, and the whole evolutionary game be over before it began.

The only mechanical solution to the problem of the enlarging cell is division by fission, which restores an economically high ratio of surface to volume. Thus reproduction by fission in protozoans (single-celled organisms) is the inevitable result of nutritional necessity. Successful nutrition requires the cell to reproduce itself in order to save its life, with the ultimate result that it tends to save the life of the species too. That is, the living cell which divides itself into many other dispersed and independent units of the same kind has a much greater chance of surviving in one or more of its successive twins than has our hypothetical single cell merely maintaining the status quo.

Hence *growth* and *increase* early become characteristics of successful living matter. For reproduction by cell division alone is meaningless except in terms of nutrition and survival. All that has happened "genetically" so far is merely the habit of having progeny. That is, the heredity of all the successively twinning cells is identical with that of the original cell, and nothing new has been added genetically. Then if two separate strains of protozoans should each happen to achieve by mutation one new and valuable trait, each valuable trait would be lost to the other strain, since there is no way of combining them if reproduction is by fission alone.

This combination of new traits is possible only by the *fusion* of two separate heredities. The first step in this direction is conservative and incomplete: two of the barely visible, slipper-shaped protozoans called *Paramecium*, after reproducing for an indefinite time by simple fission, will suddenly lie close to each other in conjugation and trade parts of their nuclear hereditary material back and forth, after which they separate and go about their business of reproduction by fission again. They never actually fuse into one cell, but merely trade hereditary goods. Only by the fusion of two parent-cells can an offspring cell enjoy the advantages of joint heredity and pass on the traits of *both* ancestries.

This process of fusion as opposed to fission of cells, curiously, has its aspect of nutrition also. In some single-celled organisms, the line between nutritional (food-obtaining) ingestion and sexual (gene-obtaining) fusion is ambiguously thin: thus in the fertilization of *Trichonympha*, a symbiotic protozoan of roaches, the female cell or gamete to all intents and purposes "eats" the male gamete. (The invasion and expropriation of a cell's cytoplasm by viruses—naked gene-like material in search of cytoplasm—is a suggestively related phenomenon which occurs, some researchers think, in the instance of cancer.) The great possibilities of this new sexuality are evident in another single-celled organism, *Paramecium aurelia*, which has eight different "sexes"; *Chlamydomonas* has ten sexes, five "male" and five "female," all reacting with varying degrees of intensity to their opposite sexes.

The food economy of animals, as a departure from the plant method, entails other important consequences. Needing only carbon dioxide from the air, water, and sunlight for photosynthesis, plants can be and mostly are sedentary or at least passive to the movements of water and wind and animal-carriers. But with predatory, fully animal ("holozoic") nutrition, animals are obliged to develop *locomotion*. Environmentally, plants are in a sense more "autonomous," depending as they do only upon ever present or very common things like water and air and sunlight; but animals have a more precarious dependency upon *finding* the scarcer substances, plant and animal food. Plants find what they want where they are, but animals mostly move about in order to *encounter* what they need. The simpler plants, in this sense, respond to or "know" aspects of physics and chemistry only, but animals need also to become the first botanists and zoölogists, so to speak.

Given the basic animal postulate, then—an economy predatory upon plants and other animals—the first necessary corollary of this is locomotion or self-directed movement. It is true, of course, that some plants (the "exception" mentioned a few paragraphs back), the saprophytes —"rot-plants" like fungi and bacteria—also became predatory upon animals and other plants. Like animals, saprophytes also gave up photosynthesis and lack chlorophyll. But these largely simplified, degenerate parasites depend on fantastically lavish reproduction for survival and on the movement of body fluids in their hosts, rather than on developed locomotion. For this reason we cannot very well say that the significant thing about animals is predatory nutrition alone—for animals share this with saprophytic plants—but rather locomotion as well. In animals, locomotion in the service of the new mode of nutrition meant that the organism inevitably had a much greater contact with varied environments and a relation to them which was necessarily active rather than passive. In the long biological perspective, the development of such food-seeking locomotion must be viewed as the foundation of the greater intelligence—richer awareness of the environment and ability to take more aspects of it into account and to respond to them—that animals have as opposed to plants.

The single-celled protozoan animal (for from now on we shall be dealing primarily with the animal ancestors of man) has, however, further severe limitations. The size of one cell, even when enriched by the double heredity of fusion, is stringently limited by surface-volume ratios; hence the internal complexity of the cell and the variety of things it can do are also limited, if only because there is a sheer mathematical limit to the number and kinds of chemical molecules that can be contained within one cell. It is true that a glance at the Ciliata (Infusoria) alone would indicate that the possibilities within these limitations are enormous, even so. But these are largely varieties of

7

structure, and none of the protozoans *do* anything drastically new or different.

The engineering problem barring further evolutionary change is this: the need for greater size (for number and variety of molecules), but with size basically limited in protozoans (by surface-volume ratios). The protozoan predicament was solved by the invention of a *society of cells,* the many-celled metazoan, which in a sense is the first moral invention of living matter. Some protozoan cells, in dividing and redividing, evidently found that there were advantages in sticking together. For example, in a sphere of associated cells like *Volvox globator* there is more economical locomotion; *Volvox* also has the earliest of cell specializations, that of some into male and female cells, with the rest of the body cells developing by fission alone. This metazoan has its cake and eats it too, for it has the advantages of body-cell fission and germ-cell fusion alike.

In *Hydra* additional advantages were reaped through a minor change in body plan. Instead of the hollow sphere of *Volvox globator,* *Hydra* has a sack-like shape with specialized tentacles or arms surrounding this opening to direct food into it. Thus *Hydra* has a mouth and an internal food-gathering cavity, in addition to the germ / body-cell specialization already found in *Volvox.*

Without any question, all the incalculable complexities and advantages of later kinds of life derive from the enormously greater scope afforded by this scheme of a commonwealth of cells. The multicellular organism can *do* more things than a single-celled one. Not that every given cell can do everything the metazoan organism does, for size still limits variety of functions in one cell. But metazoan cells can *specialize,* some doing one thing, others another, and the total organism enjoys all the benefits of the specialized activities of its component cells. The job of becoming any kind of cell whatsoever, the job of remaining the source for the specialization of cells (that is, reproduction sexually of a whole new individual metazoan animal), is handed over to the germ cells, while somatic or body cells branch out into all the specializations of the metazoan organism. Thus it is that the evolutionary prehistory of any species can be clearly read in terms of what body cells specialize out of what others during the embryological development of the new individual.

But body cells in the fully developed organism can reproduce only other cells of their own kind, and the price of specialization is the loss of this "totipotentiality" of the germ cells. That is, the more specialized body cells become, the more they lose the germ cells' ability to reproduce the whole animal. This is a small enough matter so far as the species is concerned, so long as the germ cells can reproduce new individuals of that species, but it is often a critical matter to the individual animal. Cut up a starfish, and some parts may produce new individuals. Cut, less drastically, an earthworm in halves, and each half may produce a new individual by somatic-cell division alone. A lizard may lose most of its tail and still regenerate a new one; but the loss of even one mammalian finger means that it is gone forever. Similarly, the undamaged neighboring cells in a cut or burned finger can reproduce enough of their kind to fill the gap; but highly specialized nerve cells have very limited ability to regenerate or to repair. (The logic of these facts, incidentally, suggests that the most precious and most irreplaceable group of cells, since the most specialized within a larger whole, is the individual human being.)

For death, properly speaking, enters the world with metazoans. A single protozoan cell, it is true, can suffer destruction, but its "sister"- or "daughter"-cells—which are itself, genetically speaking—live on theoretically forever. But when metazoan cells become so specialized in the organization of the whole that they cannot live independently if anything happens to a part, then the disorganization of the whole is ultimately fatal for all its parts.

Among metazoans, flatworms already realize a structural corollary of the animal organic postulates: given a nutritional interest in the *organic* environment (which animals and saprophytes have), given the possibility of structural specialization in the massive sense (metazoans), but given also locomotion in the molar whole-metazoan-body sense as well (animals alone)—then the animal will have a front and a rear, as it moves through its environment. Logically, then, the greater awareness of the environment will necessarily tend to be localized in the front part, which first meets the new environment—and our metazoan has a head. Thus flatworms have heads and tails where *Volvox* is only a globe.

But success brings new problems. With food taken care of, a problem arises about waste products. With increasing size, metazoans can no longer rely on excretion of waste products through the surface of the body, for a majority of cells may be interior and not on the surface of the body. Thus flatworms have devised a simple multiplication of interior "surfaces," a system of tubes to drain the interior of the animal, like canals in a swamp. This is a good enough makeshift for the liquid end-products of the animal's metabolism; but what about the solid parts of foodstuffs that are not digested and never become part of the organism?

The sack-like *Hydra,* it will be remembered, had a mouth and an inclosed food-cavity—but this mouth had to double as an anus. After eating, Hydra merely threw up the undigested solid particles of food through the same opening through which food had come in. The crinoids did hardly much better. Crinoids had an anus in the middle of the food-collecting grooves. That this plan of organization is extremely poor architecturally is indicated in the later development of the animal. The anal pyramid rose higher and higher above the food-collecting arms, to attempt a separation—with the result that it could shower waste material all over the food-groove area and not merely over the inner portions, as formerly. (Organisms, the first "knowers" around, and evidently on their evolutionary own, have to get their knowledge in experimental hit-or-miss fashion. Compare the poor arrangement of the trilobites, among the earliest joint-legged creatures to have eyes: the stomach was poorly located in the middle of the head, so that the larger the stomach, the smaller the brain; increasingly incompetent and a prey to fishes with much better architecture, the trilobites are long since extinct.) In roundworms the innovation of an anus distant from the mouth was made; and for the first time a complete alimentary tube permitted the advantage of continuous feeding, successive and discriminated stages in the process of digestion, and a one-way traffic for food.

At this point in evolution, animals are increasing in size, but they still have to get around for their food. Among protozoans there were three methods of locomotion, but methods increasingly archaic for metazoans: by means of flagella (long whip-like lashes), cilia (tiny surface threads that beat like oars, in undulations like a field of wheat), or by means of the flow of actual body contents into protruded pseudopodia ("false feet"), as in amoeba. But as metazoans increased in bulk and weight, the relative surfaces on which flagella and cilia could operate correspondingly decreased. The third method—the amoeba's protean flowing—can be done by one cell but hardly by a group of cells each with its own cell wall, and it is impossible in animals large enough to need body-stiffening structures for support. In a fashion better suited to their size, some free-living flatworms can move by muscular contractions and old-fashioned cilia combined. But roundworms can *crawl* by massive body movements on the sea floor, a new method of locomotion, though one limited to two dimensions.

Lancelets, however—for example *Amphioxus,* a primitive chordate or gristle-stemmed animal without skull, brain, heart, jaws, or true fins —soon rediscovered the third dimension by the invention of a new type of free swimming. This was accomplished by a side-to-side undulation, which remained throughout evolution the most efficient means of aquatic progression until man himself invented the screw propellor—even the advanced mammals, like whales and dolphins, which returned much later to the sea, use this method first invented by lancelets. Lancelets were able to do this by means of an elastic but firm gristly interior rod, the notochord. The logic of the notochord arises from just this to-and-fro undulation. The now more highly developed and paired antagonistic swimming muscles have to have something solid to pull themselves against (and to which the whole animal is attached), lest they cancel out each other's action.

In the lancelet the anus is also shifted forward, and the entire rear of the animal is committed to swimming muscle. In doing this, lancelets had invented not only the beginnings of a backbone but also a full-fledged tail. The gain over the roundworms in food-obtaining ability was of course considerable; for, whereas the roundworms had to content themselves with whatever fell to the ocean floor, lancelets could go after food anywhere in the water. To this extent lancelets are a more efficient model for a food-gathering mechanism than roundworms—and if (as is obviously desirable) our metazoan is to increase in size, food-gathering efficiency is certainly an advantage. Thus swimming chordates in the sea, with their gristly interior support, can manage to be much larger than any roundworm or flatworm, both because of this support and because they can obtain food more easily. Thus chordates, like the basking shark, ultimately grew to sea-monster size.

Since all living things by definition have irritability and response, the beginnings of specialized nerve cells are obscure and arguable. Not arguable, however, is the fact that the enlarging metazoan needs interior communication and co-ordination of parts. In any case, coelenterates (gut-possessing animals like *Hydra*) have the first nervous *systems*. One of the most interesting early nervous systems is found in the starfish. Here there is a simple ring of nerve cells around the central mouth, with branching nerves into each arm. Since the starfish, physically, can crawl in any direction, it is clear that this nervous system avoids an anarchy of arms when food is available, lest he starve to death like Burian's ass. The mouth-ring tells the muscles, so to speak, where to go and get the food. This general arm-and-mouth pattern is a basic and familiar one: *Amoeba* embracing food with momentary pseudopodal arms and engulfing it through a makeshift mouth; *Paramecium,* with busily lashing cilia sloshing food particles down an oral groove; and *Hydra,* which is scarcely more, structurally, than arms filling a gut through a mouth. The mouth is one of the very earliest inventions, critically necessary for animals as opposed to plants; and its biologically regnant position in the center of nerves and arms is thus early signalized.

The enlarging metazoan has another problem in addition to nutrition, locomotion, excretion, and nervous co-ordination of parts: that of circulation. When specialized interior cells lose a functional relationship to the surface, just as wastes must be carried off in nephritic (proto-kidney) drains, so also must food material be carried to them. In the possession of a circulatory *system,* specialized for this purpose, the segmented worms have made an advance over the flatworms and the roundworms. It is such circulatory systems, as much as anything, which permit increase in metazoan size and further specialization in parts.

But the mobile organism also requires *protection* from the hazards of the environment, especially when predatory vegetarians become predatory carnivores and when the variety and numbers of animal-eating animals increase. Some animals, the mollusks, regressed to a state which was sessile (or able to move with difficulty, but largely sedentary) in the adult, achieving the easy protection of shells before the battle with the environment wrought any further specialized adaptations. The price of protection was the loss of adult locomotion, a high one in terms of future evolution. Shelled mollusks lacked varied problems and contact with the outside world. A larger biological view than the selective one we have taken here must take this into account. The emphasis in the present biological section has been upon the *cumulative* adaptations of lines *ancestral* to man, of whose animal improvisations he is the heir. Of course the multiple adaptations of later animals do not mean that earlier adaptations, or adaptations alternative to man's direct ancestors', have not survived. The adaptation of the oyster is still good enough for its purposes. But the difference remains that man has more *purposes* than an oyster. The shelled mollusk never experiences a great enough variety of things to develop either advanced intelligence or radically new body structures. In fact, unquestionably the most intelligent of the mollusks are the shell-less squid and octopus, which gave up the shells of the early cephalopods and developed protections alternative to shells. The octopus has, instead, the double camouflage of changeable protective skin coloration and a smokescreen of ink to cover its retreat, besides having a better eye to inspect its environment than other mollusks have.

This ancient engineering problem of living things—protection versus speed and mobility—is one that still vexes naval architects and aeronautical and space-ship engineers. In their wrestling with the problem, animals developed further adaptations which had enormous later consequences. Some of the ostracoderm ("potsherd-skin") fish preserved mobility-with-protection by a kind of dreadnought armor plate: they are armored with bony plates all over the skin. The shark, on the other hand, has its external armor reduced to tiny denticles, so that whatever nipped at a shark had the inside of its mouth bitten by the shark's skin-teeth. The armored ostracoderm is the battleship; but the shark, like the destroyer, sacrifices armor for speed. The squid, like the shark, has also chosen speed over protection: with its internal cuttlebone support (similar in function to the shark's cartilage), the squid moves much faster than the shelled mollusks. But the octopus' changeable protective coloration, ink-screen, and superior eye, together with the jet-propelled means of escape in its funnel or siphon, are all *defensive* adaptations only, and the beak of an octopus is not to be compared as an offensive weapon with the mouth of a shark.

When chordates began to get as big as sharks, the older type of mouth, suitable for eating only soft or very small objects, became more and more inefficient. The older mouth had been largely a sucking organ, although in some cases it could be protruded or could grasp feebly. Some of the ostracoderms had slightly movable bony plates in the region of the mouth, but these were of very limited value. Arthrodires, fish whose bony armor was jointed at the neck for this purpose, had to bite by moving the whole upper part of the head against a rigid base— and more strangely still, the "teeth" of the arthrodire were actually projections of dense bone, so that uniquely among animals they actually bit with the jawbone itself. On the other hand, some of the segmented worms, the sea centipedes (Eunicidae), had a kind of jaw, but no real teeth. Efficient *seizing and chewing*, however, are the first and necessary steps in transforming the flesh of one large metazoan animal into that of another. That this problem is real is shown by the fact that an entirely separate line of animals—insects, spiders, and crustaceans— actually turned *legs* into jaws.

It was shark-like creatures which made the two major improvements on the old animal mouth—the benefits and significance of which continue to echo down to the days of the most modern primates. The "spiny-form" fish (Acanthodii) were the first gnathostomes, or "jaw-mouthed," animals as such. But jaws without teeth (Arthrodira, Eunicidae) are hardly better than teeth without jaws (ostracoderms). Sharks stumbled upon the idea of teeth, and in an odd way. We have seen how the sharks reduced the old body armor into defensive denticles, like a file in effect, on the skin. Some of these, on the "lip" of the gristly gill-arch, developed into a formidable offensive weapon, and thus sharks were the first animals to have both a hinged jaw and true teeth. Admittedly, the shark has only gristle, and no bone, in its jaw— but just the same the shark's mouth is efficient enough for its purposes!

But ostracoderms and sharks were by no means the last word in marine engineering. In both armor and swimming support the more modern bony fish made a better technical compromise than either the bone-plated ostracoderms or the skin-denticled, gristle-spined sharks. Fish devised a more discriminating protection of important parts (the skull), the purely secondary defense of scales, and the further development of the old chordate swimming support into a limy and hard but jointed system—the *internal skeleton*. Considering the variety of fish alone—and ignoring the whole great evolutionary structure built upon it—this invention of the internal skeleton was evidently an unqualified engineering triumph. Among later descendant forms, the fifteen thousand kinds of fish are rivaled in variety and number only by the birds.

No animal knows the evolutionary future. But the enormous advantages of an internal "endoskeleton" over an outside "exoskeleton" can be seen by humans through an evolutionary hindsight after the fact. The ostracoderms have all disappeared, though the modern cowfish in its bony box somewhat resembles them; and the shark family is limited in variety of forms. True, the mollusks solved the problem of growth within a hard case, and in a number of ingenious ways: simple expanding cones with flat doors, volcano-shaped or single hump-backed shells, sometimes even jointed back-shells as in the chiton clinging to the tidal rocks on Bermuda beaches, spirals of increasing bore-diameter, bivalves with the lips of the two shells added to for inclosing more space and the hinge-joint increasing its angle, the chambered nautilus forever moving into a larger living-room—and so on. But the evolution of mollusks into sixty thousand species was never more than alternative geometrical solutions to their immediate predicament of growth. For admirers of form, mollusk shells rival diatoms; but, like them, their variety consists only in varying formal solutions to the same set problem.

The significance of the skeleton, in fact, can be well brought out by comparing it as a structural solution with the different solutions to the body-support problem that other later animals made. Already, in the sea, the "joint-legged" arthropods made a brilliant invention of a light-weight body-support material, chitin, which has been called the first plastic. The more than six hundred thousand species of insects alone within the arthropod group surely serve to indicate the very great possibilities of this new model for living-machines. The chitin-armored arthropods—with gills protected from drying out by chitin shields—and walking on chitin-tube legs, were as a matter of fact the first animals of all to emerge onto the dry land. But the same serious problems in having an exoskeleton remain in their construction as had plagued echinoderms, mollusks, and even some of the chordates. That is to say, crabs and insects alike must still expensively discard the hard outside exoskeleton like an outgrown piece of clothing, in order to increase in size, being meanwhile unprotected until a new covering can be grown. Nor, on land, can they afford to have their size and weight render them shapeless before growing a new skeletal covering; thus water-supported arthropods like crabs and lobsters can grow larger than any land insect or spider—which makes the fantastic fears of some imaginative writers about man-size insects preposterous. And when aerial flight is added into the equation of engineering requirements, it can readily be seen that the insect has a number of problems of weight, materials, body size, and nutrition to juggle.

The structural impasse on insect size lies, in addition to its chitin exoskeleton, in its respiratory system as well. This consists of tubes into the body communicating with the outside air—as feckless a method of respiration as the old body tubes of the ancient flatworms were for excretion. The diameter of any insect therefore runs up against the laws of the diffusibility of gases; and consequently no insect's body can ever be much larger than a man's fist, so long as it is saddled with its archaic respiratory methods. And since all insects are too small to afford a large specialized central nervous system, no insect can ever compete in intelligence with large mammals, though remaining a great nuisance to them.

As might be expected—could any animal so far have viewed the evolutionary past behind it—the answer lay in specialization, centralization, and systematization of the function. This had happened many times with the more efficient systems invented earlier: the *nutritional* system (the animal mouth and central gut of *Hydra*, the roundworm anus, and the chordate food-storing liver—in place of the every-man-for-himself in the cells of the colonial Protozoa); the *locomotor* system (the change from the diffuse cilia of *Paramecium* to the molar body movements and associated specializations of the worms); a *body-support system* (the notochord of the lancelets and the jointed skeleton of fishes); the *excretory* system (the change from the random tubes of the flatworms to the proto-kidney in each body division of the segmented worms, and from this to a still more efficient aggregation of these "nephridia" into a single pair of kidneys in the backboned animals); the *circulatory* system (the dorsal-ventral blood-vessel plan of the segmented worms); and the *nervous* system (the nerve nets of coelenterates like *Hydra*, in place of the diffuse irritability of *Amoeba* and the lack of nerve communication in *Volvox*). The same general principle of specializing and centralizing a function into a *system* still needed to be applied to respiration.

It was a more tentative emergent from the water, therefore, much later than the arthropod insects, upon whom the future of large land animals rested. Of course the mollusks, sharks, and fish all had gill systems which were efficient and centralized means of obtaining oxygen in the water, but these were not adapted for sub-aerial dry-land existence. As is often the case, another problem provided a means for the solution. Some of the bony fish encountered a shortage of oxygen in the stagnant shallow waters they invaded, and they supplemented their insufficient gill-obtained oxygen by gulping air at the surface of the water. Using what was originally perhaps only a recess in the gullet with abundant blood vessels, in time they had a true air-breathing lung. This organ has survived as such in the lungfish, which can survive the drying-up of its pond by rolling up in the mud and starting to breathe, and in two survivors in modern crossopterygians. But in most other fish this lung was revamped into another organ, the swim-bladder. This is a useful pressure- or depth-sense and also a ballast organ for adjusting the specific gravity of the fish by secretion and resorption of gases from the blood—much as a submarine's ballast tanks are used—to enable the animal to rise or sink in the water without continuous muscular effort. Since these air-breathing fish could now live out of the water, some of them began aggressively crawling out of the water—probably to obtain the abundant food that land-living arthropods like the insects provided. Thus it was that land-and-water craft, the amphibians, first emerged upon the land as air-breathing animals with lung respiration. The stegocephalians (whence salamanders and frogs are derived) also reinvented legs—this time out of fish-fins and in a more economical pattern of four legs, instead of the six of insects and the eight of spiders and scorpions.

But, for all that, amphibians lived a double life and were still reproductively bound to the water. They had to return to the water to lay their eggs, and each amphibian individual had to make the same evolutionary journey from water to land that its ancestors had done, and in its own brief lifetime. Adult, land-frequenting amphibians could of course escape aquatic predators, and there were no other animals on land except the insects which were their food. Still, their damp skins required that they stay close to water or at least operate in conditions of shade and moisture—a condition which hampered them in their pursuit of insects, many of which can live in hot, sunny, and very dry situations. But, more important, amphibian eggs and their tadpole young in the water were just as vulnerable to aquatic predators as were fish-eggs and fish-fry, even though the few which survived to adult land-living might escape this. The reproductive energy required of amphibians is almost as prodigious and wasteful as that of fish.

A new-model animal, the reptile, solved the two problems of amphibians. The first of these solutions was the *shelled* reptilian egg. This invention was dependent on the successful synthesis of ureates, as a safe mode of storing nitrogenous wastes within the shell, now that wastes could not be excreted into the water from an egg laid on the dry land. Then the replacement of the moist amphibian skin by a scaly reptilian one, coupled with the new reptilian egg, not only allowed both adult and young animals a full emancipation from the water but also enabled reptiles to invade drier environments. The reptiles were now the largest and most efficient land animals, without rivals, able to follow insect prey into the hottest and driest environments. Apparent heirs of all the land, they were free to change their food from insects to large land and water plants and soon even to become carnivorous, as the variety of reptiles proliferated. Some reptiles (Ichthyosaurs, "fish-lizards") reinvaded the sea, and others (Pterodactyls) even learned to fly.

However, cold-blooded reptiles were the helpless victims of temperature changes. The importance of this fact is evident when it is remembered that the specific heat (amount needed to raise the temperature 1°) of the mixed gases in air is much less than the specific heat of a liquid like water. You can burn your finger badly on the hot gas two inches above a lighted match, but it takes many more calories of heat to bring a pot of water to boil. Thus specific heat was no great problem for water animals. Temperature changes in vast bodies of water are slow, and minimal at that; but even daily—and, much more, seasonal—changes in the air above the land are relatively enormous. For this reason, no reptilian species has ever invaded a really cold polar environment, and many reptiles did not survive the Pleistocene Ice Age. Indeed, hibernation in winter (much as some mollusks "estivate" or become dormant when shallow waters become too hot for them) is the only alternative of such reptiles like snakes as have invaded regions of marked seasonal fluctuations of temperature. However, the shelled reptilian egg did necessitate internal fertilization, and courtship introduced a newer inter-individual process with great importance for future selection and variability.

Two offshoots of the reptiles—birds and mammals—created warm-bloodedness in the world, as both had to if they were to be active in winter or in cold climates. As a consequence, both mammals and birds can range from tropical to polar climates with their own internally maintained temperature control. Still, reptiles did break through the carnivorous vertebrate tradition of fish and amphibians; and among the reptiles the great variability of the dinosaurs is a result. However, temperature changes which were very considerable ultimately came in geological time. Many reptilian species could not meet these new environmental changes, which also drastically modified their plant and animal foodstuffs, and they became extinct. Other reptiles disappeared from some regions which they have never reinvaded—like the snakes of the island of Ireland, long before St. Patrick!

While birds escaped many of their land enemies through flight, the bird egg represents no great change from the reptilian egg. "Reproductively," the advance birds made was a *social* one, that of greater post-natal care of their young than reptiles have—and one based perhaps on the heightened inter-individual associations incidental to courtship and breeding behavior in birds. It is interesting, too, that the first original mammalian invention was not in new reproductive technique but rather the new inter-individual one of *nutrition.* Thus we find mammalian suckling of the young in the duck-billed platypus and the spiny echidna, which still lay eggs in reptilian or bird fashion.

The marsupials improved on this in having a protective pouch, within which the fetal live-born young could be nourished through teats. Modern mammals made a still greater stride. They not only retained the egg within the body after fertilization, dispensing with a shell, but also nourished the growth of the fetus for a longer period by means of the placenta—a kind of temporary "endoparasitism" of the young upon the female inside her body. The earliest-known placental mammals are found in the Cretaceous rocks of Mongolia; their teeth resemble those of modern insectivores, but they may have eaten a number of foods besides insects. Everything suggests that the evolution of placental mammals began in a cold climate. For one thing, the standard mammal has *hair,* comparable in insulating function to the feathers of that other warm-blooded group, the birds. For another, egg-born young must of necessity be much smaller at birth than adult animals, and hence have a dangerously high ratio of heat-radiating surface to heat-producing volume. This would have no special significance in warm climates—indeed, in the tropics, even the adults of some mammalian species are quite tiny or slender—but in the Arctic, globularity and bulk are another matter. The retention of the young within the warm maternal body until they are as large as birth size permits would be a distinct advantage for survival in the Arctic. For all these reasons, the evolution of the placenta may have taken place in an Arctic climate, which the early mammals had invaded by virtue of their warm-bloodedness.

In any case, this improved nutrition and protection in placentals together achieved an enormously greater reproductive efficiency and economy. A mammalian female need produce in her lifetime at most only dozens of offspring, to an amphibian's hundreds and a fish's thousands, in order for the species to survive. The value of these animal inventions of teat and placenta is testified to by the veritable explosion of radial evolution (further variations built upon these basic ones) in mammals during the Tertiary period. From their first faint origins in the late Triassic (some 180,000,000 years ago) the teated mammals made gradual but steady advances through the Jurassic (beginning 155,000,000 years ago) until the placenta was invented in the Cretaceous period (beginning 115,000,000 years ago), and it was on this that the spectacular flowering of mammals in the Tertiary was founded. Their double nutritional dependence—endoparasitic (placenta) and ectoparasitic alike (teats or breasts)—also illustrate another grand evolutionary theme culminating in *Homo sapiens:* the increased inter-individual dependencies of physically separate animals upon one another, a theme independently illustrated by the social insects and birds.

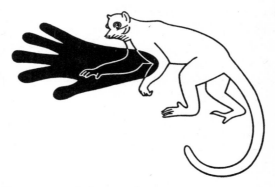

2. The Primates Take to the Trees

The mammals' addition of the placenta to the older habits of suckling and increased post-natal care of the young was an organic gain of great value. The best way to judge the "survival value" of any adaptation is, of course, to ask "Does that species in fact survive?"—or perhaps, even more precisely, "Does that adaptation itself survive?" In other words, we must note the number of adaptations that are built out radially in all directions on the basis of the original adaptation—an evolutionary process called "adaptive radiation." Another but not quite so good an index is the increase in size of the animal type throughout evolutionary time (Depéret's law), as in *Eohippus* to modern horses.

In both respects, variety and size, mammals make a creditable showing. In fact, as far as size is concerned, a mammal takes the grand prize for all animals that ever lived, barring not even the thunderously big dinosaurs—land lizards or marine monsters alike—that reigned in the time of the earliest mammals. This leviathan of animals is the great Blue Whale. More significantly, another mammal, man, has invented a new kind of non-genetic evolution or non-bodily "adaptive radiation," by which he hopelessly outclasses all other living species put together. As we shall in fact see, man has made blind bodily adaptation obsolete and unnecessary as an evolutionary technique; and within his own species he has to some degree abolished the evolutionary significance of new heredity and natural selection.

But all this was later: the future of mammals was by no means evident in the age of reptiles, when mammals first appeared. In variety and ways of life the reptiles led the evolutionary parade. In nightmarish size too the dinosaurs, well-named "terrible lizards," overwhelmed all creatures that lived or ever had lived before them. By contrast, the earliest mammals were small, furtive, obscure, and numerically rare animals. With a conservatism that reached back to the first amphibians, they were still insect-eaters. In turn, mammals were preyed upon by the frightful meat-eating lizards. In those days, the chances of the earliest mammals must have seemed very slim indeed!

But out of the nettle danger, the mammals plucked an incomparable flower of adaptation. Both their capture of agile insects as food and their necessary avoidance of being food themselves—and the mammal-hunting reptiles were sufficiently agile—alike put a premium on mammals' developing an *acuter awareness of the environment.* This meant both improvement in the senses and the ability to make neuromuscular reactions with maximal speed. All evolutionary progress heretofore, to be sure, had come from discovering and taking into consideration some new aspect of physical reality or from solving by organic invention the problems arising from an organism's new demands on life for nutrition, protection, speed, and the like. But mammals raised deliberate attentional activities to an unprecedented pitch and consequently had an intelligent awareness of the environment far beyond that of any lizard.

These functions of observing, remembering, and comparing new observations were mostly a matter of increase in size of a newer part of the central nervous system, the forebrain or association areas. The first birds had much the same enemies as the first mammals, but birds escaped danger by adaptation to flying. Flying probably puts severe weight limitations on a central nervous system in birds, or else some other limiting factor is operative. In any case, for all the vivacity and agility of birds and complex instincts rooted in the basal ganglia (old part) of their brains, mammals in general outclass birds in cerebral intelligence (of the larger, new part of the brain). Mammals as a whole, therefore, foreshadow the striking specialization on cerebral cortex which came in the primates and culminates spectacularly in man.

The value of simple nervous co-ordination is clear in its own history alone, apart from any other nervous-system adaptations—for the speed of this function has improved throughout evolutionary time. For example, mollusk mentality within a comfortably protective shell is impossibly slow by human standards. A nerve impulse in a fresh-water mollusk travels only 5/16–8/16 of an inch a second, that is, barely 94–150 feet an hour. Even in slugs, which have given their very name to slowness, a nerve impulse travels around 19 inches a second, or a little over 1 mile an hour. In king crabs a nerve impulse from brain to muscle goes at the rate of some 10 feet a second, and in frogs the rate is a respectable 70 or 80 feet a second. Human beings are out of this class entirely, even with the relative differences in size taken into account. For in ourselves the speed of nervous impulses is 400 feet a second, or over 250 miles an hour. Since the purpose of nerves is co-ordination and communication, in purely functional terms therefore a human nerve is ten thousand times as good as a mollusk's. While mollusks evidently do not need such speed in order to survive, the general survival value of nervous functioning is surely indicated in the great and continuing improvements made on it in evolutionary time.

What we have just described is a qualitative refinement in nervous tissue. But mammals have also surpassed reptiles in quantitative terms too, both relative and absolute. For example, the brain of the massive stegosaur weighed only about 70 grams, or 2½ ounces. Its "hip-brain," or the ganglia which controlled the tail and hind legs, was actually much larger than its cranial brain. By contrast, even the brain of a sheep—which is not a particularly brilliant mammal—weighs 130 grams, greater both in absolute size and even more so relatively to body size. Of mammals somewhere near the size of stegosaurs, an elephant has 5,000 grams to the stegosaur's 70, and the whale 2,050. More than that: while the stegosaur had only an ounce or so of brain per ton of body weight, the elephant has 1 pound of brain for every 500 pounds of body weight—some sixty times the ratio. Indeed, if a mouse weighed only as much as 4½ pounds and kept the same ratio of body to brain weight, then the mouse's brain would actually weigh more than the monster stegosaur's. So far as strength is concerned, nothing could stop one of the great dinosaurs when it was on its way; but while it is all very well to be able to go where you are going, the reasons for going and what is seen and understood on the way are even more important.

Much improved over reptiles (in having large brains, warm blood, the placenta, and suckling of the young), mammals did well in adaptive radiation or further variations built upon these basic patents. Porpoises and dolphins, for example, returned to a fully marine life, and among their fellow-Cetacea the whale newcomers to the sea became much larger than the marine lizards had ever been. The larger size of marine over related land animals is, interestingly, an engineering matter related to the strength of materials: the strength of a column of bone increases only as the square of the diameter, but the body weight of an animal increases as the cube. Armored dinosaurs put just about as much body weight into bone as is economically possible for endo-skeletal land animals, and are not surpassed in this even by such huge and heavy later mammals as the elephant and rhinoceros. But marine vertebrates, whether mammal or reptile, have their body weight supported distributively by water displacement, instead of having it concentrated on two or four columns of leg bone. If, therefore, whales became bigger than the biggest sea lizards, it must have been for other adaptive reasons than this simple matter of strength of materials.

Other mammals made other adaptations. The toothless Edentata were conservative: many of them remained insect-eaters, and some of them, like the armadillo, developed defensive armor. The Sirenia such as the manatee are peaceful, inconspicuous vegetarians and scarcely venture out of shallow estuaries; there are not many species in their order. On the other hand, the Ungulates, which tried out a wide variety of models of feet and toenails, are a highly successful order. Some—like the many-varietied antelopes, the giraffe, and the elegantly peris-sodactyl horse that walks on the nails of its middle fingers—relied upon speed in running for safety. Some, like the oxen group, rhinoceroses, and antelopes, developed defensive horns. Others, like the rhinoceros, elephant, and hippopotamus, relied upon great size and thick skins; the camels upon adaptation to a very dry environment; and still others, like the pig, upon equally formidable tushes and reproductivity. The Carnivora remained meat-eaters but set out for larger game than insects, some on the land (cat, dog, and bear families) and others semi-aquatic (seals and walruses). The Rodentia did well with their specialized gnawing teeth (rats, mice, squirrels, beavers, and porcupines) —in fact not a single family of rodents has become extinct since the appearance of their order in Eocene times. Moles, shrews, and hedgehogs (Insectivora) retained the eating habits of the original mammals, but their other habits were varied, some of them becoming earthdelvers. Chiroptera, bats, took up flying.

These last deserve special comment, as showing the significance of an adaptation alternative to that of birds. Bats' invention of flying was not "original" in point of evolutionary priority—for insects, pterodactyls (reptiles), and birds had separate patents on flying before them. However, it was original in method, for bats fly with their hands, but birds with their arms, and pterodactyls with their monstrously developed "little" fingers. This method of bats brought no great additional advantage, unless hanging by the thumbs can be counted one. Rather, the improvement of mammalian bats over flying insects and birds is again a *sensory* one, in this case functionally related to flight, and no mere juggling with minor structures: bats have a new space-sense. This is based on ultra-high-frequency sonar (periodic squeaks of modulated amplitude, the frequencies so high as to be mostly inaudible to us), with highly developed directional hearing to measure range and bearing of the object. Thus, while birds break their necks and wings flying into windows and insects blunder stupidly against screens and into spider webs, bats are capable of flying rapidly around a pitch-dark room as crammed with obstacles as an old attic, without ever touching anything. Bats are therefore adapted to blind nightflying. Indeed, the adaptive radiation of bats is impressive, for these sonar-equipped mammals include fruit-eaters, insect-eaters, and even fish-eaters, as well as blood-suckers. But bats have been able to compete with birds only at night and in restricted environments. The sight of birds is far superior; and in variety of food habits and habitats and in number of species the palm must go to birds, and not bats—perhaps, as we shall see, because sight is intrinsically a better sense than hearing.

No animal can know beforehand whether its new adaptation is a really first-class invention like the fish's backbone, the arthropods' chitin, the amphibian lung, the reptilian egg, and the mammalian placenta—or a relatively picayune specialization like the bat's sonar, the elephant's trunk, the rhinoceros' horn, or the saber-toothed tiger's long canines. All makes of animal and all their gadgets, so to speak, must stand grueling road tests. Only paleontological hindsight can judge the relative value of adaptations for survival.

One generalization does emerge nevertheless: Cope's "law of the survival of the unspecialized." This is another way of saying that the animals which survive are those close to the main lines of evolutionary development representing major animal improvisations. These animals enjoy the benefits of all the large-scale inventions of their evolutionary ancestors but do not make the dangerous specializations—expensive but relatively less useful—that land their less canny relatives at the end of evolutionary limbs. In biology it is the quality of the engine that counts, so to speak, and not the white-side-wall tires. And so it is that the present-day unspecialized opossum is better off than some of its specialized marsupial relatives. These rejoice in the names Diprodontidae and Dromatheriidae; but they are known only as fossils. And probably, too, the wily opossum will survive the somewhat specialized Australian kangaroos and wallabies. Such "relict" animals as the opossum are those which retain their sound primitive characteristics and seem able to stand all manner of vicissitudes in their limited environment.

Still, new evolution cannot occur unless some forms strike out anew. But who can say, in the growing tree, which twig in the crown is to become the main trunk, and which a lower branch? The culmination of specialization in the reptiles is in the limbless snakes (among reptiles that survive) or in the winged pterosaurs (among those that are extinct)—and not in the mammals, which by and large still have the four legs of the oldest amphibians. Among vertebrates, birds are the most specialized, not the mammals. The baleen whale is the most specialized mammal, and after it perhaps the vampire bat, not man. The Primates, to which order man belongs, are by no means the most specialized of the mammalian orders. Nor is man himself the most specialized of the anthropoids, in purely physical terms. Man is, relatively speaking, a "relict" animal, like the opossum among marsupials, with very high actuarial chances of surviving. The difference is, however, that man's kind of evolution proceeds apace, but the opossum has not changed much throughout geological time. This fact suggests, as indicated in a later chapter, that some kinds of specialization peculiar to some groups of men (certain non-adaptive culture traits) may not survive, but it does not mean that man as a species is finished.

The point we began with, and should always keep in mind, is that animal adaptations must serve useful purposes. But the statement that living matter's activities are meaningful reactions to reality and serve organic purposes must not be confused with a "teleological" argument. Teleological rationalizers, having rightly observed that life achieves ends, make an inference from this that "it must all have been planned that way beforehand"—which is not necessarily true at all. When living matter has immediate problems, it must solve them or die; and when it perceives desirable present ends, it seeks them. Organic evolution appears to be no more than a constant hand-to-mouth improvisation, and organisms give no appearance of knowing where they are ultimately going.

This view requires no assumption of a planning Will outside the organism and has nothing to do with a mysterious, long-range "orthogenesis." Orthogenesis supposes predestination and a whole blueprint of the future laid out beforehand from the beginning. Psychologically, it falsely imputes the purposes and plans of the microcosm (organism) to the macrocosm (environment); this may be purposeful (comforting) human rationalization, but it is quite wrong about the location of will and purpose. Biologically, orthogenesis pretends that the future problems of later species, and environmental situations and relationships which have not yet occurred, somehow directively controlled the past and control the present, in shaping organisms to remotely foreseen and planned ends.

This is nonsense and should be pointed out as such at this stage of our discussion. The first five-fingered amphibian was not planning a monkey's or a man's hand: it was trying to use fish fins to push itself out onto the land; and for good (fish) reasons these were the five fin-stiffeners it happened to have for the job. Furthermore, environments hand nothing to organisms on silver platters: it is the organisms that have the problems, not the environments. As we will see later, tender-minded teleological thinking is a fantasy about the world that has its only real grounds in the actual infantile situation of long dependency in the human animal. Orthogenesis is a viewpoint that probably could be held only by an animal that was shaped in the human kind of family; neither preying lion nor preyed-upon antelope would be so deluded.

These theories are soothing fictions (with purposes!) to deny the painful but obvious reality. Teleological views do violence to the plain facts of evolutionary history, to the tentative starts, the desperate gambles, the fatal mistakes, the blind struggling, the pitched battles, and the gallant unaided fight of life for its own existence. There is no evidence of intervention from outside, no umpire to suspend the rules when the going gets tough. Teleological views also do violence to the obviously unsentimental nature of reality. Reality is. It does not negate or reverse itself upon organic petition. Whatever reality is ultimately like, it certainly does not behave toward organisms like an anxious, uncertain, overprotective human mother; nor is it like a vengeful, angry, frightening father either.

If life be compared with a "game," the rules certainly cannot be suspended or changed, the game is "for keeps," and there is no welching on IOU's: the stake is life itself. But organic evolution appears to be a struggle of life with an impersonal adversary, neither friendly nor unfriendly, an adversary that life does not really know—but which ceases to be an adversary when life does know. For the organism has then *achieved its purposes* through knowing—adaptation to and exploitation of—stern physical necessity. All genuine knowing is tested adaptation to reality of an organism which has a purpose in knowing.

This use of the word "know" may seem inappropriate to those who would prefer to keep it exclusively for man's behavior. But this both overestimates what man does and underestimates what other organisms do. A plant root knows down from up, that water is wet, and a good deal of complex chemistry besides. Animals may not be articulate (i.e., lack language) about what they know, and they may not be able to share this knowledge with their contemporaries (i.e., lack culture), but they can pass on their adaptations genetically to their offspring. If this process is not to "know" that much of reality, never mind: perhaps some other word will have to be used to point to this behavior of all organisms. Meanwhile, it is clear, plants and animals—and men too—do not know more than their problems press them to know; indeed, organic life in general appears to discover reality or the rules of the game only piecemeal as it goes along.

We have dealt at such length with the general animal and mammalian context of man because these facts of evolution are needed to show us the nature and meaning of the human animal. A final glance at the mammals will help us further in placing man. By the late Eocene, roughly 50,000,000 years ago, the basic types of mammals had become established. Most of the surviving groups were differentiated by late Oligocene or early Miocene times (say, some 20,000,-000 years ago), which followed the Eocene. But the great days of the mammals, except for man, are evidently nowadays already in the past. Some groups, conspicuous in Oligocene and Miocene times, have long since become entirely extinct. The four ice ages of the Pleistocene (beginning 1,000,000 years ago) wiped out a number of other mammals, and man himself has exterminated and is exterminating others.

Still other mammalian groups, for all their warm-bloodedness, have retreated to the easy tropics, leaving no relicts in the arctic, subarctic, or even the cold temperate regions to make vigorous and new adaptations. Such out-of-date mammals include the tapirs, the once proud and widespread elephant family (early man himself probably aided in the extinction of the Siberian mammoth), the dwindling rhinoceros group, the ferocious but obsolescent lions (extinct in Europe and almost so in Asia)—and even man's primate cousins, the gorillas, which are rapidly becoming rare animals. Possibly in the time of man none of these animals will survive except under man's special protection or in his zoos. Bears (which are omnivorous) and bats and cetaceans (which include types with a variety of food adaptations in a number of diverse environments) all appear to have better chances of survival than have elephants and lions and gorillas. Many ungulates—cattle, sheep, pigs, and horses—will no doubt remain, as will the dog, only because of man's domestication of them.

But the most important group of mammals, on whom the future of evolution rested, have not yet been discussed: the Primates. While the other mammals were achieving horns, hooves, and thick hides, claws, flippers, wings, and fangs, and were invading desert, ocean, and air, one group of mammals, the Primates, took to the trees. Only the light-weight, yard-long *Hypsilophodon*, among all the dinosaurs, may have been tree-living; but even if it was tree-living (on this scholars disagree), its teeth show it was harmlessly vegetarian. Thus there appear to have been no carnivorous tree-living dinosaurs—so the Primates escaped all the land-living great lizards that enjoyed eating them, thanks to those marvelous plants—trees.

Primates got away from their land enemies just as effectively as birds did, but they paid a much cheaper price for this in specialization than did birds. For the primates kept unspecialized the ancient five-fingered hands bequeathed them by their oldest ancestors who came to the land, the amphibians. These hands they improved in prehensility, or grasping ability, by climbing about through the trees. The result was a very great functional improvement, but with surprisingly little anatomical change. The more a paw is a flipper or a wing or a hoof, the less it can be potentially anything else: too specialized or too hasty adaptations have left their fossil shipwrecks through all the rocks of the paleontologist. The cleverly grasping hands of the tree-living primates are a modest change—compared with the spectacular hand-wing of the bat, the horse's delicate walking on one fingernail, or the thoroughly mammalian whale going back to the sea and masquerading as a fish in its outward form. Nor is the monkey's hand anything like so bizarre a specialization as the flying with the little finger of the extinct pterodactyl. The primate hand, which man has removed from all probable future specialization, may yet afford the most elegant example in all evolutionary history of Cope's law of "the survival of the unspecialized."

In more ways than one, arboreal habitat was the evolutionary salvation of the primates. For another thing, the primates' change in the trees from the almost exclusively insect diet of early mammals to an additional diet of tree fruits foreshadows the omnivorousness and variety of diet in modern man. Certainly primate teeth are not so specialized as those of many other mammals, such as whales, elephants, the saber-toothed tiger, and rodents like the beaver. Tree life is also involved with the making of nests by some primates. This habit has had unanticipated and far-reaching consequences and deserves more attention than it usually receives.

The disposal of wastes is for all living matter as important as the getting of food; even the one-celled amoeba collects its wastes into a tiny "contractile vacuole" which when large enough moves to the surface and is ejected through the cell membrane. Wastes were a problem for *Hydra,* crinoids, and flatworms. The segmented worms had a plumbing convenience or "nephridium" in each room or somite of the body; in vertebrates these are combined into two kidneys. Emancipation of life from the sea had to await the synthesis of ureates for nitrogenous wastes in the shelled reptilian egg. Disposal of wastes is no very great problem for animals that wander about on the land. But nesting is a different matter.

With a number of nestlings kept together in a limited space, to be protected and fed by adult birds until they can fly, the old problem of waste disposal arises again in birds. Various instinctual mechanisms deal with this problem in different species. In some birds of prey the nestlings back up to the nest rim, using specially developed muscles to project the feces clear of the nest. In most passerine and some other birds, the droppings are encased in gelatinous sacks secreted by the intestine; the parent-birds eat or carry these sacks away. Some woodpecker species mix their nestlings' refuse with sawdust to aid removal. Some birds with domed nests (e.g., willow warblers) eject the fecal sacks onto the outer nest rim outside the entrance, whence the adult birds remove them. And in many species of birds the nestling will not defecate until the parent taps the cloaca with its beak, even if it must wait pleading a long time with upturned posterior. All these adaptive instincts, in both nestlings and adult birds, cease operating when the young leave the nest, and hence are clearly adapted to prevent nest-fouling and contagion.

The circumstances of primate nesting are rather different from those of birds. For one matter, primate young are usually born singly—and hence there is no question of avoiding infection from other nestlings, as in the bird clutch. For another, primate nests are used both by adults and by the young primarily as sleeping places at night. The young are not left there permanently, as with fledglings, while the parents forage for food. On the contrary, the primate baby accompanies its mother everywhere, clinging to her fur, and shows signs of fear and anxiety when separated from her. Moreover, primate nests are abandoned should they become fouled. But given prehensile hands in both adult and young, there is no insurmountable problem in moving the young, as would be the case with birds. Tree-living in primates, then, is associated with an intenser relationship of the mother with a single baby at a time; but this is also involved with the problem of the infant soiling the mother, whom it always accompanies. We know little enough about the cleanliness habits of the apes—and yet it is difficult not to see, foreshadowed in the primate predicament, the beginnings of those social demands and cultural invasions of the individual's own physiological autonomy which are so prominent in *Homo sapiens*.

Placed beside the fate of the sense of smell in birds and in primates, to be discussed in a moment, this may be a factor in "the organic repression of smell" remarked on by Freud in the case of man; this is even visible in the evolution of the vertebrate brain, which from fish to primates devotes proportionately less and less to the sense of smell. It is also possible that these factors have partly influenced the human animal's extraordinary attitudes toward its sexuality. Only a few human societies, and at their peril, have culturally invaded the ancient mammalian adjustment of mother and young to each other or the old physical closeness of the primate mother and her child. But cleanliness habits are not instinctual in man, though in most environments good biological reasons remain for instituting them culturally.

Thus the biological problem handled by instincts in the various species of birds must now be handled by culturally instituted learning in the various human societies—an invasion of individual physiological autonomy by cultural controls. Cleanliness demands, or the relative lack of them, are part of the atmosphere of adult expectancies and attitudes toward children and differ from group to group. The tone of cleanliness training is therefore a good index of the emotional conditions surrounding the socialization of the child and coloring the way it is made to take on the culture patterns arbitrarily provided. The problems of conditioning peculiar to primate infants which cling to the mother are clearly another consequence of the tree-living habit of the primates. And though a land animal, cave-dwelling and house-building men still have the same problem as the nest-building apes— a problem increased by the social habit of living together in large numbers. Some of man's sinfulness is dirtiness, not sexuality.

Taking to the trees had still other profound effects on the primates. Brachiation, or "arm-walking" through the trees, develops much greater maneuverability of the limbs, especially of the forelimbs, than does the simple fore-and-aft gait of land quadrupeds—whose legs, besides, are needed for almost constant rigid support. A horse's foreleg, for example, is useless for scratching any part of its body; but monkeys can hunt body lice almost anywhere in their fur. The human shoulder blade and collarbone are built on the basis of this arboreal primate maneuverability, and the shoulder in man is virtually a universal joint. More than that, getting about in the trees—especially in a wingless creature—demands accurately developed position-assessing and distance-gauging eyes, if the brachiator is going to make that next limb safely. There is no doubt that the primate stereoscopic eyes, added to the flexible shoulder and grasping hands, give them a much richer visual-muscular space consciousness than most land animals have. With their eyes on the sides, not the front, of the head, land animals see separate halves of the world—and, when they do see it, can't do very much about it with their limbs except walk through it two-dimensionally. On the other hand, the primate ability to "monkey" with things quite literally puts them more in touch with reality, a matter which always has great learning possibilities in it.

Stereoscopic or space-conscious sight needs two eyes set apart from each other *in the same plane* and not in two separate parallel planes. Such stereoscopic eyes each see *almost* the same thing: the right eye sees a bit more around the right side of an object, a bit less around the left—and vice versa with the left eye. Also, the farther the object, the acuter the angle made by the lines from eyes to object; the amount of convergence thus made by the eyes and the lens muscles' focusing for far and near vision are also part of the total space-sense. Up to a point, the closer the object, the more obtuse this angle becomes; but at a few inches in front of the nose, the fusing of two slightly different images into a sense of farness and nearness breaks down, and we begin to see double. Exhaustion and alcohol can also break down these co-ordinated eye reflexes—but this is a small price to pay for stereoscopic vision. Some mammals whose two fields of vision partly overlap—or can temporarily be made to overlap by rolling the eyeballs convergently forward—have a small stereoscopic region, but only straight ahead. Hence a cow has to roll her eyes and swing her head around until what she wants to see stereoscopically falls into the overlap region in line with her nose. Some rabbits have this overlap region behind the head, and thus have a highly practical notion of how far away an animal pursuing them is. A parrot, by cocking its head and looking at the same object from two slightly different angles, can probably get a stereoscopic effect. But none of these makeshifts is nearly so good as the built-in stereoscopy of primates.

Though life in the trees increased the biological importance of sight, it also brought about a loss of acuteness in the sense of smell. Smell depends on close contact and moisture, and distance from the ground invariably affects it adversely: in the open air, bits of the thing smelled diffuse as the cube of the distance and are soon diluted beyond perception. (However, with flat surface winds, both hunted and hunting mammals can develop great acuteness in smell.) Thus eagles, which fly at great heights to survey large hunting territories, have to rely on acuteness of vision; they have a much poorer sense of smell than land animals hunting the same game as eagles do. Condors, also very high flyers, could in fact well use a sense of smell to detect the carrion they feed on; but condors and vultures have to depend on eyesight too, just as the eagle does. Even birds like hawks and owls that hunt closer to the ground depend on sight, not smell. This is especially striking in the case of the owl, which hunts at night—when conditions of moisture would actually be better for smelling than in the daytime. Thus smell-poor owls develop very good eyesight.

It is not an ancestral lack: reptiles have a better sense of smell than either their bird or tree-living primate descendants. In each case it was living high in the air that led to recession of the sense of smell. For land-living grazing mammals went on to develop a sense of smell much better than any reptile's, and so also did hunting mammals, notably dogs. (Indeed, if a dog's olfactory membrane were spread out, it would be larger than half its outside skin surface; the same membrane in tree-descended man is only as big as a fingernail on each side. Almost half the cerebrum wall in dogs is devoted to smell; in man only one-twentieth.) Actually, the sense of smell goes back to the earliest land animals, and taste to the fishes or earlier, so both have a respectable antiquity. It must be admitted, however, that for purely technical reasons sight is a sense intrinsically superior to smell. Smell depends on very limited stretches of space and time: even a skunk's passing by is a sensory datum which hardly lasts more than a week or extends more than a few miles, since perishable and diffusible-particles of the scent substance are necessary for smelling.

By contrast, sight responds to a much more fundamental aspect of reality than mere molecules of a particular chemical substance. It responds to an energy which is the absolute in velocity in the universe, light. The eye can therefore register stimuli originating light-years away in space and time. No animal sense can do better than that. The evolutionary value of sight is also underlined in the fact that the human eye in one respect has reached ultimate perfection. Experiments have shown that one molecule only of rhodopsin or visual purple in the human eye can cause a psychic response to one single quantum of light. Since a molecule is the smallest possible unit of a chemical compound and a quantum the smallest unit of light energy, there is plainly no progress possible in sensitivity. And if, as some people seem to believe, man is organically contemplating a new extrasensory contact with reality, he would do better to hitch his perception to this absolute, rather than to merely *psycho*kinesis. For the best neural velocities we know are only a poky 250 miles an hour, while light travels some 11,179,800 miles an hour, a bit over forty-four thousand seven hundred and nineteen times as fast.

All through evolution, species have moved from proximity-senses to distance-senses. Touch, depending on actual contact, is the earliest sense of all. Next in appearance are taste and smell, hearing and sight. In fact, a rough idea of the evolutionary position of any animal can be gained from knowing merely the repertory and relative development of the animal's senses. We know of no physical medium to which a future sense is likely to evolve a response. If the human eye is already perfect in sensitivity, all that seems possible would be to extend the range of this sense. Color vision already discriminates the frequencies within the visible gamut; but a sense might further respond to ranges beyond this spectrum. True, we can already feel infrared rays or radiant heat; yet conceivably we could respond immediately by a new sense to such frequencies beyond heat and light as X-rays and radio waves.

But this would be pointless. Man's intelligence is several eons ahead of his body in this. Man will never need an X-ray sense or a radio sense or a Hertzian-wave sense in organic terms, since he already has extra-organic ways of manipulating and apprehending these frequencies in his own machines. But this was also unlikely to happen in evolutionary terms, because organisms adapt only to realities with relevant survival value to them. Actually, until man, there was no intelligible modulation of radio waves—let us grant this much, that it is intelligible —in nature, to which adaptive organs would have any relevance or survival value. The same is also true, certainly at present, of cosmic rays. But if survival depended on intelligent response to intelligible modulation of cosmic rays, there is no reason to doubt that animals could adapt a sense to these too. But, once again, man *knows* all these things without needing to evolve senses for them. His mind is too fast to permit or to need such genetic evolving.

In the sense of hearing we have a "stereo-auditory" idea of the *direction* of sound, but only if the sound comes from a direction to one side or the other of a plane splitting the head in half midway between the ears. The reason for this is that the sound waves in such off-center hearing move so slowly that they hit the near ear an appreciable time before they hit the far ear—and from this we can tell direction. If the sound comes from somewhere within this plane, then we have to cock the head around experimentally until one ear is nearer and the other farther from the source of the sound, and only then can we tell its direction. The *distance* of the sound does not enter into this process; so, unlike the case of seeing, we do not actually sense distance in hearing itself. We judge the distance from remembered comparisons and anticipated volumes and other learned cues. Thus sight gives both the range and the bearing of the object, but hearing gives only the bearing. This is another reason for the technical superiority of sight over hearing.

The sense of hearing in primates is not demonstrably better than that of some of the preyed-upon, grass-eating land animals; and dogs have a discrimination of ultra-high-frequency sounds beyond the reach, probably, of any primate ear. But at least the physics of sound in air caused no great loss of hearing in the trees, as did the chemistry of smell in air for the anthropoids at least. This is a fortunate thing, since speech depends on hearing. Bats, too, can hear frequencies of sound inaudible to the human ear. But man need not envy dogs and bats overmuch. Sound is a sluggish communication medium anyway for an animal that can already move about physically faster than sound. And meanwhile we can step up the velocity of human speech, for what it is worth, by converting slow sound into fast radio waves and back again—which is something neither dogs nor bats can do.

Primates were fortunate that their particular problems forced them to concentrate on the queen of the senses, sight. Primate sensory improvement over other mammalian orders is confined to sight alone. Only the later primates—and not even *Tarsius,* as was once thought—among all the mammals, have the "yellow spot" in the eyes. This is a patch on the retina of the eye which the animal can turn on an object for especially clear vision—at the same time keeping a lesser but serviceable visual grasp of the larger field or context. Huxley believes this yellow spot is the sensory basis of human attention and mind concentration. We might also speculate further that it underlies man's symbolic selectivity, discrimination, and sense of parts and wholes and contexts as well. If this is true, it is quite consistent with the old mammalian habit of *paying attention to the environment,* though here in a more precise and intellectual manner. Increased primate discrimination in sight is again evident in color vision. Comparative studies so far indicate that among mammals only the primates, and perhaps only the anthropoids, have developed color vision, which discriminates minutely among the wave-frequencies of light.

Tree life influenced the primates in other ways also. Climbing and "arm-walking" tended to give the torso a vertical habitus—with the hind limbs used for standing, crouching, and sitting, and the fore-limbs primarily in climbing, brachiating, and feeding. "Handedness," of course, is the foremost primate characteristic. In fact, it is much more correct to call the majority of monkeys "four-handed" than "four-footed" animals, though lemurs and some monkeys, long before the anthropoids, had front- versus rear-limb specializations and differences, which were to become so conspicuous in man.

Among arboreal primates the raising of the snout from the ground and reduction of the sense of smell, coupled with these limb habits, together influenced the shape of the skull. The lower, typical lemurs rely on the sense of smell and are dog-faced. *Tarsius*, however, relies primarily on sight, has a retracted muzzle, and is monkey-faced. The habit of feeding the mouth with the forelimbs—thus freeing the muzzle from having to grasp as well as to chew food—is clearly as much related to the retraction of the muzzle as is the retreat in importance of the sense of smell. For there are parallels in other animals: the re-tracted face in the squirrel, marmot, raccoon, and the cat family are correlated with the forelimb grasping of food. Some sit up on their haunches and some (like the lion) rest the weight on the belly and chest while feeding; but all these animals use the front paws to help the mouth handle food. By contrast, dogs, which mainly use their jaws, and grass-eating animals like the horse have to have the muzzle ahead of the eyes in order to feed, and so have long muzzles rather than flat faces. (The flat-faced bulldog, a glandular monster bred so that it could breathe while bull-baiting—an eighteenth-century pastime —and the flat-faced Pekinese, actually bred by the Chinese so as to look like a lion, are domesticated exceptions to this; but both bulldog and Pekinese have some difficulty in eating and would probably not survive outside domestication.) It is interesting to note that the "dog-faced" baboon is also a four-footed walker on the ground. Though it is a forelimb feeder, its quadrupedal habit and formidable use of the teeth in fighting somewhat complicate the matter.

However, no body part like the skull can be understood in simple descriptive terms. In itself, the skull is already a complex of mechanical and functional relationships; and, more, it is part of the larger organism as a whole. It is over-simplified, therefore, to think of simple one-way causality when such changes occur, for influences are undoubtedly mutual. The functional organic complex includes hand-locomotion, hand-feeding, loss of smell, retraction of the snout, flatness of face, and stereoscopy of eyesight. We can now put together the elements so far discussed only separately. In a tree-living animal which must grasp and hold onto limbs securely (whether by forearm brachiation or by four-handed locomotion), space-gauging eyesight is a vital matter; four-legged land animals have no such critical concern with gravity and eyesight. Thus the more stereoscopic its vision, the more safely it can move about in the trees. But the same tree life that developed handedness and enhanced the value of sight at the same time reduced the possibilities of the sense of smell; and meanwhile the reduction of snout and of smelling increased the possibility of developing stereoscopic eyesight on the plane of the flatter new face. Likewise, arm-walking and hand-feeding are related to the vertical torso position, to the retreat of smell and the snout, and to the advance of sight. To get it all in requires a jawbreaker of a sentence: a brachiating, handed, vertical, tree-living animal can feed a non-grasping mouth reduced in prognathism in a stereoscopically seeing, flat-faced rather than snouted smelling animal! All these things are functionally and mechanically related to tree-living—the basic adaptation of the primates.

Wood-Jones pointed out that tree-living also means a reduction in the size of the primate family, that is, in the number of offspring born at one time. For the primate mother cannot take care of many infants at once as easily as a land-living animal can. And if the baby is to cling to its mother's fur as she moves about, we can see the further value of hands *in the infant* of an animal that hands its way through the trees. (Of course there are adaptations alternative to clinging to the mother:

tree-living has not resulted in reduction of family in birds and squirrels, which nest, or in opposums, which carry their young.) At the same
time, the vertical torso of the mother and the reduction in number of
young bring about additional changes in the mother: the two lines of
teats—commonly along the abdomen or in the groin of other mammals—
in most primates are reduced to two breasts placed on the chest. The
baby can then cling to its mother's upright torso and feed without
being upside down itself—besides which, when sitting, the mother can
hold the now single baby in her arms, in a way no non-primate mother
ever can.

But with fewer young, better care of them is necessary if the species
is to survive—a trend long evident in evolution. Better care, in turn, is
related to the lengthening of the period of dependent infancy in primates. Of course, better care by the mother can be plainly seen in primates, even in comparison with the care other mammalian mothers
commonly give their young. But in typical mammals the mother is
usually alone with her litter: the male is not around, except seasonally
for breeding. Clearly, better care of the young would be greatly enhanced if the male—already characteristically strong and powerful
through natural selection, from battles with other males for mates—
could be persuaded to stay around and lend his powerful protection to
mother and young. Wood-Jones thought that in primates "the bond of
the helpless offspring keeps the male in attendance." This explanation
we find rather unconvincing and biologically rootless: it states the fact
as its own explanation. We would like to offer an alternative though
admittedly more complex explanation, which so far as we know has
never been made before.

The primates are predominantly a tropical and subtropical order,
an ecological fact plainly related to their arboreal, fruit-eating habits.
Except perhaps for the Himalayan langur and the Japanese macaque,
no sub-human primate lives in really temperate climates, and certainly never in arctic—though warm blood allowed several other mammalian orders (as well as birds) to invade the coldest regions. This warm-
climate habitat seems to be true of extinct primates as well. From the
first, primates were pretty consistently arboreal, and continuous forests
of fruiting trees require milder climates than do conifers; moreover, a

forest containing a collection—one kind or another—of continuously fruiting trees would likely be found only in the tropics or subtropics. Furthermore, in Asia and Africa, the Eocene and Oligocene were moist and equable in climate, with extensive forests; it is precisely in these areas that the greatest profusion of fossil primates has been found —in particular, the various *Dryopithecus* species of India and Africa, whose tooth structure is undoubtedly ancestral to man's.

The generalization "tropical or subtropical habitat" holds true for even the most specialized and most modern sub-human primates, the anthropoid apes. Without exception the great apes prefer forested or even jungle terrain—even in the case of the largely ground-living gorilla, or the chimpanzee which is about equally at home on the ground or in the trees. The availability of trees for retreat from enemies is perhaps critical for primate creatures without horns, sharp claws, long tusks, wings, thick hides, swift-running hooves, or the like. Even the gorilla usually retreats to a tree nest at night; still, it would seem that a gorilla male could hold his own with any natural enemy in his habitat, should he choose to remain on the ground and make an issue of it. The more impressive reason for jungle habitat would seem to be the matter of tree-fruit diet.

The case of humans is significant by virtue of its very complexity. There is no doubt that anthropoids became humans partly through surmounting and adjusting to the hardships of the four Pleistocene ice ages during the last million years. In fact, most students would agree that the possession of fire is a critical distinction between men and apes. In this we concur, not merely because the presence of fire is an objective fact conveniently easy to determine in archeology and human paleontology but also because the possession of fire is a fact of *cultural* order—and the possession of culture, unique to and universal in man, is the major criterion of the human. Even more strongly, a good case could be made that the possession of fire is a first fact of the culture which is still universally possessed by man everywhere—even in the tropics, where fire is evidently less important for the survival of anthropoid creatures than it was in the Ice Age north.

The Ice Age also saw the conversion of anthropoids into the carnivorous animal, man. Once again, since primates lack the bodily hunting equipment of carnivores like lions, the habit of hunting large animals for their meat was made possible only by other cultural inventions—weapons. The hunting of animals for their furs as human clothing was also an adaptation to the cold climate. But fire also was significant in preparing this kind of flesh food taken up by animals whose ancestors were fruit-eaters and largely vegetarians. Thus fire and furs were needed to survive the cold, and flesh and fire were related in eating. Man is therefore the uniquely cold-climate anthropoid—a warm-climate primate forced to invent culture (fire, borrowed furs, and flesh-hunting with manufactured weapons) if it was to survive in the regions glaciated during the Ice Age.

But the matter is not quite so simple as this. Clearly, man is not an ape *physically adapted* to a cold climate (but only *culturally* adapted, and hence human). In fact, man's relative bodily hairlessness and "linearity" of physique both point back unmistakably to the tropics. For one thing, he would scarcely have lost the fur otherwise typical of the mammals (and even of all sub-human tropical anthropoids) *because* he did not need it in the Ice Age! Only the prior cultural possession of other animals' furs could in this circumstance conceivably allow him to dispense with his own, and that is unlikely. Man does not lack hair because he has clothes; he had to have clothes because he lacked hair. Hence the probability is that hairlessness in an anthropoid is a tropical trait, and hairless man's immediate ancestors must have been relatively hairless tropical apes. This adjustment to the tropics therefore meant that a hairless anthropoid was "caught short" by the Ice Age and forced to alternative, uniquely human, cultural adjustments, if it were to survive in glaciated regions.

Man's "linearity" points to the same thing. Not only does an arctic or cold-climate animal need fur or feathers or blubber to insulate its warm blood, but an arctic animal also tends to be more compactly spherical than linear, in order to reduce surface heat loss. In the tropics, on the other hand, warm-blooded animals need a relatively large surface in order to diffuse the heat produced by the body. Man's characteristic linearity in this respect is undoubtedly the trait of a tropical animal. As a matter of fact, this contrast (though on a smaller scale) is evident even within the single species of man. Indeed, the "bean-pole" bodies of the tall thin tribes in the hot Nilotic Sudan are even more extravagantly linear than the bodies of most humans, while the bodies of Eskimos, who live in the full Arctic, seem to have been selected for more short, rotund, and fat-insulated bodies. Thus for many and diverse reasons man's ancestry points back to tropical fruit-eating anthropoid apes. This fact, as we shall now show, is critical for other aspects of man's human nature as well.

Now in the tropics there is a lack of marked seasonal change in temperature. Vegetable foodstuffs like fruits are therefore available fairly evenly throughout the whole year. If food is available all year, the young can be born at any season; and if the climate is warm, they may safely be born without any further adaptation of their own. This continuous availability of food is in marked contrast with the situation in temperate or arctic regions: the seal, for example, must breed in relationship to seasonal food supply. If, therefore, the primate young may be born at any season, then obviously they may be conceived at any season. Furthermore, an adequate food supply permits continuous association of individual adult animals. A continuous food supply, therefore, is the enabling factor behind non-seasonal sexuality. If those individual animals which tended to breed non-seasonally throughout the year had therefore more offspring than those which bred only seasonally, then there would be selection for permanent, non-seasonal sexuality.

The primate male, therefore, remains in attendance upon the female not so much because of any new and mysterious "paternal instinct" but rather because he has a genetically selected, permanent, non-seasonal sexual interest in the female. Simply to name the phenomenon —male attendance upon the female and her young—by a term like "paternal instinct" and then to suppose that the term explains the phenomenon is mere word magic. No lower animal is so absurd as to lack biological motivation for its behavior, and there is no reason to suppose that the great anthropoid ape males should suddenly have turned sentimental over their young. Human and anthropoid social fatherhood, no less than mammalian motherhood, has a sound and discernible biological basis. The cohesion of mother and child in the mammalian family is nutritional, the adhesion of the male to this group is sexual in motivation. That the anthropoids do tend to a permanent, year-round sexuality and do tend to a new kind of animal association, the familial, is ultimately, we believe, a matter of primate food-ecology.

If other tropical animals, with food equally available all the year around, do not in fact have permanent non-seasonal sexuality, then this must be owing to other traits peculiar to primates. We are inclined to view these as being related to primate sociability, additionally based on another factor: the closer association of individual adult animals, related psychologically to the closer association of the tree-living primate mother and her singly-born infant.

As usual, we can get some perspective on man only by looking at other animals. We have suggested that the new kind of animal association in the higher primates, the familial, was ultimately based on primate food-ecology. Contrast the food-ecology—and hence the "social organization"—of the little rodent *Dipodomys*. Hundreds of these kangaroo-rat mounds have been gassed and then excavated to discover their inhabitants. Invariably, investigators found in them either a solitary female, a solitary male, or an adult female and her young—never an adult male and an adult female living together. As soon as their short mammalian dependency is over, all the young, both male and female, must leave the mother's burrow and set up on their own. Biologists believe that scarcity of food in their desert habitat is the reason: each adult animal builds a separate mound in the center of the large area from which it gets its food. But with two adults feeding from the same protective burrow, the food terrain would have to be uneconomically large and their trips for food unprofitably long and, in fact, dangerous. Therefore these desert rats live a solitary life in which adults visit each other for sexual intercourse but never live together.

The *family* is not a habit of mammals as such! We are so accustomed from childhood to animal fables like that of Donald Duck and his nephews, and to the casual nature-faking which imputes human traits to animals, that we come to take our human nature too much for granted. The reader will forgive such literal spelling-out—but the alarming and significant fact is that *ducks do not have uncles!* What needs to be emphasized is the biological uniqueness of the higher

45

primate tendency toward a new kind of animal association, the family organization; and what needs to be examined into is the biological mechanisms on which it is based.

Nor do all animal societies by any manner of means have, or need to have, the same set of biological causes. Food drives, not sexual ones, are the primary basis of association in many insect societies that have hives but not families. When the young worker-bee is about three days old, an instinct stirs her to feed the older grubs, her younger sisters, with honey and pollen taken from the common store of the hive and gathered by still older workers than herself. On about the sixth day the so-called "salivary" glands of the young worker-bee begin to swell, and with their growth the instinct to use them begins functioning. These glands secrete special fluids. The younger grubs cannot digest raw pollen. So the young worker turns from feeding older grubs pollen to feeding younger grubs the prepared fluid from her own "salivary" glands—and meanwhile the older pollen-eating grubs, when hatched, turn around and feed pollen to still unhatched older grubs. But from the sixth to the tenth day, the worker with mature salivary glands does little else but nurse the younger grubs—one of the few cases in which invertebrate adult animals feed the young, in this case not the worker's own young. So it is that, while the worker is a lifelong virgin sexually and is never called upon for the exercise of reproductive functions, she nevertheless has specialized feeding organs and "maternal" instincts based on them—though her "motherhood" comes earlier, rather than later in life. For as she grows older, she gives up her nursing role and takes over a "man's job": she goes out to earn a living, to gather and bring home pollen and honey for the whole hive. Thus the worker-bee is first nutritionally a mother and later economically a father—though she is never either genetically. Reproductively, the hive is a kind of "meta-organism": for just as in *Hydra* certain cells are specialized for reproduction, so also among bees a separate organism or group of cells (the queen bee) is specialized for reproduction—with or without the co-operation of another specialized group of cells, the drone. Recently there have been discovered communication-dances of bees relating to food location. Thus bees have not only social cohesion but also a kind of "language," both growing out of food needs.

The "social organization" of ants is instructive in having similarly clear and visible its organic and biological foundations. Anyone who has idly watched ants will have noticed that, while apparently randomly and abstractedly wandering around, ants may rush up to each other, stroke each other with their antennae, and seemingly kiss each other. "Kissing" it may be, but it is not for the usual mammalian motives. One of the ants is hungry, not amorous. Sometimes they kiss only briefly, and then rush off separately in apparent boredom, frustration, or indifference. But sometimes they stay together for some time, one of them at least showing evident eagerness and interest in the process. For ants have a kind of economic or social organization based on food exchanges. If the ant being solicited is well-fed, the two of them will raise up the foreparts of their bodies, and one will produce from its mouth a drop which the other eagerly swallows.

This liquid comes up from the crop, which Forel aptly calls the "social stomach." The crop is a large reservoir in the front of the ant's abdomen, between the gullet and the true stomach, and only when food passes a valve from the crop to the true stomach does the food become the private property of the individual ant. Until then it is still completely "collectivized." All this can be demonstrated by a simple experiment. If a few ants are fed honey colored blue with a harmless dye, the crop can be seen colored through the thin portions of the abdomen. Soon, in a few days, the whole ant community will show a bluish tinge—thus evidencing the velocity and promiscuousness of this property-exchange. In this way we can see how the social cohesion of the ant nest is based on instinctual exchanges of food—"instinctual" in the quite hardboiled biological sense of the automatic working of a genetically given body structure. While there is any food at all, the individual members of the ant community are physically structured to share it. Ant social organization, whatever men may think of it, is rooted in their bodies.

This same rooting in anatomy is true of ant "domestications." Certain aphids or plant lice live in symbiotic association with some ant species, in a manner based reciprocally on protection and nutrition. No ant species has developed mouth parts which can suck plant juices, and thus tap this rich source of nourishment. Aphids and coccids, however, have a proboscis designed to do just this—but they apparently need the biting jaws of some such species as the ant to protect them. Aphids buy this symbiotic service by means of an incomplete digestion, whereby they pass out drops of sweet "honey-dew" which the ants eat with relish. It is this satisfaction that is behind the ant's protection and care of the aphids. In wars between different species of ants, some ants will protect their aphids before their own grubs and may go so far as to build little "barns" over the sucking aphids to protect them from predators—for ants can produce more ant grubs, but they cannot reproduce more aphids.

(The same non-sentimentality in nature is also plain in human domestications, quite apart from what man may contrive to think about them. The domestication of the dog does not depend upon its worship of the superior creature, man; nor does it depend upon man's passion for a faithful companion. Dogs were, at least initially, a domestication reminiscent of the jackal's dependence on the lion. Dogs loved Old Stone Age man because of the abundant garbage he produced. For the bones of dogs are found in the refuse heaps near Old Stone Age camps, but not within the camps. The bones of dogs showing domesticated traits are found within the camps only in the New Stone Age, and their domestication depended on man's exploitation of the dog's vastly superior sense of smell in hunting the animals which man killed, the scraps of which he may have thrown to the dogs after taking the best parts to eat for himself. Man's semi-domestication of the reindeer is based on this animal's passion for human urine, and it recalls the ant's "domestication" of the aphid. The pig, like the dog, is also at least partly self-domesticated; for the pig is interested in human feces and the offal produced by primitive man. Another scavenger, the chicken, may have become domesticated in a similar manner. The cat was first attracted to human habitations in Neolithic Egypt, because of the rats and mice abundant in this grain-growing early civilization. It is still a question, however, whether the cat has any interest whatever in man save as a direct or indirect provider of food.)

Some of these social mechanisms of insects we have been discussing are very complex, but for all that they are still firmly based on their

48

anatomy and physiology. Ants and bees pass crop contents from mouth to mouth, and some ants additionally eat the honey-dew of aphids, but termites have an elaborate system to exchange food in many ways. Like ants, they regurgitate some food, which is only partly digested; and, like aphids, they dispense partly but more fully digested food at the anus, only some of the valuable substances being assimilated in the animal's own gut and the rest being passed out for the consumption of other termites. One reason for this is the termite's diet of cellulose: to break down cellulose chemically requires the presence in the gut of special micro-organisms, but these can be obtained by young termites only through eating the feces of older termites that already have them. This is why termites must be social insects, since termite physiology cannot operate in the absence of termite social organization. But this is not all: some of the food which is digested and absorbed by an individual termite is worked up in its "salivary" glands to provide nu-trition for others. And, finally, some termite castes secrete fatty sub-stances from their skin. These are not only agreeable but allow the various castes to recognize each other in the unending but necessary moisture-preserving darkness of the termite nest. As bee-dances per-form a function of language in finding food, so also food substances enable termites to communicate necessary information about caste.

Given our own mammalian dispensation and an easy assumption of its self-evidence, we may perhaps be surprised to find food exchanges going not from adults to infants but from infants to adults. Neverthe-less, social organizations can be and are based at least partly on this seemingly reversed situation. This is the case with wasps. Adult wasps do not exchange food with one another. But there is a physiologically necessary exchange between adults and infants. The reason for this is the wasp diet, which is mainly flesh. But the adult wasps that do the hunting of the flesh do not so much need it as do their grubs. The grubs need protein for growth; the adults need sugars as fuel for their flying. This has given rise to an interesting bargain: after the worker wasp has fed the grub its protein diet, the worker taps the grub's head, and the grub then gives out a drop of sweet liquid from its salivary glands, which the worker eagerly sips up. The grub, by giving up this sugary stuff, bribes the worker to her protein-hunting task for the grub's benefit; and the worker, no longer needing as much protein as she captures, uses the grub to provide the sugars she does need. In physiological fact, then, we can say without metaphor that wasps in a nest are metabolically members of one another.

To summarize: the organic roots of mammalian and anthropoid and human social organization are quite as clear as those of insect societies. Indeed, in the later evolution of land vertebrates, we can see the same massive (though quite independent) trend we have just described in the evolution of these later land arthropod societies of insects—the trend toward *meta-organisms* or societies, in which individual animals form larger genuinely functional and organic units, and separated from which the individual metazoan is either meaningless or unable to survive. The basic mammalian invention was nutritional, as seen in the primitive egg-laying mammals (platypus and echidna) which suckle their young—a close physiological relationship between individual animals if there ever was one. Birds' improvement over reptiles in parental care is also a nutritional association: most birds gather food for their young to eat, and some regurgitate partly digested food from their own bodies for their fledglings. Bird courtship and mating are also more intensely inter-individual affairs than is the case in reptiles. The next step that mammals take beyond suckling is the marsupial one. In marsupials eggs are not laid, but the young are born alive, in a very immature state; for a long while they live in a semi-fetal state in an external teat-supplied pouch on the mother's abdomen. As they become more and more mature, they venture out of this pouch for longer and longer periods until they are fully independent.

(The "marsupial" pattern of adults protecting their young by various means inside their bodies must be very useful to survival, since it has been independently invented many times by other animals. The Surinam toad, for example, places its immature young in receptacle "cells" which honeycomb its back. Some fish protect their young in their own mouths or in external pouches of the body. Of course neither toad nor fish has the truly marsupial pattern—they do not nourish, but only protect. The viviparous or "live-birth" pattern of keeping the egg within the body until the hatching stage is also an adaptation of obviously great value, inasmuch as it too has been independently invented many times. Some reptiles even have it (viviparous snakes), and indeed even some fish; in fact the viviparous pattern is found in a few invertebrates. But in none of these cases is the pattern fully mammalian in nature, for the mammalian fetus or newborn infant feeds from the mother as it grows. The unborn of these other groups feeds upon a limited food-capital settled on it once and for all in the egg.)

The next step mammals take in intensifying the functional relationships between individual animals is the plainly physical one of the placenta—once again nutritional, as in the earlier case of suckling. This is a logical progression indeed. From being "ecto-parasitic" on the mother outside her body (as in platypus, in suckling), the mammalian infant increases its dependency by a kind of semi-detached residence in the marsupial mother's pouch; and from this ambiguously halfway stage in marsupials, the fetus in placental mammals goes on to a full and unambiguous "endo-parasitism" within the mother's womb, taking the materials for its growth from her very bloodstream.

As a social unit the mammalian "family" had similarly tentative beginnings. Originally it was made up of the female and her infant offspring only. Added to that, it lasted a short time only—for any "social" relationship between them was based solely on the body structure of the female, physically specialized to feed her infant young. A characteristic mammalian "family" of this kind is illustrated by seals. Here the two sexes meet only seasonally, and the cubs are born when the mother is alone. At the season of plentiful food, the females foregather with the males, bringing along the newborn cub and perhaps also an immature cub from the previous year. At the feeding grounds the female breeds with a bull, and soon thereafter they separate, to remain separate the rest of the year. The seal bull thus has a minimal relationship to the mother-cub "family." He is the male progenitor physically, but hardly a father in the social sense. Many mammalian females, in fact, do not even consort with the male until the young are gone from her and able to fend for themselves—for the males will attack and kill as rivals their own young. The bird "family" too is dispersed in a season, and even birds that pair for longer periods may have several such "families" in one single season. None of these associations of parents and young is notable for its duration.

While all infant mammals have a period of helplessness right after birth, the time of dependency in most of them is a remarkably short one from the human point of view. Colts, calves, kittens, piglets, and pups become self-sufficient adults in relatively short order. (An exception to this is interesting in itself. In elephants, whose young are also long dependent, we find both increased intelligence and increased teaching of the young by adults—possibly related to the herding of both sexes of adults with the dependent young. But the "long dependency" of baby elephants may be more a correlate of *long life* in elephants as compared with other mammals. In man it is by no means a simple matter of long life, for many other factors operate, e.g., actual physical infantilization, to be discussed in chapter 5.) But, by and large, most mammalian infants swiftly become self-sufficient adults. Only in the primate order does something new appear to be happening. In their social organization, primates in a sense "infantilize" the juvenile animal, both because of increased maternal care and because of the increased paternal association of the male with mother and young. Or, from another point of view, the young animal is increasingly ectoparasitic and dependent upon adult animals of its own species.

This is part of a long trend in evolution toward larger integrations. The cells in colonial protozoans became increasingly dependent on one another, until, like cells in a metazoan individual, they could no longer have independent existence. Similarly, the primate infant becomes increasingly dependent on adult animals, to a point where it can no longer exist, much less become human, without them. The close and actually physiological integrations of insect societies are a quite independent illustration of the same trend. The trend in primates is unmistakable, for the changes are progressive as the evolution of the primates proceeds. The facts can be neatly tabulated. In the roughly evolutionary sequence of lemur-monkey-ape-man, the offspring tend to be smaller, more helpless, and more immature at birth. Dependency increases from lemur to man, and the suckling period is progressively extended. An increasingly longer time is required to learn the adult method of locomotion. Progressively more time is needed to achieve social independence, and sexual maturity at the same time is increasingly delayed as the animal reaches a progressively longer life. The accompanying table will show that as we pass from the lower primates to the monkeys, and from the apes to man, a number of interesting and significant things are happening.

COMPARATIVE TABLE OF INDIVIDUAL DEVELOPMENT IN PRIMATES

Species	Length of Pregnancy	Status at Birth	Period of Dependency on Mother	Learns To Walk	Suckled for:	Capable of Social Independence	Sexual Maturity	Social Organization	Longevity*
Lemur	111, 145 days (two species); multiple births; other primates usually single	Relatively very large, mature, with senses functional	A few hours or days	Within first week, usually	Several days or a few weeks	Within a few weeks	Within a year	*Tarsius* in pairs; but some lemurs are gregarious	25 years
Monkey	Marmoset, 150 days; macaque, 163 days; rhesus, 166 days	Relatively large, mature, with senses well developed	A few days or weeks	Within first month, usually	Several weeks	Within 2–4 months	Within 2 or 3 years	Mostly gregarious; harem-forming in some baboons	15–45 years, depending on species
Ape	Gibbon, 209 days; chimpanzee, 235 days	Relatively very small and helpless, with senses partly functional	3–6 months	Within 6 months, ordinarily	Several months	Within 12–18 months	Within 8–12 years	Gibbon: family bands; orang: ?sexes apart except at mating; chimp: bands of 4–14 (av. 8.5); gorilla: groups of 2–4 nests; maximum known 16	25–45 years, depending on species
Man	266 days	Relatively small and helpless, with senses partly functional	At least a year	Within 18 months, usually	1–2 years	Within 6–8 years	Within 10–14 years	Exogamous family groups within larger societies	Depends upon time† and country; in U.S. a male born now may expect to live 67 years; a female, 72 years
Trend from lemur to man	Lengthening of the period of gestation	Smaller, more helpless and immature	Dependency increases	Longer time needed to learn to walk	Length of suckling extended	More time needed to achieve social independence	Puberty progressively delayed	Tendency for family to emerge in higher primates	With human culture, longevity distinctly increases over infrahumans

* Figures based on known *maxima* of life in individual animals in captivity; since the *average* span of life in wild animals is less, and only the average (not the maxima) for humans has been given, the contrast in longevity between man and the infra-human primates is probably much greater than the table indicates.

3. The Anthropoids Climb Halfway Down

Among the primates of the Old World are four living species whose many similarities to man have led them to be called anthropoid or "man-like" apes. The gibbon and the orang-utan are Asiatic apes, the chimpanzee and the gorilla, African. Their exact evolutionary relationship to man has long been, and still is, somewhat a matter of controversy. We say "somewhat" only, because on some questions scientists are agreed. That none of these apes is a direct ancestor of man is a settled question, for each of them has specializations divergent from man's own. But at what point "hominids," or animals leading to man, branched off from the anthropoid stem is at present a question wide open to legitimate difference of scientific opinion. Many physical and functional, geological, and geographical factors are involved, and these are differently assessed by different scholars. Nor are all the fossil facts at hand on which to base anything like a final opinion. Furthermore, since they are different species, nothing which is true of the apes is necessarily true also for man. Still, man is at least a "speaking cousin" of the anthropoid apes, and their study not only is suggestive but also throws considerable light on the origins and nature of man.

The gibbon is found in south China, the Malay peninsula and archipelago, and on the island of Hainan. By far the most numerous of the great apes, the total population of gibbons is in the tens or even the hundreds of thousands. The lightest in weight of all the anthropoids (11–15 pounds), the gibbon is also incomparably the greatest aerialist, flinging itself with confidence and unconcern over wide spaces in the trees. Its specialization for tree life is signalized in its anatomy. It has the longest arms in proportion to torso of all the anthropoids, and the bones of its very long-fingered hands are actually curved palmward to aid in brachiation. The gibbon is a very agile animal. It is not only the most expert climber among the anthropoids but also the most expert bipedal walker, running along with its arms held about shoulder height as balancing-poles, and sometimes standing on its short legs with support from its grotesquely long arms. Physically, the gibbon is generally regarded as the remotest of the anthropoid relatives of man, for the limb proportions and general skeleton of the gibbon is as highly specialized for arboreal locomotion as man's is for terrestrial. Gibbons are the only anthropoids that do not make tree nests for sleeping.

Socially, however, the gibbon seems somewhat less remote from man than it is physically. Gibbons unquestionably live together in family groups. Though Spaeth on one occasion came upon a "bachelors' club" group of males alone in the morning, conversing in typical male gibbon tones in the trees, this is not usual. Occasionally solitary animals of various ages are seen, but most of the time they are found associated in family groups of father, mother, and two or more young ones in various stages of growth. But since gibbons also live together in bands, it is at times somewhat difficult to discern the family grouping very closely. The transition from marked band gregariousness to clearly emergent family life seems to lie between gibbons and chimpanzees.

The other evidence available seems consistent with this in-between status of the gibbon. The "dimorphous" contrast in body of the sexes is not so marked in gibbons as it is in chimpanzees and gorillas; but, for what the observation is worth, some students consider that gibbons are more reserved toward men than toward women, some captive individuals showing very marked preferences. Still, the pre-eminence of the gibbon family bond over that of the band is clear, no doubt since breeding is definitely not seasonal. The permanence of the male-female association into families is somewhat uncertain, even though the father-mother-offspring family is usually distinctly visible. Gibbons even appear to be monogamous.

The gibbons are very interesting to students of man in another direction. Most of the mammals have highly developed *listening*, for protection from their enemies. Some of them, both preying and preyed upon, have occasional *production* of sound which serves one or another biological purpose of communication. But this inter-communication among individual animals is heightened to such an extent in gibbons that it can only be fairly characterized as *vocalization*. For the gregarious gibbons are, if anything, even noisier than bands of monkeys. The white-cheeked gibbon, for example, has a voice of great compass, and one type at least has a vocal sac which appears to have some functional connection with vocalization.

It is not only in volume and in incessant use that gibbon vocalization is remarkable. Boutan has observed five vocal expressions for states of satisfaction or well-being, four indicating states of illness or fear, four of an intermediate state, and one used when the animal is in a state of great excitement—a total of fourteen distinguishable vocalizations. These vocalizations, however, do not have the value of words. They are, rather, expressions of body feelings or awareness of agreeable, disagreeable, or dangerous situations and events. But it is at least a "pseudo-language," if we are careful to define what we mean by this. Perhaps it may best be characterized as "phatic" communication, that is, it succeeds in spreading information about an individual animal's state of mind, or it communicates a generalized emotional tone throughout the band so that all its members come to have the same attitude toward a situation. Sometimes it binds the group to biologically useful common action—as when one group of gibbons asserts a claim of territorialism and, by this kind of vocalized warning or bluff, substitutes for an otherwise necessary physical clash between groups in protecting its foodstuffs. Fruits form 80 per cent of gibbon diet, but they also eat eggs, young birds, and insects.

The usefulness of gibbon "phatic" communication should not be underestimated. Indeed, it is no easy cynicism but a sober statement of fact, that a quite surprising amount of human communication remains strictly phatic, for all its employment of articulate words. For example, the purpose of poetry, notoriously, is to communicate feeling—to make the hair stand up on the back of the neck or to stimulate fantasy so that we feel communication has taken place when it has not ("Life like a dome of many-colored glass stains the white radiance of eternity")— and not to make genuine or verifiable statements about the structure of the universe. But also much, if not most, of the language of lovers, advertising, political argument, philosophy, theology, and (as with the gibbons) the diplomatic *démarche* has no necessary relationship to objective realities outside the speakers but only to emotional states within them. Indeed, in each of these cases, objective statements of fact would not serve to secure the desired purposes! Thus even the most articulate of the primates, man, still often uses phatic communication. Gibbon talk is at least a kind of social hormone, to communicate emotion and to unify band action. Gibbons stamp with joy and displeasure; and so do we. For the rest, the gibbon seems to be a standard primate, since its adaptations of senses, physique, temperament, band organization, and vocalization alike are suited to quick flight rather than to aggression—or even to defense, though a band may attack in concert if one of its members is molested.

The other Asiatic great ape is the orang-utan. The name "orang-utan" comes from two Malay words meaning "man of the woods"—a description beautifully appropriate to suggest not only its caricaturing of man but also its solitariness. With its expression of a disappointed Diogenes, the orang is in great contrast to the highly sociable gibbon— one of those facts that make the study of the primates at once complex and fascinating. The orang is the least gregarious of all the man-like apes. Some students state that, except during the mating season, the adult males live alone, though other equally qualified students doubt this. It is also said that females bear their young alone, though they may have with them one or two semi-dependent young in addition to the baby, and several old females may be found together, sometimes with young. Related to their somewhat solitary habit, no doubt, is the fact that orangs are largely silent.

The orang is heavier in weight than the gibbon, adult males averaging 165 pounds and females about 81, which may explain the fact that the orang is only second among the anthropoids in climbing ability and third in four-footed walking on the ground. It is the last of all in bipedal walking, which it does in poor fashion on the outer edge of the partly curled-up feet. However, since the orang is found only on the large jungled islands of Sumatra and Borneo, walking is evidently not of prime importance for them. In fact, orangs live mostly on wild fruits. Their life-span is 40–50 years. Bodily sexual differences among them are greater than among the gregarious gibbons, but the bearing of this fact will remain unclear until we know more about orang family formation than we do at present. Orangs build nests in the trees for sleeping, and avoidance of excrement is well attested to in captive animals—two facts which may be related, since fouled nests are abandoned. Orangs also rely on caution, cunning, and concealment for safety rather than on aggressive attack or even defense. On the whole, in fact, orangs are arborealists second only to the gibbon, but, unlike the later, orangs are certainly undistinguished for locomotion on land.

The lively chimpanzee is the most widely distributed of anthropoid apes, being found in many thousand square miles of equatorial Africa from the west coast to the Lake Tanganyika region. Third in climbing ability and third in bipedal walking, they are first in quadrupedal walking among the anthropoid apes. Though markedly arboreal and plainly unsuited for life in open treeless country, chimpanzees nevertheless spend an appreciable portion of their time on the ground. They can stand and walk erect briefly and for short distances, but chimpanzees find this way of getting around relatively difficult. Possibly their weight has something to do with it, since adult males average about 110 pounds and females 88; and possibly also their way of walking explains this difficulty. Sometimes the feet are flat on the ground, and sometimes the toes are curled inward to support the weight on the outer border of the feet—certainly the chimpanzee foot has not anatomically settled on how the animal shall walk. Generally they walk in a quadrupedal position, but not flat-handed like baboons: the hands are half-closed, and the weight rests either on the knuckle joints or on the backs of the end and middle finger bones. Since its arms are relatively long and its legs relatively short, the chimpanzee often uses its arms in "crutch" fashion, swinging the legs and light pelvis between them. But for all its indecision about methods, so far as speed on the ground is concerned the chimpanzee is the fastest of the anthropoids. A chimpanzee can easily run away and escape from a man with its half-quadrupedal, half-bipedal scuttle; and once in the trees, no human Tarzan is half a match for it. Chimpanzees are more defensively aggressive, perhaps, than gibbons or orangs and will bite in defense at real or imagined aggression against them. Like the orang and the gorilla, chimpanzees make nests in the trees. Their attitude toward excrement is variable but is generally one of avoidance. It is well established that chimpanzees have red-yellow-blue color discrimination, which even some of the monkeys like the macaque have.

It is in their social traits that chimpanzees are most interesting. They are highly sociable animals and—except for an occasional solitary old male cast forth by younger males—they always live in bands made up of a single or associated families. The male is supreme in the family group and may have appropriated to himself as many as three or four females. In French Guinea these groups range from 4 to 14 individuals, averaging 8.5 and often containing more than one male; in any case, females make up about 65 per cent of chimpanzee groups. The chimpanzee is notoriously active sexually, and Bingham suggests the order of increase in sexuality as monkey-ape-man. Certainly in chimpanzees copulatory play is frequent and variable even in sexually immature animals, including heterosexual, homosexual, masturbatory, and exhibitionistic activities. The social stimulation of other chimpanzees and even of other anthropoid species (including man) tends to increase the amount of sexual excitement and the frequency of its expression. A characteristic statement concerning the chimpanzee family is made by Sokolowsky:

The troop consisted of a large adult male, a few younger females, and a young male. The old male was even in captivity the undisputed guardian and ruler of all the other members. He kept himself aloof up at the top of the cage, seated on a board, observing and controlling the doings of the others. If a quarrel arose he sprang down from his seat, and made an end to it by blows and bites. He never indulged in games or sports, but preserved his austerity which was respected by the others. The sexual appetite of this male was very interesting to note. He was very exacting in this respect, and demanded repeated intercourse every day with his females. For this purpose he sprang down, and seized one of the females who even if she struggled at first had to yield finally to his superior strength, and submit to copulation. When he saw the young male attempt intercourse with the females, he sprang on the couple, and drove the young male off with bites and blows. The young male succeeded in effecting intercourse only when he waited until the old male was asleep, and then made advances to the females who accorded. From my observation the old male exercised his power and strength in a despotic manner, and demanded sexually implicit submission.

Sexual relations continue during pregnancy, but after birth and until the baby is weaned there is no relation whatever between the sexes. That is, the status of lactation determines the intercourse of the sexes. This is an interesting point, for it means that in chimpanzees the female's functions as mother and as mate *alternate* in stretches of time, whereas in humans maternal and sexual behavior are relatively simultaneous.

The sexuality of primates is complex. The apes (and many of the Old World monkeys as well) have a menstrual cycle instead of the seasonal oestrus or "heat" characteristic of other mammals. It is possible that the chimpanzee is sexually the most active of all the anthropoids. In relative size of male genitalia, chimpanzees are by far the largest and most potent; and the others probably follow in order man, orang, and gibbon, with the gorilla last. In prominence of female genitalia, chimpanzees are also first by far. But though chimpanzees are exceedingly active sexually, they are equaled in this by baboons and numerous other monkeys. The active sexuality of baboons is interesting, in view of the fact that some species are polygynous or harem-forming. Indeed, this heightening of sexual activity in the male has parallels in other harem-forming mammals, like the bull and the goat. It seems highly probable, therefore, that active sexuality in baboons may serve harem-forming functions, with a bearing on heightened sexual selection in the male; in monkeys, active sexuality may be in the service of social cohesion in bands, and not in the service of greater reproductivity as such. It is not our purpose to make invidious distinctions among the primates with respect to sexual activity. The objective evidence is incomplete, and observations on captive animals may be weighted on the side of sexually more active younger males. It is possible, however, that first place may go to monkeys, chimpanzees, or baboons, and not to man—though in human males there is extraordinarily great variability in sexual activity, and humans may further be more motivated to hide their sexuality, since they are also more conditioned to inhibit it. All that can be said with some assurance is that man ranks high among the primates in sexual activity, as primates rank high among mammals in general.

Students of the primates have other interesting information for us as well. In some primates the food drive is of greater importance to the species than we might have expected. In some cases the survival of the young is at stake, and food satisfactions bind the mother emotionally and protectively to the young. The licking of the baby among monkeys and apes is performed for the sake of the mother, and only incidentally, if at all, does this in itself benefit the baby. The baby is in a sense attractive to the mother: the mother craves the fetal fluids as she does the placenta. Even fighting for the baby may be initially or partly a hunger drive, for she will similarly cling to and defend against aggression the placenta, which she eats. (It is significant among humans—for all their "organic repression" of smell, and to whom all other physiological odors are more or less repulsive—that the newborn and very young baby "smells good" to the mother, a fact not immediately apparent, perhaps, to the human male.)

Primate mechanisms sometimes seem to "slip a cog" however. Finding the nipple is the result of trial-and-error behavior *of the baby*, equipped with its fierce sucking reflex. The infra-human primate situation is that of the baby sucking the mother, and not of the mother suckling the baby. Infra-human primate babies are equipped with more rigidly canalized aggressive behaviors in this respect than is any human baby. Food altruism is evidently not responsive to some vague, instinctual "mother love," and certainly not to the disciplines of cultural morality—for monkey mothers have been observed to take food from the baby's mouth and put it into their own, although the mother's cheek pouches were already distended to capacity. It is a simple matter not of sentiment but of superior strength. Among caged rhesus monkeys en route from India, when fed sparingly on a new diet, the mothers almost uniformly fought their infants away from food, and eight or ten mothers actually killed their infants. Thus it is evident that it is the physiological functioning of the breast, and not the moral mind, which motivates maternal behavior in monkeys.

(In humans, too, it is not the tuition of morality and culture that is pre-eminent in mother love—indeed, in some societies like our own, these actually aggressively interfere with sound organic functioning. The physiological gratification of the mother is behind the prodigies of care of her baby. Males lack this and are far more inclined, on occasion, to be restive under the demands of parenthood. And if women are thus mysteries of emotion to men, the reason is simply that males do not have female bodies. Primate males, including human ones, are no help whatever in suckling the young—and often, for their own reasons, an active hindrance. Male pediatricians have even been known to pretend, with their bottles and clever formulas, that men can do anything better than women, including nursing, and hence they sensibly take over the infant from its mother. It must be admitted, however, that the mammalian breast has been at this complex biochemical job for rather a longer time than even the most experienced pediatrician. The psychiatrically oriented person even gets the impression at times that some pediatricians dislike children and dislike maternity, and enter the profession only to put the proper male stamp on the process.)

In chimpanzees there is clear paternal discipline of the young, including both scolding and the physical persuasion of bites and cuffs. The sexes in chimpanzees are about as different from each other dimorphously as human sexes are, but dominance in the band may be by either sex. Instead of a single leader, also, with the other members of equal status, the chimpanzees have rather a serial system of dominating and being dominated by the other individuals in the group —like the "pecking order" in chickens. Such moral fatherhood as occurs in chimpanzees, therefore, appears to rest on no more respectable ethical grounds than greater physical strength.

In contrast to the dour, lethargic, and solitary orang, the chimpanzee is highly active, vivacious, imitative, and uninhibitedly vocal, adding to his repertory of chatters and cries the drumming of trees and of the ground. Sometimes chimpanzees will imitate each other in parades or stomp-dances on the ground, even using rags or sticks in the process. But such apparent games are nonce-events; they are dependent upon physical proximity and direct imitation, and they never achieve the status of time-transcending, traditional culture. The one serious disagreement among experts is on whether the chimpanzee is wholly vegetarian or partly meat-eating. The probability seems to be that it is primarily vegetarian, but it undoubtedly supplements this diet with insects—notably its own or a friend's body lice—the eggs of birds, and possibly in addition an occasional small animal. Of one thing we are sure: it is never exclusively or even predominantly carnivorous.

Many experts believe that the chimpanzee is next to man in intelligence. The Yerkes, however, reasonably expect that the gorilla would be, in view of the more pronounced resemblance in structure of the nervous systems in the gorilla and in man. It may be that the former judgment is colored by human preferences. The gorilla is sullen, untamable and ferocious, shy, wary, and slow-moving. The chimpanzee, on the other hand, is more lively, tractable, gregarious, and "humanizable"—besides being of smaller size, and less dangerous to man than the gorilla. The fact is that psychologists know a great deal about the intelligence of the chimpanzee, whereas the gorilla's is relatively unknown. Meanwhile, it should be stated that gregariousness and amiability are not quite identical with intelligence. And if gorillas do not go out of their way to show affection for their human hunters and captors, this can scarcely be adduced as evidence against a respectable I.Q.

Physically, in any case, the gorilla is undoubtedly the anthropoid closest to man. This largest and most powerful of all existing anthropoids (including man) has come down out of the trees even more than the chimpanzee, and certainly more than the orang-utan or the gibbon. The heavy gorilla, which may weigh up to a quarter of a ton, is understandably the poorest arborealist of the four anthropoid apes, being fourth also in climbing ability. But it is second in bipedal skill and second in quadrupedal. If the gibbon and the orang are predominantly tree-living and the chimpanzee almost equally at home on the ground or in the trees, the gorilla is predominantly terrestrial. The gorilla is a formidable animal. Tests on immature gorillas have shown a muscular strength two or three times that of a strong man. The strength of the adult male gorilla is not exactly known, because of his uninterest or active lack of co-operation in the administration of such tests. The great size and weight of the gorilla discourage tree-living. But the accompanying great strength of the creature makes it safe for the gorilla, alone of the anthropoid apes, to live largely on the ground.

The gorilla is physically impressive. Its dark eyes are deepset in the head under enormous beetling eyebrow ridges. The nostrils open forward (rather than downward, as in the bridged human nose) and are surrounded by thick gristly rings flat against the face. The head seems large and towering, but a great portion of it is devoted to massive jaws. These jaws have peculiar molars, premolars, and projecting canine teeth, all set in a discontinuous and unevenly projecting line in a U-shaped palate and lower jaw. The apparent skull height is misleading, for part of the upper skull is employed in the service of these great prognathous or forward-projecting jaws: adult male gorillas have a high "sagittal crest" of bone, like a wall or keel running fore and aft on the top of the skull. Mechanically, this crest is identical in purpose with the projecting breastbone of birds, for it serves as a solid support and separation for muscles pulling in opposite directions: in the bird it is the flying muscles, in the gorilla the powerful muscles of the jaw. In fact, the bony shelf behind the great brow arches is actually almost horizontal, the apparent low slope of the forehead being made up of jaw muscles too. Only a small, ovoid space is thus actually available for inclosing the brain.

The gorilla has a thick neck for good mechanical reasons: the point of juncture of skull and spine is not centrally under the skull but at the bottom rear, and therefore the gorilla needs large neck muscles to keep the massive snout and jaws from rocking forward and downward onto its chest. This is shown, too, in the greater length in gorillas than in man of the backward-jutting spurs of the upper vertebrae (especially the fourth and fifth from the top) which anchor these neck muscles. The whole spinal column is curved concavely forward in the gorilla, and he lacks both the graceful shoulder-neck and the elegant lumbar, "small-of-the-back" recurvatures of mankind. A gorilla's arms look odd to those accustomed to human proportions: the upper arms are relatively very long with respect to the very short forearms—indeed, this grotesquely long upper arm is the major contributor to the fact that the gorilla's arms as a whole are actually much longer than his legs. His reach may be 9–10 feet, though his height is only 5–6 feet. His thighbone is not only relatively but also absolutely shorter than man's. There is a marked differentiation in front and rear paws, the hand being wide, webbed, and thick, but the foot long and with the beginnings of a heel. Monkeys tend to have chests that are very deep front-to-back, but rather narrow from armpit to armpit. However, deep as the gorilla's chest is, it is wider still, and hence he has a proportionately broader back and shoulders than monkeys have. With this immense chest, a thick protruding abdomen, and heavy arms reaching below the knees, the gorilla is clearly constructed for strength, not speed.

In walking, the gorilla places its longish foot flat-soled on the ground. In this, as well as in its incipient heel, it most nearly approaches man among the anthropoids. But with its forelimbs the gorilla customarily "knuckle-walks" and rarely moves about without holding onto objects with its arms or supporting itself at least partly with the arms. With this gait, it is slower on the ground than humans, and, while a sane man would not choose to stand his ground and wrestle with a gorilla, a healthy man could probably outrun a gorilla if he elected to make it a contest in speed. Heavily built as it is, the gorilla is a fairly skilful but cautious climber and relatively clumsy in the trees, even as compared with the fairly heavy orang. Thus in locomotion the gorilla is really neither a brachiating acrobat in the trees nor fully bipedal on the ground, but ordinarily an imperfect and undecided quadruped in a semi-erect position.

The social and sexual organization of the gorilla is still much disputed. It must be admitted that argument arises chiefly because we do not have enough knowledge about the animal in these areas. The consensus of opinion is that the gorilla is moderately gregarious, living in bands smaller than those of the chimpanzee, with females more numerous than males. The typical gorilla band has as many as five associated families, feeding in the same general locality and making their tree nests at night in the same general area, though not quite so close together as those of the individual family units. Monogamy is inferred from the fact that these family nests are usually two of large size, with or without associated nests, presumably of immature young, smaller than the parental nests. Feces-dirtied nests are abandoned. Males may become solitary with age, but ordinarily gorillas are nomadic in groups, in search of their predominantly plant food. The gorilla is mostly a silent animal, though perhaps less silent than the orang, and capable of loud vocalization and chest-drumming.

The nature of gorilla sexuality is not established. One student contends that there is a rutting season when the males call the females, after which the males remain with and defend the females from aggression; another rejects this view and states that the gorilla is monogamous, the mates remaining together throughout the year and indefinitely. Evidence and opinion tend to agree on the relative permanence of matings, but gorilla monogamy is not really proved. The same ignorance prevails concerning the physiology of sex as concerning its sociology. Our "knowledge" of the gorilla is therefore, to a degree, a well-blocked-out awareness of ignorance, though some of the final facts may indicate transitional developments.

The geographic range of the gorilla is limited. One race, the "mountain gorilla," or *berengei,* with darker, longer, and thicker fur, lives in east-central equatorial Africa, especially in the Mountains of the Moon, near the eastern border of the Belgian Congo. The other race, the coastal or "lowland gorilla," rejoices in the scientific name of *Gorilla gorilla gorilla* and lives in west equatorial Africa, especially in Gabun and the Cameroons. It must be classed as a rare animal, and the estimated total number of gorillas in the world is less than ten thousand. Despite strict protection, the gorilla probably is gradually dying out. Von Oertzen summarizes the situation well:

The gorilla appears to me, although it is the highest of the apes, very likely an animal which in its genetic development has been betrayed into a blind alley. For this anthropoid belongs to creatures with a double nature, which have acquired a little, never enough of, the many qualities needed in the world to carry on successfully the struggle for existence. It is not so circumstanced, within the boundaries of its natural gifts, that the species is assured of the greatest possible length of life. It is neither a skilful climber nor an enduring runner. It has the powerful jaws of an animal of prey, but nourishes itself on plant foods. It has the strength of an athlete, but prefers to save itself by flight rather than attack. Its means of speech are limited.

Lachrymal glands occur in the animal, but because of anatomical characteristics and the small amount of secretion, the gorilla does not shed tears. It is an irony that the gorilla cannot even weep for its ultimate demise.

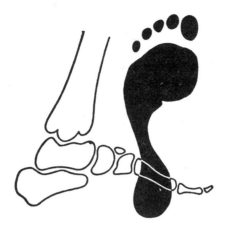

4. Man Stands Alone

The tradition that man is a fallen angel finds little support in either paleontology or physics. If for his manifest behavior man must be regarded as a fallen creature, it is much more likely that he is an ape fallen from arboreal grace than that he is a fallen angel. The sobersided biologist, who would rather seem ingenuous than be gullible, has a terrible time wrestling with angels! Now a featherless biped like man could easily be a *descendant* of angels, once flight was lost (cf. the flightless moa, rhea, and ostrich)—though man's left-over hair looks a good deal more like mammal fur than bird feathers. Angels are said to have been "created." What this statement means operationally we do not know, unless it means that angels or something very like angels reproduced them. The problem, then, is to find *ancestors* for angels. With paired arms, legs, and wings, ancestral angeloids must therefore have had six limbs. Arthropods? But crab gills could not stand the drying-out of flying; and insects, with six legs *and* a pair or two of wings, have eight or ten limbs when we need only six. Besides, insect tube-respiration makes an anthropoid-size angel impossible. Some angels, however, are said to have a double pair of wings. Eight-limbed arachnids? But we have no flying scorpions or winged spiders; nor do our sources mention chitinous exoskeletons in angels. So crabs, insects, scorpions, and spiders are out as angel-ancestors.

Their peculiar history suggests that angels are warm-blooded. But birds have already accounted for their forelimbs once, and cannot have both arms and wings; besides, it appears that mammalian behavior caused the Fall. Bat ancestors? Same problem as birds: we need six limbs for angels, and the best the bat and bird descendants of amphibians have is a banal and stultifying four. Thus angels are flying mammals (but not bats) derived from an aquatic form that was neither crustacean nor insect, neither arachnid nor amphibian. Out goes our last hope, the whales; besides, the heaviest of all creatures does not seem much cut out for flying. Also, his arms are already flippers.

Cherubim as winged heads? But this so shirks problems of nutrition, respiration, circulation, and excretion as to be biologically implausible. Besides, with no organs below the neck, what about suckling and parturition, which on internal evidence (mammalian behavior) are required of angels? "But angels are immortal—if they behave—and hence do not have to reproduce (which would in fact entail misbehavior)." We do not believe it: an organism as big as an angel must be a metazoan, because of the surface-volume ratios in protozoans—and all metazoans are mortal. Thus, if angeloids are to survive, they must reproduce, i.e., misbehave, and therefore lose their immortality anyway! As for seraphim, their zoölogical description is ambiguous: flaming serpents or six-winged with two feet—a flat contradiction. But snakes (as our sources correctly state) lost four limbs; and no reptile has gained eight or, if arms are assumed, ten.

Engineering-wise, the physical possibilities of angels are equally discouraging. Even the most magnificently portrayed wings are aerodynamically too small: their long clean shape suggests speed enough for "messengers" (as their name implies), but they are not broad enough to support such a heavy creature. Also, an angel of moderate avoirdupois, say 150 pounds, would need a breastbone jutting out some 6 feet to support the flying muscles; and since an animal this big must be a lung-breather, this model of animal has very difficult engineering problems of morphology and metabolism. Flying, even more than brachiation, requires a strong pectoral girdle at the expense of a light pelvic girdle. But how about suckling the young, quite apart from the necessary arm length? Pectoral mammary glands anterior to the huge flying muscles seem impractical—even if the pelvic girdle were a small egg-laying one like birds'. On the other hand, the pelvic-girdle requirements of mammalian birth and bipedality in so large and heavy a creature appear impossible in an avian form. But if angels are not flying mammalian bipeds, then they are not angels. And if, besides being ancestorless themselves, they do not suckle their young, then they can hardly be immediately ancestral to *Homo sapiens*. It really is quite a problem! (Meanwhile, if mammalian behavior was a long-established habit of his ancestors, it seems quite unfair that man should be the first to be punished for it.)

For compelling technical reasons, therefore, this long-traditional biology of man is highly untenable. The shape of the human hand and foot, man's sexuality and social organization, alike force upon us the belief that *Homo sapiens* is descended from a large arboreal ape. He was a renegade, if one prefers it this way, whose irremediable sin lay in turning his back on traditional primate tree-living—but refusing, for all that, to revert to the orthodox four-footed gait for furry land animals and wilfully setting forth on a dangerously radical, bipedal career. Man's original sin was not so much the eating of the fruit of the tree as in climbing down from it. For man is the unique anthropoid who finally and unregenerately came down out of the trees, to become completely and irrevocably bipedal.

Of course bipedality, as such, is not wholly an unprecedented phenomenon in evolution. Although all the heavily armored dinosaurs were quite understandably quadrupedal, some of the large dinosaurs (the carnivorous megalosaurs and coelurosaurs, as well as the ornithopods and therapods) raised themselves from the ground and achieved a bipedal, or at least a kind of "tripedal," posture with the heavy tail and hind legs. (Mathematically, of course, a tripod is the most economical of all, since three points can define a plane, i.e., three legs can give support at rest, as in a stool. But ever since lancelets and fish, vertebrate animals have tended to be bilaterally symmertical, and an uneven number of supports always has come from a tail added to the two hind legs.) It is interesting that the bipedal dinosaurs—both the herbivorous and especially the carnivorous ones—had proportionately larger brains than the quadrupedal dinosaurs. But this was evidently not enough: the forelimbs were not backed with enough brains, and, besides, their nervous tissue was elaborated primarily in the service of the huge hindquarters. The arms dwindled in most cases to absurd vestigial appendages, and the jaws remained pre-eminent in eating. Instead of becoming arms and hands, the forelimbs of the heavy vertical reptiles seem rather to have become useless left-overs. For reptiles in general had rather simple old-fashioned amphibian paws, with none of the clever prehensility which the primate hand developed from tree-living.

Some of the lighter reptiles seem to have achieved a fast bipedal running, with the tail and forelimbs used as balancing organs; these in time became specialized in the flight of birds. But the bipedality of birds is one in which the forelimbs are committed to the purpose of flying; and in the large, heavy, flightless moa, rhea, and ostrich, the wings were already too much specialized to serve as anything but (again) the balancing organs of bipedal runners—which was right back where they started from. The cynical Greek, who, hearing a philosopher define man as a "featherless biped," brought him a plucked chicken, was not really meeting the whole issue.

Some marsupials, like the kangaroo and the wallaby, and some rodents, like the jerboa, have a tripedal hopping gait and a posture reminiscent of the upright dinosaurs; but once again the merely pawed forelimbs appear on the way to becoming vestigial. More than that, the semi-erect position of dinosaurs, birds, and kangaroos required constant fighting of gravity and ended in the ossification of the tendons of the dorsal muscles of the trunk and leg; in the jerboa the metatarsals are fused into one bone, as in birds. Hopping, moreover, is mechanically much more complex than four-legged ambling. (Still, one of the primates, *Tarsius,* achieved it, to become the best of all vertebrate hoppers, far surpassing frogs. This big-eyed, big-eared little primate snaps itself so swiftly from one limb to another that it is a matter of "now you see him, now you don't." Moreover, it kept its hind paws intact in the process, obtaining increased leverage by extending the foot *backward*, whereas the horse extends it forward and loses a paw for a one-fingered hoof. That is, by enormously extending the ankle bone, *Tarsius* has achieved an additional limb-lever: the leg extends forward from hip to knee, backward from knee to ankle, and foreward again with the long ankle bone, with a full set of well-developed foot bones at the end of this to boot.)

As for the anthropoids, the great apes achieve at best only a temporary and precarious bipedality, which must constantly call upon the forelimbs for help. Thus we see that, of all the placental mammals, only the primates (and some of the primitive Insectivora) retained the old amphibian limbs unspecialized; and among all the mammalian orders, only the primates evolved from four-footed to "four-handed" animals, by virtue of their tree-living. Torso verticality in trees was perfected by the brachiating primates; the primates, too, began a fateful front- and rear-limb specialization. All the anthropoid apes (as well as baboons and some other monkeys) show a marked tendency to take to the ground. But only the heaviest of them, the gorilla, became primarily terrestrial—and its preferred land gait was quadrupedal knuckle-walking. Thus only man achieved a completely bipedal gait, with the primate hands completely "emancipated" from walking—or from brachiating, flying, or swimming, for that matter.

Thus man's bipedality is bipedality with a difference. It is big-brained and mammalian, unlike the reptile's. It does not have a specialized commitment of the forelimb, as in the bird. It has better than the paws of the jerboa, the kangaroo, or the vertical dinosaurs: it is bipedality backed by the tree-fashioned hands of primates, their stereoscopic eyes, and their elaborated mammalian brains.

The single most spectacular physical trait of human beings is just this bipedality—a fact noticed as early as the ancient Greek philosopher Anaxagoras. The effects of this revolutionary change still echo throughout human anatomy and physiology; it may in fact have made organic evolution itself obsolete, as we shall see later. For, although otherwise a rather generalized animal—as compared successively with anthropoids, primates, and even mammals as a whole—man is undeniably "specialized" in all his functionally bipedal traits. The human foot is an improbable thing. Physically, it is quite as specialized as the horse's and just as clearly constructed for a particular kind of locomotion: the lengthening of the foot gives increased leverage to the leg, much as does the lengthened middle finger of the horse or the ankle bone of *Tarsius*, and the heel gives support.

The importance of heels in giving man a stable kind of four-point support with the balls of the feet is best realized when it is lacking. In the remoter provinces of China such as Yünnan, many of the older women still have bound feet, an artificial deformation in which the foot is curled over until they walk on the backs of the toes, with the heel in the air. This merely two-point support gives these women an unstable "peg-leg," tottering kind of gait, which old-fashioned Chinese gentlemen profess to prefer. Not even the toe-dancing of classical ballet resembles it, strictly speaking. For in ballet it is precisely the critical use of her heels momentarily (or tripod support with her male partner) that enable the *première danseuse* to execute her more picturesque effects. The double arch, lengthwise and crosswise, gives resilient firmness of support, as well as some flexibility for bipedal balance—a far more complex matter mechanically than quadrupedal balance. In fact, by using the heel, outer border, and ball of the foot as the minimal tripod basis of support, man can even stand on one leg—and characteristically does, when resting, among the natives of the Nilotic Sudan in Africa.

There are also pelvic changes for the attachment of muscles to aid in maintaining bipedal balance. But human balance is easier for the fact that the center of gravity of the body lies exactly within the vertical line passing through the center of the skull, the pelvis, knee, and arch of the foot. By contrast, the axis of a gorilla's torso makes an X with a plumb line passing through its center of gravity; thus the gorilla must hang onto something, knuckle-walk, or fall forward onto his teeth. The great lengthening of the legs in man, especially of the thigh bones, gives additional leverage and stride in bipedal walking. The large human buttock is a bipedal specialization also, for the buttocks of other primates—though often spectacularly colored—are small in size and serve sexual and sitting rather than bipedal purposes. The pelvis in man is also more massive, since the entire weight is now supported on only two legs.

But, as is always the case in living organisms, a change in one part brings functional or other changes elsewhere in the body. The broadening of the pelvic basin for the sake of posture can hardly be unrelated to the function of pregnancy. Carpenter had considerable difficulty in telling a wild male gibbon from a female in Siam (except for the broad hint of a baby clinging to her); but in human beings the dimorphous distinctions of the sexes are marked, and especially in the pelvis. The broadening of the pelvis is not merely a matter of specialized bipedal walking functions alone; indeed, the longer-legged male is surpassed in pelvic breadth by the shorter-legged human female. Obviously, therefore, this aspect of human sexual dimorphism serves reproductive purposes. (Amazingly, gibbon pregnancies often pass unnoticed in zoos—which can scarcely be the case with human pregnancies.) The wider pelvis in the female is the enabling factor behind the bigger-skulled, bigger-brained birth among humans. For man has continued the increasing specialization on brains in mammals in general, in primates, and in anthropoids.

Comparative studies show that the smaller species in any one group of animals devote relatively more weight to brain than do larger species in the same group. For example, in mammals, the brain-to-body proportion in the mouse is 1:28, but in the whale it is 1:40,000. Similarly, in birds, a small songbird has 1:27, an ostrich 1:800. It is as if, regardless of the expense in the small animal, there were an irreducible minimum absolute amount of brains for the purposes of that kind of animal. Or, to put it another way, the biological advantages of brains outweighed even their high proportional weight in small animals. Now, taking account of this trend, according to his body weight among mammals, man ought to have about a 1:300 ratio, somewhere between the actual 1:250 of a large dog and the 1:350 of a full-grown sheep, which would bracket man in body weight. In point of fact, however, the proportion in man is *over seven times* what it ought to be on this basis. Man is away out of step in this matter—indeed, although he is hundreds of times as heavy as a mouse, man's 1:40 proportion respectably rivals the 1:28 of a mouse. More than that, his 1:40 clearly outdistances the 1:112 in the female orang and 1:157 in the male (who approximates man in body weight) and the 1:150 to 1:200 of the gorilla (his nearest competitor in intelligence).

In terms of absolute weight of the brain, man of course by no means has the heaviest. But though man is very far from being the largest of the mammals, his showing in absolute brain weight is nevertheless spectacular. His body weight ought to put his absolute brain weight somewhere between the tiger's 290 grams of brain and the sheep's 130. But in actual fact, man's 1,400 grams of brain place it third to those of the very largest mammals of all: the whale's 2,050 and the elephant's 5,000 grams of brain. But even this is not the whole picture. More of the newborn infant in humans is committed to brains than in any other warm-blooded creature regardless of size, from sparrows to whales. Among warm-blooded animals, small songbirds have 1:27. Among mammals, mice have relatively very large brains (1:28) in the adult animal. But in the newborn human, fully one-seventh of the total weight is brain! The small face of the baby seems almost crowded off the skull by its bulging brain. The newborn baby's brain is relatively so monstrous, as regards the adult of the same species, that the rest of the body seems almost an afterthought. This is all the more noticeable with respect to that other human specialization, long legs—which have to wait until years after birth for their major growth. The head height of a child doubles in becoming the head of an adult, the torso triples, and the arm length quadruples—but the leg quintuples in length in growing to the adult size. That is to say, humans are born with big brains that relatively soon after birth (considering the total life-span) grow still bigger, but only much later do they get around to growing long legs: humans have to wait until life is more than a fifth over to get their maximum leg length, but they already have the bulk of all the brains they are ever going to get, before life is one-twentieth gone. By contrast, the smaller brain of the gorilla baby has more nearly finished growing at birth, and most of the growth of the gorilla skull after birth goes into jaws and mechanically related parts—a poor bargain indeed.

Perhaps men should take pause from the fact that, although their brains weigh absolutely more than women's (because men are larger animals than women), nevertheless women's *ratio* of brains to body is superior to men's. Possibly man, when he finds woman thinking circles around him, may take rueful comfort from this fact, for what it is worth; with his lesser proportion of brains, his poorer biological endowment, what can you expect! The fact is, however, it is not so much the amount but the quality of the brain tissue that counts in individuals. The absolute weight of the individual human brain has no particular relationship to the person's intelligence: the biggest brain known was an idiot's, and one of the smallest was that of a famous philosopher. What is important, and alone significant, is that the human species is bigger brained than other animal species.

Hence, no matter how you look at it, *Homo* is fully entitled to the description *sapiens*. Biologically considered, the brain seems almost a voracious organ. Indeed, as the evolution of the brain has proceeded, the human brain has "swallowed" its own spinal cord. That is, the brain has taken over more and more of the spinal functions, bringing former reflex actions under the control of consciousness and will. Responses via instincts, therefore, give way to the more flexible choices of intelligence and learning. Furthermore, among all the mammals, man has the smallest spinal cord relative to his brain. Even in the living anthropoids, the cord is larger in proportion to brain size than in man.

Another superiority of the human brain lies in the overgrowth of the association centers, in the newer part of the brain. When looked at in evolutionary sequence, this "neo-pallium" of the brain seems to sweep forward like a wave, swelling over and engulfing the old smell-brain of the archaic mammals, and, metaphorically at least, bulging the forehead to a vertical position and shoving the reduced face downward and under the skull. The causality of the matter, of course, is nowhere near so simple but depends upon complex organismic-functional relationships. A more accurate explanation would have to take account of other necessities and other enabling factors, which we shall now describe.

Since the hand is fully freed for feeding and since vertical human posture allows little possible come-back for the sense of smell, the ape snout and jaws can retreat still further in man from their jutting prognathism. At the same time, a skull with a lesser commitment to face (and especially to jaws) can then devote relatively more space to brain—for there is probably an upward limit to the total head size possible, even when born through the enlarged human pelvis, further enlarged in the female. In both man and gorilla the major growth of the face and jaw occurs after birth. Thus, in a skull which is consequently more compactly spherical at birth, there is the largest possible cubic volume per longest diameter.

This reasoning seems logical, for Weidenreich has shown that this "brachycephalization" (or increasing roundheadedness) is still occurring even in recent mankind. Weidenreich regards it as one of the mechanical finishing touches on upright balance. This widening of the brain case and the shortening of the jaw do of course facilitate head balance in the more fully erect bipedal posture, just as the front-back flattening of the chest and broadening of the shoulders help the poise of the torso in bipedal man. But this mechanical explanation, true as it is, does not perhaps exhaust the significant functional facts. For the widening of the brain case is absolute as well as relative, and, as the skull broadens, there is an almost incidental improvement in another function, that of seeing. The more widely apart stereoscopic eyes are set, the more obtuse becomes the angle of the lines from eyes to object and the more efficient technically the stereoscopic vision. Widely spaced human eyes are not merely more "beautiful" eyes, they are functionally better eyes. (Indeed, if we could stick them out on side turrets like a hammerhead shark's, they would be still better; fortunately or unfortunately, human evolution shows no sign of this development. Men are merely less squinch-eyed than apes.)

Meanwhile, in the rounder, less snout-jutting skull, the smaller jaw muscles make mechanically reduced demands for purchase on the skull vault; their more right-angled line of pull makes the jaw a more efficient lever system too. Man lacks, and for these two reasons certainly does not need, the specialized sagittal crest required in the male gorilla to separate and to support the antagonistic muscles of its immense prognathous jaws. Nor has man the same thickening of the arches above the eyes, which the gorilla needs mechanically to keep from crushing its eyesockets by the pull of its jaw muscles. With less prognathism, the palate and lower jaw in man are of course more C-shaped than U-shaped. With this shortening of the dental arch, the line of teeth in man becomes—for the first time in primates—not only continuous (without gaps) but also even (non-jagged in profile). The projecting canine tooth at the outer corners of the prognathous jaw is somewhat useless in a shorter rounded jaw, and it is particularly reduced in length—almost to that of the incisors and premolars flanking it. Animals which must grasp with the teeth, such as horses, usually have to have these front teeth, or incisors, "procumbent" or forward-leaning. But handed man, with less jutting jaws and a change in the angle of muscle pull, can now bite with incisors vertically edge to edge. Therefore, instead of a "simian shelf" inside the retreating chin of the anthropoid ape, man has a vertical chin, open at the bottom—a doubly neat solution, since it does not crowd but rather increases the flexibility of the tongue and throat muscles which man uses in speech. The fanning-out of jaw-muscle attachments in a smaller area above the ears means, however, that a man has to tilt his hat, or even take it off, when he is eating. A small price indeed for his bigger brain!

This general "globularization" of the skull, then, is probably more than a merely incidental mechanical fact related to posture; for the head remains part of the whole body in more ways than one. In the last analysis, this increasing roundheadedness may be a functional solution of the brain versus pelvis reproductive problem—in which the brain, in its own fashion, has won out. Some anthropologists, fearful of Lamarckian heresy and not wishing to be accused of "orthogenesis," are willing to see the validity of mechanical adjustments only if these are uncontaminated by any manifest biological purpose. But this runs the far greater risk of supposing that all these complex—and obviously related—changes are without function or meaning in any evolutionary sense. That organisms do not pre-plan their purposes surely does not mean that they never do achieve purposes!

If one may assume that the "purposes" of evolutionary change must be the purposes which actually do become accomplished, then all these related changes seem selectively organized for the ultimate purposes of the largest possible brain that still has to be born through a pelvis. In choosing which traits to regard as directive or pre-eminent in such a complex, we are forced to regard as such those traits which the animal itself has adaptively "chosen" in its own development. (This does not mean that primate fetuses have been consciously and competitively planning big brains since away back yonder, but it does mean that primates who accidentally happened to have bigger brains for one reason or another got along better adaptively in the long run, the real world being as it is.) In man this is fairly easy to see, since brain subordinates face and jaw in the skull and in fact overshadows the rest of the whole body in the newborn baby. From early mammals to man, evolutionary development has cumulatively gone in the direction of more brain; and in the growth of the individual human being also the emphatic insistence is upon brain. Thus all these mechanically associated traits must be viewed as having ultimately aided, accidentally or otherwise, in serving the major function which does in fact end in being achieved. For the size of the brain case has been the consistent winner in every play of the game.

Meanwhile, of course, there are other related changes in the skeleton. With less jutting jaws, increasingly round skull, and a more fully vertical posture than in the apes, the joining of the skull with the backbone is more centrally under the skull. This means that the skull can now be largely supported by gravity and does not need the thick muscles at the back of the neck in apes. Since the neck-spines on the upper backbone are likewise reduced in length (no longer being required for such massive muscle attachment), man has a slenderer neck than the anthropoids and probably at least slightly greater ease in looking around. The upper backbone has a "cervical" neck curvature, not present in knuckle-walking primates; this is related to upright posture and also helps the poise of the skull and absorbs shock.

At the other end of the backbone, the pelvis rotates part of the way with the torso from a pronograde (horizontal) to an orthograde (vertical) position with reference to the hind limbs. Very evidently, however, the first four-legged amphibians had not foreseen this remote contingency of vertical man. Mechanically, the pelvis is not able to rotate the necessary full 90° for the torso to be fully vertical; hence the lower backbone must curve in the lumbar region to make up for this. The S-shaped thigh-bone of anthropoids (and early man) straightens out and lengthens at the same time. Thus modern man has an S-shaped spine and a straight thigh-bone, rather than the reverse. One student points out, indeed, that the lumbar curve is not even inherited in the species but develops only when the baby sits up and walks: it is thus so recent as not to be phylogenetic (evolutionary) but only ontogenetic (individual) in development.

Certainly man has had troubles with his pelvis! Some changes have been made necessarily with the change from support of soft internal organs, hung like washing from the line of the backbone, to support of the slumped jumble from below. The flat abdomen is justly admired in man, for it represents a genuine muscular achievement when it occurs. For support from below, man used an inward-curled tail, the coccyx, which ever since animals gave up swimming had hardly been much used in mammals except to give tripod support or to switch off flies. Some of the light-weight New World monkeys, it is true, learned to hang by their tails—a really clever idea, at least as clever as the elephant's trunk, but not, apparently, with much future to it. But as the tail is, after all, a part of the backbone, no such internal changes were needed in monkeys; it is only in the heavy, more vertical Old World anthropoids that the external tail was given up, and for the same reasons as in man. Nevertheless—in skull, backbone, femur, heel, and pelvis and in everything having to do with full and free standing on his own two feet—man stands alone, because he alone stands.

Exactly when all this happened—for it plainly has happened—has long been, and still is, a matter of controversy. For good if somewhat technical reasons, experts disagree over which changes preceded which others. For example, recent fossil evidence seems to indicate that the vertical body precedes, both in time and in causation, the globular skull in man. A healthy scientific situation prevails, for no sooner do two gigantic apes turn up in fossil form from Asia, than South Africa counters with a passel of unquestionably bipedal man-apes. The continuing flow of facts is the best thing that could happen, for fantasies proliferate where facts are few.

But scientists are only human, and one healthy hooter at shaky hypotheses has chosen to look at the whole thing with his tongue in his cheek and with deft pinkings of nationalist trends in science. The French tradition in anthropology, Hooton points out, is to regard man as a very late development, almost of proto-historic times (for of course the French too are only latecomers to historical eminence). The French consider that the only fitting ancestor of modern man is Cro-Magnon man, an intelligent and artistic product of the caves in southern France—to the exclusion of the "German" Neanderthal man, a brawnier but stupider race (in terms of brain capacity), whose general type has been found elsewhere not only in Europe but also throughout much of Asia and Africa. The German tradition in general has been to derive man in comparatively recent geological times from a generalized giant anthropoid, taller even than Wagner's supermen or King Friedrich Wilhelm's soldiers, but related to the gorilla, chimpanzee, or orang-utan. Klaatsch even took the extravagantly "racist" point of view of deriving the modern human races from different anthropoid-ape ancestors!

The Americans have a larger appetite for ancestral time depth. W. K. Gregory, basing his conclusions on a wide range of anatomical characters (but especially the teeth), believes that man probably arose from a generalized and progressive anthropoid-like *Dryopithecus*, whose five-cusped molars are of a type ancestral to man; fossils of the *Dryopithecus* group are found in many parts of Europe, Africa, and Asia in Late Tertiary (Middle and Upper Miocene) times. Hooton also believes it is somewhere in this general region of paleontological time and geographical space that some giant *Dryopithecus*-descended ape first took to the ground and thus made the first fateful steps toward humanity. On the other hand, understandably, the British place man's ancestors in the still remoter past: Sir Arthur Keith and Le Gros Clark once thought that man branched off the anthropoid line as early as the Oligocene, while G. Elliot Smith and Wood-Jones would insist that there is no ancestor of man among all the primates above the tarsioid level!

With a large sympathy (based upon a very large knowledge of comparative anatomy) the internationalist Weidenreich would include not only Neanderthal in *Homo sapiens* but also even *Sinanthropus pekinensis* of China and *Pithecanthropus erectus* of Java, because of what he believes is their genetic and morphological continuity. As regards the evidence available at present, it seems clear that Weidenreich is right in regarding man as emerging from a welter of genetically related hominid types, and he is joined by the weighty opinion of Dobzhansky in considering living mankind as a single polytypical species. The position of Weidenreich and Dobzhansky has the advantage of making the apparent situation in the past consistent with the obvious situation in the present, so far as the promiscuous outbreeding of hominids is concerned.

On the paleontological period and place of man's branching-off, there seems no need to derive him from primates as remote (and as specialized) as *Tarsius*, even though a tarsioid may have been ancestral to the later primates that include man. Man's teeth are undeniably dryopithecine; so some one of the species of *Dryopithecus* must have been in his ancestry. And the features which man shares with modern anthropoids (blood groups, lack of tail, terrestrial tendency, eye and brain characteristics, etc.) undoubtedly place man with the "man-like" apes. The present evidence is impressive for the position that man is derived from a giant arboreal anthropoid ape, which took to ground-living somewhere between south-central Africa, and central, southern, or western Asia, in very early Quaternary times (some million years ago) or even earlier in Miocene or Pliocene times. Meanwhile, the point where one draws the line between proto-hominids and *Homo sapiens* depends upon many and diverse criteria in different scholars. Also, there is not one single "missing link" but many, one at each parting of the ways. Possibly, in time, the welter of small and bootless taxonomic skirmishes will be given up in favor of a functional view of man: the first bipedal ape with fire and tools.

But what caused this bold and precedent-shaking event of full bipedality in the primate world? One theory suggests a change in climate associated with the uplifting of the Himalaya Mountains and the consequent cutting-off of central Asia from rain-producing and jungle-growing monsoons: the trees disappeared, and our ape was perforce left stranded on the ground. But the linearity of man, his relative hairlessness, his clothing, and his culture-based carnivorousness suggest that the proto-humans, like the anthropoids, were warm-climate-adapted animals, caught off base by the Pleistocene Ice Ages, not by Himalayan cataclysms. The cataclysmic theory is not quite satisfying for other reasons too. As Hooton unanswerably put it, apes can brachiate a good deal faster than forests can recede. Many students believe the ancestral ape came down to earth of its own free will, motivated to enlarge its diet, and was able largely to stay down because of its great strength.

Still, this could be done in temporary forays, without relinquishing the pleasant fruits of the trees or their primate protection. Besides, all the great apes still live in forested regions, for all their terrestrial tendencies. It may be that the anthropoids were simply such successful animals that they grew progressively in size, obedient to "Depéret's law," much as the elephant and horse families grew progressively bigger throughout their history. If so, the result of this would be that tree-living became more and more inconvenient for locomotion and suitable only for nightly retreat. For it is to be noted that the anthropoid apes, on the whole, became progressively more terrestrial as they became larger and heavier and progressively poorer brachiators. Certainly the modern anthropoids have not been grounded by any disappearance of forests in their habitat. Furthermore, for all its predominantly terrestrial habits, the largest of the anthropoids, the gorilla, is still a strict vegetarian, with no interest in hunting land animals to parallel the chimpanzee's incidental diet of birds' eggs, insects, and perhaps birds themselves. The proto-hominid may have had less a dietary lure than a *vis à tergo* to keep him grounded: his increasing weight. He simply got too big to float through the air with any very great ease.

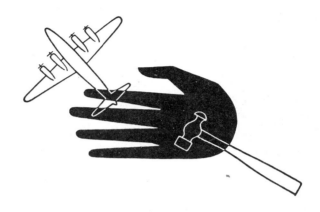

5. Man Hands Himself a New Kind of Evolution

Early man was an earth-bound ape, with empty hands. But it was these same empty hands that changed completely the whole manner of evolution in man and made him unique beyond all comparison with any other living creature. Seen in its separate aspects, the human hand is nothing special. Five-toed paws were part of the original pattern of lungs and legs of even the early amphibians, and they are thoroughly commonplace in later land animals descended from the amphibians. For man to have five fingers would be the usual thing to expect: it is the pterodactyl's little-finger flying, the bat's long-fingered wing-hand, the bird's arm-wing, and the whale's hand-flippers that are the anatomically clever, the functionally spectacular, variations on the basic pentadactyl theme. Human hands are not unusual, either, as the freed limbs of bipedal animals: there are plenty of instances of this, from reptilian dinosaurs to marsupial kangaroos and mammalian jerboas. Nor is the hand unique as a grasping organ in man: many of the tree-living primates were even four-handed, and thus two up on man—whose specialized foot has lost just about all its one-time prehensile skill.

The uniqueness of man's hand is functional, not physical. Of course his primate ancestors' sojourn in the trees did greatly improve the grasping ability of the old amphibian-reptilian-mammalian paw. It is also true that the fully opposable thumb in man is a further improvement on the primate hand. But in purely physical terms, monkey hands could probably do nearly everything a man's hands could. The main significance of the human hand lies in its being one member of a functional complex of hands, brains, and eyes.

When man, heir of four limbs, uses only two of them for walking, his clever primate hands are then finally freed from use in any kind of locomotion whatever. They can now be used for purely exploratory grasping. The advantages of this are not to be underestimated. Some New World monkeys, it is true, have prehensile tails, but these are still largely locomotor in function; besides, the tail has the grave disadvantage of not being ordinarily in the monkey's field of vision. A better case of exploratory prehensility is the elephant's trunk—perhaps significantly combined, as is man's hand, with great intelligence. But the elephant's trunk is mainly used for feeding; and, besides, there is only one of them. Nor do elephants have stereoscopic vision, to put together a muscular with a visual space-sense. Still, a sensitive grasping trunk is not to be sneezed at as a biological advantage. At least in the past, the elephant family had the adaptive radiation that often shows up in a successful animal type; for elephant-like creatures once made themselves at home in a variety of environments from Siberia to Sumatra, from England to Africa, and from Saskatchewan to South America. But judgment must respect the fact that all of these are extinct, some of them with man's assistance, except for the elephants of Africa and of Southeast Asia—and these too are dying out.

Emancipated hands are not enough: many dinosaurs had them, but they lacked sufficient brains. Intelligence is not enough: elephants have a great deal of intelligence behind their trunks, but they do not have stereoscopic sight; the prehensile-tailed monkeys are intelligent too, and they have stereoscopic vision as well, but they do not ordinarily see their tails. Stereoscopic eyes are not enough either: for the intelligent, tree-living apes have them, with color vision and the yellow spot in the retina to boot. It is the combination that counts. Man has paired grasping organs, fully in his field of vision and wholly freed from locomotor duties, in a stereoscopic-sighted, big-brained mammal—and these add up to the answer.

Anaxagoras claimed that man had brains because he had hands, but Aristotle argued that man had hands because he had brains. When the implications of these statements are better understood and the dust of battle has settled a bit, modern anthropologists are inclined to give the decision to Anaxagoras rather than to Aristotle. But hands, brains, and eyes are a case, really, of hens-and-eggs causality; nor did it all begin, strictly speaking, with man. For in all primate evolution they influence each other mutually and develop progressively together; and the ability to "monkey with things" that man got from his primate ancestors is still one of the keystones of human nature. Certainly such hands and eyes and brains put an animal into closer object-relationship with reality and enlarge the animal ego in the technical sense of increasing awareness and testing of reality. Very literally, such an animal as man has more *contacts* with reality.

But when we remember the conflict of brains and snout for possession of the skull (the total size of which is limited by pelvic birth), it is probable that the mouth is also part of the hand-brain-eye complex. Eating is just as much a function of the primate hand as are tree-acrobatics. Food, as much as safety, both available in the trees, probably took the primates originally into the trees. And at least some students believe that food available on the ground brought them down again—after a refashioning of locomotion itself in the service of nutrition. When primary grasping with the snout is given up, the sense of smell is less important as a guide. But if snout-smelling gives pleasure in feeding, hands will now share in the pleasurable accomplishment of the basic organic satisfaction, eating. While smell still plays a large role in eating enjoyment, the relative insignificance of the snout anatomically and of smell functionally indicates that they are overshadowed in man.

The matter is probably more complex than this. It should be remembered that grasping the mother's fur is part of the association of food and security in primate babies. It is significant too that in human babies the two major reflexes fully prepared at birth are the "sucking reflex" and the "grasping reflex" (such that a baby can actually support its weight and hang from a bar tightly grasped in its hands). Also, one gets the decided impression in watching older babies that half the fun of eating lies in playing with the food. All in all, it seems quite probable that human hands have an "erotized" interest in handling things, which is borrowed from their pleasurable association with feeding. Anatomically, man has obviously moved beyond a mere nutritional "oral" interest in his environment. His hands show a controlling, manipulative concern with non-nutritional *objects*, with a desire and an ability to coerce reality beyond his own body and body-contents, or potential body-contents like food; just as, similarly, the permanent human breast and heightened sexuality evidence a persistent and organically rooted inter-individual interest in other *persons*.

In this hand-brain-mouth-eye complex, the close brain-eye tie-up is quite clear: we have only to look at the large optic lobe in the brain of later animals to see this. The brain-hand nexus is very evident neurologically, for the nerve-supply of the hand is almost fantastically rich—even in so archaic a sense as touch, the hand (as compared, say, with the thigh, the leg, or the back) is developed in discrimination and sensitivity to an extravagant degree. The hand-eye connection is easily appreciated on study of muscle-sense, stereoscopic seeing, and space-awareness in man. The hand-mouth relationship is shown in several ways. The newborn human baby is very undeveloped neurologically, that is, many of its nerves do not grow to make final connections with muscles until a couple of years after birth; and, in this context, the neurological maturity of the sucking and that of the grasping reflexes is particularly striking. Furthermore, the representation of the lips in the cerebral cortex is quite enormous in comparison with other parts of the body. Also, in a baby old enough to sit up, anything that the eye can see and the hand can grasp is immediately sent to the mouth for consultation and confirmation.

The price in irreversible specialization in his foot, which man has paid for this new significance of the hand, seems a small one indeed when its advantages are noted. For it must be admitted that the human foot is now as hopelessly specialized as the limbs and appendages of most other warm-blooded creatures, and it is difficult to imagine its ever being useful for anything but bipedal walking. The accidents of evolution rarely give an animal a chance for more than one or perhaps two adaptive specializations of any organ: the more exactly and efficiently an organ is adapted anatomically to some special aspect of the environment, the more fatally dependent it is on the accidents of environmental change. The large-scale extinction of animal species in the past fully illustrates this fact. It is as if that species goes farthest which holds off its physical specializations as long as possible; it can then build its own minor specialization on as large a collection of prior major animal accomplishments as possible.

But this suggests a greater planning and self-consciousness in organisms than is really visible in evolution. The value to organisms of getting a hold on things must be a general one, for it is found in many kinds of animals. The general idea of hands has been stumbled on again and again in evolution, from crabs and scorpions and their claws to the various backboned animals (the two-legged dinosaurs, and "three-legged" wallabies and kangaroo rats) that sit or stand up to use their front paws in holding things. In this light, the hand in man is a venture backed by the biological capital of all the long line of body patents to which he is the heir, in the main line of amphibians, reptiles, mammals, and primates. But the double arch of the human foot—that came from changing from the land to the trees and then back again from the trees to the ground—shows that man's line has already taken all his probable chances at adaptive specialization of the hind limbs. As far as the foot is concerned, man is now in the same evolutionary boat as every other specialized animal: an adaptation, once made, is a hostage to fortune and a commitment to future evolutionary fate. The human foot has "had it."

The great bargain that this specialization represents in man, however, removes him from any comparison with any other animal. The human hand is the adaptation to end all adaptations: *the emancipated hand has emancipated man from any other organic evolution whatsoever*. With man, genetic evolution and organic experiments have come to an end. Without involving the animal body and its slow, blind genetic mechanisms, man's hands make the tools and the machines which render his own further physical evolution unnecessary; they replace the slow, cumbrous, expensive, uncertain, and painful mechanism of organic evolution with the swift, conscious, biologically free, and painless making of machines.

Nothing like this has ever happened before in evolution. Machines not only can do man's flying, diving, and superhuman seeing and hearing for him, but also *they do his evolving for him.* (Indeed, in a cybernetic "feed-back" machine like a thermostat—in which the results of its action are automatically scanned by the machine to correct and modify its future action according to man's preconceived, built-in intentions—man is already creating a quasi-organism, with one sense and a part-brain, after his own image. Nor does it invite disrespect to realize that with his brain man can build mathematical thinking machines better than his own for their particular purpose.) The critical fact is that the making of machines is done with no narrow and irreversible commitment whatever of man's body. With human hands, the old-style evolution by body adaptation is obsolete. All previous animals had been subject to the *autoplastic* evolution of their self-substance, committing their bodies to experimental adaptations in a blind genetic gamble for survival. The stakes in this game were high: life or death. Man's evolution, on the other hand, is through *alloplastic* experiments with objects outside his own body and is concerned only with the products of his hands, brains, and eyes—and not with his body itself. True, a flaw in the design of an experimental jet plane may kill a pilot, but that does not make the human race extinct or even wipe out aeronautical engineers as a species.

It is an error to suppose that a spider's web is in this sense a "tool." For, besides being instinctive (a genetically given function), the spider web is merely an autoplastic extension into space of its own non-living substance or metaplasm. No more is a bird's nest a "tool," since neither insight nor tuition and neither memory nor experience plays any part in this instinctual activity. Even the most generous interpretation would allow temporary or accidental nonce "tools" only to anthropoids. But then these tools are not socially hereditary, for the best that apes have is insight or imitation-by-contiguity, and not human culture.

It is not only the genetic freedom of man's new kind of evolution that is significant; one has to consider also the fantastic speed of it as well. It took millions and millions of years from fish to whale to evolve a warm-blooded marine mammal: but man evolved submarines from dream to actuality in a mere few centuries and at no genetic price in physical specialization. It took innumerable genera of birds uncountable eons since *Archaeopteryx* for their autoplastic experimentation with flying: but man, in only some fifty years since Kitty Hawk, flies not only as well as birds but actually far better. In objective physical terms of speed, altitude, and range, man already flies faster than sound (something no bird will ever do with moving wings), higher than any bird (since birds must breathe the open air), and farther than even the most miraculous migratory bird (with its settled complex of methods, materials, and metabolism). Even by the admittedly crude evolutionary criterion of gross size, man's airplanes are even now far larger and far heavier than any eagle or condor, whereas a bird as large as an ostrich is already permanently grounded. Man makes a new model of plane and tinkers with its mechanical "bugs" much more cheaply biologically and more efficiently and quickly than any bird can modify its form by evolution.

Since man's machines evolve now, not anatomical man, he has long since gone outside his own individual skin in his functional relatedness to the world. The real evolutionary unit now is not man's mere body; it is "all-mankind's-brains-together-with-all-the-extrabodily-materials-that-come-under-the-manipulation-of-their-hands." Man's very physical ego is expanded to encompass everything within reach of his manipulating hands, within sight of his searching eyes, and within the scope of his restless brain. An airplane is part of a larger kinaesthetic and functional self; it is a larger ownership of reality by the questing ego of life. And airplanes are biologically cheap. For, as unconcernedly as a man changes an auger for a reamer in an electric drill, he exchanges the joystick of a plane for the driving wheel of a car. Without being, through specialization, a biological amputee, he attaches all sorts of prosthetic devices to his limbs. This *evolution-by-prosthesis* is uniquely human and uniquely freed from the slowness of reproduction and of evolutionary variation into blind alleys from which there is no retreat. Man, with tools as his projected body and machines the prosthetic creatures of his hands, is not merely a promising animal biologically: he makes every other animal wholly obsolete, except as they serve *his* purposes of prosthetic metabolism, locomotion, manufacture of materials and of biological medicines.

This new kind of human evolution is fully proved in the positive sense by man's conquest of reality. All the standard biological criteria, save one, can be applied in his case. As monkeys go, man is a large animal. In number of individuals, man is certainly now the most common large mammal on earth, and his numbers are increasing. In range and in variety of environmental adjustments, no other animal remotely rivals him. But this new kind of evolution is further proved negatively in terms of the striking inapplicability of another biological criterion—that of adaptive radiation. Man himself has stopped evolving physically in any massive or significant way. The basic type of man, the human species generously conceived, has been much the same since 500,000 to 1,000,000 years ago. This is an astounding thing in an animal as spectacularly successful biologically as man is. *Man is the only successful animal never to undergo adaptive radiation.*

We have seen that adaptive radiation is the commonplace of evolution: with each new and successful animal discovery or invention comes a variety of divergent additional adaptations built upon the basic patent. Thus when the arthropods added the achievement of land existence to chitin and exoskeleton, the insect group taken alone proliferated into some 600,000 or more separate and distinct species. The verticality of *Homo sapiens* is a change of at least the magnitude of the arthropod change of habitat—indeed it is actually far greater— and yet *Homo sapiens* exists in only one species! Now it is true that in the races of man we find objective and measurable differences, some of which (though fewer than one imagines) are genetic in nature. But the extraordinary thing is that racial differences in man are neither *radial* adaptations in the exact sense, nor are they even racial *adaptations*.

The first point is quite plain. Whatever changes of whatever scale have occurred all the way from proto-hominids to the type we choose to designate *Homo sapiens,* it is quite obvious that one race is not evolving its hands into hammers, another into pincers, and still others into screwdrivers or chisels. This kind of process is entirely absent in man. The reason for this is that man's genetic promiscuity and geographical getting around have always prevented the genetic and geographic isolation necessary for the rise of divergent animal species. True, this mixing of races and of stocks is a very slow process in time —one that waits upon such large-scale events as the great invasions out of central Asia, the almost explosive medieval migrations of peoples outward from Arabia and Scandinavia, the discovery of the New World, and European imperialism in Asia and in Africa. But slow also is the tempo of generations in man.

Some students have reasonably pointed out that these conditions may not always have been exactly the same throughout the history of *Homo sapiens.* Washburn estimates that in the hunting and gathering stage of culture, there were probably only about 7,000,000 human beings in the entire world. This poverty in absolute numbers and the dispersal of people owing to the way of life would favor the conditions of relative geographical (continent-wise) isolation, the accidents of "genetic sampling," and the genetic drift which are evidenced in the fact of races today. But this relative inbreeding of early man can never have been absolute; for, as Washburn conservatively points out, "Each living race has had at least one hundred times as much of its human ancestry in common with all the other races as it has had alone." Furthermore, Hooton considers that the primary race-making stage in man's biology ended about 15,000 to 20,000 years ago, at the close of the Pleistocene.

It is an old and still respectable opinion that modern races represent local climatic types. It is argued, for example, that the non-projecting nose and fat-padded slit eyes of the Mongoloids are adaptations to a cold, dry climate. This seems plausible; but one might well ask such reasonable questions as "Why then the projecting cheekbones?" and "Why then their hairless bodies?" It is easy to see that one could quickly become lost in a tangle of *ad hoc* arguments, depending on which climate one wished to rationalize, for men do move about. In this case, however, the argument is a good one, for we have every reason to believe that this same general human type has lived in central East Asia since the remotest human times. The immediate next question would be, "Why has this alleged climatic type not been modified as it moved southward?" Certainly Singapore is not cold, or Siam dry, and yet Mongoloid and Chinese types have retained their racial identity in these new climates.

The answer to this would be easy. Even if the southward drift of Mongoloids in Asia began long before the slow pressure of Chinese culture from north China (beginning in the Shang Dynasty Bronze Age), Mongoloids remain Mongoloids wherever found in Asia, because in slow-breeding man they have not had enough time yet to change genetically. The trouble with this argument, however, is that it is inconsistent with the case of the American Indian, an ancient offshoot of Asiatic Mongoloids. The American Indian has certainly been in the New World since the end of the last Ice Age, and probably before— a rather longer time ago than the Chinese Bronze Age. In the New World the Indian has certainly been placed in a great variety of environments, from the Barren Grounds of northwestern Canada to the rich woodlands of the southeastern United States, and from the cool, dry highlands of Peru and Mexico to the dank, hot lowlands of Amazonia and the Caribbean islands. And yet, with all this greater time depth and with all this variety of climate, the American Indian is essentially the same unspecialized Mongoloid from Alaska to Patagonia!

Surely the genetic and geographic isolation possible with two whole empty continents open before them was much greater for the American Indians than when hunting tribes were, relatively speaking, crowding one another out of eastern Siberia across the Bering Straits. The great difficulty is that if the race-climatologists demand a still longer time for genetic change than the period since the end of the Ice Age, they do so at their peril. For with the Ice Age comes a great change in just that climatic stability on which such adaptation depends, and the whole argument falls to the ground.

We are therefore prepared to agree that genetic drift in early man has made for large-scale, continent-wise differences in race. But we cannot see how the observed genetically stable types could have threaded their way so successfully through immense ranges of time and into such climatically diverse areas, if racial traits are simply adaptations to climate. For if once adaptive, why not always adaptive? The fact is, slow-breeding man gets around too fast—indeed, climates themselves change too rapidly—to account for the observed anthropological facts.

Once again, if races are adaptive types of man, we have to enlarge the scope of the term *Homo sapiens*, so that we may call upon the larger reaches of time that seem to be needed to explain the observed genetic facts. The definition of man in niggling taxonomic or minor anatomical terms misses the genetic boat. And so far as the major races of man are concerned, there must be other factors operating than simple climatic adaptation.

In any case, with the enormous rise in absolute numbers, the increased migrations of man in at least historic times, and still greater mobility in modern times (with consequently increased geographic and genetic impingement of one group upon another), the relative outbreeding of historic man is increasingly dominant over the relative inbreeding of early mankind. Therefore, in this absence of genetic and geographic isolation, whatever imaginable variations arise in physical man of the future, these will never assume the scale of differences of species. Thus, even if these physically differing varieties of man happen to be adaptations (and not something else), the adaptations would remain the genetic property of mankind at large. In other words, because of the constant and indeed increasing inter-breeding of groups in *Homo sapiens*, any "adaptive" variations that should arise in one race of man would remain genetically available to the whole species.

Perhaps this can best be explained in terms of genes, those units of heredity, each of which has a definite position on one of the rod-shaped chromosomes in the nucleus of a germ cell. In joining together at fertilization, germ cells add to the total gene potential of an organism by the fusion of two heredities. But fission in the production of specialized body cells means a subtraction of possibilities. That is, a fertilized germ cell can give rise in the new individual to more different kinds of cells than can any already specialized kind of body cell. For example, a nerve cell—by virtue of its high specialization at the end of many body-cell divisions—is poorer in genes than is a fertilized germ cell. In becoming a nerve cell, it has lost a germ cell's potentialities for becoming any kind of body cell whatsoever; more than that, a nerve cell has lost much of its ability to reproduce, by fission, even another nerve cell, with the result that only very limited repair and regeneration are possible when a nerve is injured. Meanwhile, the germ cell, by not specializing, has retained its "totipotentiality," i.e., the power, on fusing with another germ cell, of giving rise to a whole new individual made up of all kinds of cells. In human beings these germ cells are segregated from the body cells in the earliest divisions of the fertilized ovum. Thus these germ cells retain their ability to be ancestral to any kind of body cell (in an individual of the next generation). But the body cells, in giving rise to a new individual (in this generation), gradually lose more and more of their genes as they are specialized more and more into the various parts of the individual's body.

Something of the same kind is true of animal species. The more specialized an animal species is, the more genetic possibility has become somatic actuality. A species with selective adaptation to an environment *and with genetic or geographic isolation from closely related species* (which is one of the basic criteria of what constitutes separate species) is poorer in genes than the total mother-stock. That is, any one species of animal is poorer in total variety of genes than is a whole group of related species. For example, there is a greater variety of genes in the sum total of South African antelopes (springbok, steenbok, hartebeest, duiker, eland, nylghau, gnu, etc.) than there is in any one of the species alone. But a springbok's adaptations are not a bit of good to the gnu, or the gnu's to the springbok, so long as they are genetically isolated from one another as separate species. As a result, the non-inter-breeding of these species makes the great total variety of antelope genes mutually unavailable in the separate species.

Contrast this perfectly normal situation in animals with the atypical case of man. For all its spectacular variety, mankind is obviously a morphological and genetic unity. (Indeed, the fossil evidence, e.g., the Mount Carmel finds, suggests that this has been true since the most ancient past.) Mankind appears to have arisen, with different local gene concentrations, from a large and miscellaneous mass of closely related proto-hominids inhabiting much of the Old World. But, instead of further differentiating into gene-impoverished separate species (like the South African antelopes), these local varieties of *Homo sapiens* maintained at least enough genetic contact with one another for all modern races to be able to interbreed—with the result that the species *Homo sapiens* is fantastically rich genetically.

In this remarkable fact, man is obviously once again a different *kind* of species from any wild-animal species. The total number of germ cells contained within even one pair of a wild-animal species could probably reproduce all the limited traits and variabilities (hair color, etc.) of that entire species; but man is genetically far too complex for this. Spuhler has ingeniously calculated human gene-loci (the actual locations on the chromosomes of the controllers of identifiable hereditary traits) as being of the order of 20,000–42,000. But even ignoring the fact that each gene-locus is not necessarily limited to controlling only one genetic trait, the treasure trove of alternative human genes is too enormous for traits of even one major race to be contained within the germ cells of a single pair of human parents.

Suppose, for the sake of argument, that man scrapes along with a bare 30,000 gene-loci. Suppose, also, that there were only two alternative possibilities for each gene (e.g., yellow versus black skin) in human beings. This is, of course, a great over-simplification of the facts; but, conservatively, we would then have genetic possibilities of the order of $2^{30,000}$. In other words, all the human beings who have ever lived throughout the Pleistocene period have not scratched the surface of possible gene combinations in *Homo sapiens*. Actually the human kind of animal may not especially need such an extravagant adaptive potential. But in survival terms this biological booty of genes in man is fabulous. Very probably, descendants of *Homo sapiens* will still be around when the last of all the antelope species will have become extinct, even in zoos. The representative from Buncombe County may get gasping fits at this disclosure and the Senator from Mississippi blow a gasket, but the fact is that man's best biological future lies precisely in his present out-breeding behavior: it is not his sin, but his salvation.

6. Father Comes Home To Stay

Man's vertical posture, which gave him hands, was laden with far-reaching consequences. But even these are overshadowed in significance by the fateful results of a new kind of animal association in the higher primates, the tendency toward familial social organization. As developed further in man, this social artifact, the family, is firmly and visibly rooted in human biology—quite as the symbiosis of ants and aphids is based on their respective mouth-parts and metabolism; as ant society depends on the "social stomach"; and as termite organization rests on cellulose metabolism, coprophagia, food exudations, and hive specializations; quite as worker-bee tending of the young depends on the nurses' "salivary" glands; and as wasp nurturance derives from reciprocal specializations in sugar and protein metabolism in adults and grubs. In distinct but equally valid fashion, human society is biologically based upon the human body, and most especially upon the human breast and human sexuality.

No wild animal has the permanent breast. The female in *Homo sapiens* uniquely possesses such a specialization alone of all the mammals—with the exception of the domesticated milch animals which are man's own creations long after the fact of his humanity. This anatomical feature in humans, however, is more than a mere "domesticated" trait and is certainly more than a merely cosmetic creation of sexual selection. It is, rather, one of the causes of human domestication itself, in a complex chain of mutually related factors.

In the mammals, milk secretion provides the physiological basis of the association of a mother and her offspring. The nourishment and protection of the young by the adult animal profoundly affects both mother and young in the association. Since more of the offspring are enabled thereby to survive, the female may also enjoy a greater economy of reproductive activity. This relation of survival of young to reproductive economy is, of course, a theme running through all life. It is found not only in mammals but also independently in birds, reptiles, and amphibians. The latter need lay fewer eggs than fish do, since the grown amphibian escapes its aquatic enemies when it comes onto the land. In turn, reptiles need lay fewer eggs than amphibians, since the reptile young also escape aquatic enemies. Birds need lay still fewer eggs than reptiles, since nesting in trees (for a majority of species) and the feeding and protection of the fledglings by the adult birds bring a still higher percentage of survivors—added to which, flying allows adult birds to escape many of the ground-living enemies of amphibians, reptiles, and birds.

The mammalian "society" of mother and young is the forerunner and the basis of more complex mammalian societies; and much the same survival purposes are served in both as were served in the earlier adaptations mentioned. The gain through protective association of mother and young is still further increased among the hooved animals, where herding habits secure the mutual protection of adults by adults— and with still greater economy of reproduction. In non-herding animals like cats, with only brief maternal care of the young and no mutually protective association of adults, the individual animal must soon be an adult itself and on its own. But the herding habit means a higher survival rate in both young and adult animals. The herding antelope and cattle species can therefore have fewer young at a time and fewer total young per female than do such prolific solitary animals as cats, rabbits, or even non-gregarious primates like some of the smaller lemurs which have litters.

Herding together also multiplies the danger-warning senses of the individuals in the herd. Hence it is not uncommon to find herds among preyed-upon grass-eating mammals, just as flocks are not unusual among preyed-upon or migratory birds. Some of the larger hooved animals with the herding habit develop the further specialization of horns as a defense. To hunt these large horned animals successfully, the smaller carnivorous animals (such as those of the dog family) must themselves unite to hunt in a pack. The sexual specialization in horns in male herding animals undoubtedly still further serves reproductive economy in the female—indeed, in some ungulate species the females have horns too.

Still more marked sexual specialization occurs in some hooved animals. Heightened sexual activity seems hardly needed in species that have gained greater reproductive economy—at least it is not needed for purely reproductive purposes. Significantly, harem-forming herders, like the bull and the male goat, are notorious for ebullient genital activity in the service of herd polygamy—precisely in those forms which became man's domesticated animals. Horns and heightened sexual activity in males alike serve herding-societality; and this in turn affects both the reproductive economy and the sexual dimorphism (udders) in the female. These were the potentialities on which man built his own protective domestication of such animals.

Life in the trees secured for primates the same protective advantages for both young and adults as birds have through flight and nesting; but among some primates the living together in hordes additionally got the same advantages as herding animals have. The effects on reproduction, from the double security of tree life and of group association, are clear. The tree-living tarsier is less prolific than the land-living pig; furthermore, the gregarious monkeys (and even the only partly arboreal anthropoids) are still less prolific than terrestrial herding ungulates. Once again, the tree-living horde primates are less prolific than dogs, which, for all their hunting in packs, nevertheless have multiple young like the solitary cat and rabbit. Both the horde-habit and tree-living, therefore, must be held jointly responsible for the marked reduction in number of offspring among primates. For, in general, the gregarious primates (monkeys, gibbons, and chimpanzees) are still less prolific than non-gregarious primates, such as many of the lemurs.

In fact, the same gradations exist among the primates themselves, when associated with additional factors. Within the primate group, the growth of maternal care is progressive, from lemurs to monkeys and from apes to men. And, as we have seen, from lemur to anthropoids the offspring are on the whole smaller, consistently more helpless and immature at birth, and relatively larger-brained and smaller-bodied. In the same order the period of dependency upon the mother lengthens, and a longer time is needed to reach the adult manner of locomotion. Similarly, the period of suckling is extended from the lemur's several days to the monkey's several weeks, and from the ape's several months to the human's one or two years. In the same sequence sexual maturity is progressively delayed, and life is lengthened. (One might even suppose that in civilized and indeed in some tribal societies the official sexual functioning of the individual may be still further delayed by the lag in economic or social maturity of the offspring.)

In man there are other factors related to increased life-expectancy in the individual, in addition to the increased protection of the newborn and dependent young. That is, the longevity of the individual adult animal among hominids also increases in the same progressive fashion. By judging the age at death from the skeletal remains of individuals, some interesting contrasts are found between Neanderthal man and later Old Stone Age man. In Neanderthals only 5 per cent lived beyond 40, but 10.8 per cent survived this long in later Paleolithic men. Moreover, in Neanderthals 40 per cent died as children of 11 years or less; but in later man, only 24.5 per cent died this young. In fact, 1 per cent of later Old Stone Age men actually lived beyond the age of 50. We also know that longevity has progressively increased throughout historic times. For example, the mean death age in the eleventh-century fortress town of Scarborough, England, was 39 years; 8 of 143 individuals lived to be over 60, and the oldest was 74—far different from the corresponding modern figures. A progressively more civilized state (or the absolute size of the community?) also appears to increase the life-span. For example, 25 years was the upper limit in more than half of 32 native Tasmanians examined; only 2 reached 60. The mean death age of 189 West African Negroes (the Royal College of Surgeons skull series) was 30 years, with only two surviving beyond 60; of 600 Pecos Indians living in New Mexico between A.D. 800 and 1835 only 60 reached 65 or more, and only 3 were in their eighties. We have no evidence that the potential duration of human life has increased biologically through the ages. The differences are due to the reduction of life-hazards, that is, they are *cultural* and not biological as such; but since survival through the breeding period has biological consequences, there is no reason to deny that the kind of culture men have, has real adaptive significance and survival value. In modern civilized circumstances, life-expectancy has been further increased, at first largely through reduction of the newborn death rate and through the conquest of children's infectious diseases. But the same trend toward longer adult life is clearly continuing, with the management and control of the degenerative diseases of post-mature adulthood.

Among all the primates, therefore, a longer pregnancy period, longer dependency of the young, and longer life are all correlated with increased maternal care and increased reproductive economy and also, roughly, with increased sexual dimorphism, increased genital activity, and increased sociability. These factors are evidently related to one another causally.

Marked dimorphism of the sexes is no isolated variable but is clearly related (among other things) to an increased permanency of the sexual drive. The Yerkes regard the increasing permanency of the sexual drive in the anthropoids to be of the order gibbon, orang-utan, chimpanzee, and gorilla; and all the available evidence indicates that, in this, man caps the anthropoid climax. The anthropoid family of female and offspring *plus* the male has obviously been instituted by the fact of the male's increasingly permanent, non-seasonal, year-round sexual interest in the female. This can hardly be unrelated to the fact that the female changes reciprocally, too, from an oestrus or seasonal period of heat to a year-round menstrual cycle, with probable modifications of lactation as well. The question is not entirely settled yet as to whether all the anthropoid apes, or which of them, have oestrus or menses, although the latter seems to be the case in Old World monkeys and apes. But it is very plain from watching ape behavior that all the anthropoids tend toward permanent and non-seasonal as well as highly active sexuality.

However, the matter cannot be so simple as this. If it is granted that the primates do tend to have non-seasonal sexuality, then why do other tropical animals, with the same access to food the year around, not have permanent sexuality also? Also, possibly the increased sociability as much affects the permanence of the sex drive as the reverse. Furthermore, it is not at all self-evident why animals which have fewer offspring (as primates do, compared with other mammalian orders), a longer gestation period, a longer period of infant dependency—and more young surviving to maturity as a result of increased bi-parental protection—should necessarily *specialize in heightened sexual activity*. With such multiply increased economy of life, for purely *reproductive* purposes one might well expect the exact opposite to be true!

The answer undoubtedly lies in the fact that among anthropoids, as among humans, sexuality in its heightened form serves *social* rather than immediately procreative purposes. Köhler, one of the most careful observers, has remarked on this in another context:

I can only repeat that even the strongest expressions of sexual behavior gave a very naïve impression, and the drive under its normal conditions of functioning merge constantly into the rest of the "social" or communal, life of the group. The sexuality of two chimpanzees is as it were less *sexual* than that of the civilized human being. Often when two chimpanzees meet one another, they seem to "sketch," or indicate, movements, which can hardly be classed definitely under either the category of joyous or cordial welcome, or sexual intimacy.

Sexuality is also very clearly a component in the dominance-submission social or "political" hierarchies of anthropoid species, with no possible relationship to reproduction. Often, for example, an immature or weaker male will use protectively a "breech presentation" to an older or more aggressive male, and with a kind of gestural shorthand seems almost to employ this as a symbol of subordination. As Kempf writes, since "submission as a homosexual object is implicated with biological inferiority in the infrahuman primate, this is probably the phylogenetic root of man's conscious, ineradicable recognition of homosexuality as a biological deficiency." It therefore strongly suggests special pleading, in the long line of apologists from Plato to Gide, to allege that genital sexuality additionally serves or should serve to heighten homosexual as opposed to obviously heightened heterosexual bonds in *Homo sapiens*. The arguments are not sufficiently convincing biologically; and there are alternative, more consistent, psychological explanations of this widely prevalent aberration, which we will present later. In any case, neither anthropoid nor human sexuality can be understood in purely procreative terms, since genital activity of whatever sort far surpasses reproductive needs.

It is also biologically footling to say, as have two recent authors, that "the prolonged helplessness of human infants conduces to the formation of a family group"—for this is to suppose that *results achieved* are the *dynamic causes*. Besides, just how does helplessness do any conducing? On the contrary, the existence of a family group based upon identifiable drives is the enabling factor behind the development of prolonged infantile helplessness. That drive in the male is clear. The drive inducing the anthropoid or the human male to stay more or less permanently with the female, to drive away enemies, intruders, or rivals, and incidentally to protect her offspring, is the male's sexual interest in the female. The anthropoid and the human male alike stays to form a family not because of extraneous cultural or moral fiats after the fact, but because biologically speaking *he wants to;* not because of any tender and special *ad hoc* paternal instinct toward the helpless little ones but because of powerful organic drives within him toward the female.

A comprehensive, holistic view of the evidence shows several things. This new animal invention, the family, is a biological phenomenon; it is as rooted in organic and physiological structures as are insect societies; it is, strictly speaking, a symbiotic relationship which has modified all its members; and in its growth there has been a cumulative causal relationship of all the factors involved. Klaatsch suggested a quarter-century ago that the permanent breast is perhaps related to permanent sexuality, but he went no further into possible causes. As we shall indicate in later chapters, there is evidence that the heightened inter-individual relationship of nurture between mother and infant has also influenced the heightening of that other inter-individual relationship between mammals of sexuality (and vice versa), since the infant-that-was and the adult-to-be are in time the same person.

As for the "symbiotic" relationship between mother and child and the reciprocal influences of this, no doubt whatever is possible. On the one hand, the physiological response of the mother to the baby is rooted in a complex hormone structure of the female, such that milk-production occurs automatically within a few days after giving birth. The infant, on the other hand, indicates its side of the relationship not only in its increased dependency and infantilism, an extraordinary enough event in itself biologically, but even more spectacularly in those few responses in which it is not immature. That is, although the connections of nerves with skeletal muscles are not complete in humans until something like 29 or 30 months, the neuromuscular complexes concerned with sucking are present and fully mature at birth. The human baby even carries over still the now unnecessary "grasping reflex" of the ape baby for holding on to its mother—helpless as the human baby otherwise is! The sucking and grasping reflexes are strong proof of the infant's part in this relationship.

The psychological facts are as clear as the physiological ones: genuine mother love and maternal care are based upon the pleasure of gratifying a fundamental structural and physiological function in the mother, suckling. The presence of certain kinds of portal skin is the invariable and unmistakable sign of the pleasure-reward for effective relationship of the organism to the external world, and in this respect the nipple must be classed with the mucous membranes. Just as importantly, the infant learns the basic human lesson of inter-individual response in the species, through gratifying its fundamental nutritional need for very rapid post-natal growth, so that body may catch up with brain. It is well to recall here also the fact of the greatly disproportionate part of the brain in humans that represents the lips.

If love means advancing the biological interests of another, from a feeling that this person is a part of one's self, then mother love fulfils this definition amply and exactly. And the human baby who soundly learns that its greatest physiological pleasure is obtained with another person's body never forgets this knowledge, rooted as it now is in his very autonomic nervous system—that ancient and unconscious smooth-muscle nerve-net where the tides of animal appetites and feelings surge, deep below thinking and far earlier than words. He has learned to embody the main biological meaning of human nature: the *togetherness of individuals,* now in a love which shares both in pleasure and in very body substance, and later in a humanity to be built on by a shared language, a shared cultural symbolism, and shared institutional structures. His basic humanity, therefore, depends upon successful functioning of human physiology.

Luckily, there are always enough women who respect themselves as women to serve as models for those who do not. It is possible to counterfeit love; but the result is an emotionally mutilated, counterfeit human being. Thus the child may be taught by his mother's hysterias that libidinal being-with-another-person is or should be ridden with anxiety or tortured with mixed feelings and dishonesties, and he learns from this that appetites are sins and that what he is, is basically shameful. Or, worse still, a child may be taught in essence that there is no love to be had in another's body, and his only pleasure resources are in his own body or in his own mind; he is not taught by love of the Other, the not-self that lies outside his own organic skin. Clearly, then, a society's attitudes toward women and toward maternity will deeply influence its psychological health and all its other institutional attitudes. Clearly, too, what the child learns—in his blood and bones and beyond all rationalizing—will permanently shape his feeling toward other human beings. And cumulatively! For the individual human is the sum of all his social relations. It is a tragedy of our male-centered culture that women do not fully enough know how important they are *as women.*

Since the permanent breast and the wider female pelvis are themselves instances of contrasting physique in the two sexes, it is clear that sexual dimorphism is also one of the factors involved in the human family complex. It is interesting that, among other warm-blooded animals with marked sexual dimorphism, birds, there is the same somewhat prolonged association of the sexes and increased protection of the young, coupled with this sexual dimorphism—especially since the brightest dimorphism and the protective association may last only through the breeding season. Indeed, permanent mating does occur, for whatever reasons, even in some species of birds.

In humans, all three individual members of the symbiotic trinity of mother-father-child are affected. Dependency in the infant increases in evolutionary sequence, together with increasing maternal care and more prolonged suckling. The reason that the newborn baby may commit more of its birth-weight to the human specialty, brain, and relatively less to a largely helpless body, is precisely that it enjoys this protected dependency and fostering by the mother—for the body is much more mature in other non-primate newborn, for example the colt, the most important and conspicuous trait of which is the different equine specialization in long legs at birth. In the human, the bigger globular skull containing the brain (with all the complex relationships we have already described) is limited, of course, by the extent of pelvic dimorphism in the female. Thus the large skull of the newborn baby and its related bodily immaturity are functionally correlated with the marked sexual dimorphism of wide pelvis and permanent breast in the female. And, to repeat, the whole emotional pattern of greater closeness in the mother-child bond has ultimate effects upon the more intense inter-individual bond between the sexes. (Is it more intense, or have we only forgotten?)

Indeed, it seems probable that the specialization in maternity and in infancy, so to speak, of two members of the trinity would not be possible unless the sexually bound male were increasingly protective of the family. As we will show more fully later, *Homo sapiens* is, strictly speaking, a domesticated animal; and domestication is defined as special protection from wild enemies, special provision of food, and special genetic modifications through human selection. Even in these symbiotic terms, there is a literal congruence of definition and of fact in humans. As protector and provider, the male is just as much the human "domesticator" as is the food-giving and food-preparing female, and both make sexual selections which mutually affect each other's dimorphous traits and the fate of their young.

The male's dimorphous specialization in strength and agility—shown in his larger bones, larger muscles, lungs, and heart, and more red blood corpuscles per cubic centimeter for large surges of aggressive activity—is certainly the final result of sexual selection by the female; her dimorphous traits result in turn partly from sexual selection by the male (who was once an infant). In biological terms, under the conditions of life of early man, that male with this greater strength stood a better chance of getting a mate in fights with other males, and hence a better chance of breeding offspring; and the family protected from wild enemies by that greater strength would have a better chance of surviving. This male specialization in strength must indeed have happened early in humanity or have been inherited from our ape forebears; so the argument that sexual selection means nothing now, when nearly all adult males reproduce, has little weight; and, even so, sexual selection may still operate in modern humans, though on a lesser scale perhaps than in early man and for other protective traits possibly than sheer strength. For it seems probable that the pregnant human female or the female with a newborn infant could not as well fend for herself in the "wild" state of isolation from the male—if only because such a presumed state has nowhere survived, and never occurs among humans. To the same end, the later cultural sanction of marriage, everywhere the norm, further reinforces the economic responsibility of the male toward the mother and child.

This marked mammalian dimorphism of the human female, the "domesticated" trait of the permanent breast, then, is at once the organ of the infant's increased, domesticated dependency and a sign that the male must have increased his "domesticating" protective attendance to facilitate this mother-child development, quite as much as it is a sign of male sexual selection of females. To give now the more complete picture: the child could not increase its dependency without being met in this by the increasing nurture of the mother; but the mother could not increase her domesticated sexual dimorphism for this purpose without the protective attendance of the male; but the male increases his attendance upon the female because of a heightened inter-individual (genital) drive, which is ultimately based in life-history terms on that other heightened inter-individual (oral) relationship of mother and child. It does not matter much where one begins in this self-intensive circle of causality: in human symbiosis no anatomical or physiological factor exists independently, *even though these are present in different individual bodies,* any more than any member of the human family exists as a "wild" or solitary monad, whether as infant or as adult. This functional togetherness of individuals is the essence of human nature: it is openly visible in the very physiques of women, children, and men.

Looked at biologically, sexuality and sociability are thus seen to be even more tightly woven together in humans than in anthropoid apes. It is true that sexual relations, in many primitive societies, may appear to be a matter involving only two individuals—for premarital promiscuity is not at all uncommon among primitive and indeed among civilized adolescents. Nevertheless, society always has its attitudes, its cultural pressures, and patterns concerning sexuality. It never permits sexuality to be a merely physiological matter, but persists in having interventionist opinions even as regards non-inter-individual acts (autoerotism, bestiality) and biologically inconsequential (homosexual) acts. And if mere sexuality as such is hardly regarded as a personal matter, reproduction is categorically a concern of every society—the more especially of primitive societies which are organized around kinship ties. Moreover, the full adult social state in all societies is a procreative membership in a biological family—not necessarily monogamous, as we shall see, not necessarily lifelong in duration, but nevertheless a condition toward which all adult human animals permanently strive.

This striving is motivated by sexual love. Man is neither a fallen angel who has lost his morals nor a reformed ape who has given up his "lower" nature and has somehow risen "above" the mammalian dispensation. Man has not ditched his mammalian inheritance. On the contrary, he has invested and built his evolutionary future ever more solidly upon it. For all her angelic nature, the human female is plainly neither avian nor egg-laying: the human female is in every significant respect exuberantly *more mammalian than any other mammal.* Among mammalian infants, the human infant is *as extravagantly infantile as they come.* And among male animals, the human male is too (at least for constancy if not for prowess) without doubt *the best mammal in the business.* In these circumstances, with father come home to stay, it is clearly the inescapable predicament of *Homo sapiens* to become human.

7. And Makes It Legal

Since, in our society, we are given quite strong representations that a marriage should be instituted before a family is begun—and not a family formed, with marriage later as a shotgun sequence—we are likely to have a mistaken view of the real historical order of events. Anthropologically, however, the family came first, and marriage arrangements grew out of it, rather than the reverse. The family is a biological universal in humans, but marriage is only a cultural sanction. The form of marriage is therefore a contingent cultural variable. While the irreducible minimum of one male and one female is found everywhere in the family, there may be (and are) cultural variations on the marital theme. A good deal of our would-be psychologizing in this area of culture is no more than the rationalization of our own parochial patterns. This normative tendency is found also, unfortunately, in some anthropological writing.

Thus Edward Westermarck (with Sir James G. Frazer, one of the genuinely great scholars of an earlier anthropology) labored long to prove that the Victorian ideal of monogamy was the ultimate norm for all human beings—despite the fact that the data cited in his three great volumes on human marriage constantly contradict his thesis. Human beings are "instinctively" neither monogamous nor polygamous nor promiscuous nor anything else, so far as manner of heterosexual expression is concerned (indeed, as we shall see, their very heterosexuality is at least partly a life-history product of learned responses, not a narrowly instinctual given). Furthermore, the studies of Dr. Alfred Kinsey and his associates have shown that monogamy is merely a cultural—perhaps, for some, impossible—ideal and not the actual pattern of behavior, even in our own society. In any case, the sexual behavior of the human male as they describe it leaves no doubt that often he is so urgently sexed as to strain the confines of formal monogamous marriage in his manner of sexual expression.

The possible monogamy of gorillas—as well as the evident polygamy of some other great apes and monkeys—argues nothing, of course, concerning *Homo sapiens*. To explain a supposed evolution of culture on the basis of a non-existent sequence in biological evolution is to commit the "animal series fallacy" indeed! Man, in fact, has all the forms of marriage he has been able to think up. Nor will we be disposed to belittle his imagination, when we take a look at the facts.

This human ingenuity in contriving cultural forms wreaks havoc on our local folklore and thought-habits, when these are paraded as universal human psychology. For example: despite our fixed notions of basic male jealousy, the pattern of polyandry, or the marriage of several men to one woman, is an ethnographic fact; in the Marquesas Islands of Polynesia, the marriage of a number of non-related males to one woman is the normal and preferred form of marriage. And despite our perhaps well-observed convictions on sibling rivalry in our society, the normal and preferred polyandry of the Toda in southern India is usually "fraternal," that is, a number of brothers share one wife. More than that: the Kaingang of Brazil have several forms of marriage, 14 per cent of the choice of forms being polyandrous; and polyandry, both fraternal and non-fraternal, appears to be one of the class-stratified forms in the complex system of Tibet. The sexual privileges of a man's brothers with his wife (though the right to such sisters-in-law is not strictly "marriage") is found among the Haida, Tenino, Trukese, Shoshoni, and Kota—in fact, in 41 societies, or more than half of those on which Murdock found pertinent data available for his recent comprehensive cross-cultural sampling.

When it comes to polygyny—that form of polygamy in which a man takes more wives than one—the cases are extraordinarily numerous. Indeed, polygyny is permitted (though in every case it may not be achieved) among all the Indian tribes of North and South America, with the exception of a few like the Pueblo. Polygyny is common too in both Arab and Negro groups in Africa and is by no means unusual either in Asia or in Oceania. Sometimes, of course, it is culturally limited polygyny: Moslems may have only four wives under Koranic law—while the King of Ashanti in West Africa was strictly limited to 3,333 wives and had to be content with this number. The custom of concubinage, official or unofficial, or the taking of secondary wives and concubines, is very widespread in both Asia and Europe and elsewhere. Among the Nayars of Malabar, we even have the custom of ciscisbeism, or the taking of male concubines by the women of the tribe: "male mistresses," as one puzzled college student put it in an exam!

This extreme case is worth looking at in detail. Among the Nayar, the daughters of an extended family (or group of female kin) are all officially married before puberty at the same time to the same one man. But the marriage is never consummated sexually (though Westermarck believes that this official husband has the *jus primae noctis*, to avoid the fear of defloration among the Nayar). At the end of three days they are formally divorced, and the man dismissed with presents, never to appear again on the social horizon. Later, when the daughters are grown, they may enter into more or less permanent sexual liaisons with Nayar men. But these men are never accorded the status of husbands, since (according to Hindu law) a woman may enter into only one legal marriage in her lifetime. These lovers have no status in the house, no authority over their own biological children, and no economic obligations to them. The real male head of the family is not the lover but the woman's oldest brother—who is of course related to her by blood, whereas the lover is not even married to her. If any man is regarded as the legal father of her children, it is the man she married as a girl, before puberty—the absentee husband who categorically could *not* be the biological father, even were the brief marriage ever consummated.

Nor is this the whole story of Nayar marriage. Nayar women may also choose consorts, simultaneously with their Nayar lovers, from among the younger sons of the neighboring Nambutiri Brahmans. These Brahmans have a very strict system of primogeniture, that is, inheritance by the oldest son only. In order to keep family property intact, only the eldest son in any Nambutiri family is allowed to marry and to have children; younger sons are forbidden to marry. Thus, in the case of a liaison between a Nayar woman and a Nambutiri younger son, we have a culturally defined divorcée consorting with a culturally defined celibate! This is a curious framework indeed within which to produce children.

But one important fact must be stressed. Though elsewhere in the world it is usually an adult male in the woman's *marital family* ("family-of-procreation") who has authority over her children, nevertheless there is still male "parental" authority in the Nayar family—but here vested in a member of the woman's *kin-family* ("family-of-origin"). In other words, biological male paternity and adult male authority—in most of the world both vested in the husband—are here divided between the mother's lover and the mother's brother. But biological male paternity there is, and avuncular male authority there remains!

The cultural *form* of marriage must never be confused with the biological *norm* of the family. For nearly every institutional pattern in our own tribe encounters grave exceptions elsewhere in the world—which fact thoroughly destroys any naïve suppositions we may have that our marriage patterns are somehow necessary or natural. Is it "natural" to trace descent through the father? True, cases like that of the patrilineal Chinese are very common; but we also have the matrilineal Zuñi and many others. Indeed, since maternity is a far more obvious biological relationship than paternity, a good case could be made for regarding matrilineal descent as the "natural" pattern, and our own patrilineal descent the artificial social one.

In many tribes, in fact, there is the curious custom of *couvade*, in which the man takes to his bed when the child is born and pretends to suffer the pangs of childbirth—while the woman takes off obscurely to do the real job of childbearing. This is a dramatic and symbolic way of asserting his paternity and "magic" relationship to the child which is otherwise not sufficiently obvious to these peoples. But even if we have established "legal paternity" in this or other ways, is it therefore natural and normal for the child to take its family name from the father? Well, this is common enough in the world for men to retain their honor. But we also have the pattern of its taking the matronymic instead from the mother. Nor is this all: sometimes the child does not take its name from either parent—but the parents, instead, take their names from the children. Thus in a number of tribes, instead of the familiar Scandinavian pattern of "Svenson," "Jensen," or "Lavransdatter," we have the pattern of "John's-father," "Anne's-mother," or "David's-parent," which is known as *teknonymy.*

Do we still feel, because of our European background, that it is somehow natural for the first-born son to inherit the bulk of his father's property or, since he is the oldest and thus wisest, to take care of his younger brothers and sisters with it? It is true that this kind of primo-geniture is a common enough thing. But we also have the opposite pattern of ultimogeniture, in which the last or youngest son inherits from the father. This is the case among a number of Siberian reindeer-herding tribes. As the older sons mature and the father's herds enlarge by natural increase, he gives his elder sons portions of his herd in payment for their help, and they separate off and seek different tundra areas for the reindeer to graze on. The youngest son, left at home with his aging father and with an increasing proportion of the burden of herding falling on his shoulders, naturally inherits the bulk and residue of the herds when the father dies. To the Siberians the pattern seems both inevitable and just. It is also effective "old-age insurance."

Do we make the hidden assumption that a marriage contract— whether it is monogamous or polygamous or whatever—must somehow in any case be "until death do us part"? This is of course by no means necessary. In Tibet, in Abyssinia, and also in parts of Persia and Arabia, there is "term marriage" for a specified period. Among the Shi'ah Moslems, the period contracted for may be only a month or even a day, but any children ensuing are legitimate and have the right of inheritance from the father. This *beena* form of marriage is particularly common among North African traders, who must be absent from their permanent homes for long periods of time, in seasonal travels over deserts. As one anthropologist sardonically put it, "*Beena* and marriage are the difference between six months in the penitentiary and life imprisonment." But must there not be, in any case, a marriage ceremony? By no means: the Kurumba in the Nilgiri Hills of India have no marriage ceremony; nor, in fact, do most American Indians, beyond a mere socially recognized living together. To lack a marriage ceremony is not at all the same thing as lacking the institution of marriage.

Do we think there is something inevitable in the authority of biological parents over children? If so, we soon learn that our tribal custom is not necessarily universal. In the Andaman Islands in the Gulf of Bengal, a child is repeatedly adopted by other parents than his own—until his real disciplinarians amount to practically all the adults in the whole horde and not merely his own biological parents. In Samoa the people live together in large joint households, and the authority over all the inmates of the house, whether adults or children, is the authority of the house headman, and not the child's mere biological father. Thus we have in Samoa a merging of parental and political authority. So far as the immediate care of the children is concerned, this is actually a responsibility of their older brothers and sisters and not so much one of their actual parents. (As a result, both Andamanese and Samoan personality are said to be much more standardized than is personality in occidental Christian societies. In our tightly knit and exclusive nuclear family, so far as conditioning in the early years of the child is concerned, we put all our eggs in the one basket of two individual parents only. But in the Andamans, essentially all the adults shape all the children, and the result is a fairly standardized person. In Samoa, authority is generalized to apply to both adults and children, and the headman is *paterfamilias* to the whole household. With older children ruling younger children, Samoan personality tends to the same dead-level "gang conformity" which American parents sometimes complain of in their own children.)

In the Trobriand Islands of Melanesia, a boy does not obey his

biological father at all but rather his mother's brother. For the Trobrianders have the curious fiction that there is no such thing as
biological fatherhood. Hence the only male of the adult generation
who is blood-related to a boy is considered to be his mother's brother
or maternal uncle. That is, the boy's mother and his maternal uncle
have the same mother (the boy's maternal grandmother) and thus are
to be considered related by blood; but the father is merely the husband of a boy's mother and is not regarded as being related to him
by blood. In addition to this "avunculate," we have some cases of
the "amitate." In Tonga, a Pacific island, if a girl wishes advice and
guidance, say about marriage, she goes not to her biological mother
but to her father's sister. This is because, in a patrilineal system of
descent, the paternal aunt is regarded as the nearest female blood
relative of the parental generation (that is, the girl's father and her
paternal aunt are both descended from the same male, her paternal
grandfather).

But in these matters of descent and authority, what if we have a
whole family of brothers married to one woman, as among the Toda
of southern India? Which of the brother-husbands, then, is the child's
father? This is taken care of by the "arrow ceremony," which establishes
a purely fictive social fatherhood over the child for one of the husbands. Thus, in some cases, a boy's social "father" might actually be
biologically only his paternal uncle; and, likewise, his real father may
be socially relegated to the position merely of "father's" brother and
co-husband.

Or does it seem to us inescapable that a man must owe economic
obligations specifically to his wife and to his children? There are
many exceptions to this common pattern. In the Trobriands, a man's
prestige depends upon how many harvested yams he can pile up not
before his wife's but before his sister's house: there a brother is considered the "natural" and lifelong protector of his sister—for is he not
related to her by blood? On the other hand, a man's wife must categorically be unrelated to him by blood, and so too are his children
regarded. Thus, if a Trobriand man were a fortune-hunter, he would
take care to court the only girl in a family with many brothers. A
much-besistered woman would be a drug on the market; worse yet,

a woman with no brothers would have a low value in the marriage mart, since she had no visible means of support.

It seems logical to us that adults must of necessity give economic support to children; but this is not quite true in all cases. For example, among the Mentawei of Indonesia, marriage (and the consequent position as head of a household) is a semi-religious status for a man. Many men cannot afford to get married until late in life, if at all; for becoming a household head means retiring from all economically useful activities, because of one's semi-sacred status. Besides, there has to be a household first, of which to become the head! Thus a man must have his family first, so he can afford to get married—or for marriage to have any point anyway, as they see it. A man is therefore motivated to live quite faithfully with one woman for a long time, even though he is technically a bachelor and presumably free, for the express purpose of producing children by her, preferably sons. Later, when a man's sons are adolescent and able to support him in the style to which he would like to become accustomed, he marries their mother, formally adopts his own biological sons, and retires to the exalted position of married man. The sons then take over the responsibility for supporting their father (and perhaps grandfather too), until the sons in turn can produce a big enough family to afford to get married on. In the Western world, it is the young woman who is fighting for the status of marriage; but among the Mentawei it is the old man!

Economic obligation is of course a recurrent feature in marriage systems all over the world. The principle of investment seems to be operating in East African Bantu polygyny. Here a man seeks to collect as many wives as he can, because women do most of the agricultural labor, and wives are an economic asset, rather than a liability. Far from resenting it, the women like the system. As my friend Prince Akiki Nyabonga of Uganda puts it, a woman can hold her head up more as one of the wives of a man of substance than she could if she were the only wife of a poor, second-rate, monogamous husband. In some of the East African tribes the attempt to introduce missionary monogamy wrecked the joint labor system of the women, the ambition of the men, and hence their whole agricultural economy.

In other regions it was the women themselves who most successfully resisted changing the system of polygyny.

Another phrasing of this basic Bantu system occurs among the Pondo of South Africa. In the Western world, since status is conferred by the man, it is the woman and her parents who are concerned about marrying her off advantageously. But among the Pondo it is the mother who is concerned about getting her sons married off—and married as many times as possible. If we imagine that there are emotional apron-strings which everywhere make a mother reluctant to lose her son in marriage, these are certainly not visible among the Pondo! An ambitious Pondo mother thinks not of losing her son but of gaining daughters-in-law. The reason for this is that the daughters-in-law form a labor pool under the direction of the mother and thus enhance her prestige, social position, and wealth. To be sure, the mother-in-law herself originally entered the family "on the ground floor" as a mere daughter-in-law, marrying into the patrilineal group from outside; but now she has a chance to recoup and gain the benefits of a lifetime of hard work. In Western society an over-protective mother might reproach her son for not loving her, because he left her to get married; but a Pondo mother might reproach her son for not loving her, because he had not married often enough for her to hold her head up as a woman of means!

In much of the world a woman ordinarily marries partly to obtain the economic support of the man for herself and her children. But a common remark one hears among old Plains Indian warriors is that a man gets married to have a woman to take care of him. The reasonableness of this attitude can be seen in the fact that, in the old days, the woman tanned the skins, sewed and embroidered the clothes and moccasins for the family, sewed and set up and took down the tipi, gathered the berries, prepared and cooked the meat and other food, packed and unpacked all the gear in traveling, bore and cared for the children, and in general acted as the common dray-horse for the whole Plains economy. But only the man's job had any importance or prestige: he was wholly preoccupied with war-like activities and with obtaining "medicine power" from animal supernaturals.

The economic motive is plain in Eskimo marriage also. In the hard arctic environment the real economic unit is not the individual but the male-plus-female. The Eskimo give us a most clear-cut picture of economic symbiosis of the sexes, or the social dimorphism of males and females in the family. Thus, even before a boy is married, he brings home animals he has killed, and his sister makes them into food and clothing for both. After marriage, the economic unit is still more clear. Though some Eskimo have a strict property-monogamy (or wife-ownership by the man), a man may lend his wife to another man who wants to go on a hunting trip, but whose own wife is incapacitated from traveling either by pregnancy or for some other cause. This is easily misunderstood as sexual promiscuity. It is, in fact, quite the contrary: a strict property-monogamy. A man owns his wife exclusively, including her sexual favors, and hence may dispose of them as he chooses. Thus a man will beat his wife if she goes off with another man without his say-so; but he would also beat a disobediently faithful wife if she refused to go off with another man when her husband told her to. The critical fact is that a woman's economic services in chewing boots, repairing fur clothes, and the like are absolutely necessary to a man on a long hunting trip. But these services are monogamously and exclusively owned by one man; he lends these services (including the much less important sexual rights incidental to them) to another man, who might return such a loan at some future date. The Chukchee of Siberia, who travel around considerably with their reindeer herds, have developed this Arctic system into an arrangement called "companions-in-wives," in which a herder makes a number of reciprocal wife-lending contracts with other men in various parts of the territory.

The full social significance of the adult marital status is brought out by one of the most extreme cases the anthropologist has ever encountered. In parts of Polynesia there is a system that can only accurately be called by the grotesque name of "institutionalized unmarriage." Throughout the South Seas there is great emphasis on primogeniture, that is, on the rights and status of the firstborn in any family. Both religious and political structure depend upon this, for the high chief (the eldest son of a senior lineage) is a semi-sacred personage, the living representative of the divine line going back to

an ancestral god. Sometimes these firstborn-of-firstborn priest-king
became so excessively sacred and so hedged about with taboos tha
a kind of prime-ministerial "talking chief" arose in some islands to d
the actual political job of ruling.

But the exaltation in rank and privilege of some individuals in
society can be effected only by a corresponding degradation and dis
franchisement of others. Younger sons of cadet lineages were there
fore in a social-marital status that more than remotely recalls th
predicament of the younger sons of Nambutiri Brahmans in souther
India. Thus, in Tahiti, in the Marquesas Islands, and elsewhere i
Polynesia, there grew up a kind of institutionalized youth group
whose members were never permitted to get married, whatever thei
age. That is to say, some individuals were "frozen" in a stage o
adolescent activities, in which they remained socially, for the rest o
their lives, regardless of their chronological age. The institutionalize
youth group was presided over by the high chief's daughter, th
taupou, or village hostess, who had to remain a virgin as long as sh
held the position. The function of the youth group was, partly, t
obtain a high-ranking chief as her husband, and hence was one o
entertainment. They chewed the pepper-kava root to make the cere
monial drink for visitors, they did the dancing and the other enter
taining, and they also provided sexual hospitality for distinguishe
visitors.

To remain a member of the youth group, one had to kill all th
children that happened to be born out of the replete sexual activity o
the group. The individual who happened to be married might als
join the youth group if he chose, but had to leave husband or wif
and kill all children born of the union previously. The youth group
to be sure, were unencumbered socially and economically with chil
dren; but on the other hand, and more importantly in Polynesia
terms, they could never enjoy the prestige of a head of a lineage. Th
chief's daughter, the village hostess, had to remain chaste not so muc
because of any South Seas sexual prudery, but rather because sh
was to be saved for marriage to the most distinguished visitor of all
the firstborn-of-firstborn of another lineage, a neighboring village chief
It is easy to imagine the impact of this institution on the eighteenth

century sailors of Captain Cook, who, after a long voyage around the Horn, were greeted at the Marquesas by a number of unclothed young women who swam to their ships, bringing fruits to eat, and offering themselves to the visitors. The now-undeserved reputation of the South Seas probably comes from the account of this great sailor, which was widely read in the eighteenth century and (though now expurgated for boys' reading) in the nineteenth as well.

We can understand, too, how shocked even a far-traveled sailor like Captain Cook could be when he witnessed (as he says in his account of the voyage) certain events at the "court of the queen" on another of the islands. What these doughty voyagers were encountering, obviously, was various forms of "institutionalized un-marriage" in the youth groups of the Polynesian islands. In these, the symbolic paternity and privilege of one section of society enforced permanent symbolic youth upon others. The senior lineages alone had the prestige of procreation, but the caste disfranchisement of younger lines imprisoned some of their members in permanent social adolescence. To be sure, these *kahioi* were not denied sexuality. But these societies threw the sop of irresponsible sexuality to the *kahioi* and meanwhile robbed them of the social status of founding lineages.

Ethnography provides a welter of instances of non-monogamous sexual institutions. But it is now universally accepted among anthropologists that complete theoretical promiscuity, unbound by incest taboos, never occurs in any human group. Both the institution of marriage itself (whatever its form) and incest taboos (whatever their scope) together militate against the possibility of complete sexual promiscuity. The fully adult human social status, though all individuals may not reach it, is still the marital status, which by its very nature places exclusions upon sexuality; and still more effectively and bindingly than marital claims, the kin-taboos on human sexuality negate all possibility of promiscuity.

Closely related to the universal fact of the family unit among humans is the universality of incest taboos within the nuclear family (its breeding members and their immediate offspring only). The categorical imperative can be stated in various ways. Every breeding member of a family-by-marriage must be categorically unrelated by blood to the opposite breeding partner or partners. No member of a family-by-birth may have intercourse with (much less marry) any other member of that family to whom he is related by blood via parentage. No family-of-origin of a given individual can be the same as his family-by-procreation. The "oral" family of dependency must be abandoned for the "genital" family of responsibility: no individual may have the same role in his two families.

Human incest taboos are not instinctual or biological. They are, rather, the initial (and universal) cultural artifact, deriving immediately from the universal fact of familial social organization in humans. For secondary incest taboos vary widely in their range—and hence can scarcely be instinctual if they can be modified by mere culture change, even so minimal a change as state legislation. However, one incest taboo can be categorically asserted to be found everywhere in all human societies. Nowhere, and under no circumstances, may a son have sexual intercourse with, much less marry, his biological mother. Nowhere may the individual have the object of both oral and genital love in the same person. For this would be disruptive of the family; and in this sense the Oedipus complex is universal. To be sure, Malinowski has stated the now well-known but not theory-destroying facts that such cultural aspects of the family as economic responsibility, authority, and theory of descent (among the Trobrianders) diverge from our own cultural notions. But until Trobrianders marry their mothers, the generalization must be allowed to stand. Indeed, the fact of the mixture of races and human polytypy (as we shall see) suggest that extravagant out-breeding may often provide an escape for some individuals from exorbitant incest anxiety, such that they flee "incest" within even so large an extended "family" as their own race: some beachcombers run away from home to marry foreign women in far places.

Nearly as universal as the mother-son taboo is the prohibition of intercourse of the father with his daughter. Recently an alleged exception to this, that of the ancient Iranians, was discussed in the professional literature; but here the "father" and "daughter" involved are evidently classificatory or terminological, rather than nuclear family kin. In special cases, however, exceptions do appear to occur, though these are excessively rare. Thus certain high nobles are allowed to marry their own daughters among the Azande of central Africa; and among the East African Thonga, an important hunter may have coitus with his daughter preparatory to a great lion hunt, in which he may be killed. But nowhere are such marital or coital relationships either common or allowed to the general population. These exceptions indicate no more, perhaps, than that the stronger male imposes the rules and hence, in a few cases of the socially powerful male, may himself violate them.

The basic pattern, therefore, is the prohibition of intercourse between the child and its parent of the opposite sex. It is clear that the reason for this is inherent in the very nature of the family itself: the human female is at once the necessary oral object of the infant and the genital object of the male—her body, so to speak, the battleground of divergent biological interests.[1] For the family to be instituted in the first place, it is categorically imperative that the male anthropoid do not automatically kill the offspring—stallions will kill colts if they can, and buck rabbits their young—but permit it oral-dependent access to the female. But by the same token, in humans, the filial male is forever categorically forbidden genital access to the mother.

1. The repeated occurrence of a taboo on intercourse during lactation, in widely separated societies which could have no cultural connection with each other, may partly derive from this fact. Relations are prohibited in Dahomey until the baby is weaned, and in the Congo sometimes for two or three years, until the child can run about. The Liberian Mandingo abstain from marital relations for three years after the birth of a girl, but four years after a son is born. On the Gold Coast, some groups abstain for two years for a child of either sex.

But the examples do not come only from Africa. The Abipones of Argentina practice marital continence for three years, until weaning; the Huron Indians, for two or three years during the child's nursing, remain apart. In British New Guinea, coitus may not be resumed until the child can walk about—otherwise it would sicken and die. On Yap, a Micronesian island, the husband may not have sexual commerce even with other wives or with prostitutes, until his latest child can run, lest it fail and sicken. In Fiji the husband must actually live in a separate hut, a celibate for the duration of the suckling period of the baby, which lasts from one to three years. To prevent mishap to the child on resuming sexual relations with his wife after the period of abstinence, a Wagogo man must give the child a protective magical drink—an interesting compulsive defense against unconscious aggression.

The situation in chimpanzees is suggestive also: the Yerkes state that until the baby is weaned and milk is no longer produced, even the sexually active chimpanzees have no intercourse with the mother, though relations may occur throughout pregnancy; and Mme Abreu's conclusion is that the condition of milk-production determines the relations of the sexes—a situation which in chimpanzees may have actual hormonal counterparts.

The extremely long dependency and non-instinctual modifiability of the human infant are no doubt important factors in making the incest taboo *seem* instinctual in man. It is perfectly clear that in infra-human mammals nothing operates which either can or does prevent the son, when sexually mature, from mating with his mother; and the same intercourse of son with mother is of course, in time, physiologically possible in humans also. (No doubt "dog" is so widely an opprobrious term among human groups because these near-universal companions of man, for all their opportunities to learn, do not obey even the most basic of human incest taboos.) But once the human family is instituted, the same marked dependency of the infant, which (on the one hand) requires the close nutritional tie with the mother, entails (on the other hand) an infantile helplessness removing it without question from any competition with the father; furthermore, the long delay in sexual maturity makes the whole question purely academic for a long time. Meanwhile, the very non-instinctual and unconditioned nature of the child's responses permits the inculcation of the incest-taboo during all his long span of latency, until at maturity the incest-taboo has become a permanent—and remains a lifelong, rigid, seemingly instinctual, and studiously unexamined—introjection, that is, a piece of unwittingly got learning that appears to be part of himself but is really only "second nature."

The child possesses the breast, the father the sexuality, of the mother: on this biological bargain the family is founded. It is thus the long infancy of the child, together with the paramount strength of the father, that makes this rule become so deeply impressed as to seem instinctual. The cumulative effect of culture on all humans, too, makes the process so to-be-taken-for-granted as not to be necessarily witting or conscious in the individual father: it does not seem *his* moral fiat, because he never questioned its traditional rightness, least of all as applied to himself! Such is the categorical imperative arising from the fact of the human family: the mature sexual love of women is permitted only if the woman so loved is *not* the woman first loved in infantile fashion. Conceivably, this settlement may also affect the instituting of a father-daughter incest-taboo, in a "what's-sauce-for-the-goose-is-sauce-for-the-gander" fashion. This is evidently feebler than the original mother-son prohibition—for, although the daughter is as much an oral competitor for the mother as is the son, the daughter can never become a sexual competitor like the son.

Beyond the universal biological fact of the extravagant difference between the dependent immature infant and the adult male, paramount in strength in the family, incest taboos very quickly become culturally divergent. Ordinarily, the prohibition of sexuality of infants with parents is extended to include a similarly lifelong prohibition of sexual relationships between siblings: if parents are forbidden their children, their children are forbidden one another. But the father is perhaps not so motivated to feel, and thus to express this prohibition: certainly there are authenticated exceptions to this general rule, in the brother-sister marriage customs among the royalty of the Peruvian Inca, the ancient Egyptians, the Hawaiians, and perhaps some others. Likewise, the children-of-siblings (that is, first cousins) very commonly marry in European royalty and nobility. Such exceptions again prove that incest-taboos are not innate or instinctual, but only that the taboo is less binding on the monarch and the privileged than on the commoner—or that the morality of the symbolic patriarch, the ruler, is not necessarily the same as that of the commoner, the son. That the pattern of sibling-marriage among rulers may sometimes extend to the upper nobility as well is clear in the fact that the "nomarchs" (or viceroys of regional "nomes") in ancient Egypt also sometimes practiced brother-sister-marriage. The probable reason for the custom, in both royalty and nobility, was to preserve status, purity of blood, and intactness of inherited property—factors which would operate almost as strongly among the nobility as among royalty.

Of course, when one reaches the matter of cousin-marriage—that is, of merely quasi-siblings outside the nuclear family—it is evident that incest feeling is wholly arbitrary culturally. Indeed, it is a well-known ethnographic fact that "cross-cousin-marriage"[2]—of the daughter (or son) of a brother with the son (or daughter) of a sister—is preferred in

2. The language of kinship terminology is admittedly intricate; but so are the facts. In this field the experts very much need their precision of diction. This fact is amusingly demonstrated by a moment's reflection on the examination "boners" of college students, who thought they were saying what they were thinking, but would never think of saying what they did: "Cross-cousins are the

many groups; and in others it is even required. But it is a different matter with "parallel cousins"—cousins who are the children of two brothers, or of two sisters—who, biologically, are just as closely related as are "cross-cousins"; furthermore, cousins who are the children-of-two-brothers are no more and no less related to one another than are cousins who are the children-of-two-sisters (as least as we view the facts of life!). In other words, we consider that first cousins are related to first cousins equally whether they are descended from two brothers, or from two sisters, or from (the separate marriages of) a brother and a sister. However, the same tribe that requires cross-cousin-marriage may either permit or forbid the marriage of parallel cousins, depending entirely on the sex of the linking relatives, their parents. For example, in a patrilineal system, first cousins who are the children of sisters may marry, since the cousins are "descended" from their fathers, viz., the unrelated husbands of the sisters (and not from their mothers, the sisters). (If the husbands had been brothers, the following ban would fall.) But first cousins who are the children of two brothers may not marry, since they are patrilineal blood kin through their fathers, viz., two brothers descended from the same father (the cousins' common grandfather). However, should the theory of descent in the tribe be matrilineal, the forbidden marriage would become permitted, and the permitted marriage forbidden: brother-descended-cousin-marriage would now be permitted (because males here do not transmit descent), but sister-descended-cousin-marriage would now be forbidden as incestuous, since the cousins are matrilineally descended through their mothers from the same grandmother. Much as one might wish to believe that incest avoidance rests on the rock of the instinctual, and not on the shifting unsure sands of our own indoctrinated psyches (this is what makes philosophical absolutists!), no one can pretend that mere genes, bearing the bright banner of instinct, could thread their way through this maze of fickle cultural contingencies.

Curiously, the extreme of cultivated, human incest-anxiety is found among the materially most "uncultivated" people in the world, the

---

children of parents of opposite sex," or "The children of a brother and sister are cross-cousins." As far as the present writer goes, he will apologize for his language in this paragraph when the tribes involved apologize for their behavior.

aborigines of central Australia—who certainly put into a cocked hat any cherished notion one might have of the instinctual nature of incest-taboos. Not the most intricate, but the most easily explained, is the Arunta tribe's system of eight patrilineal marriage-classes. (The writer once had the firm conviction that he grasped the principles of a sixteen-class Australian system that was reported in the professional literature; but if there exist thirty-two-class systems, he politely and respectfully wishes never to hear anything about them.) The Arunta system works in this way: each Mr. A *must* marry a Miss Alpha and a Miss Alpha only, their children being D's; each Miss D must marry a Mr. Delta, their children being Betas; each Miss Beta must marry a Mr. B, their children being C's; and each Miss C must marry a Mr. Gamma, their children being Alphas. Conversely, each Miss A must marry a Mr. Alpha, their children being Gammas; each Miss Gamma must marry a Mr. C, their children being B's; each Miss B must marry a Mr. Beta, their children being Deltas; and each Miss Delta must marry a Mr. D, their children being A's.

	Moiety I	Moiety II	
Section One {	A —	α	} Section Three
	B —	β	
Section Two {	C —	γ	} Section Four
	D —	δ	

The A's, B's, C's, and D's constitute one "moiety," or out-marrying half of the tribe, and must marry into the opposite moiety of Alphas, Betas, Gammas, and Deltas; more specifically, the members of each marriage-class must marry into one other class, and into that class alone, viz., A's to Alphas, B's to Betas, C's to Gammas, and D's to Deltas. The class-descent of the children is determined by the sex of which parent is in which marriage-class. Thus a boy is never in the same class with his father and can never compete with him for available wives; but a man always finds himself back in his paternal grandfather's marriage-class, so that patrilineal descent in the alternative classes of the same moiety remains clear and recurrent: A—D—A, B—C—B, α—γ—α, and β—δ—β. On the other hand, a woman's children always belong in the opposite moiety from her, their class depending upon the still different class of her husband, their father. (Any mere genes wandering into this ballpark have got themselves involved in a real big-league game, compared to which Tinker-to-Evers-to-Chance is sandlot kid stuff.)

Of course this is a gross over-simplification of Arunta sexuality. All that we have described so far are the *unawa*-relationships (that is, the reciprocal relationship allowing for potential marriage between A-Alphas, B-Betas, C-Gammas, and D-Deltas). For the primitive Australian has a nicely graded horror of incest. The marriage of an A with an A is wholly unthinkable, for it violates moiety-, section-, and class-exogamy (or "out-marrying" rules); besides, this would be like committing incest either with full or classificatory sisters, or paternal great-aunts. The forbidden marriage of A and B would be only slightly less horrifying, since it violates moiety- and section-exogamy rules; but after all, at worst, it is only of the order of your daughter's son's wife in our terms. The forbidden marriage of A and Gamma would obey the rules of moiety-exogamy and section-exogamy perfectly well, but unites the wrong marriage-sections; but whatever classificatory hell there might be to pay for this, this is—while strictly reprehensible, understand—a matter only of the order of a great-grandfather's competing for his daughter's daughter's son's wife.

Take the case of Mr. A's young daughter, Miss D. In the *atna-ariltha-kuma* ceremony, Miss D has sexual access not only to Messrs. Delta and Messrs. Gamma but also to her *ipmunna*, Messrs. C; indeed, in some circumstances, she even has access to her *mura*, Messrs. B, who are otherwise ordinarily taboo as the *ipmunna* of her "fathers"! But as for Mr. A himself and the Beta ladies, while not yet officially marriageable *unawa*, they are (after all) his *unkulla*, and sexual relationships with them obey all the rules of moiety-, section-, and class-exogamy; even the most straitlaced Arunta would not view such affairs as "incestuous," for they merely unite the wrong classes in the right sections. And so far as we are concerned, it would take the combined matriarchs of Savannah and Richmond to trace Arunta kin ties in this case anyway.

That the Arunta marriage system is not instinctual is proved by the fact that a good proportion of the waking life of adult Australians, when meeting members of other hordes, is still devoted to learning just what whose relationship is to whom (that protocol or indulgence may be governed thereby)—after, of course, they have thoroughly learned the system itself as children. It is small wonder that the central Australian tribes have evolved an elaborate sign language with the hands, for use when hordes with mutually unintelligible languages meet and need to go through their respective genealogies. Nor have we mentioned that other matter of totem membership; but fortunately, in the case of the Arunta, this has nothing to do with sexual or marriage relationships. For all his freedom from the alleged curse of material property, the Australian Bushman is still burdened with much social baggage! For in his system, sexuality with three out of every four females is ordinarily forbidden by incest-taboos, and only one in eight is a possible wife. This may be a hardship, when chiefly polygyny and the sparseness of population in the central desert of Australia are remembered; still, one never competes with his "fathers," but only with his paternal "grandfathers" and "brothers"—that is, if he can find any wife at all.

The extension of incest-taboos to other relatives than the nuclear family is a remarkably simple matter, in a unilinear system of descent through only one parent (matrilineal or patrilineal), which is by far the commonest in peoples of the world. That is, many tribes extend the native term for "father" to connote the brothers of the biological father, and the term for "mother" to denote the sisters also of the biological mother. Thus a child of one's classificatory "father" or "mother" is the individual's classificatory "brother" or "sister," and hence such marriage is forbidden as incestuous. All that must be done in such a simple system, to find out whether sexual or marital relationship is permitted, is to look for a significant linking terminological relative within the forbidden degree.

Early anthropologists like Morgan (on whom Marx based his fantasies) believed that the original social organization of mankind was based entirely on kinship ties, and that only later was the abstract principle of the territorial "state" or group formulated. This envisages human societies as growing by simple multiplication from unitary biological families. The theory has the advantage of simplicity; but it has the disadvantage of illogic. For incest-taboos in the family must already have driven the individual from his own (extended) biological family in search of a mate—hence of necessity there must have been some kind of relationship with other non-kin groups. Something like a territorial peace-group or social "in-group," or marriage-by-capture among separate warring groups, must therefore have existed with the human family from the beginning.

It might be interesting to know whether ape hordes are blood kin or mere territorial "sodalities." But this would prove nothing about man, since he is descended from none of the anthropoids available for study. However, the logic of family structure, the best inferences from comparative ethnography, and the best reasoning from analogy, when taken together, may give us some leads. Since the population of early man must have been scattered and sparse, the society of early man must have been something between the present social organization of gorillas and that of such sparse environment-pressed tribes as Fuegians, Kalahari Bushmen, some Asiatic hill tribes, and Eskimos. (Eskimos, true, have an astute knowledge and skilful manipulation of their difficult environment; but the feeble cultural techniques of early man, in however benign an environment, would make for the functional equivalent of a "difficult" environment. Besides, there are those who believe that earliest man was booted into humanity by a harsh environment.)

Earliest man, then, must have lived at best in a smallish group of biological families, loosely and weakly associated into nomadic territorial groups. The relative separability of the single family from the horde, and the size and permanence or fluidity of the territorial group, might well have varied locally within wide limits—might perhaps have varied even seasonally in higher latitudes, as governed by ecological, economic, and other conditions. The actual degree of cohesiveness in the band organizations successively (as we go north) of Plains Indians, Mackenzie-Yukon Indians, and Eskimo strongly suggests this.

On the one hand, the advantages of group living to a relatively defenseless land animal—subject to the hazards of the food-gatherer, the limitations of the lone hunter, and the luck of the fisherman—would appear to urge toward larger aggregations than the single family. But, on the other hand, the total available food supply and inter-male aggressions (for males must fight for adulthood and its prerogatives) might well counteract some of these advantages. Still, the need for mates remains, and these may not be obtained within the local group if it is made up only of close blood kin. So man must have had "society" from his earliest humanity, and in this the steadily visible unit is the nuclear family, with or without its larger kin-extensions.

The various forms of human marriage are merely the varying solutions-by-social-contract of this common problem of leaving the childhood family for a new one of maturity. And marriage, probably, has achieved the final domestication of man. For it has him doing all manner of antic things that can have nothing whatever to do with natural selection or survival. Still, as a self-domesticated animal, that's his choice, and that's his business.

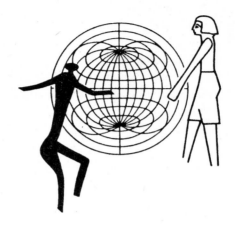

8. People Are Different

Genetically, the human species is "polytypical." The implications of this biological fact are most remarkable—and are even now only becoming more fully understood. Some of them might be listed as follows:

1. Races are not species. It is an error to suppose that racial differences in man correspond in kind, if not in amount, to the differences between animal species: human races are not emergent species in any imaginable sense.

2. The incessant cross-breeding of various groups of mankind—which seems always to have been the case even in early man, and which is increasing very greatly in modern man—would assimilate any such emergent species, even if they existed. For all races of man are interfertile; and, in the absence of geographic and genetic segregation in man, such species could never become separately established.

3. Besides, there is no adaptive radiation whatever in *Homo sapiens*. Brilliant as the invention of hands has been biologically and adaptively, man has built no bodily specializations of any kind on these hands as

such. Functionally, hands vary not at all in racial terms; nor are there in man any adaptations isolated at the ends of divergent non-inter-breeding racial radii.

4. In adaptive terms, man seems not to be evolving at all since he first appeared as man, except in minor perfectings of his vertical posture. But even such mechanical adaptations, like "brachycephalization" or increasing round-headedness, are characteristic of the whole species, not merely of races: these adaptations of one part of his own organism to other parts of it are adaptations coming to be shared by all mankind.

5. Man's material evolution is alloplastic and not autoplastic, anyway. He makes matter outside his body evolve like prosthetic pseudo-organisms, through his own intelligent conscious experiments; these machines make unnecessary any blind adaptive fumblings with his own genetic body. What is evolving is his brain's knowledge of reality, not his body's hit-or-miss adaptations to it. Only in mankind's universal vertical specialization—and in the possession of the hands that make such alloplastic evolution possible—do we find facts of immediate evolutionary magnitude.

6. It is incorrect to speak of "the separate races of mankind." What we construe as "races" are statistical inferences based upon genetic facts. That is, all true racial traits are inherited through the germ plasm but can be seen only in the actual living individual. However, the individual often carries in his germ plasm hereditary traits that are not manifest in his particular body. Thus two brunets can have a blue-eyed child. Likewise, many traits may be inherited and not be statistically significant racially (like having six toes). Or many statistical traits (like stature) may not be wholly hereditary. Furthermore, the number of races we come out with depends entirely on the minuteness of our statistical analysis, and the differing classifications are valid on different levels of abstraction. But, whatever traits we choose and whatever level of analysis we wish to make, the actual statistical distribution of these traits does not for a moment permit any inference of more than relative "separateness."

7. Not only do humans have no adaptive radiation, but their racial traits may not even be adaptive as far as races are concerned. Racial

traits probably have more significance for the survival of the species than for the survival of "separate" races.

8. The living races of man do not represent stages of evolutionary development or the adaptive progress at large of races at all.

9. In fact, there are changes in man that have no immediate reference to natural selection: for example, all the racial traits of self-domestication in man that go beyond the universal traits resulting from his human-symbiotic domestication.

10. More than that, these changes incident to domestication are not so much evolutionary as devolutionary (for example, fetalization).

Some of these matters have already been touched on earlier in this book; we will discuss in this chapter those that have not. Taken as a whole, they make the biology of man utterly unique and altogether fascinating. But even more important, knowledge of human biology gives us a firm basis for ethical and political decision, as we will attempt to show in later chapters. Likewise, it relieves us of any further concern for certain bogus problems of human organization.

In the first place, human polytypicality means that we cannot speak of a "typical" human being, unless we leave out all racial traits from the discussion: for no individual can be black and white and yellow and red and brown at one and the same time! The "typical" human is hard enough anyway to find statistically. Suppose for a moment we took an over-simplified statistical view of the situation. Assume that we could plot on a bell-shaped curve all the variations in a single trait (say, height) that occur in man. Then if we generously took the middle half of the graph as representing the "typical," we would have one chance in two of finding the typical as thus defined. Then suppose we made 10 graphs of 10 unrelated traits. Our chances of finding a typical individual would then be 2^{10}, or one chance in 1,024. If we took n traits (and remember that man has between 20,000 and 42,000 gene-loci controlling his genetic traits), then the chances are that this "typical" specimen may never have existed throughout the entire history of *Homo sapiens!*

One can hardly dispose thus cavalierly of a whole species—by suggesting that a typical member of the species probably never existed. Actually, the reasoning above is full of holes. To obtain the above statistical chances, we would have to assume that the trait plotted on each graph was functionally unrelated to all the traits on every other one of the graphs—an absurd assumption to make of any living organism! (For example, all male white cats with blue eyes are deaf, because these traits are sex-linked in one of the chromosomes.) Actually, of course, some of these graphs could not be made: some differences cannot be plotted as gradations of the same continuum (as linear height can, but as color variation in skin cannot). Men actually vary in *alternative* traits and not merely in continuously varying linear traits. The fact is that man is polytypical in his racial traits, and typical only in his human traits. A typical human being has two hands, two stereoscopic eyes, and two double-arched feet—not two yellow hands, two blue eyes, or two brown-skinned feet!

One error in thinking about race is unfortunately very common; but fortunately it is one on which the scientific evidence is quite unequivocal. This is the notion that the various living races represent evolutionary stages in the development of man—as though the "lower" races were living survivals of earlier human stages of development. Most people have a more or less clear idea nowadays that modern man has evolved from more primitive fossil types, like the shorter, low-browed, stooping Neanderthal "cave man." But they make a wrong inference if they suppose that any living race is somehow "closer" to this cave man; that is, if they assume that one race is physically more "advanced" than the others and that these others in serial order are consequently more "primitive." This can be shown with elegant finality to be nonsense.

Now it does seem that some human traits in some humans are "advanced" in the evolutionary sense, and that others are "primitive" (though we will show later that these designations are wholly misleading when applied to "fetalized" man). But for the moment there does seem to be some justification for saying that the "advanced" traits are those specializations which are most exclusively human and most divergent from the ancestral norms, while "primitive" traits are those conservative ones shared with primitive fossil types of men—and even with our primate ancestors. Thus the white skins, blue eyes, and vertical faces of some Caucasoids are "advanced" specialized traits, since primates in general are dark-skinned, dark-eyed, and prognathous in facial profile. Similarly, the brown skins, dark eyes, and protruding jaws of most Negroids are conservative or "primitive" traits, since these traits are shared with the primates.

This does not mean, however, we can jump to the conclusion that Negroes are therefore a more primitive phrasing or type of man in the evolutionary sense. Such a conclusion rests on only a narrow selection of the available evidence. If we take other traits, the argument turns somersaults. For example, a long thigh-bone is a genuinely advanced "humanoid" trait, when contrasted with the shorter femur of Neanderthal man and the still shorter femur of the gorilla and the other great apes, our closest living primate relatives. Thus the long thigh-bone of some modern groups like the Patagonians (Mongoloid) and the Scots (Caucasoid) is progressively advanced over the thigh-bone of Neanderthal or the primates in general. Likewise, the more developed human heel is a "humanoid" specialization, which is advanced over the merely incipient heel of the gorilla or the zero heel of other anthropoids and primates. But in both these humanoid traits—long thigh-bone and more pronounced heel—Negroes as a race are the most advanced of all living humans! If we took only these traits and ignored other ones, then we could "prove" that the Negro was the most advanced in the evolutionary sense.

Even more offensive to objective scientific method than the restricted selection of evidence, however, is the falsification of further evidence when it is used. For example, when it has been rationalized that the Negro is "inferior" on the basis of brown skin, eye color, and prognathous jaw, it is then further supposed that all his other racial traits, like frizzly hair and thick lips, necessarily support this position. But open eyes in the Primate House of any zoo would see that the monkeys and the apes have lank hair and thin lips (for all the prognathism beneath them). Thus the thick lips and frizzly hair of many Negroes—far from indicating any "racial inferiority"—are actually badges of their most pronounced humanoid specialization in these traits. Furthermore, some Negroes are actually a sooty-black in skin color rather than brown, and this is as much a specialization from the general primate brown as is a "white" skin. Therefore, the blacker the Negro's skin, the more humanoid the specialization!

We must face the dreadful facts straightforwardly: relatively profuse body hair clearly places the Caucasoids closest of all living races to the lower primates, while Mongoloids and Negroids are more advanced in their humanoid hairlessness. But, on the other hand, the Negro's broad flat nose and the Mongoloid's low-bridged one are both more "primitive" than the Caucasoid higher-bridged, long, thin nose; while, in this respect, the "Armenoid" nose (mistakenly called the "Jewish nose," since the Jews are not a race but a traditional religious community) would seem the most advanced of all human noses. Once again, a lumbar curve in the "small of the back" and protruding buttocks are distinctly human traits, as contrasted with the ape's forward-bowed back and small buttocks. But in both lumbar curve and buttock protrusion some Negroids surpass all other human races: indeed, among the Hottentots, the "steatopygous" buttocks project from the lumbar region almost horizontally, like a shelf.

But we must not neglect the claims of the Mongoloids to an exaggeratedly human status. Most human front teeth or incisors are half-moon-shaped in cross-section, but a specialized form of incisor sometimes found is new-moon-shaped, concave on the inside surface, or "shovel-shaped" in cross-section. Statistically, the shovel-shaped incisor has a much higher incidence among Mongoloids than among other races. Likewise, in eye contours of specialized human form, the Mongoloids largely monopolize the whole field.

More complete evidence thus destroys the claim of any race to evolutionary "superiority." Thus a Nordic may take evolutionary pride in his specialized blue eyes, white skin, high-bridged nose (but some "Armenoid" Jews surpass him in this!) and curly hair (but here he must take a poor second place to some Negroids!)—only at the expense of soft-pedaling the highly reprehensible hair on his chest and shame-facedly scraping off his matutinal beard as assiduously as possible. Among Mongoloids, even though Eskimos have on the average the largest brains, specialized Mongoloid eye contours, and a high incidence of shovel-shaped incisors—still the prize for being "most human" cannot be awarded to Eskimos, because they do not have the longest thigh-bone, because their hair is straight, and because they are not the most advanced in loss or gain of pigmentation. Negroes might vaunt their thick, everted lips, but not the prognathism behind them; their long legs, but not the brown skin on them; their kinky hair but not, perhaps, the long dolichocephalic skull beneath it; a relatively hairless face, but not the dark eyes in it; a marked lumbar curve and handsomely humanoid buttocks, but not their regrettably lower incidence of shovel-shaped incisors. The truth is that even when only a small set of traits is considered, no single human race has a monopoly on all the "advanced" evolutionary traits. Nor does any race lack some "primitive" traits. White skins persist in being hairy; shovel-shaped incisors may come in a prognathous jaw; and peppercorn hair grows out of a dark skin.

Scientific candor, however, requires mention of the nearest to an exception we know to the above statements, the case of the primitive Tasmanians. This group appears to have a *clustering* of primitive traits, in their dark, hairy skins, dark eyes, prognathism, low receding foreheads, and flat noses. The Tasmanians may therefore represent a genuinely unspecialized phrasing of *Homo sapiens.* But even so, Tasmanians show the "advanced" trait of markedly curly hair; and the case is further weakened in the fact of their extremely short ("advanced") faces. Perhaps the question is somewhat academic, however, since the Tasmanians are extinct as a race. But Tasmanian primitive traits are trivial in scale and in significance, when contrasted with their human bipedality and handedness. The generalization remains that the living races of man can*not* be placed in any linear or evolutionary "ladder" order from "high" to "low" in objective physical terms. (Perhaps this is even true for some fossil human races, for Cro-Magnon man averaged a higher cranial capacity and longer thigh-bones than does the modern European.)

So far as the much-touted head form is concerned, racist arguments get into most embarrassing logical difficulties, as they did in World War II. Nordic long-headedness, true, is conveniently shared with Mediterranean Italians—but it is also, most inconveniently, shared in even extremer form with Abyssinian Negroids. Besides, most Germans are not "Nordic" anyway in the trait of long-headedness—actually, the Scandinavians they fought are far more Nordic in this respect (and in blond hair and in blue eyes) than the mixed Germans are. Worse yet is a fact which would distress both Hitler and his critics alike: round-headed humans (Hitler was round-headed) represent a more *progressive* trend in humanoid head form than the admired Nordic long-heads! This would appear to be a sufficient *reductio ad absurdum* of racist special pleading.

Nor can we be sure that "advanced" human traits are advanced in the truly evolutionary sense of being adaptive. Man's modern racial differences are not necessarily adaptive to present environments. It is a superstition as old as the Greeks, for example, that the Negro has kinky hair because it was frizzled by the hot tropical sun and that he has a dark skin because of a kind of cumulative tanning, which in some mysterious Lamarckian fashion became hereditary. It is a modern wrinkle of the theory to suppose that these changes were adaptive. There seem to be several weak spots, however, in this line of reasoning.

In the first place, it is not immediately apparent to the heating engineer just why either a dark skin or kinky hair is adaptive. If insulation from a hot tropical sun is required, then longer and looser hair which trapped many air spaces would be more efficient thermodynamically. (But no, that will not do, because Caucasoids have that, to insulate them from the cold!—and also why do Mongoloids, who live in the same high latitudes and even colder continental climates, have long hair that is merely straight?) Actually, the Negro in Africa has short, tight, kinky hair—which in some of its extreme forms actually leaves the bare skin exposed to the sun's rays between knobby "peppercorns" of hair. Likewise, a dark skin absorbs heat rays more readily than a light skin does—and it is not very clear just why Negroes need skins adapted to keeping them warm in the tropics. Indeed, many such alleged racial "adaptations" may actually be maladaptations. As a matter of fact, we could cling to the belief better if our logic did a flip-flop: a better case could be made for supposing that a dark bare skin (and nearly bare pate) can better radiate body heat than a light-colored hairy skin can. But this at best leaves our Negro "adapted" only so long as he stays in the shade; he is severely maladapted as soon as he steps out into the sun. Also, one is a little puzzled as to why the Negroid Melanesians, in the same hot moist climate as the Negroid Africans, should by contrast have immense mops of kinky hair, sometimes a yard in diameter, on their black heads.

In the second place, Negro traits may have nothing to do with environmental influences in Africa. The present world distribution of dark-skinned peoples—in a great arc from West Africa at one extreme, through southern India, and into the Melanesian islands of the Southwest Pacific on the other—constitutes some of the evidence for a hypothesis that Negro peoples came into Africa from other latitudes, in fact from another continent. Also, even the most far-flung dark-skinned peoples (from the Congo to the Pacific islands) are all predominantly agriculturalists. This fact suggests that they had contacts with the southwest Asiatic cradle of agriculture and may have entered their present habitats only eight to ten thousand years ago—when their complex of racial traits must already long since have been formed. And if environment is king so far as skin color is concerned, some sharp-eyed reader is going to raise the question as to why the lighter-skinned gorilla race lives in the same West African lowlands as the darker-skinned Negroes—while the darker-skinned form lives among the lighter-skinned Negroes of the East African highlands. The environmentalist would have to beg off as best he could by saying that separate primate species are involved (though the environments are the same) and, besides, the East Africans are not a pure race—so please don't bring up any more questions like that.

Then what about the "separate" races of man? Here the anthropologist is back on the safe ground of professional consensus: it is a mistake to suppose that human races are genetically quite "separate." We have already noted earlier that, physically, all the races of man have many times more human traits in common than they have racial traits, even with relative separateness. A very simple mathematical calculation shows the fact of human genetic relatedness in another way. Assuming one male and one female parent for each individual in the series, the number of ancestors a living individual has only fifty generations back—which takes us only to the Middle Ages—is, theoretically, 2^{50}. That is, for fifty generations (of twenty years each) for the last thousand years, the number of grandparents would double with each generation: two parents, four grandparents, eight great-grandparents, and so on. Now, numerically, 2^{50} is 1,125,899,906,842,624. But we know quite surely that there were never 1,125,899, 906,842,624 individuals alive to be our individual's ancestors during any one generation of the Middle Ages: the total population of the entire world in the Middle Ages was considerably under half a billion, a figure reached only in the mid-seventeenth century. But, furthermore, 1,125,899,906,842,624 is a figure immeasurably greater than the total number of all the human beings who have ever lived in the entire world since *Pithecanthropus erectus*. Yet, even so, to go back to the Stone Age of, say, half a million years ago, we need, conservatively, $2^{25,000}$ ancestors mathematically, not a paltry 2^{50}, which is far too picayune a figure. These calculations, of course, refer merely to the ancestry of a single living individual and must be multiplied by a figure which is the sum of all the other living human beings whom we regard as "unrelated" to this individual and to one another—a product which in a race-proud individual might exceed the total number of atoms in the solar system.

The fact is that the more race-proud a man's ancestors were, i.e., the more inbred, the fewer the actual ancestors this individual has had. Indeed, where we can actually trace it historically in European royalty, there is a startling numerical "loss of ancestors" and a corresponding increase in individuals who must double up as ancestors in several lines or in several ways. There is little doubt that the Cockney may easily have more individual ancestors than the king. Also, the lowly, despised Anglo-Indian has certainly more than the Cockney. Meanwhile, Charlemagne was probably an ancestor of all three—though the Anglo-Indian might also claim descent from the Emperor Asoka, Chandragupta, and Jenghiz Khan to boot. Likewise, Alfred the Great (ancestor of European royalty and of Charlemagne) is probably related to Sun Yat-sen via at least one line (possibly the late Joseph Stalin's), if you take common Stone Age ancestors into account.

Obviously, our actual genetic ancestors were fewer in number than the theoretically possible ones; even if all of them are ancestral to us in one line or another, the total number of human beings in 500,000 B.C. is far too few unless most of them are ancestral to us in thousands of multiple ways. Only past inter-breeding and complex duplications of ancestry and the blameless innocent marriage of unbeknownst fifth (or a hundred and twenty-fifth) cousins can account for this stupendous "loss of ancestors." Plainly, the farther back one goes, the more likely he is to find an individual ancestral to him in two or more lines. And, similarly, the farther back we go, the more likely we are to find a common ancestor of two or more living individuals in the same social group. (The writer, an "Old American" of barely over three hundred years' standing, used to go duck shooting with a friend in one of the old pre-Revolutionary villages of the United States. It occurred to us once that we were probably related. Some genealogical research established that we were indeed seventh cousins twice removed—his rural ancestors had married earlier than the writer's urban ones and had slipped in a couple of extra generations since the eighteenth century— all of which was a gratifying discovery, but got us no ducks.)

No doubt many of the so-called "poor whites" in the Appalachian backwoods are each descended from Charlemagne in a dozen different ways apiece, but never found the time, the money, or the energy to look it up. This crossing and re-crossing of lines is the same fact that is attested to in the common sharing of the bulk of their genes among all present-day races and among all individuals within a "race" (however defined) to an even greater degree. Biologically, all men are at least distant cousins, if they are not literal brothers in one generation. With this slight rephrasing, the moral perception of the ancient Aramaic traders and teachers and travelers is sound physical anthropology.

In a polytypical species like man's, whose types inter-breed, it is much over-simplified to think of a mere "branching" of human races from one single hominid bole. A many-trunked banyan tree, which sends new trunk-roots down to the ground from its branches, is a better basis for conceptualizing the facts. But even this is a poor figure for analogy. In mankind's family tree there has been as much convergence of roots and branches as there has been divergence. If the part above the ground is what we know historically as *Homo sapiens* and the part below the ground as paleontological hominids, then we would have to imagine the paleontological "roots" of the tree as having anastomosed (or grafted onto each other organically)—quite as have the branches, to our knowledge, in anthropological history. This strange reticulated or net-like organism might then somewhat resemble mankind as it is genetically. (In this, human races are like dog breeds. It is a known fact that the "Doberman pinscher" was put together by a dog breeder of this name, out of pinscher, mastiff, shepherd, and hunter strains. Subsequent in-breeding and selection stabilized the new "breed" traits; and now this hodgepodge of canines wins prizes at dog shows, on the basis of masquerading as a "pure race"!)

For polytypicality and inter-breeding do make mankind at large just such a net-like unitary genetic organism. Von Uexkull puts the matter picturesquely:

> The difficulty of picturing the species as consisting of numerous individual organisms and yet being an entire organism itself, depends only on the fact that the separate creatures do not perform their actions at the same rate or at the same place. Let us imagine the species as, for instance, a large shoal of fishes hunting a great quantity of pteropods, and followed in turn by a number of sharks. We at once get the impression of a huge organism, pursuing and pursued, which now spreads out, but fundamentally remains the same throughout. At one point speed, at another slowness, at one point coloration, at another light, here sharp sight, and there a keen sense of smell, act for the preservation of the whole. So long as the whole retains all these properties, it will continue its existence unchanged, although that essentially consists of perpetual flight and pursuit.

This concept applies with special force to *Homo sapiens*. Mankind is at least three such great shoals of individuals—white, black, and yellow, with many admixtures of each. So conceived, the human species can easily be seen as an enormous independent organism, with a character of its own and with tremendous longevity. We shall later present linguistic and cultural evidence to show that, in humanly significant terms, groups of men *can only be understood* in their functional relatedness to one another and as members of one another. But for the moment we wish to deal only with the literal fact of the matter in genetic and biological terms.

Polytypicality in humans is a biological phenomenon with very great survival value. Its potentialities are certainly as great as those arising from the exchange of nuclear material by two paramecia; its promise for the future is surely as magnificent as was the first joining of two heredities in the sexual fusion of two single cells. Indeed, human polytypicality is an extension of the same process, though on a far grander scale; and the increasing scope of human exogamy (or out-breeding) is not merely our historic fate but undoubtedly also our evolutionary salvation. Suppose that some nearly world-wide catastrophe occurred, say a great atomic cataclysm. If some individuals on its margins were to survive on the basis of skin color (that is, some colors would reflect or absorb the rays selectively more or less than others), then mankind could still regenerate itself, and in all its former varieties. For with genetic mixture, the color of the individual's skin is not necessarily equivalent to the skin colors his genes are able to reproduce; the more racial out-breeding there is, the more this is the case. Plainly, the theoretical limit of human exogamy is biologically the most promising, and we neither can nor ought to do anything about it. In our hypothetical atomic conflagration, the genetic richness of *Homo sapiens* would therefore give continued viability to the species, for all that one apparent race (like the Doberman pinscher among dogs) had temporarily ceased to exist. For this reason, again, we cannot say that racial variations necessarily have any adaptive survival value as such to the race—though mankind at large enjoys the survival advantage inherent in all possible racial variations. For—who knows?—at some still farther future, perhaps the other human skin colors may have some survival value for the species.

However we look at the matter, the fact seems to be that *man's racial differences are quite without any immediate small-scale evolutionary significance whatever*. Another reason for this is that man is no longer subject as an individual to the full effects of natural selection and to the other evolutionary mechanisms which operate on wild animals. As soon as the first hunter in the first human society shared his kill with older men and with women and children or fought off some human or wild enemy, these dependents ceased to be wild animals relying for survival on their own efforts and were removed as individuals from the operation of natural selection. In human groups the conditions for survival—whether of mystics, Babbitts, schizophrenics, or idiots—are largely set by the unwitting cultural "choices" or learned preferences of the society itself. Thus man as a culture-bearer is largely the arbiter for the survival of individual human animals—and not nature. Therefore, if nature does not set the conditions for selection, it is difficult to see how "natural selection" could operate on individual man.

This reasoning is supported by a number of other facts. For in the technical sense, man's biological nature is precisely that of a domesticated animal, that is, of a self-domesticated animal. This fact was noted as long ago as the end of the eighteenth century by the great anthropologist Johann Friedrich Blumenbach. Hahn defined a domesticated animal as one in which man had for generations intentionally influenced nutrition and reproduction. The variations which occurred (hair form, pigmentation, and the like), Fischer and others have regarded as biologically neutral, neither adaptive nor anti-adaptive. So far as humans are concerned, anthropologists would agree that, once again, no "genealogical ladder" of mankind is possible in these terms, because the diverse traits of domestication are biologically random.

Man fits all the criteria now used to define a domesticated animal. These are: a *controlled food supply,* which man's cultures secure for him; *human selection of traits,* for man's cultural selections control the traits of "breeds" of men just as the animal breeder's choices and preferences shape the appearance and the heredity of a breed of dogs; and *protection from natural enemies,* which man's social habits and cultural inventions achieve for him. (But if man-in-society constitutes the "natural" enemy of man-in-another-society—a point to be discussed in a later chapter—it may be that selection continues to operate, not in terms of individuals, but in terms of societies.)

The many traits which man breeds into his domesticated animals, but which are uncommon or lacking in wild forms, are very easily observed. For example, while both blondness and pure blackness are rare among wild animals (the rare black panther and the black bear are exceptions), nevertheless in all his own domesticated animals—whether horses, cows, pigs, cats, dogs, or chickens—man has created both blond and black forms. White breeds of domesticated animals, as it happens, would be severely disadvantaged in the wild state, quite apart from their higher visibility to natural enemies, and would probably not survive out of domestication so far as those depending on a sense of smell are concerned. In all animal groups, individuals that lack pigment are poorer in sense of smell than are the darker individuals. (For instance, white hogs in Virginia commonly die because they cannot discern through smell the difference between the poisonous *Lachnanthes* root and other roots they feed on, though pigs ordinarily have such a good sense of smell that in France they are used instead of dogs to sniff out underground truffles. Parallel cases are the white rhinoceros in Africa and white sheep in southern Italy, which sometimes eat poisonous grasses.) The reason for this deficiency is that in animals with a highly developed sense of smell, both the olfactory mucous membrane and the entrances to the olfactory organ are normally deeply pigmented. Thus when pigment is bred out, the domesticated animal's sense of smell is also injured, probably to an extent endangering its survival in the wild state.

The similar traits for which man must be adjudged a domesticated animal have now been plentifully demonstrated by physical anthropologists. For one conspicuous example, the "natural" color of man both as a primate and as a mammal ought to be brown—but *Homo sapiens* has such extreme "domesticated" forms as the blond Scandinavian and the black Gold Coast Negro. So far as pigmentation goes, the microscopic structure of the Nordic eye is identical with that of a blue-eyed rabbit; and human blondness of hair is of the same order as blond hair in domesticated pigs and horses. Variable hair form, present in man, is also notable in dogs, from the Mexican "hairless" to the shaggy Scotch terrier. Long head hair in some humans is paralleled by that of Angora cats, goats, alpacas, and the like. The curly hair of some poodles and the curly feathers of some fancy breeds of fowl are strictly comparable to the frizzly hair of the Negro as traits of domestication. It is a wry commentary that Barnum's "wild man from Borneo" should in his frizzly hair actually have the most domesticated form there is (short of the Hottentot's peppercorn hair), since the hair of most wild animals is straight. There are, of course, no "wild" human beings living in a "natural" state; all human groups live strictly within the technical conditions of domestication.

The great variation in size of domesticated animals (the Shetland pony and the Percheron or Clydesdale horse, the Chihuahua and the great Irish wolfhound, the Bantam and the Rhode Island Red) are paralleled in humans by the Pygmy versus the tall Scot, by the Negritos of Malaya versus the tall Patagonian Indians, and by the shortish Hopi versus the more than tallish Nilotics such as the Watusi. Indeed, recent fossil finds (*Meganthropus, Gigantopithecus* versus *Pekinensis* and *Pithecanthropus*) strongly suggest that the same variability in size among modern African Negroids already existed in the proto-hominids of Asia at least. This tendency toward variability even seems to be a trait of all the anthropoids, where conditions of breeding and group living may tend to parallel the human state: we have mentioned the two "races" of gorilla, but primatologists also count two orang-utan races, three chimpanzee, and five gibbon races (if siamang is in-cluded). In man, one function (among others) of living together in societies is so obviously the protection of variability that terrorist "right-thinking," both communist and mccarthyite, is quite plainly anti-eugenic. A democratic live-and-let-live policy, therefore, is basi-cally necessary for the best operation of human biology.

The "domesticated" matter of diet in man deserves further empha-sis, for nutrition is everywhere fundamental in biology. In the long view of paleontology, nothing so clearly announces the fading of a promising phyletic future as a narrowed and finicking diet. It is all the more ominous when there is actual anatomical specialization exclusive-ly for ant-eating, blood-sucking, or the like, and not merely a phys-iological specialization, like the panda's preference for the leaves of a certain species of bamboo or the silkworm's preference for mulberry leaves. Too fine an adjustment to one small facet of the environment leaves the animal all too vulnerable to a minor environmental change in just that feature. If that bamboo bough break, so to speak, the whole panda family is in for a phyletic fall.

On the score of diet, *Homo sapiens* is among the safest of all animals, because he is omnivorous. His heredity is a mixture of happy accidents. His mammalian ancestors ate insects. His primate ancestors learned to eat fruits and plants as well. And by Pleistocene times (if not ear-lier) the early humans were also carnivorous, as witnessed by the abundant Old Stone Age spear and arrow points used for killing animals. Man's omnivorousness gives him unusual ecological elbow-room; for since he can subsist on a variety of diets, he can invade almost any environment. (The omnivorous potential of the bear family is the major reason why bears, like man, have invaded a variety of environments from the boreal to the tropical, and from the Himalaya highlands to the semi-marine habitat of the polar bear. But some of these bears specialize; only those that continue to be omnivorous have the same safety as *Homo sapiens*.) Man's tooth structure clearly indicates—from biting incisors and tearing canines to grinding molars and premolars—the omnivorous potentialities of man. Whatever racial variations occur (like the shovel-shaped incisor of Mongoloids) have no meaning as an "adaptation" to a given food.

The significant thing is that everywhere man's ecological adjustment to specific food staples is an entirely cultural phenomenon, dependent upon traditional habits only and hence modifiable, and is never anatomical or genetic. Any change of environment by migration, any climatic change in the environment itself (e.g., man's neo-primate carnivorousness in the Pleistocene), and any change in cultural habits, all leave man free to adopt new diets. On the one hand, man everywhere remains basically omnivorous, since even the meat-eating Eskimo eat some plant foods, and since even the rice-eaters of the Orient eat some meat and fish. No race, that is, exists within nutritional conditions which would either facilitate or require anatomical specialization. But above and beyond this, the slow but steady mixing of the genes in slow-breeding man is still sufficient in itself to counteract any radial specialization, even if this incipiently existed. Meanwhile, there is nothing in a mouth with a shovel-shaped incisor, for all the rice-eating habits of its owner, which prevents it from eating sweet-and-sour pork, a well-cured sea slug, cuttlefish-walnut, bamboo shoots, or a twenty-five-year-old egg.

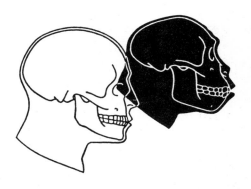

9. Man Climbs Back up His Evolutionary Tree

Close attention to the nature of race shows (again, as in the case of hands) that man is not only a new species but also an entirely new kind of animal. Race in humans, we have seen, is not a question of old-fashioned animal speciation, that is, the usual adaptive radiation of a successful animal into new experimental forms. Race is something different in the evolutionary sense. Racial traits are not true radial changes in the basic animal, nor do they seem to be pure and simple adaptations to local environments. Also, natural selection can have no bearing on the racial traits of a self-domesticated animal, certainly not on the racial level as such. Races are the technique that a poly-typical animal has fallen on to multiply its hereditary potential: it is a new way for the varying parts to depend on one another genetically, for the survival benefit of the whole reticulated species.

This is in itself an extraordinary enough phenomenon in evolution. But how astoundingly revolutionary this animal is, has only recently been suspected—when it became increasingly clear that, in a sense,

Homo sapiens is evolving backwards! The reader will recall our reluctance in the last chapter to use the terms "advanced" and "primitive" to designate various physical traits of race. This was not because a white skin (or a very black one) does not represent genuine specializations away from the conservative or unspecialized primate and mammalian brown color—for both very plainly do. It is not even because we could legitimately insist that a racial trait parading as "advanced" must by definition be an adaptive one—for it may be ultimately adaptive on the species level, though not on the racial. It is rather because it seems to the anthropologist highly dubious to call a human racial trait "advanced" when it is actually regressive in primate or mammalian terms.

That is to say, racial differences may represent not so much a progressive evolutionary branching out as a kind of regressively crawling back down the evolutionary limb. Man seems to be not so much putting forth new adaptive traits in a land animal as he is ransacking his genealogical tree for some possibly overlooked genetic fruits. As we have seen, the primates are on the whole rather conservative unspecialized mammals. And we have already suggested that, in the progressively increased dependency of young primates on their parents, the primates are "infantilized mammals"—that is, they specialize extravagantly in the initial mammalian depending of infant on adult animals. But even more surprisingly, man seems to be a "fetalized ape."

For example, the great apes have thick beetling eyebrow ridges and great prognathous jaws, both of which are fully developed only in the adult animals but are not present to the same extent in the newborn young. Likewise, there is every reason to believe that man's protohominid ancestors also had beetling brows and projecting jaws, for the early fossil forms (notably Rhodesian man) show these same traits, though in diminished form as compared with the anthropoid apes. When these facts are put together in serial form, it becomes clear that *the more modern man becomes, the more he resembles the infant ape.* Figuratively, it is as if hands turned out to be so incomparably superior to jaws in grasping, and brains so much more important in skulls than jaws, that man back-tracked even on his hominid ancestors' lesser commitment to jaws. In other words, modern man *retains the* rounder head of the infant ape and does not go on to develop the projecting brows and jaws which are characteristic of the adult apes. Or, from another point of view, modern men do not grow up to the adult physical characteristics of early men. Physically, man is increasingly infantilized.

The bearing of this on race differences is interesting. For different races have retained in differing degrees, and in different traits, the forms characteristic of the infant. For instance: if the infant ape and the infant human both have smooth brows, then the Mongoloid, who lacks marked supra-orbital ridges, has retained this infantile condition to a greater degree than has the Caucasoid, with his discernible and sometimes heavy ridges—but not even the Caucasoid "matures" to the extent of having the beetling brows of the gorilla or even of primitive early man. For ease of reference the term *paedomorphic* or "child-form" is applied to traits resembling the infantile, while *gerontomorphic* or "old-man-form" refers to those specialized traits most fully developed in the old male of the species (e.g., the gorilla's sagittal crest is "gerontomorphic"). Having big brow ridges, then, is also "gerontomorphic." That is, old male gorillas have heavily projecting supra-orbital ridges—far more developed than those of infant gorillas or even of grown female gorillas. Similarly, old Caucasoid males have more marked brow ridges than do Caucasoid babies; and Caucasoid females retain a greater infantile smoothness of brow than do the males of the same group. For this reason, given his own racial norm, the Caucasoid is likely to consider the Mongoloid male both "younger" and "more feminine" in the brow region, since the Mongoloids are "paedomorphic" in this trait. In other words, we find it hard to judge how old a Chinese man is, if we have to depend on the signs we would look for in a Caucasoid male, but which are lacking in Mongoloids. The stately and noble brow ridges which contribute no little to our idea of Caucasoid male beauty are therefore an old male ape trait. Women, children, and Mongoloids are much more human in this respect. Baby apes also have eyebrows and eyelashes, which are lost in the adult—so long eyelashes in women are paedomorphic, and plucked eyebrows bring them to resemble old male apes. However, curiously, shedding tears is a gerontomorphic human trait, since apes do not have it, though human babies shortly acquire tears and "paedo-morphic" women long use them!

Some fetalized traits are characteristic of all human beings, others are found differentially in the various races. Let us take a few important examples of the universal traits first. One of the most conspicuous traits involves, of course, the skull. In the smallness of the human face and the largeness of the brain case, all human beings have shown a tendency to prolong the fetal state of apes into their adult human state. Keith shows, interestingly, a possible reason for this: "A suckling monkey, clinging to its mother's breast, has to carry its head in the human position; hence the central position of the foramen magnum in the skull of newly-born apes. Movement of the foramen magnum sets in when the suckling period comes to an end. This infantile state has become permanent in man." As usual when the face is involved, it is useful and instructive to look at the brain. It is immediately evident that *Homo sapiens* persists for a long time after birth in the fetal stage of active brain growth in monkeys and apes. In both the rhesus monkey and the anthropoid gibbon the active period of brain growth is reached at birth, at which time about 70 per cent of the adult size has been reached; after birth, monkey and gibbon brains grow at a rate corresponding to the rate of body growth. In the gorilla and chimpanzee there is a short post-natal period of rapid brain growth, but 70 per cent of the adult brain size is reached early in the animals' first year. But a human baby—huge as its brain is at birth—has only 22 per cent of its adult brain size. A rapid increase persists during the first and second years, but 70 per cent of the adult size is not reached until early in the third year and 80 at the end of the fourth year; that is to say, the brain continues to grow, but the rate of increase declines until about the thirty-sixth month after birth. Thus the human baby persists for several years in an activity which is fetal in monkeys. The actual physical configuration of the skull points to the same conclusion. Fetal and infantile anthropoids have bulging, prominent foreheads, smooth in the brow. In chimpanzees, gerontomorphic transformation takes a great leap with the coming of the permanent teeth, the frontal bone rotates to make a low or receding forehead, and large supra-orbital ridges are formed.

152

But in man the bulging fetal form of the forehead is retained through-out life; indeed it may even heighten somewhat.

From this viewpoint, man's whole life seems to slow down to let his brain grow. Monkeys and apes appear to race through all the same cycles as man. But for both brain and intelligence to grow, man needs more time for learning. Thus a rhesus monkey has an intra-uterine period of 166 days, is infantile 1.5 years, juvenile 6.5 years, and adult some 20 years; a chimpanzee is intra-uterine 235 days, infantile 3 years, juvenile 8 years, and adult some 30 years, the first 20 of which are the fertile period in the female. To the chimpanzee times man has added over a month to intra-uterine growth, 3 years to the infantile period, 6 years to the juvenile, and some 20 years to the adult, most of this in the post-mature period. Biologically, *it takes more time* to become human. Obviously, too, it is the human brain and human learning which gain particular advantages by this biological slow-down.

The above "fetalizations" are more or less the case with all human beings. But some differential fetalization is clearly at the basis of race differences. For example, all human babies have "button noses." But only Mongoloids, and to an extent Negroids, retain this infant form. Caucasoids tend to develop long, high-bridged noses—the most extremely gerontomorphic form of which is to be found in some aged Armenoid males, with their great beak-like prows. Similarly, all human individuals have at one period of their existence an epicanthic fold over a corner of the eye. But, as Bolk has pointed out, this transitional stage has become terminal in some races, such as the Mongoloid. The same is true in Mongoloids with respect to infantile protuberant eyeballs.

About 70 per cent of the Hottentots also retain this "Mongoloid" combination of low nasal bridge, epicanthic fold, and protuberant eyes. This does not necessarily mean that the South African Hottentots are racially descended from East Asiatic Mongoloids; it means merely that, whereas nearly all Mongoloids retain this common human infantile combination, only some 70 per cent of Hottentots do. Likewise, in certain defective developments of Caucasoid individuals, we have the combination of traits in "Mongoloid idiots." This does not mean that there has been a "throwback" to an earlier inferior Mongoloid "stage" of human evolution, however; it means merely that deficiency of growth (from the ovum of a mother near menopause) has left these individuals developmentally in an earlier paedomorphic stage that is not characteristic of normal Caucasoids. In other words, Mongoloids, Hottentots, and "Mongoloid idiots" can all *stay put* at the same paedomorphic way-station, because they are all human.

It was such glandular contexts of growth that led Keith, the first great champion of Bolk, to formulate his endocrine theory of the origin of racial characters. For example, we know that various glands control different aspects of growth and different physical features. In conditions of glandular imbalance, we sometimes get very short or very tall stature, hair that is very fine in cross-section, a lantern-jaw and big extremities and other bone anomalies, an apparently yellowed skin, an unusual growth or distribution of body hair, and the like. It is easy to see, therefore, how differing glandular patterns might be related to differing racial characteristics in these same traits. In an enthusiastic book (we need more such!) Keith's follower, the younger Marett, has gone on, perhaps sometimes tenuously, to relate these to soil minerals (which sometimes affect glands) and climatic conditions. The whole matter is still under debate, but it remains a fine example of the unexpected inter-disciplinary nature of the study of man. One point remains provocative: anatomically, it is interesting to note that the thymus gland is very large in children and evidently has a longer functioning during the growth period; but with the coming of puberty and the activity of the sex glands, it decreases in size and no doubt in functioning. Unfortunately, however, we know very little in detail about the precise functions of the thymus gland. Meanwhile, it goes without saying that anthropologists will welcome any new information that the endocrinologists turn up regarding the thymus gland, for it will undoubtedly help them to understand their own scientific problems.

Numerous racial traits can be viewed in Bolk's terms. For example, many fair-haired and light-eyed Caucasoid babies become darker as they grow older; true "Nordics" retain this unpigmented state on into adulthood. Likewise, the relative fairness of Caucasoids as a whole is a retention into adulthood of a transitory intra-uterine stage characteristic of all human beings. Mongoloid and Negroid bodily hairlessness is similarly the lifelong loss or remaining in a hairless stage of the fetal ape—and not even the hairiest old Caucasoid male ever catches up with the hairiness of body typical of all the anthropoid apes. The dark skin color and the out-thrust lower jaw of some Negroids are both geronto- morphic traits; Mongoloids are intermediately paedomorphic and Cau- casoids most extremely paedomorphic in these particular features. Once again, however, no racist capital can be made out of these facts: every race has a mixture of paedomorphic and gerontomorphic traits or occu- pies a different position from other races on the paedomorphic-geron- tomorphic line (sometimes high, sometimes low) with respect to one particular trait. There will be no prizes given for "most paedomorphic" or "most gerontomorphic" to any human race; that is, none is more gerontomorphic in all its traits than any other race, and no race lags behind in humanoid paedomorphy more as a whole than any other race.

This interpretation of man as a "fetalized ape" puts an entirely dif- ferent light on racial traits and forces us to discard the terms "ad- vanced" and "primitive" entirely, at least as far as the evolution of man is concerned. For example, the specialized white skin of the Caucasoid can hardly be called "advanced," when it is actually the retention of a primitive stage of development in an ape fetus. Similarly, the body- hairlessness of Negroids and Mongoloids is not so much "advanced" as regressive, both in the embryological and in the evolutionary senses. By the same token, the prognathous jaw of Negroids is not quite "primitive" when it is actually the developed gerontomorphy normal for all the anthropoids and early hominids—but which the other races (and especially the Caucasoid) fail of achieving. These facts behoove us to give up all notions of making invidious distinctions in racist terms —the more especially since present-day man does not quite know what these mean and does not know where on earth paedomorphy and geron- tomorphy are taking us anyway!

Actually, the races have *specialized variably in the paedomorphy of different traits.* This makes the alleged evolutionary adaptiveness of racial traits recede even further. But one might hazard a guess: these experiments in paedomorphy are *phenomena of domestication* in an animal with increased dependency of infants upon adults and of spe- cialized adults upon one another. For racial traits have nothing to do with the evolutionary survival of the individual, and they evidently have nothing to do with the survival even of races. Racial traits can then only serve to increase the survival potential of the whole species. Thus single cells depend on one another to make a metazoan organism; infant mammals depend for survival on adult animals of their own species; primate infants from lemurs to man have progressively increased this dependency; children depend on parents to make them human; individuals depend on one another in a society to shape a culture or set of common attitude-stances; and races, we suspect, do ultimately depend on one another to increase the survival chances of *Homo sapiens.*

The increasing dependency we have found in primates and in man is directly related, we believe, to the physical "infantilization" of human racial traits. The increased human protection of infants has removed them still further from the necessary adaptations of wild animals to nature. Human babies need not so much adjust to nature as to their parents. Different races of this self-domesticated animal have, so to speak, specialized in different babyish traits: in their breed-differences, men do not so much please nature (adaptation) as they please themselves (domestication). For race-differences are breed-differences created by man—probably on the initial basis of accidents of "genetic sampling" when man was a rare animal and widely dispersed, but later enhanced and preserved through "genetic drift" and varying ideas of "beauty."

Actually, of course, physical beauty in human beings is not an absolute, but an aesthetic judgment that varies from group to group. It takes a conscientiously cultivated sense of artistic "genre" even to see the beauty in other races: thus the most beautiful human beings of their own kind whom this anthropologist has ever seen are in each case a toss-up between an old Kiowa Indian woman in Oklahoma and an ancient Mongoloid woman seen in Darjeeling, an English lady and a young farmer in western Virginia, a fiercely dark Kandyan noble in Ceylon and a superb pure Negro woman on the Gold Coast of Africa. One can admire them all, on the same grounds as one does the very straight forelegs of a purebred Scotty, the thin muzzle and nostrils of an Arabian horse, or the severely rectangular outline of prize beef cattle.

"Beauty" for any group, significantly, is the approximation to its racial norm, a kind of aesthetic ethnocentrism—and "beautification," those techniques and procedures which enhance these traits or simulate them. Thus the naturally pink cheeks of Caucasoid women are painted pinker, their white skins made whiter cosmetically, and red lips redder. The preferred blond hair is often achieved chemically, and its normally wavy pattern simulated artificially. Similarly, the naturally long heads of Negroes are in some groups lengthened by cranial deformations or made to appear longer by the style of hair-dressing (e.g., the Mangbetu), and big lips enlarged by labrets (Ubangi). Likewise, the naturally small feet of Mongoloid women are sometimes made still smaller by binding. And among the characteristically hairless-skinned American Indians, the scanty natural body hair is often removed by depilation, even of eyebrows and eyelashes.

The achievement of "beauty" is of course not the only motive for body-mutilation, but it looms important among the several motives; even so, in most cases the mutilation is an appreciated sign of group-membership. Perhaps, too, the native rationalizations as to why these things are done are not so important as the fact that they are done. Thus some American Indian men claim—certainly falsely—that the pulling out of eyelashes and eyebrows improves their eyesight (which is surely important for hunting and warring peoples). Similarly, a traveler reports the native story that Ubangi men first put lip-plugs in their women's lips to make them ugly to slavers. Possibly this is colored by the traveler's taste in women; for it hardly accounts for the competitive enlarging of lip-plugs when the danger of enslavement is gone and when the largest lip-plugs give the women a better competitive position in the marital market of their own tribesmen. Among Chinese who still deform the feet, the increased sexual attractiveness of the women as a motive for the deformation has remained conscious, certainly among gentlemen of the old school in Kunming.

Not to be forgotten, either, in such traits as are genetic, is the oedipal component in such judgments of "beauty." For if the male selects a mate who resembles the females of his family-of-origin, this type-inbreeding will affect the "genetic drift" and cumulative standardization of a family line. Thus adult racial self-approval parallels and reinforces any genetic influence arising from increased human identification of adults and infants.

Both long hair and beards are "domesticated" traits strongly suggesting human sexual selection. Moreover, both sexes are motivated to modify the length, color, texture, and style of both hair and beard in accordance with fashion cycles far more rapid than the possibilities of genetic response in popular "breeds" of men and women. Caucasoid males have been shaving to please their women since at least Sumerian Bronze Age times—but they still have to perform this masochistic and pseudo-paedomorphic rite with no help from nature. The *culture* of the razor meant that women select not for genetic beardlessness but for the accommodatingly clean-shaven state. Fortunately, this leaves Caucasoid males able to grow beards again, should fashions in men be fickle and women change their minds. But as a cosmetic creature, man doesn't have time for mere evolution.

In the eye of evolutionary time, therefore, the response to racial traits of "beauty" is at least as variable and biologically trivial, as purely aesthetic and emotionally arbitrary, as preferences for breeds of dogs. It is absurd to state that in the evolutionary sense a beagle is better than a bloodhound, or a pointer superior to a poodle, so long as the traits of these animals are established entirely by man's own aesthetic prejudices or practical purposes, and not by nature. A Nordic is no more "higher" than a Melanesian in the evolutionary sense than a Buff Orpington is "higher" than a Rhode Island Red. Any prejudices which exist are human prejudices only, not judgments of nature. Genetically, only a preference for human beings as opposed to chimpanzees or poodles has any biological weight or moral stature.

Not that nature has not seemed to conspire to thrust a sound appreciation of *Homo sapiens* upon us. So far as the traits of the whole species are concerned, they are a collection of adaptations that have necessarily been successful; and we do not have to rely upon an admiration for mankind to be able to value the metazoan revolution, the backbone, amphibian legs liver and lights, mammalian reproduction, or primate brains, eyes, and hands. The biological false starts and failures have been left behind. On purely technical grounds—of protozoan surface-volume ratios versus metazoan cell-specialization, of gaseous diffusion limits in tube-respiration versus lungs, of chitinous endoskeleton versus the vertebrate endoskeleton, and the like—man is the best animal there is. The positive achievements of all our animal ancestors are not to be denigrated in false modesty just because we happen to be possessed of them.

The biochemist Henderson has rightly pointed out the unique "fitness of the environment" for the growth of life on earth—a succession of adaptations of organisms to environment that seem almost magical, because they have all been made on this planet, under conditions which we must suppose are at best cosmically rare. We need a sun as a continuous external source of energy, but we must not be too close or too far lest life burn or freeze (i.e., the possibilities for complex chemical combinations be less than optimal). It is a grateful fact that water, the nearest to a true "universal solvent," should be the most plentiful liquid on earth, rather than ammonia or the various hydrocarbons that are limited in the solutions they can make. It is most convenient too that water, uncharacteristically of liquids, should stop contracting four degrees above its freezing point and begin to expand—lest seas and lakes freeze from the bottom up. Gaseous carbon in the air's carbon dioxide is almost too much to hope for—since, of all elements, the peculiar chemical nature of carbon makes it the most precious to organisms—but there it is. Somewhere in the universe organisms may be based on sulphur instead, but their metabolism must be infinitely less complex than our organic carbon chemistry. The chemically inert krypton, xenon, and argon in the air are pointless accidents, but the abundant presence of oxygen for all kinds of fundamental chemical operations is a priceless boon. Rocks and soil of relatively insoluble silicates and aluminates are necessary as a stable stage for higher life. Earth is a rare place.

Now that life has made him, man can look back (as Huxley shows) and begin to see just why his actuality rests at every point on this particular evolutionary process and no other. Speech and conceptual thinking, hands and alloplastic evolution, brains and animal societies, all rest upon prior necessities. A metazoan organization of cells was needed for size and specialization. Sexuality was necessary for the combining of heredities. The inner and the outer skin of the gut-owning coelenterates underlie efficient nutrition. A circulatory system, as in the worms, was a prerequisite for further size. A free-swimming type like the lancelet rationalized the head-tail axis and the collection of the senses and nervous system. A backbone and an inner skeleton were imperative for the land existence of large animals. Lungs were another need for a land animal large enough to afford a brain, and so are the vertebrate kidney and liver.

To be sure, legs for land movement have occurred in various patterns of four, six, and eight or more—but four limbs are behind the evolution of hands. Hence amphibians, with backbones, four limbs, and lungs, won the future over six- and eight-legged arthropods, whose small size (due to skeleton-molting and tube-respiration) forever condemned them to instinctual behavior. Reptiles emancipated life from the water; the warm blood of birds and mammals released them from the hot tropics. But bird flight lost the chance for hands, limited animal size, and thus also imprisoned the birds in instinct. This misses another advantage of warm blood, for a stable inner environment furnished by warm blood is necessary for the finer functions of a brain (which in humans is exquisitely sensitive to any defects in blood supply, has alternate routes to insure it, and makes exorbitant demands on the circulatory system). Hence mammals, and not birds, were the warm-blooded precursors of animal size and non-instinctual thinking.

Mammalian reproduction rescued animals from the enormous wastage of their offspring in earlier animals. Tree life preserved primates from the blind alleys of other mammals' specializations, and tree life perfected sight as the greatest of the senses. Fetalization (and big brain) required an arboreal species with singly-born young. Fruit-eating and tropical habitat achieved primate social organization, and size probably drove the anthropoids back to the ground. But only man stands, and man alone has free hands. Climatic catastrophe shaped man to culture—fire, clothing, and meat obtained by weapons—and anthropoid family association further nurtured the fetalization necessary for a prolonged period of learning. Hands emancipate man from autoplastic evolution, and his enormous learning brain gives him alloplastic freedom. And the heightening of all mammalian traits in the anthropoids gave man the closeness of emotional ties which alone can build the human animal.

We shall in later chapters go beyond this biology and seek to prove that speech, human sexuality, and all the cultural institutions of man could only have arisen in precisely this kind of animal—in a familial animal with a pronounced infantile oral dependence and with a permanent non-seasonal genital drive in adults, with nuclear families that are nevertheless immersed in a larger horde. It is man alone among animals, to whose oedipal predicament culture and speech serve as adaptations. Nor could speech itself have evolved in a merely horde-animal, but only in a familial one, as we shall seek to demonstrate in a later chapter.

If man is so elegant a creature, then why was he not planned that way in the first place, without all this ignorant blind evolutionary hugger-mugger? The answer is that this is what the world is like. Living matter has to do its own planning, as it has to do its own experimenting with reality. To the argument that a humanistic view of evolution appears "teleological," we can only reply that organic evolution appears to have humanistic ends: certainly living matter has achieved them. But arriving blindly at such ends—through living matter's progressive adaptations to the nature of reality—does not necessitate any theological pre-planning by an entity either anthropomorphic or paternal. Where has a god been all this time, throughout all evolution, if not within life itself! As for indifferent reality, it just is. It has never snitched on the rules to give any animal a break. Why should not man have pride in his animal evolution? A greater lack of humility lies in those who would try to pretend that the physical universe is anthropomorphic and, disappointed by the serene indifference of the universe to these narrow standards, seek to deny the whole brave evolutionary process that has brought man where he is.

When living matter, from protozoans to primates, perceives desirable immediate ends, it seeks them. Man is the cumulative product of all his animal ancestors' ends-seeking. What it is imperative to realize is that this humanism is not the old anthropocentrism which made man invidiously "different" from all the "lower animals" and hence tends to exclude him from their ranks. On the contrary, it is an enlarged pride of ancestry which includes the whole evolutionary gamut of life. It points specifically to all our animal ancestors for the many stupendous achievements of which we are (or should be) the grateful residual heirs. It is not a narrow vanity of man himself alone: it is a reverence for all life. It takes a long-perspective biological view to see properly why man is the cumulative triumph of animal striving that he unquestionably is. And the argument that man is the best animal there is, can be well defended on the purely technical grounds provided by evolution itself. Until competing intelligences are known from other planets, this is where we must stand.

The important large-scale fact, meanwhile, is man's humanity as a present achievement and not his small-scale racial differences, for whatever these may portend in later human (not racial) evolution. All racist arguments, we have seen, fail on their own properly biological grounds; they do not take sufficient cognizance of the new genetic significance of the whole reticulated polytypical species. Even as regards ultimate survival, the critical differences among groups of men may no longer be the physical ones—whether the inside of the front teeth is flat or concave and whether hair is present or absent on the back of the hands between the upper knuckle joints. The ultimate survival of societies may consist rather in *what the people in them believe* —their value-geometries, their *cultural* speciation. The creation of cultures is the technique, as the social organisms engendered are the means and unit of survival in mankind.

For this is a shockingly new and quite revolutionary kind of animal. Man's hands—the tools, machines, and food these hands have created, and the human self-domestication and alloplastic evolution these hands have achieved—have made purely genetic body evolution obsolete and last era's model in design. The traits men share *as human beings* are the critical ones physically. The important thing in man is what the animal sees, not the color of his eyes—and what he thinks and does about what he sees. In his seeing, it is his common stereoscopic vision and sense of perspective that are important. In his thinking, it is his large learning-rich fetalized brain. And as for his doing, without any doubt, the critical thing is whether the animal has hands, not whether the hands have hair between the knuckles.

10. Man Starts Talking

For reasons that are plain in the baby's long dependence on the mother, man is libidinally a very mouthy mammal. For the human mouth is not only the means of eating it is in other animals; it is also, in the beginning, the organ of human inter-individuality between mother and child. It is very appropriate, then, that the mouth should additionally—through the astonishing invention of language—have become the main organ of human inter-individuality finally and permanently.

The organic erotization of the mouth in our species cannot fail to impress any honest observer. When hunger arises in the newborn baby (no longer perpetually provendered by the placenta), the early beginnings of problem-consciousness emerge, and the baby awakens. When this happens, it is notoriously the mouth which both unmistakably summons the inter-individual aid and aggressively seeks the succoring of its needs. And after a downright lustly enjoyment, gluttonous and without shame, of the process of satisfying appetite, the baby sinks again into the sated sleep of a citizen with a sound organic homeostasis and peace of mind. But the human mouth is more than an opening for food intake. For simple purposes of muscular innervation and control, the brain cortex representation of the lips might well be relatively small—and yet, as we have seen, it is very great, and surely not fecklessly so. In the older waking infant the mouth joins other organs in exploring the world, and on the more knotty problems it is invariably called into conference with the hand and the eye. And the endless echolalia of the somewhat older babbler—who has discovered some of the moist and noisy tricks which the mouth and tongue, lips, larynx, and lungs can do—is obviously playing with pleasure. Anyone who disagrees with these views on the libidinal importance of the mouth need only light another cigarette and larrup into this heresy, park his chewing gum and set to, grab another coke and lay it on the line, or stop sagely sucking his pipe and set us straight on the matter.

Among the anthropoids, vocalization seems primarily to serve social purposes, under which might be included, perhaps, the sexual. The solitary orang is also a silent animal, except possibly in the interest of discovering its apparently only temporary mate. The orang is not prominent among primates and among anthropoids either for sexuality or for sociability. After mating, it is believed that the male lives alone and does not fraternize even with others of his own sex, while the female orang retires to bear her young alone. Significantly, this least gregarious of the anthropoids is also the least vocal.

The gorilla, which is mildly sociable in single families or small multi-family bands, is only a little less silent than the orang. But when producing the fearsome sounds with which he warns away enemies, the gorilla is just as likely to thump upon the upper chest with his fists or boom away by drumming trees or the ground as he is to vocalize. We would not think of suggesting that either silence or sound-production has any necessary bearing on intelligence—but it is the chimpanzee, which loves company above almost anything, that is the notorious chatterer. However, it is probably the gibbon, gregarious in large noisy bands, to which first prize for vocalization among other anthropoids than man must be given. This much is certain: compared with other apes, the gibbon's volume of sound stated in decibels easily outstrips their intelligence ratio. Some gibbon species are almost unbelievably loud in vocalization—using a laryngeal sac and a monstrously over-grown hyoid throat-bone to inform whole jungle neighborhoods of its state of mind.

This we say advisedly; for it is probably only the state of his mind about which even the most articulate gibbon is able to inform his public. Careful studies of the white-cheeked gibbon (*Hylobates leucogenys*) have disclosed a gamut of expressions which might rough-ly be translated into human speech. Five of them would correspond to "mmmmm" (meaning, roughly, "ti kai" or generally OK), four to "ow" (definitely "boohow," "kaccha," or "not up to snuff"), four to "hmmm" (non-committal attention), and one to "yippee" ("wow!"). But none of these, however, when closely examined, can be said to have the semantic status of true words. They are at best vague "phatic" com-munications, which convey no detailed information about the struc-ture of the universe; they are actually no more than unclassified in-telligence concerning the individual ape's physiological or emotional state. All that is conveyed, quite literally, is a "tone of voice." Even the "conversations" of the ape Senate or Union League club probably do no more than set and maintain the relaxed emotional tone of the group, well-fed, free from danger, and uninterested either in sexuality or in fighting on a mild morning. (The conversation of human adoles-cents commenting on the infinitely varied passing world also consists, almost exclusively, in such group-conformity-making pejoratives, en-comiastics, and intensificatives—though some hard-pressed parents have been known to state that the total number of expressions does not reach the white-cheeked gibbon's fourteen.)

In spite of their lavish use of vocalization, sight is nevertheless more important for communication among tree-living primates. As the Yerkes say, "Mutual understanding and transfer of experience among apes are dependent rather on vision than on hearing, for the animal reads the mind of its fellow, interprets attitude, and foresees action rather as does the human deaf-mute than as the normal person who listens and re-sponds to linguistic vocalization." Apes don't tell each other much. Our great and largely unaware dependence upon speech-cues highlights this marked difference. A blind monkey would be much more out of things mentally (to say nothing of physically) than would a blind man—and all because of the existence of human speech. Likewise, a merely deaf monkey would be much less incapacitated socially than a deaf man is. Sight thus remains the most important sense, even socially, in the infra-human primates.

It is the sociability of animals that is behind the possibility of even phatic communication among them; and speech could never originate in a solitary animal. In fact, vocalization among primates roughly increases with their gregariousness. It is also much on a par with the vocalization of other herding animals; but since the primates need these danger-warning cues even more than do land animals (who have various other defenses and also a better sense of smell), this is doubtless the reason the primates have developed vocalization to such a great extent. But, even so, the best vocalizations of the most gregarious gibbons are not speech.

What seems to be needed (when we make the proper biological comparisons) is not mere animal association as such, but specifically human social organization: nuclear families within a larger society. Primate horde society is too diffuse in its relationships for incipient semantics to "jell." No doubt the speech of proto-humans was still largely phatic in nature. Indeed, a surprising amount of human speech —political, diplomatic, economic, social, theological, philosophical, aesthetic, and amatory—still remains largely phatic (communicating or seeking to induce merely an endocrine state, emotional state, or manipulable "state of mind"), for all its pretenses at semantic respectability. But what is needed for the growth of language is clear:

1. Commonly experienced contexts of meaning, the particularities of which are not too immediately destroyed in the diffuseness of a group.

2. Extremely close organic-phatic libidinal ties, to bring about the blandly accepted, the multiple taken-for-granted agreements which inhere in and make up all arbitrary semantic communication.

3. Long-continued, stable, and intense emotional ties for the repeated experience of contexts by the same particular individuals.

4. An infantilized animal whose exaggerated dependence on adults of the same species makes *them* his primary "environment" during the

long time after birth when he is being shaped for essential membership in the species—that new generations may take on the "domesticated," non-real symbolic systems of the adults.

5. An animal with a large brain, and not merely large but "fetalized," i.e., uncommitted as yet to mechanical instincts (the bodily-inherited past experience of the species); a brain with "neurobiotactical" freedom to learn, to structure its growth on its experience, to build its nature out of its nurture—since no language and no symbol system that any human mind ever works in is in its content "instinctual."

All these conditions are encountered only in *Homo sapiens*. Humans alone are fetalized, domesticated hyper-mammals with the necessary oral-dependent and intensified sexual traits; the human brain alone is huge precisely in those association areas that show persistent coping with human symbol-synthesis; and humans alone have the necessary social organization of society inclosing the nuclear family.

More than that, the phatic conditions are still visible in the human family. Many mere males have noted in bewilderment the acute phatic prescience of a mother when her child is concerned: she somehow knows when it is hungry and when it has had enough; when it is thirsty and when it is soiled; and when it is tired, ill, or merely in a bad temper. Close emotional concern, endlessly repeated contexts, the infant's idiosyncrasies of expression, and the mother's own organic receptors all give her a large and continuing intelligence about the child. The phatic closeness of lovers also commonly reaches fantastic extremes of precision. And a wise husband in time learns he can hide nothing from the phatic prescience or "feminine intuition" of an experienced wife, who understands him all too well.

By contrast with apes (who, moreover, have no genuine semantic communication whatever), the great social burden that even phatic verbalization still bears in humans is quite enormous. Nothing is more infuriating to some people than a spouse who does not keep up even a reasonably intermittent flow of phatic reply, but holds to an unpermitted and thoroughly suspect emotional privacy. And at a really successful party, after the second drink any initial pretense at intellectual commerce begins to collapse into phatic nudges, pats, punches, pawing, and verbal face-making. Nor is anyone fooled into believing that an exchange of polite opinions about the weather between two thoroughly sober people has any real concern with or bearing upon current or proximate meteorological events: in this, people are taking the temperature and assessing the humidity of the inter-individual weather, not the earthly.

Constant association alone, and with only feeble emotional ties, can commonly carry the burden of much new phatic context. Even with a constant companion like a college room-mate—who has attended the same classes, read the same books, seen the same entertainments, and known the same people—one can convey incredible amounts of meaning and evoke large constellations of understanding merely by a breath noise, a certainly more than "non-committal" grunt, a lifted eyebrow, a modulated cough, or a minimal body movement. Everyone also knows how often new sub-languages or argots arise among secretive ingroups like criminals, adolescents, and others with their own special libidinal ties.

In these ingroups the emphasis is on exclusiveness—the same which is provided in the family unit. But in all these ingroups, phatic communication is built on a semantic language already in existence and available; hence they are not quite appropriate examples. So far as the family, too, is concerned, communications might remain wholly phatic and nonce-events that happen only once—to disappear with contexts and to die with its members. What is needed for semantic speech is a de-emotionalizing of private phatic language to make it common social coinage. To be sure, phatic communication of attitudes is necessary for the very existence of the family; but meanwhile, as the individual family continues to exist, these learned habitual and *familiar* situations become more and more burdened by common memory of specific contexts, more and more colored by individual personal idiosyncrasy, and richer and richer in private emotional connotation. It is only the further necessities of inter-family communication—in the flux of cyclic break-up and re-formation of the family—that force the private and the ineffable to become the public means of common understanding. Once again, it is only the human kind of social organization, of the integrated, stable, close family within the framework of a larger non-familial society—both deriving from the oedipal situation and universal incest-taboos—that uniquely satisfies this precondition.

The late Edward Sapir, one of the great minds of our generation, has with characteristic insight described the purely linguistic aspects of this process:

It is likely that most referential symbols go back to unconsciously evolved symbolisms saturated with emotional quality, which gradually took on a purely referential character as the linked emotion dropped out of the behavior in question. Thus shaking the fist at an imaginary enemy becomes a dissociated and finally a referential symbol for anger when no enemy, real or imaginary, is actually intended. When this emotional denudation takes place, the symbol becomes a comment, as it were, on anger itself and a preparation for something like language. What is ordinarily called language may have had its ultimate root in just such dissociated and emotionally denuded cries, which originally released emotional tension.

Both the evolutionary and the individual life-history evidence fully support Sapir in the thesis that phatic communication precedes the semantic. (Something like this, in fact, seems already to have occurred in one of the vocalizations of gibbons studied in Siam: when one gibbon band meets another at the edge of their respective territories, both bands use this cry, which ranges from the pseudo-angry to the apparently murderous—but with no accompanying openly belligerent action. This mutual vocal abuse is a symbolic substitute for action, a statement in inter-band diplomacy which has much the same function as a politico-economic treatise establishing historic legal title to territories.) But always the nonce-communication of emotion must be transformed into a symbolic gesture of reference: the "m-m-m" of rich personal connotation must become the "good" of wider and more impersonal denotation.

All that we need do is to adduce the evidence of the biological framework within which this linguistic process Sapir described occurs. For it is all these social factors—plus the human mouth, brain (and perhaps hand)—that are the biological enabling factors behind the growth of language. The uniquely human erotization of the mouth and the significance of this in terms of human inter-individuality have already been amply described. And as far as the human brain is concerned—that elegantly, sometimes meretriciously, homeostasis-manufacturing organ

—almost its entire superiority to the gorilla brain rests solely in its grotesquely overgrown frontal association areas. Such a brain can (and does!) put into symbolic equation any two remotest aspects of reality, if it needs to. Schizophrenia is in this sense merely such private symbolic apposition, such willed putting together of differentnesses (as forced by inordinate affective need) that achieve no social consensus semantically.

The symbolizing function as such appears to be generic, characteristic, and intrinsic to the human mind. Even the primates can be shown to have some limited capacity for symbolic thinking. But paying attention to *selected aspects* of the environment (if only by default of completer knowledge), in accordance with the organism's limited purpose, is a fundamental characteristic of all living matter. The rock a beetle crawls over is merely a beetle-path; it does not at this point belong to the science of geology—its metamorphic origin, the molecular weight of its contained compounds, their isotopes, and their valences are all matters of indifference and do not exist for the beetle. The odd thing is that it takes purposes to make facts. Man's symbols are a new biological way for animals to have purposes.

Conceivably the hand, as we have suggested, also contributes to the total paradigm. For just as tools are man's "projected" body, the prosthetic creations of his hands, so too semantic symbols can be viewed as his mouth-tools and brain-tools. Through these he manipulates and experiments with a thus "introjected" outside reality—that is, with selected aspects of it. It is not a somatic, autoplastic taking-into-the-body of a concrete part of the world: the symbols are magic screening devices to let man see only what he wills to see through them. Now the meaning of a physical tool is no more and no less than the human purposes it serves; the symbol, similarly, depends upon arbitrary selective human interest in the universe.

What must be insisted upon is that these selections are heavy-laden with the affective purposes of the organism. True enough, without continuously handling things, man can experimentally manipulate them through his symbols. But he must continually make reality-tests of his conclusions from time to time, lest he remain imprisoned in a pleasant private psychosis or dangerous dream. His wishes are not the world.

Organic preference is always nibbling away at the clean-cut austerity of apprehended realities. The "heart's desire" may never be able to "grasp this sorry scheme of things entire" but is ever willing to "shatter it into bits" of convenient size at least. Symbols are a new biological bridge between the "pleasure principle" of organic need and the "reality principle" of the environment; but in using symbols, human wants sometimes overwhelm realities.

Symbols are always insisting that they are the essence of reality. Still, a symbolic world cannot stand on its own feet without any outside referents—for all that a symbol is ultimately an artifact of human biological purposes—any more than tools can have any relevance or meaning as tools without the "inside" factor, man's organism and its purposes. But since a symbol-system is fundamentally affective in origin, even individuals sharing the same culture will in some wise have subtly differing symbol-denotations and symbol-connotations; indeed, much speech is intentionally exploitative of this; and some speech is used to preserve intellectual privacy.

Worse yet, the symbol-systems of other societies may be hopelessly incommensurable with our own. To be convinced of how completely out-of-touch with reality some men can become, we have only to look at the symbolism of some other society than our own (or even at the postulated "truths" of some sub-society within our own, such as the other political party)! An expert linguist named Smith has tried to impress this sophistication on his listeners, and it is a very good and appropriate thing that he also happens to be in our State Department. In fact, there is evidence that the atomic bomb was angrily dropped on a Japan eager for surrender, because the news agency Domei mistranslated for English broadcast one crucial word—*mokusatsu*—contained in the reply of the Japanese Cabinet to the Potsdam surrender ultimatum. It was given as "ignore" rather than properly as "withholding comment [pending decision]." The proper implication was that the Cabinet had the matter under serious positive consideration: the atomic bomb need never have been dropped. Hidden connotations are the terror of human languages. Phatic ape "territorial" language may be "internationally" understood; but human languages are very often mutually unintelligible in discussing the same "reality."

The fact is that even related languages, like the Indo-European Latin and Greek, at times show the same conceptual incommensurabilities. Humboldt long ago pointed out that the Greek and Latin terms for "moon," though they designate the same thing, go about it with different ideas in mind. In Greek, *mēn* indicates the moon's function to "measure" time; but the Latin *luna* (from *luc-na*) is concerned with the moon as a "light"-giving body. Thus the two languages, in their vocabulary-making, have quite legitimately attended here to two very different attributes of the moon; and nothing can be proved against the Romans, just because all the Germanic languages, Sanskrit, Persian, Hindi—and even Zend and Old Bulgarian—happen to agree with the Greeks from historical habit.

Sometimes, of course, symbolic structures become so extravagantly loaded with cultural mythology that with a little thought we can see them even in our own most sacredly rational behavior, the economic. Consider the humble "nickel" as a symbol. The physical fact of a nickel is hard, objective, real. But its real function and meaning is a tissue of cultural fictions. We pretend, preposterously, that a nickel is "equal" to a pair of shoelaces, a package of five slivers of chicle-tree sap, a bottle of sweet caffeine-containing carbonated water, or a couple of magical documents from a stamp-vending machine. For a nickel we can (or once could) even sit in a bus—driven by a gentleman to whom we haven't properly been introduced socially and who owns no part of the bus personally—and confidently expect that, in obeying a fantastically intricate web of agreements (wages, company franchises, union contracts are but part of it) and quite without any verbal exchange (you must not talk to him!), he will in good time and in fair condition deposit us at a longitude and latitude everyone loosely and dubiously pretends is "Times Square." A nickel is "equal" to all these things and more, depending upon our whimsy or organic wish in the matter. But no one in his right mind would presume for a moment that in any objective physical-science sense a pair of shoelaces is equal to a pack of chewing-gum is equal to a coke is equal to the services of the United States Post Office is equal to a trip cross-town. We city slickers know a thing or two: we can tell a hawk from a handsaw!

Of course, the sober scientific literalist can wreak still further havoc upon the supposedly "hard" reality of this economic myth. A nickel is not made of nickel but is largely copper. Nor does it have five times as much copper in it as a "copper" (which in turn is partly tin). It is only by courtesy "equivalent" to one-twentieth of an (alloyed) "silver" dollar—indeed, you can buy in the open market more pure silver for a paper dollar than is contained in a silver dollar. The paper equivalent is traditionally a promise to pay on demand a certain weight of (in this case pure) gold. A glance at the Periodic Table of elements would show up all these "equivalencies" as nonsense chemically. Meanwhile, people are no longer allowed by law even to own one of these paper promises in the form of "gold certificates," much less to exercise their alleged right to exchange it for monetary gold. And so far as the fixed "worth" of a dollar is concerned in terms of organically useful wheat or beef, the symbol-mythology actually changes so rapidly that even the most obtuse are easily convinced that money is indeed a cultural myth. A dollar is a solemn "Sir Roger de Coverley" dance, a codified psychosis normal in one cultural subspecies of this animal, an institutionalized dream that everyone is having at once.

A symbol never is the thing: it stands for it. Nor are symbols ever coincident with "unities" inherent in nature: the only "natural" unity is all reality itself! It is symbols, rather, that carve out of total reality the organically chosen aspects of it to which the organism elects to attend, to the calmly outrageous ignoring of all the rest of that which is. Characteristically enough, we often make in our symbolisms arrogantly subjective statements that are not really so in the cosmic sense: a "good" beefsteak and a "good" book have nothing whatever in common, except that they both please a given intricate featherless biped at the moment. In a god's-eye view of the world there is no particular reason to select beefsteaks or a specific book for denotation or singling out as "good." Furthermore, Hindus and vegetarians will dissent from the one dictum, and the Bill of Rights gives firm constitutional backing to a preference for W. H. Auden over Gerard Manley Hopkins.

That is, we call "good" indifferently two things we would not dream of confusing with each other objectively. If we choose—now a carbohydrate like sugar and now a hydrocarbon like gasoline—to impute this "goodness" to, the choice is meaningful solely with respect to our immediate total organic purposes: the biochemist and the internal-combustion engineer are under no illusions about the diverse chemical reactions of sugar and petroleum products. But we blithely use the same term for quite different denotations. Nor are our connotations or implicit subjective attitudes necessarily the same, even when we appear to be agreed upon the same denotative entity. Thus a "collegiate Gothic" chapel means one thing to the benefactor of the college, another to the Dean of the School of Religion, and still other things to the art historian or the man of taste, the geologist, the lightning-insurance salesman, and the cultural anthropologist. Even tools are not tools without human purposes behind them; and symbol systems have still more to do with yearning organisms than they have to do with reality. They are both, tools and symbols alike, organic artifacts.

The whole phenomenon of language testifies eloquently to this factor of preference and choice in man's dealings with the universe. And yet, despite the biologically revolutionary nature of both tools and symbols, they are both in the great tradition of serving organic purposes. As a science, modern linguistics is one of the least generally known; but it is nevertheless one which has extremely important lessons to teach us about man. One difficulty is our naïve tribalism, which affects even (or perhaps most especially) our philosophers; indeed, until the analytic philosophy of modern symbolic logicians like Russell and Whitehead, Ogden and Richards, Carnap and others, no one ever examined rigorously the very instrument, language, that synthetic philosophers had used throughout history in building their metaphysical universes. In finding a large consensus in language among the co-speakers of our own language, we are far too easily able to take the fact of language for granted and to consider its forms inevitable and necessary in their logic. Intellectually, we are in the position of the American farm-boy as a soldier in Germany who, when having a large equine animal pointed out to him as a "Pferd," stoutly insisted that "Well, it may be *called* a Pferd, but it sure as hell acts like a horse!"

Another difficulty is that we are ludicrously journey-proud in our parochial ignorance concerning language. Most persons who study a "foreign" language learn at best only French, Spanish, German, or Italian, in these days even Russian, decreasingly perhaps Latin and Greek, and, as an extreme of the recondite, Sanskrit. None of these, however, is a truly *foreign* language—but only one of the divergent dialects (now mutually unintelligible) of the Indo-European family of languages descended historically from the same original source. When we re-encounter in all these dialects much the same repertory of formal structures, we have an absurd sense of having encompassed all the possible variations afforded by comparative language study. We think we have been to Bangkok when it is only to the next county seat. We must learn Navaho and Nootka and Nam—or some other non-Indo-European language—to have any legitimate sense of how alarmingly variable and arbitrary a thing a given language is, and how little it mirrors the structures of reality. Indeed, as we shall see later, the "structure" we find in reality is, much of the time, merely imputed to reality by the structure of our language.

Even so, any student of some other Indo-European language than his own, if he keeps his ethnographic ear alert and the eye of his mind open, soon learns that the denotations (things pointed out) and the connotations (the meanings implied) of words in one language are not quite the same as the connotations and the denotations in another language. If this were not so, the difficult job of translating from one language into another could be performed by an electronic dictionary-machine, as some naïve enthusiasts have claimed could be done. However, the German "Herr" is in many subtle ways not at all the same as the English "Mister." Even in the case of the French "spirituel"—the apparent cognate of English "spiritual"—the meanings are surprisingly divergent. The French word connotes the sprightly and the intellectual, the English word the lugubriously moral.

Yet even here, in translating from one Indo-European language into another, we are misled by the fact that we usually encounter in the "foreign" tongue some rough approximation of meaning with the original. At worst, when it is "hiver" in France and "inverno" in Italy, it is still recognizably "invierno" in Spain. And a Swedish "vinter" is only a little colder than an English "winter"—even though the unpredictable Russians unregenerately and unilaterally call it something else again, "zima," which all right-thinking people will have no trouble agreeing is an intransigent error.

The greater difficulty is that the Eskimo (who ought to be authorities on the phenomena of winter) do not agree at all with the speakers of Indo-European languages as to just what the "unitary" phenomena are. When we speak of "snow," for example, we are comfortably convinced that we have got hold of something unitary and objective in nature. Snow is snow, whatever you *call* it—and most of the people of Europe, plus half those of India, the Persians, and the Icelanders, would agree to this. But the Eskimo have numerous categorizings of nature to our one. If it is wind-driven flying snow, it is one thing; if it is snow on the ground, it is (to them) obviously another; and if it is packed hard like ice, as in snow suitable for an iglu, still another concept (and word) is used. In English, on the other hand, we get off the Eskimo subject pretty badly, and if the snow is partly melted or refrozen, we call it "sleet," which is something else entirely.

The fact is that (from a god's-eye point of view) there is just as much discernible "objective difference" between Eskimo wind-driven-snow-in-the-air and snow-packed-hard-like-ice, as there is between English water-vapor-frozen-into-feathery-hexagonal-crystals and melted-and-partly-refrozen-snow. We are sure we are discriminating objective physical realities in "snow" versus "sleet." And so we are. But the Eskimo are quite as justified in considering the two together, if their vocabulary-connotation is interested in the air-borne nature of the snow rather than its past temperature phases. And they are quite as justified in making further finer discriminations concerning its position or state which we habitually neglect to make.

It is tempting to suppose that the Eskimo may be more concerned about the temperature situation now, because the categories he has contrived through time help govern his adaptive organic behavior—in such life-or-death matters as building a quick iglu (out of snow-packed-hard-like-ice when there is a dangerous amount of wind-driven-snow-in-the-air), rather than going hunting (with a fine crust of snow-packed-hard-like-ice on the ground). But this is too easy a rationalization: the discrimination of "sleet" versus "snow" might also be a life-or-death matter to an Englishman racing his week-end Jaguar down country lanes—but his language had these terms long before automobiles were invented. The truth is that the "rationality" of any language is limited or non-existent. Whatever accidents of linguistic history long ago led to the presence of both "snow" and "sleet" in the English dictionary, any rationality in the matter now is entirely the modern Englishman's, in making appropriate additional discriminations between accelerator and brake.

All that we can say with any sureness, then, is that the Eskimo are lexically alert to more faces of winter than we are and that they see different faces than we in the storm. (Or, to change the figure, vocabularies and nature are a good deal like hog-butchering: the same hog can be cut up "Boston style" or "Chicago style" and the pork still sustain life and taste equally good.) In either case, Eskimo or Englishman, any conviction that basic realities are being dealt with arises merely from the real fact that different vocabularly-categorizings exist. As soon as the human infant learns to speak any language at all, he already has a "hardening of the categories." They are different, this we know, for our language tells us so.

All languages have these airy incommensurabilities with one another. For example, as Whorf shows, the Hopi word *liasa'ytaka* covers all classes of agents that fly—except for birds, for which a separate term is employed—whereas English discriminates "dragonfly," "airplane," "pilot," "angel," and "bird" too, as well as pterodactyls, bats, kites, and bumblebees. The Hopi word, therefore, cannot be rendered correctly by "flyer" (by which we mean only "pilot") or even by the made-up English word "fly-ist," but must be further qualified as "all-flying-agents-minus-birds." For another example, English has one word to denote H_2O (with the implicit connotation that the liquid phase is meant, that is, *most* of the time!), viz., "water"—regardless of the quantity or functional category involved. But Hopi has two words: *pahē*, for considerable quantities of H_2O as present in natural bodies like lakes, waterfalls, fountains, and rivers; and *kēyi* for "water-in-containers" (by connotation man-made containers, hence by denotation "water-for-the-domestic-purposes-of-human-beings"). On the other hand, speakers of English know perfectly well that a waterfall is not a fountain, since the water in these two situations goes in opposite directions, and English chooses to attend to this arbitrary difference.

But a Hopi would stubbornly insist that both fountain and waterfall are plainly *pahē*, as any fool can see, and that's the end of it.

Any argument about the point by either Hopi or speaker of English is entirely non-rational. For no language is "there"; each has been dreamed up by different traditional societies of people. On the one hand, a word can put into semantic equation any two most disparate objects in the universe, if the society chooses—just as the dreamer or the schizophrenic can put into symbolic equation any two diverse things the individual chooses to equate. On the other hand, every phenomenon or event that can be discriminated from other "similar" events must, for that reason, be in some way different—and, if *different,* might logically just as well enjoy a distinct verbal designation! The physicist can prove to us that no two snowflakes are exactly alike, in brute objective fact. Why not give them different names then? But this would dissolve a vocabulary into an infinite number of nonce-words and would be useless for purposes of inter-individual communication. People at some point must have loved one another well enough blindly to accept the arbitrary shibboleths that make up all language. We *have to* lump dissimilarities together, and we do this in terms of hidden "functional" similarities we choose to see in them. The fact that the ways in which each one of us learned to do this are quite below the level of awareness, does not destroy the reality of this present fact.

Indeed, the only reason we can tell a hawk from a handsaw is that our vocabulary categories tell us they are different: it would be a small matter for a schizophrenic, sufficiently pressed affectively and sufficiently pushed by his purposes, to decide that in some "significant" respect hawks and handsaws are "identical." We could say, for instance, that both belong to words with an initial "ha-," but we would be likely to judge a man indeed out of his mind if he thought this similarity were meaningful or worth attending to. Even so, a lexicographer is allowed to make much of the fact in writing a dictionary and is called very learned, while a linguist in discovering the final -*s* can make a wise statement about English plurals. Each society, in its language, has a host of such implicit agreements. Meanwhile, culturally, with different vocabularies, we apperceive different symbolic worlds (both denotatively and connotatively), for all that we can suppose it is the same world involved.

All languages are made up of sound, sense, and structure (phonetics, vocabulary, and grammar, respectively). We confess we have found little that was sound in discussing "sense." Is there not, then, some sense to be found in "sound"? Are there not, in the physics of sound, discernible universals behind all languages? Physics tells us that a single note on a violin has *duration* (the length of time the note is sounded). The note also has *amplitude,* that is, volume or, psychologically, loudness (physically the actual distance, great or small, in which the string vibrates back and forth across its position at rest—a matter related directly to the measurable relative *force* used in producing the sound). These physical facts, no man can deny, are true in Paris or in Pukapuka.

The note also has *frequency* or pitch (the speed of movement of the string, or the number of vibrations per chosen unit of time past its position at rest). The violin tone also has *timbre* or overtone configuration (that is, the string vibrates not only in its whole length but also in halves, thirds, fourths, etc., of its total length, thus giving rise to secondary feebler tones of higher pitch that make up the characteristic "color" of the tone on a given instrument). Timbre is the qualitative difference between the note A on a violin and the same-pitched note A on an oboe or a flute. The basic frequency A is identical on all these instruments, but the overtones give recognizably different "colors" to the instruments—hence the possibility of an orchestra of instruments. Thus a flute has an almost pure basic tone, with overtones of only feeble amplitude; on the other hand, an oboe and a violin both have a rich (though dissimilar) variety of relatively strong overtones, that is, secondary tones of audibly high amplitude.

Now a Blackfoot or a Bontoc could both learn to discriminate an oboe from a violin, and they could do it whether they heard the instruments in Samarkand or Timbuktu. And all human beings could agree on such physical aspects of sound as duration, loudness, and pitch. Unfortunately, however, the sounds of speech-utterance involve no such agreement in their purposes. Take duration. In English, for example, the duration of a vowel-utterance indicates merely a regional "Southern drawl," or perhaps an individually idiosyncratic difference in manner of speaking. It enables us to distinguish different persons speaking, but makes for no difference in meaning of the utterances. Elsewhere, however, languages may give the individual no such harmless leeway. For example, in Takelma (an American Indian language of Washington) or in Jabbo (a West African language) the duration of utterance discriminates the vowel into long and short forms, which are fundamentally and meaningfully as different in these languages as "b" versus "p" are in English. (This of course has nothing whatever to do with the grievously misnamed "long" and "short" vowels in English: no matter how long you prolong the "i" of "bit"— "bi-i-i-i-t"—you never get the "i" of "police"; these are qualitative timbre-differences in vowels, not quantitative-duration differences.) Some languages even have distinct long and short consonants, with or without long and short vowels.

Or take volume. In English, the differing volume of sound or "stress accent" is a syllabic phenomenon; and by cultural habit at least thousands of years old, one of the last three syllables of a word (antepenult, penult, or ultima) must be stressed, whether or not a syllable earlier in the word is stressed. Thus we can say phó-to, pho-tó-gra-phy, and pho-to-grá-phi-cal—but only an ignorant foreigner would say phó-to-gra-phy or pho-tó-gra-phi-cal. This ancient and finicking rule even applies when we are arguing about something as relatively recent and new as British antidisestablishmentárians, or sagely consulting over newly discovered cures for pulmonary hypertrophicosteoarthrópathy. It is a rigid rule all speakers of correct English obey, though quite unwittingly.

Sometimes, too, in English we use heightened volume in an individually expressed nonce-manner to stress some phatically important part of the utterance. This may lead the Chinese listener wrongly to suppose that the Englishman or the American is erratically and toweringly angry when one of the latter states that "She is the *sweet*-est girl in the world" without being in the least bit angry about it; it merely means that the coolie (not the Chinese gentleman!) is likely to increase both the speed and the volume of his whole utterance when he is angry. In English, stress is further used together with pitch- or melody-patterns as "intonation"—as when Sir Laurence Olivier, without our knowing it, subtly sings his lines, but a first-grade reader recites his in a single monotone. This is done in an individually expressive manner that does not change the basic meaning, but only gives it grace and conviction. Or stress and pitch together may be used as a kind of spoken punctuation, for example, in pronouncing "John" with a falling intonation (declarative), rising (interrogative), high-rising (incredulity), stressed-falling (aghast disapprobation or shocked disbelief), or prolonged high-low intonation (as in calling to a person to summon him from a distance). There used to be a radio comedian who obtained his (some say) humorous effects solely by systematically inverting these normal intonation-patterns of spoken English. On the other hand, pitch-stress intonation in French is a sentence-wise phenomenon, used to "frame" a whole utterance becomingly, with syllabic stress quite even and minimal. And of course many languages never use volume for "stress" at all: if our ethnographic ear is not quite mistaken, the Kiowa Indians stress utterances by raising the pitch (but not the volume) and increasing the duration of the appropriate word-particle—which is very curious to listen to indeed.

Pitch or frequency, then (as we have already seen), also has its variations just as much as volume does in different languages. As far as English is concerned, pitch is merely an expressive modulation of the voice, punctuation, or sentence-melody. But in Chinese or Burmese, mere differences in pitch or melodic pattern of a syllable may discriminate different lexical words in the dictionary. Thus *ma* in the Mandarin dialect of Peiping may mean "mother," "hemp," "horse," or "scold"—depending on whether it is spoken with a high, rising, low-rising, or low-falling pitch or intonation. In Burma old hands delight to pull on newcomers the famous Burmese sentence made up entirely of *ma*, pronounced in different intonations to mean "Get the horse, a mad dog is coming"—a statement one surely has rare enough occasion to use in natural context but which well enough illustrates the point. In Navaho, on the other hand, pitch has to do not with vocabulary but with structure, that is, pitch is not lexical but grammatical. That is to say, Navaho pitch discriminates different inflected forms of the same dictionary word, indicating "declensional" and "conjugation-al" rather than vocabulary differences. Thus, while different languages utilize the same gamut of physical possibility afforded by duration (length), amplitude (stress), and frequency (pitch)—given to them all equally by the nature of sound in physics—they use them differently for different functional purposes linguistically.

All the foregoing may be designated the "quantitative" differences in ·sound. In the "qualitative" (timbre) differences of sounds, languages differ even more widely. For one thing, all languages do not employ universally the same fixed set of sounds or "alphabet." The various sound units or "letters" we use in speech differ, of course, from one another qualitatively in their timbre-configurations; but different languages use widely differing *sets* of timbres or "alphabets." Thus Hottentot, in addition to vowels and consonants, uses "clicks." These are: the sound we use to imitate a kiss or to call a dog (or old east European Jewish women use when putting yeast-breads—but not baking-powder breadstuffs—into the oven, to make them rise); the sound we use to tell a horse to begin moving or to move more smartly; the sound maiden ladies make among us to express moral disapprobation; etc. These, and their like, are used in Hottentot as actual "letters" in their spoken words. Similarly, in Comanche, some distinct "letters" are whispered, some sounded with the larynx. (It is hard to say what this must do to Comanche lovers, but we do know that the Comanche language—because no enemy linguist had ever studied this very difficult language—was safely used in the first World War to transmit in open language highly secret communications!)

Furthermore, all languages use sound-"units" that are not units at all. That is, they are fictitious in physical terms, and real only psychologically and subjectively. For example, the *k* sounds in the words "Keats," "cat," "kite," "kiss," and "cough" are not physically and objectively the same sound in each case at all—nor is "Keats," for that matter, the same objectively when spoken by a man and by a woman, say an octave higher. This is often an extremely difficult thing of which to convince people, so well have we learned these fictions in childhood. And yet each one of these sounds has measurable, objective, visible differences on a chimograph or smoked cylinder (or on the sound track of a talking movie). The k of "Keats" is as distinct from the k sound of "cough," as either is from the "back k" or q (as it happens to be spelled) of the Arabic "Qoran" or "Qattara." The last (q) we are psychologically able to apprehend as "different" only because its range is beyond that which we regard as proper for a correctly pronounced English k. Thus our supposed unitary k is not a genuinely objective phonetic unit in physics, but instead a fairly wide (though fussily delimited) gamut of sounds—psychologically recognized and "heard" by us as the same *phoneme*.

A phoneme is therefore merely a culturally subjective learned fiction, with no status whatever in objective physical reality. And it is of phonemes that all utterances in all human languages are made, of such stuff as dreams are made on. A child who does not yet speak well, merely has not yet learned sufficiently well the phonemic shibboleths, the arbitrary sound-gamuts, which his society insists upon. This, also, is what a "foreign accent" consists in: the speaker of the language foreign to him substitutes the closest phonemes provided him in his native tongue. These do well enough, but no one is fooled by it; we still recognize his phonemes as subtly incorrect in our terms. (His intonations, stresses, and the like are also liable to be incorrect. And this is why, too, naïvely rigid people find it difficult or impossible to speak a foreign language "without an accent"; they cannot give themselves over to outlandish and probably immoral foreign ways.)

The God-fearing Englishman regards it as simply silly to pronounce the t of French *tête* with the tongue-tap on the teeth a proper Frenchman insists on, and finds the t of "Tunbridge Wells" quite good enough —thus establishing himself unmistakably as an Englishman. The American either can't or is embarrased to say the French *la rue* by waggling his uvula as he ought to, and making the tight, constipated sound of the French *u* in the proper "bouche en chemin d'œuf"; he makes it good old Omaha "lah rrrew," thus betraying himself every time. But none of this is any better than the classical Chinese laundryman we joke about: this worthy who said "Belly cold" (in pleasant greeting to a customer) was not referring to an abdomen become chilly by reason

of an untucked-in shirt-tail; he was merely doing the best he could'
with the English phonemes *v* and *r*, that are lacking in his Chinese
phonemic system.

The phonemic system of any language is therefore narrowly selective
of the total phonetic physical possibilities; but, more than that, it does
violence to the physical facts about sound in nature. Nor is there a
finite list of humanly-possible sounds (laid up in some Platonic limbo)
to be chosen from. Every society has its own wilful way with speech
noises. Thus the Athapaskan Indian languages put together into one
phoneme (in their so-called "intermediate" phonemes) what we discriminate as two sounds: both our *b* and our *p* are heard by them
as belonging within the same wider gamut of their intermediate *B*.
This accounts for the fact that we sometimes spell their name "Atha-
baskan" and sometimes "Athapaskan," while we call their lake "Lake
Athabaska." This does not mean that our good friends the Canadians
cannot spell English; it means rather that the "two" sounds don't
really matter to the Indians, since to them it is "the same thing."
Thus, for us, sitting on a "bee" and sitting on a "pea" are fraught
with disastrous differences even on the linguistic level. But an Atha-
baskan (Athapaskan) Indian would be dull to the merely phonemic
aspects of the difference, however similarly he might respond to the
physical realities.

Some languages, on the other hand, discriminate sounds that we
happen to confound. In Aymara, for example (a language spoken by
Indians south of Lake Titicaca in Bolivia and Peru), the "sonant"
sounds *b*, *d*, and *g* are lacking; but our "voiceless" surds *p* and *t* exist
for them in three distinct forms each, and our *k* in six distinct forms.
That is to say, there is a "front *k*" and a "back *k*," each of which (like
their *p* and *t*) is discriminated into three forms each, viz., simple,
aspirated (spoken with a simultaneous expiration of breath), and
glottalized (spoken with a simultaneous laryngeal cough). The Eng-
lish-speaking recorder of this Indian language has no difficulty in
distinguishing "front *k*" and "back *k*" (similar to the Arabic *q*), because back *k* is lacking in English. But he has a hard time in distinguishing simple *p* from aspirated *p* ($\dot{p}$), since the *p* of English is
characteristically somewhat aspirated in his own speech. This is a

critical linguistic matter, however, for Aymara *puku* means "speckled," *p̃uku* "pot," and *ṗuku* (glottalized) "maize." Thus, while we would tax the Aymara with making fussy distinctions of *p*'s, the Athapaskans would wonder why we divided their intermediate "unit" *B* into a *p* and a *b*.

Another fact about phonemes is their curious behavior positionally in syllables. These building blocks cannot be put together in just any old way, but have to follow *morphophonemic* or "sound-structure" rules. Phonemes are as rigid as chemical elements, with regard to whether they will or will not combine with other elements. The astonishing thing about English is the fantastically complex set of morphophonemic rules that even the humblest ditch-digger obeys— implicitly, infallibly, and without ever knowing he does it. Some languages, by contrast with English, have a very simple kind of syllable structure. In some Polynesian languages, for example, *any* consonant in their phonemic system can begin a syllable, and *any* vowel-phoneme can end the syllable. The morphophonemic formula for all possible syllables in these languages, therefore, is the very simple "consonant plus vowel" or "C+V." In English, on the other hand, some consonants may be initial in the syllable, others not; and/or medial; or/and final; or one and not the other. They may also combine with certain other consonants, but not with others, plus-or-minus (in some cases) still a third set of consonants (but not others)—and so on. The formula for English (meaning an English syllable may begin with "zero [consonants], that is a vowel, *or* "any consonant minus eng," *or* etc., each comma meaning "or") is of truly hair-raising complexity:

$$
0,\ \text{C-}\eta,\
\begin{array}{c} g+l \\ k+l \\ \acute{s} \\ d|r, \\ \theta \\ f+l \\ b+l \end{array}
\
\begin{array}{c} h| \\ g| \\ t| \\ d| \\ \theta| \end{array}
\ w,\
\begin{array}{c} h \\ k \\ g \\ f \\ v \\ p \\ b \\ m \end{array}
\ y(u),\ s\pm
\begin{array}{c} k+w \\ t|r, \\ p+l \end{array}
\ s
\begin{array}{c} k \\ t \\ l \\ n \\ f \\ p \\ m \\ w \end{array}
+V+\binom{a}{\mathfrak{o}}0,\
\begin{array}{c} w \\ \pm r \\ y\text{-}0, \end{array}
\ \Big]\ \text{C-h,}\
\begin{array}{c} l+b,m,f \\ m|p \\ s| \\ s+k, \\ l,n|g \\ s+t \\ d \\ s \end{array}
\
\begin{array}{c} l|c \\ n|j, \end{array}
\
\begin{array}{c} k| \\ ks| \\ \eta| \\ t| \\ d| \\ l| \\ n| \\ f| \\ p| \\ m+pf \end{array}
\theta,\
\begin{array}{c} t/d \\ \pm s/z \\ st/zd \end{array}
$$

1	2	3	4	5	6	7	8	9	10	11	12	13	14	15

And yet our ditch-digger friend never falters, never makes a mistake. Indeed, he might take his whole lunch hour trying to dream up some syllable which did *not* obey these rules. The chances are that he couldn't do it—not even if he ransacked the onomatopoetic words in the "comic book" thoughtfully inserted by his wife in his lunch-pail —so firmly, so completely, so inextricably, and so perfectly are these complex rules imbedded in the covert, unwitting culture of his language-habits. He is rigidly corseted by culture and doesn't even know it.

But with one look at the formula, the linguist can come up with an obvious syllable, though one at first not easy to pronounce, because it so wars against our linguistic morality. For the second possibility listed in the formula says that an English syllable can begin with "any consonant minus eng" (C—ŋ). Now, although we *spell* eng "ng," this is not actually the sound n plus the sound g—but a quite different unitary sound or phoneme. This is easily proved by pronouncing "Long Island" correctly, and then as "Lon Gisland [Lon Guyland]." Linguistically deaf-and-dumb "grammar-school" teachers, frightened lest we "drop our g's" (substitute n for eng, that is), actually scare us into putting real g's in where they never existed, save in spelling. To avoid a low-class "singin' in the rain" they would have us risk "sin gin g in the rain," which we all even as children somehow rightly knew is phonemically immoral.

The Mephistophelian linguist then invites us to try putting the eng (ŋ), the sound which is final in each syllable of "singing," in the unfamiliar *initial* position before any English vowel. Such behavior occurs in "Pa ngo Pa ngo," to be sure, but eng *never* occurs initially in respectable English. If, with practice, you can do this outlandish pagan thing, then you have shattered our beautiful morphophonemic formula, possibly for the first time in your life—unless perhaps as a baby you once accidentally produced an initial eng before you knew any better.

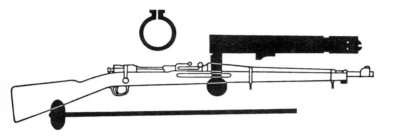

11. And Gets All Balled Up in His Grammar

All human languages have sound, sense, and structure. In the last chapter we looked at the first two of these. We saw that, once people have phonemic systems, they do not even make the same kind of noises. And once they have vocabularies, they do not even make the same sense out of the same universe. That is to say, the speech sounds men make are no more similar in different societies than are the sound-improvisations of two individual babies. In fact, any baby makes more experimental noises by far than any language seems to need; all babies have to be caught young, so to speak, and taught to narrow down their alphabet to fit that of their own social group. And as far as sense goes, humans had already made the fatal step, once they had left purely phatic communication for articulate language. Phatic communication is fairly close to universal human biology; and so long as only phatic communication is attempted, even apes in different hordes can manage to understand each other. But once societies try to make semantic sense out of things, the confusion of Babel is upon us: we not only make different sets of sounds, but in our vocabularies we even refuse to look at the world in the same way.

But how about structure in language? Human brains, we know, are very much the same in all races. Don't their cogs gear up into much the same kind of thinking machines? And don't these machines grind out much the same logic? Or, better yet, isn't it the same universe all humans are attending to? And aren't they bound to discover in it the same structures, which grammatical structure everywhere is forced to recognize? Most of us admittedly use grammar that is atrociously bad in any traditionalist sense. As far as our mother-tongue goes, we are satisfied to speak it like a native, doing "what comes naturally," and never give it a second thought—confidently knowing that we can speak "correct" grammar if we need to in any full-dress affair. We admit we are sometimes careless, but at least we do know what is right: in this our grammar is like our morals. Surely there is some final "grammar of thought," if all men only put their minds to it?

On this point the linguist must be as dour and disappointing as before: if languages differ as widely as they do, both in words and in sounds, they are even more hopelessly incommensurable with one another in structure or grammar. We might as well know the worst at the beginning: there are no universal formal categories in language, no necessary (since "logical") grammar for all mankind.

For example, Indo-European languages have "parts of speech," as the ancient Greeks and the Sanskrit scholar Panini both knew in 350 B.C. Parts of speech are not categories arbitrarily dreamed up by fusty grammarians to confuse us. They are the *kinds* of words we use in living speech, differing intrinsically according to the work they do. They function in the sentence for different purposes: as noun, pronoun, verb, adjective, adverb, preposition, conjunction, or interjection. Thus prepositions, conjunctions, and interjections never change their form at all in any circumstance. But nouns, which name things, get pluralized in English; and pronouns, which stand for previously mentioned nouns, are identified by endings or forms that tell us person (who is involved?), number (are there one or more than one?), and case (what is the action-relation of the word in the sentence?). By contrast verbs, which define action, get a different sort of ending to indicate person (who did it?), number (how many were involved?), and tense (when did it happen?).

But all the parts of speech found in English and Latin and the like are not indispensable to language as such. Chinese, for example, has no parts of speech at all—unless "full words" or roots, and "empty words" or grammar can be counted as such. A Chinese "full word" could be several of our parts of speech in function, and yet none of them in form: two specimens of *man* (noun) together *man* (verb) a boat; one of them is very *man* (manly or masculine, i.e., adjective) and easily pulls his share, but nevertheless she, the other specimen of "man," pulls at her oar very *man* (manfully, i.e., adverb)—shouting "*Man!* (interjection), this is really hard work!" There are no parts-of-speech endings visible anywhere here. The grammatical work is done entirely by the order or sequence of words. Indeed, when position in the sentence and meaning-context do not make it clear, the Chinese full word must be qualified by an "empty" grammatical word. For example, in the first or noun instance above, *man* must have a "classifier," just as in English one cannot say "a cattle" but only "a *head* of cattle." In Chinese, such classifiers—usually all translated "one piecie" in Pidgin, though different ones are used according to the object classified—are empty words with purely grammatical functions. Chinese empty words are a little like catalytic agents in chemistry: they cause other elements (full words) to combine meaningfully into a sentence, but they are not themselves affected by the process.

Full and empty words show up clearly in Pidgin English, which has a largely English vocabulary but thoroughly Chinese grammar. For example, in the phrase "Mary b'long me," meaning "my wife," *Mary* and *me* are full words which never change by inflection. Thus in the sentence "*Me* got plenty *Mary* too-much" (meaning "I am happily polygynous"), *me* is this time functionally a subjective case, whereas in "Mary b'long me," *me* is functionally a possessive case; likewise *Mary* in the sentence, since there are a number of them, is a functional plural and would show it in its ending if this were true English in its grammar. But in Pidgin neither full word, *Mary* or *me*, ever changes its form, whatever its English "parts of speech" function, and stays always the same in good Chinese fashion. "B'long," similarly, is not the same word behavioristically as the English word "belong," though it is directly derived from it. Just as *Mary* and *me* are never declined as "nouns" or "pronouns" in Pidgin, so also *b'long* is never conjugated as an English "verb" and remains forever free of any imputations of person, number, or tense. As a matter of fact, *b'long* isn't a "verb" at all, but an empty word: a possessivizing grammatical word, which means "the [full] word that follows in position is the possessor of the [full] word that precedes." *B'long* is therefore the grammatical equivalent of English apostrophe-*s* (*'s*) of the possessive case—though in Pidgin, unlike English, the empty particle precedes rather than follows the possessor word, and the possessed word, also unlike English, comes the first of all.

A few remarks should also be added to explain why some full words need classifiers in Chinese. In Chinese you cannot say simply *i jen* to mean "a man," but you must say *i go jen*, "one piecie man." The reason for this is that Chinese has a different way of conceptualizing words. In English we ordinarily have "bound" forms, that is, we conceive entities as solitary indivisible particulars, such as "man," "airplane," or "rifle." Cut a man in half and you don't have a man any more—and the same is true of airplanes and rifles. But "unbound" forms, such as in Chinese, conceptualize in terms of species or of universals, as for example such English unbound forms as "mankind," "milk," or "wood"—which are indefinitely divisible while still retaining their identity. As a result, bound forms already imply one single specimen of the entity in question. But unbound forms must specify: one *specimen* of mankind, six *head* of cattle, one *gallon* of milk, a *stick* of wood or dynamite. In fact, when English does occasionally conceptualize in unbound forms, we are forced to use classifiers just as much as the Chinese are. We must say: a fine *example* of loyalty, a good *piece* of work, a glorious *specimen* of womanhood, a single *case* of robbery. Chinese as a language is, so to speak, quite "Platonic" metaphysically; English is far more "Aristotelian." As far as that goes, Tagalog, a language of the Philippine Islands, exemplifies in its grammatical structure some of the concepts of modern physics. Like Chinese, Tagalog has "full" words, but of two different kinds, *static* (intrinsic, permanent) and *transient* (adventitious, temporary), as well as "particles" (empty grammar words)—but otherwise no sign of functionally different parts of speech at all.

Since no one of the parts of speech—or even the presence of any parts of speech whatever—is necessary to language, it follows that none of the particular "inflections" or form-categories of any one part of speech is indispensable. In fact, the very inflection of words is not necessary, for "isolating" languages like those of the Sinitic group may largely lack any inflection whatever. In a pure isolating language, there is complete mechanical separation between wholly uninflected full words and grammatical empty particles: full words are roots, and empty words are grammar. By contrast, in an "inflected" language like Latin, one can never speak the root *ama-* alone (of *amo, amas, amat*) and mean simply "love" by it—whether noun or verb as in English, or full word as in Chinese. By the same token, one didn't go around in ancient Rome saying "-s" and "-t" and expect to be understood as saying "thou" or "he," when these verbal inflections are isolated from the verb stem. In actual speech these empty particles must always occur inflectively at the ends of verbs, and only there—never connected with other parts of speech and never alone by themselves.

Thus the degree of fusion of grammar and root is not a mere matter of *writing* parts together or separate on a page, but actually a matter of the *operational behavior* of words in different languages. What a "word" is might seem a very simple thing, and very easy of definition. Actually, defining a "word" is one of the most difficult things in all linguistics. An expert linguist would never dream of indicating, by spaces in a published text, just what he thought a "word" was in a hitherto unrecorded language—until he had thoroughly mastered its grammar. It would be worth his reputation!

For this degree of *functional* fusion can run all the way from isolating languages (roots and grammar separated) to agglutinative languages (the loosely glued-together elements may at times be separate, at others not), and from polysynthetic languages (roots may stand alone, but never grammatical particles) to inflective languages (indissoluble fusion of roots and grammar into single functional words). Modern scholarship, incidentally, reveals that Chinese is not quite the monosyllabic and purely isolating language it ought to be for purposes of illustration. But Turkish is a good example of an agglutinative language, and Eskimo of a polysynthetic one. (American English, by the way, is not a very neat illustration of any one type, being at times one and at times another. The more traditional and scholarly the language, the more it retains its ancient inflective character; but good scientific prose trends very much to an isolating emphasis on position of words—and meanwhile the skyscrapers, joysticks, dreamboats, and stumblebums of our popular speech are quite plainly agglutinative.)

Therefore, since parts of speech are not indispensable, nouns are not necessarily universal either. And if nouns are not necessary, then neither are gender, number, and case—or any other declension-category found in any language! English knows this fact grammatically already, and American grammar (as we shall see) is going almost hog-wild with this new freedom, though it still hangs on conservatively to nouns as such. For example, English lacks grammatical gender in nouns—which is present in most of its sister Indo-European languages: *le* couteau, *la* fourchette, *die* Sonne, *le* sol, *der* Mond, *la* lune, *das* Pferd, kalt*es* Wasser, etc. For this reason (that of their own linguistic poverty, or rather their grammatical degeneracy), speakers of English are ready to assent to the proposition that "grammatical gender" is not necessary to meaning—but an unmerciful, purposeless burden on memory that does no semantic work whatever.

For example, in the Latin "illa bella puella," one is grammatically signalizing "the [that is, a *female* the, a single *one*, I mean the one I am *talking about* as subject] beautiful [that is, a *female* beauty, *one* single instance being meant, the *subject* of my discourse, please remember] girl [I mean, just *one* girl in case you have forgotten, the girl I am still talking about as *subject*, that is to say a *female* girl]." Now speakers of English are just as much interested in genuine biological gender as are Romans, Italians, Germans, and Frenchmen; in fact, they might argue a quicker apprehension of the femaleness of a girl (the connotation of the word already gives us a broad hint!) and of her unique singularity as an organism—without needing to be so insistently told these facts grammatically.

Worse than that, grammatical categories do not correspond to the facts of life. In the list given above, the sun is masculine in French and feminine in German; the moon masculine in German and feminine in French—though neither sun nor moon has any biological gender—while the one organism in the list that could have masculinity or femininity (horse) is grammatically neuter. Grammar is just as cavalier about the facts of life when it comes to human beings: although Roman sailors were invariably male, "nauta" is confusingly and libelously placed in the first feminine declension where no sailors belong. And how would one rationalize the flat inconsistency of the fact that in Algonkin languages the words for "raspberry," "kettle," and "knee" belong to the animate gender (as if they were persons or animals), whereas "strawberry," "bowl," and "elbow" are put in the inanimate gender?

Since English also lacks case in nouns except for the possessive (*John* hit me, I hit *John,* but I hit *John's* head), speakers of English are likewise easily convinced of the dispensability of case-endings—for word position can easily take care of subjective / objective (or nominative / accusative) discrimination of meaning, as in the altercation between John and me above. Why bother with the twenty or more cases of Finnish, or the fifteen-some of Lithuanian? Naturally, of course, the same logic applies to the English possessive case—though the speaker of English would fanatically defend the necessity of this form, since his language happened to have it.

As for case in pronouns in English, why not throw it out kit-and-caboodle also? Already we say "*Who* did you see at the party?" and "It's *me*"—revamping the old Indo-European nominative case (incorrectly used) into a new pre-verbal form, and turning the old accusative case (similarly misused) into a new post-verbal form. Case-sense is thus feeble to extinction in English, position-sense strong. But we don't even need these pre-verbal and post-verbal "case" forms. Their position before or after the verb is already self-evident both in speech and in writing. Why do we have to say so grammatically? And how does it clarify meaning in this case to have two forms for the same word? After all, Chinese gets along just fine on position alone, without burdensome inflections. For, really, there is no unclarity of meaning when case is ignored entirely: *Me* hit John, John hit *me*, John hit *me* head—using one form instead of many cases. American Quakers have long said "How *does thee* do?"—a linguistic violence for so gentle a people—

since they use a third person verb form when the second person is obviously meant, and an objective case pronoun when a subjective is meant. And many Americans can blithely say "John saw Mary and *I* walking"—to the absolute consternation of their Indo-European linguistic ancestors. But why should pedagogues fret? Surely there is nothing immoral in English becoming a more "isolating" language like Chinese and less of an "inflective" language like Latin, for this is all that is happening.

Shall we bewail the loss of the fine old Indo-European distinctions that are disappearing in American English? Or shall we rejoice that American English is becoming more efficiently streamlined by finally ridding itself of the useless formal lumber of Indo-European which does no semantic work? The answer is likely to be cast not in logical but in linguistically ethnocentric terms. It would depend on whether one spoke English (without noun gender) or German, French, Spanish, or Italian (with noun gender); and whether one spoke Lithuanian, Algonkin, Finnish, or Bantu (all of which have grammatical gender categories); or French and Spanish (that do without noun case entirely).

Ethnocentrism would triumph over logic for larger units of people also: since all Indo-European languages we encounter have *number,* doesn't this prove that the human mind has to think in terms of singular and plural, of the One and the Many? (This hoary old philosophical chestnut is merely an unwitting discovery of Indo-European grammatical number, a mere linguistic habit of some humans, and not necessarily a profound insight into the nature of reality; nearly the whole of traditional Western metaphysics is no more than such linguistic legerdemain.) Does our grammar have to count for us? Not at all. There are many languages that have no singulars or plurals. When contextually interested in more than one, these languages actually achieve a greater semantic precision in using a cardinal number as a qualifier instead. Semantically, "I have *four wife*" tells us a lot more than "I have *scissors*" or "I have *fish*"—if we are really interested in the actual number of wives and scissors and fish. Nor is English the utmost in elegantly useless finesse: some languages go far beyond English in distinctions of grammatical number. Many languages have one or more *dual* numbers, inflected grammatically throughout the whole series: "inclusive dual" (meaning we-two, that is, inclusively you-and-I) versus "exclusive dual" (meaning we-two, that is, exclusively he-and-I). Some Melanesian languages even have a *trial* number. Surely, we think, the actual occasions on which this special grammatical form for three individuals would be needed are rare enough not to require a whole set of declensional forms for it—when the simple cardinal-number adjective "three" would do the whole job in all possible instances, and do it more economically.

But the speaker of English had better not throw stones, for his language (most uneconomically) has over-capitalized the job of pluralizing. That is, English has many, many inconsistent ways of doing the same thing—and a thing which we have already agreed is not worth doing. Formally, English plurality is a disgrace: if goose/geese, then moose/*meese?*; mouse/mice, house/*hice?*; die/dice, *lie*/lice?; child/children, guild/*guildren?*; cow/kine, plow/*pline?*; tush/tushes, fish/*fishes?*; man/men, pan/*pen?*; woman/women, foeman/"fimman"?; half/halves, cough/*couves?*; cloth/cloths, *scissor*/scissors?; phenomenon/phenomena, lemon/*lema?*; datum/data, bum/*ba?*; deer/deer—is it wive/wifes or what? All this cumbrous machinery does only one thing—pluralizing. At least the Annatom Island trial number makes a further distinction, whether we choose to regard it as useful or not.

Well, we must admit, perhaps grammatical number is a dreadful, useless mess. The whole work of it could be done with simple cardinal numbers, and with much improved semantic clarity and succinctness. But surely all languages take cognizance of distinctions of *person* between the speaker, the spoken-to, and the spoken-of? Is it not critically necessary to know who does what to whom, and when "I mean you"? Not necessarily. Many languages lack grammatical person entirely and seem quite happy about it. Nor does English have a logically complete system: Navaho speakers feel the need for "fourth-," "fifth-," and even "sixth-" personal forms. And even so, in the third person possessive, English is ambiguous in "He took his hat" (whose? his own? John's?). Why, a man could go to jail for such moral slovenliness—for robbery, theft, burglary, embezzlement, fraud, piracy, or barratry—if it were a question of other kinds of property than hats! But Swedish makes it legally clear by using two words: "Han tog *sin* [own] hatt" versus "Han tog *haŋ* [someone else's] hatt." In Cree, with its obviative or "second-mentioned person," one can be even clearer, though at the price of remembering more grammatical forms: "He [A] took his [A's] hat"/ "He [A] took his [B's] hat" / "He [B] took his [A's] hat" / and "He [B] took his [B's] hat"—thus keeping all the hats and their owners semantically straight. But the price of clear title to the hat is the cost of the grammatical hat-checks. Some languages pay the price, but many do not.

So parts of speech are not universal. Nouns are not necessary. Declension is useless busyness—indeed, all kinds of inflection can be ignored in some languages. Gender, number, person, and case in nouns and pronouns are wholly arbitrary. But what about verbs? Once-burned and twice-shy, we are ready to concede beforehand that person and number in verbs may be dispensed with—but don't we need active and passive verbs to discriminate between who does and who is done to? Don't all events occur in fact (indicative) or in wish (optative) or in hypothesis (subjunctive) or by express command (imperative)—and hence the necessity of verbal mode? And isn't it unavoidable that an event occur in the past, the present, or the future? Time, after all, marches on!

So far as mode is concerned, the speaker of American English can give a clear-cut answer: the grammatical subjunctive has been obsolescent since the eighteenth century, and only a professor or a poet or a Philadelphia lawyer has any need of it; the imperative and optative modes are gone without a trace, and not missed either. Sentimental aesthetes and metaphysicians and tricky, hair-splitting statesmen in an effete Europe may mourn the passing of our subjunctive—but all a red-blooded, go-getting, two-fisted American he-man really needs is the indicative mode of flat assertion alone (i.e., no modes at all). We might believe it, but what American would say it nowadays: "If the subjunctive *be* lost, it *were* well lost"! That's Limey talk. No: if it's gone, it's gone—and good riddance too. And so far as voice in verbs is concerned, this phenomenon is oftener lacking than present in the languages of the world.

Besides, it is easy to show that grammatical tense is not really concerned with the objective time discriminations it pretends to. "I'm walking down the street, see, and I meet this dame" could actually have happened last night, last week, or last year for that matter—even though it uses the grammatical forms of the present tense. Furthermore, what objective temporal difference, please, is there between "I *write* this sentence" and "I *am writing* this sentence"? They are not different facts, just because they are different forms. And what difference is there between "I *slept* last night from midnight to dawn" / "I *was sleeping* last night from midnight to dawn" / "By dawn I *had been sleeping* since midnight" / and "By dawn I *had slept* since midnight"? That's no way to keep in condition anyway!

As a matter of fact, many languages are not grammatically interested in tense, and are not formally obsessed with time. For example, whereas English is concerned with the grammatical distinction of variously conceptualized pasts, presents, and futures (some of them duplicates, and some of them bogus), Hopi verbs by contrast are concerned with distinguishing fact, memory, expectation, and law among events. Thus when the current field of reality has a runner present, English says "He runs" or "He is running" (both meaning now), but Hopi says "wari" ("running occur," statement of fact). When the runner is not (or no longer) present, and the objective field is blank or devoid of running, English says "He ran," "He did run," "He was running," or "He had run" (various past tenses)—but Hopi still insists on the same "wari" ("running occur," statement of fact, whether the runner is present or not). Nevertheless, if the runner is not present, Hopi can express the equivalent of an English past tense by saying "era wari" ("[I] recall, running occur," statement of fact based on memory).

For futures, English says "He will run" (statement of confidence in a future event) or "He shall run" (statement of the speaker's compelling insistence that he do run in the future)—that is, an Englishman would, for Americans have largely given up the complicated "shalls" and "wills" as a bad job, and their "shoulds" and "woulds" are in a bad state too. But all through this Hopi says, relaxedly and noncommittally, "warikni" ("running occur [I] daresay," statement of expectation). English, however, gets itself into a corner if it wishes to make a statement of conceptualized law regardless of the actual time involved and is forced to double up illogically with a grammatical present: "He runs" (i.e., on the track team)—although all such actual running is in the past or in the future and at the chronological present he is conspicuously flat on his back, resting on his laurels. But Hopi can make the distinction grammatically with "warikngwe" ("running occur, characteristically," statement of law). Thus Hopi can make statements of a metaphysically precise kind which English cannot hope to through its grammatical forms; and meanwhile English must make real or fictitious time distinctions which Hopi calmly ignores.

On the other hand, Navaho verbs make grammatical distinctions that are not dreamed of in Indo-European languages like English. Navaho has separate verb-forms for an entire series of conceptualized noun classes involved in the verbal action. It is as if, conjugationally, I "handle" objects of the *living object* noun class, "handlefy" those that belong to the conceptually *long object* noun class, "handle-ate" objects of the *textile* or *flexible* class, "handle-ificate" the *"cup of tea"* class (container with its contents), "be-handle" the *rope-snake-harness* class, and "be-handle-ificate" the *burden* class of nouns, etc.—each of the verb forms, of course, being further conjugated in additional dimensions of distinctions, as we shall see.

Navaho also has a system of "aspects" in verbs, which is as pervasive as tense is in English verbs. Just as one *cannot say* anything about verbal action in English without setting it in a time framework of tense—genuine, imputed, or fictitious—so also Navaho verbs *cannot express verbal action* without making its "aspect" grammatically clear. For example, if an act extends through time ("I sleeping"—was, am, or will be sleeping, indifferently), then Navaho must use the *durative* aspect or form of the verb. If the act is completed ("I done sleep"), the *perfective* aspect is required; if customary ("I eats whenever I go to her house"), the *usitative*. If the act is continuously repeated ("I breathe"), the *repetitive* is demanded—but if it is brokenly repetitive ("I takes a drink now and then," i.e., am not duratively soused for a whole week), the *iterative* is used instead, with quite different forms. If the event is longed-for ("Lᴖrd, if she'd only write!"), the *optative* endings are used—not unlike the special forms in the old Latin optative mode, functionally speaking. If the word expresses an arbitrary selection of one of several logically sequential acts ("I gave him a sock," that is, I hit him repeatedly—either iteratively catch-as-catch-can, or with superior pugilistic skill repetitively as I chose—but mention only one of the actual sequence of blows), then the Navaho discreetly uses the *semilfactive* aspect.

Nor is this the limit of Navaho precision. If an act occupies logically zero units of time ("I set off" or "I put it down"), the *momentaneous* aspect is appropriate; if presently durative and logically expected to be perfective sometime ("He [is] walking [and he will arrive]"), then it is the *progressive* aspect of the verb—a far more subtle distinction than our English "progressive" tenses. But if the action is durative-progressive with an anticipated perfective change of state ("His hair whitens [with age]"), none of these forms can be used: it must be the *transitional* aspect. If an action is an implemented optative but negatively perfective ("I *tried* to get at him [but about six fellows held me back]"), the *conative* aspect—which gives a truly wistful flavor to Navaho stories at times. But only a Navaho could tell you whether such idiomatic English forms as "I *like to kill* myself falling off the barn" or "I *like to smacked* him when he talked like that" ought to be *conative* in aspect—since metaphysical questions of free-will and perhaps psychiatric ones of unconscious self-destructive wish enter the picture. However, we can be confident that Navaho could cope with them both grammatically.

There are of course more Navaho verbal aspects than we have mentioned—the continuative, distributive, diversive, reversative, and so on. But the writer has studied Navaho for only six months and cheerfully agrees he's a dub at it, so far as aspects are concerned. Still, the point has perhaps been established that Navaho grammar is formally preoccupied with other metaphysical distinctions than our purely temporal ones. But do not, meanwhile, forget the other dimensions of Navaho verbs! For a Navaho verb might be conjugated as transitive with regard to the nominal object, non-mediopassive in voice, semilfactive in aspect, in six persons, in three numbers, and according to the conceptual shape of the noun object involved—which would make a number of things clear but might still puzzle a speaker of English as to just when all this happens.

The reader who has patiently followed us thus far may now be prepared for the statement that symbolic systems like language have but a feeble formal grasp on total reality, that they sometimes see things that are not there, and that grammatically speaking they give the living speaker not much choice, being a compost of the wishes of dead men. No one can "say what he likes" and expect to be understood, to the extent that he has no formal choice about the saying, and his grammatical mind has long since been made up for him. Morphological "freedom of speech" does not exist. Grammar is the invisible "thought control" in our philosophical prison.

Consider an American and a Shawnee Indian commenting on the objective act of removing combustion products from a rifle barrel, in their foxhole during a lull in battle. Since both of them are *doing* the same thing, the Shawnee utterance obviously can be "translated" (reproduced anew, whole-cloth) in English, and vice versa. But they are certainly not *saying* the same thing in the structures of their respective utterances: they are grammatically busy with entirely different conceptualizations of the event. The American says, without forethought or afterthought, "I clean the gun with the ramrod"—quite as if cleaning and guns and ramrods were either important or essential aspects of the situation. Let's ask our GI friend to explain to us a little better just what he is talking about.

OK. You fellows want me to explain "I clean the gun with a ramrod"? Well, hang on tight. This is going to be as rough as a four-by-four on cross-country reconnaissance.

"I": my whole Christian tradition has taught me the total uniqueness of individual personalities. Even my dogtag asserts this again in my serial number. And yet here I am using a shopworn pronoun that anybody could have picked up before me. "I," considered objectively, am a unique event in history: there is no other male mammalian biped like me, and yet I pretend grammatically that I am completely identical and interchangeable with any other human being who speaks English. Talk about losing your identity in the Army! "I" is really everybody and nobody, if you come right down to it. It would be a hard job trying to tell my buddy, Joe Blow-Snake, just *who* an English first-personal pronoun really *is*.

"Clean": this is originally a descriptive adjective, a conceptualized *state* or condition of things, now mysteriously fouled up with being an *action*. Somehow a buck-private adjective has got commissioned as a verb; and with about as much right as some of these ninety-day wonders. "Clean" is also certainly not an unarguably objective state either, for what is clean to my Shawnee friend is not necessarily clean to me: I know about combustion products and microbes too. Grammatically I am here verbalizing into an *act* what is only a dimly hoped-for ambiguous *state* of my rifle in the future. For even if I suit myself that it is clean, there's always the Sergeant. More than that, my camouflaged "verb" is burdened with the extra gear of being transitive, present tense, first person, and singular. Now, it would be hard to argue that the hoped-for clean state is *doing anything* transitively to my dirty rifle. Also, rifles take some time to be cleaned: part of my act has already extended into the past and will have to continue into the indefinite future if this keeps up. So I really have no Army Regs justification for using a "present" tense. Better an honestly durative aspect in Navaho, if you can spare one, though the Sergeant will probably slap me down by calling it only conative. As for "person" in the verb, anyone can see who's doing it, so why bring that up? I've already told you there's only one me: we decided that "I" is Joe Blow, at least for the time being. Last time I looked, I was still here. Why keep hammering on it? Besides, how many people do you suppose *can* clean one little rifle at the same time with one ramrod anyway? Do you see me double? If you do, you better go on Ward Eight. You're going Asiatic. Come on now, let's forget that "I" is potentially any one of half a billion people who speak English: there's only one American GI cleaning this gun here, and it's me, Joe Blow. If you'll agree that the subject is singular, let's leave the question of how the verbalized state "clean" can take over my singularity and my first-personality. You wouldn't call *me* clean right now, would you? Adjective doing a flipflop into a verb, a person crawling into it. A future state claiming to be a present event. I'm feeling kind of Asiatic myself. And I thought I knew what a verb was.

"The": well, that's a way we have of pointing to things, whether they are here or not, or have been, or will be. It means that all these pieces of metal— no, not the ramrod!—are really only *one* thing, a gun, though you wouldn't think so to see it disassembled like this. Let's say that the ghost of that past and future unity, my gun, hovers over the event; I've already admitted way back that I was wrong in using the present tense. You'll just have to take it on faith that I'm going to reassemble this into a "the" sometime soon. I'll drop you a card.

"Gun": OK, OK, it's only a pile of junk now. We'd better skip this because it is no longer Top Secret that there is no gun here if the enemy should creep up on us. It just seemed important at the time to mention it.

"With": this word means a conceptual relatedness in space of two nouns, as if I'd say I wish I was with my girl. Of course that doesn't make very clear the exact space involved, because Mary is a nice girl, and won't even let me touch her, much. You could say the Marines and the Navy are "with" us too in this campaign, though the Marines are way to Hell and gone in the boondock, and God knows where the Navy is, to say nothing of our own Air Force. Some fellow Whitehead, in a book I read somewhere, says everything in the universe is "with" everything else anyway, so I'm not saying much. Besides, that's not what I mean here, because "with" claims to be spatial and sneaks over into being a cause: it means more like "by" or "by means of." That's it. It's not me, it's the ramrod that's cleaning the rifle as my agent, and I'm just sitting here yapping and persuading it. I suppose now I *and* the ramrod are cleaning the rifle if it comes to that, even though I seemed to imply earlier that I was doing it. Its like a General fights a battle at headquarters and gets decorated for bravery, though you might get the wrong impression it was us dogfaces doing it. Anyway, here I am, and here's a ramrod, and here's what was and will be a clean rifle, if it isn't now.

"A": you won't get me on that! I concede the position without a battle. "A" is one of your "empty" words. But you don't really need it here with the bound form "ramrod" (lucky I got the damn thing screwed together in one piece), and a bound form already means just one example of the thing without any more fuss about it. Been nobody as I've noticed around here talking about any Platonic "ramrodhood," now that you mention it. "A"— skip it! Forget I ever said it!

"Ramrod"? That's easy. Its this gimmick here.

During all this time our Shawnee friend, Joe Blow-Snake, has been busy cleaning his gun too—in a manner of speaking, that is, if one will permit the expression. And all he has said is one word: "nipēkwālakha." Laconic, these Indians. Does this mean *ni-*, "me" / *-pē-*, "clean" / *-kwā-*, "gun" / *-la-*, "with" / *-kha*, "ramrod"—like the traditional stereotype of Indian speech? Not at all! After all our trouble, it seems that Joe Blow-Snake has had a distinct personality the whole time: the polysynthetic particle *ni-* is a perfectly respectable and self-respecting "I." But beyond this point, Joe Blow and Joe Blow-Snake have parted company completely and have gone about their business in entirely different symbolic universes. For the particle *-pēkw-* (one dare not follow English syllable-division rules, by the way) means "dry-space," though Private Blow-Snake would have to defend his leaving the approved film of oil inside the rifle barrel—which his Shawnee connotation forbids him to, but the Sergeant requires. Next, -alak- is one of a set of Shawnee spatials and means "interior-of-a-hole"—though he is really cleaning the firing mechanism and the ejector also, as well as the interior of the rifle barrel. That, however, is grammatically ignored in Shawnee. The little particle -h- in this context means all of "by-motion-of-a-tool-or-instrument," and -a in this case means "it." Thus, what Joe Blow-Snake is literally saying is: "I dry-space inside-a-hole by-motion-of-a-tool it." But where is the verb, that "must" be there to get things done? Well, one has to admit, he has cleaned his gun in short order, perhaps even to the satisfaction of the Sergeant. But he certainly goes about conceptualizing the job differently! The identical event in the real world is conceptualized symbolically and grammatically in utterly different semantic systems. The two geometries of reference have only one postulate in common: "I."

Any language deals with reality in a serenely tyrannical way. For example, English conceptualizes *via the same grammatical forms* events which we can easily show are outrageously different in Nature. "John sleeps" is John in a *state* of unconsciousness, and not doing anything much except being, fragmentarily, John. "John reads a book" is John awake and going through elaborate sensory and psychic experiences vis-à-vis a printed page. But when "John shoots a gun," he is merely the minimal immediate cause of complex chemical-kinetic events in space quite outside John—events, moreover, for which John is given credit, but which surely belong partly to the miners, chemists, and gunsmiths who prepared the way for him. And if "John hurts Mary's feelings," even if we blame John, chivalrously but with arrant partisanship, as the sole initiator of the complex changes in Mary's psychic state, who would dare say how much of this event occurs in John, and how much of it in Mary? And when we (preposterously) maintain that "It rains"— though the same subject-verb pattern and the same verbal ending are used—who or what is this "it" that allegedly "does" the raining, unless it is the rain itself? If we must use this same paradigm, it would be more honest to come right out with it and manfully admit that "rain rains rain"—without all this tawdry anthropomorphic hullaballoo and hypothecated animistic "its."

Similarly, Shawnee is just as much a sinner as English in the eye of that-which-is. Shawnee uses the same grammatical forms for events which we are convinced are worlds apart in nature, just as are John sleeping, rain, and Mary getting her feelings hurt. Who would suppose that a movie tough slugging his girl-friend could be conceptually identical with letting a canoe-paddle slip out of one's hand? And yet, grammatically, this is exactly what happens in Shawnee: *nikwaškwitepana* for the first event, versus *nikwaškhoto* for the second. In these, *kwaškwi-* or *kwašk-* means "a condition of force and reaction, return pressure, or recoil" in good Newtonian terms, and is the same basic root used in both Shawnee utterances being discussed. Hereafter (in the mayhem) we have *-tepē-*, "locus at head," and (in the accident) *-ho-*, "locus at water surface"—both of them examples of the "spatials" Shawnee is so richly endowed with. Next is *-n-*, "by hand action," versus [zero]—since dropping something is not considered hand *action* in the way that applying the hand to another's head is. And finally we have the parallel *-a*, "cause to another [animate being]" and *-to*, "cause to the inanimate." Thus the utterance *nikwaškwitepana* is literally "I condition-of-force-and-counterforce at-the-head by-hand-action cause-to-another being"—or, freely translated, "I let her have one on the noggin." In quite parallel fashion, in Shawnee at least, *nikwaškhoto* means literally "I condition-of-force-and-counterforce at-the-surface-of-water cause-to-the-inanimate"—or, somewhat freely, "The damned thing slipped out of my hand."

If John has not yet convinced us, then surely our versatile Shawnee friend has demonstrated that analysis of nature (and the classification of events as "like" or "in-the-same-category") are governed by mere *grammatical habits*—and not by the objective structure of the real world. Thus, while English formally (and ridiculously) equates a sleeping organism (John) with a meteorological event (rain), Shawnee is no less recreant from reality in schematically equating a human head with the surface of a body of water. Psychotics and our own dreams do no worse than that! And who, again, dares say that a hawk is not in some "important" respect a handsaw?

Does not the Atlantic world enjoy an incalculable advantage over its mortal enemies in Eurasia, because we can better manipulate the referents of Einstein's $E = mc^2$—ingeniously and ingenuously conceiving reality as a verb (action or energy) equal to a noun (mass) multiplied by a squared adverb (*how fast* light goes)? Is it not convenient to know that matter is only action divided by its own squared absolute speed? What hath our grammar wrought? The atomic bomb!

The Chinese, in their way, are just as clever with symbols. They can take reality and play it on a double panpipe! The classical Chinese believed that the inner secret of reality is the *huang chung*, the pitch sounded on the mysterious "Yellow Bell," which classical China sought as the medieval West sought the Holy Grail. Each dynasty tried to find the correct absolute pitch as its first political order of business, so that man and nature might be in harmony. And if dynasties fell, then, clearly, they were off pitch All reality, the Chinese thought, is made up of *yin* (the negative, dark, moist, female principle) and of *yang* (the positive, bright, dry, male principle). The *yin* is represented by the feminine scale or *yin lü* of one half of the sacred double panpipe, the *yang* by the male scale or *yang lü* of the other. If the panpipe is spread out, it is like the wings of the phoenix—the female principle, as the dragon is the male principle. The very essence of reality, therefore, can actually be played on the sacred panpipe!

The classification by grammar of events as "like" or "in-the-same-category" is really critical for our world view. On this is based all traditional logic—and the syllogism. "If A is B, and B is C, then A is C." Philosophers take live rabbits out of the magic hat of language. The fact is, however, that we only get out of the hats denotatively what we have previously put into them connotatively. It is alarming to realize how much of traditional philosophy is merely the solemn, stately nonsense of obedience to grammatical protocol, or imprisonment in self-instituted denotation and connotation. All scientists examine their instruments to test for experimental error—but traditional philosophers never did examine *their* instrument, language! This has been done only in modern times, by the new analytic rather than the old synthetic kind of philosophy, and this shakes many semantic absolutists to the very roots of their being. Freud and the anthropologist further quietly bid us to examine that most ubiquitous of research instruments, ourselves—while our intellectual Brahmins screech bloody murder!

And yet, what have the metaphysicians done? Plato unwittingly discovered that Greek, like all the other Indo-European languages, is a noun-language—and then thought that the *logos* or the noun created all the particulars of the real world! A great stylist, he was a bad grammarian. Aristotle's Substance and Attribute represent no more than the fact that Western languages have, habitually, subjects and predicates. The linguistic structure of English shapes our tendency to see events and situations in causal terms ("It rains"), even when such analysis is not admissible and often leads us to think that an event that follows another is structurally caused by it. Is this what Hume and many later philosophers have been wrestling with, in their struggles with the concept of Causality? Are Kant's universal "Forms" of Space and Time mere linguistic habit coming to light? In his metaphysical Time mere Indo-European tense? Is space-time as much a unit as matter-energy?

The sorry fact is that our unconscious linguistic habits shape our religions and our philosophies, imprison our scientific statements about the world, are of the essence of the conflict of postulated culture with postulated culture, are involved with our wars and other human misunderstandings, and are a part even of our dreaming, our errors, and our neuroses.

Language is thus an edifying study, because it is of a very piece with all other aspects of culture. Language and culture are possessed universally by *Homo sapiens,* and uniquely by him—but they contain no universal formal categories. They make up the non-biologically inherited organismic bonds of the meta-organism, man—but they undergo no evolutionary "stages" of mechanical unfoldment or "progress" in themselves. They are arduously learned—but both language and culture are very often quite unwitting and unconscious. They differ obviously with geography and in time—yet they are taken on so early in life that men unselfconsciously and characteristically confound culture and language with the structures of the eternal universe. Though created by human need and desire, they are loaded with superfluous and non functional elements. Arbitrary, and created mostly by persons who no longer exist, nevertheless they potentially unite together any two human beings, living or dead.

As hands have changed over from their original uses of locomotion free man from all future evolution, so too have mouths from mere eating and its archaic human inter-individuality—to the creation of symbolic systems which still further enormously enhance that inter-individuality. In symbolism the hungry mouth pours out its own autistic answers, and rearranges reality to suit man's wishes—for if we could not have schizophrenics we also could not have cultures. Through symbolism the sane feed upon each other's mouths and minds like ants with social stomachs.

Biologically speaking, all human societies have speech, and only human societies have speech. All human societies have the family unit, and the incest-tabooed family exists uniquely in human societies. And only the association of families within larger societies could have facilitated the rise of semantic languages. One stands astounded at the world-creation inherent in every language and symbolic system. One stands aghast at the improbability of the whole intricate biological process. Viewed from the unimaginative infra-human side of the line, it is a positive miracle that man has wrought. *Homo sapiens,* that improbable biped, was never more improbable an animal than in his invention of symbolism. And from the safely human side of the line, one wonders admiringly: How could all these precarious and necessary biological contingencies have been so carefully and artfully assembled?

Nevertheless, can any amount of ego strength enable the individual human being ever to gaze objectively upon the face of reality, when his very humanity involves a commitment to the symbol-preferences of his fellows? By the time the individual speaks an arbitrarily structured language, he is forever swamped in epistemological predicaments and in man-created dilemmas. Language is like your favorite wife: she's all you've got, you couldn't do without her, she's the best there is—and you're stuck with it. Indeed, without language, it is safe to say man would never have become fully human. But now that he has language, will he ever be able to know reality?

12. Why Man Is Human

Everyone knows the Riddle that the Sphinx asked Oedipus as he traveled along a road alone. "What is it that walks on four legs, then on two legs, and then on three?" Many men, say the Greeks, lost their lives in not being able to answer it. But all of us now know the answer. It is man. As a baby he creeps on all fours; when he learns to walk, he stands erect; and when he is old, he walks with a cane. But the Riddle and its answer are deceptively simple. When studied and thought about, the meaning becomes deeper and deeper. For man is also the mammal whose inner essence lies in his extraordinary ability to love others of his own kind, varyingly with age and circumstance.

The fact is complicated, too, since man has a number of ways of loving, several of which he must learn in order to become human. As a child he must love in one way, but as an adult in others. Thus the Riddle that the Sphinx puts to the animal that lives in families is much more complex. Each individual is asked it at some point on his road through life. And if he cannot answer it, he dies, in so far as his full potentia! as a man is concerned. In this form the Riddle is more baffling: "Who may love, but not love the one whom he loves?" The answer is the same: man. It was in solving this Riddle that man finally became human. And it is in resolving it that each individual person finally reaches his own moral "gerontomorphic" manhood.

Anatomically, man's humanity does consist in this vertical two-legged posture that the Greek answer implies. Physiologically, his humanity rests on an exaggeration of mammalian traits, and not on their organic repression or evolutionary loss. Psychologically, it is just this exaggeration of both dependency and sexuality that brings such grave problems of inter-individual adjustment of behavior within the human family. This is no problem for the wild animal. There is no conflict between the two aspects of its mammalian behavior. For in wild animals, breeding and maternal care operate in alternation and do not occur within the same span of time. That is, the sexuality of wild animals is ordinarily seasonal. The sexes breed and separate; the offspring are born when the female is alone; and the dependency of the young is over in a season. The female's roles as protective mother and as breeding mate do not occur during the same time period; for when the next breeding season comes around, the young usually have departed. And if, later, adult son breed with mother, he may do so on the same competitive terms as any other male.

This never happens in any human society. For the universal human family is a semi-permanent living-together of both adults and young. Indeed, the bodily adaptations to the family manner of life are physically evident, as we have seen, in the actual bodies of men, women, and children. Their very sexual dimorphism and racial differences grow out of it. In humans the adult male is specialized in strength and aggression and potency for the purposes of the permanent family group, as permanent mate and as protector and as father—just as the human female has specializations of general mammalian behavior which also contribute their part, and just as the infantilizations of the human baby are at the root of several aspects of our humanity. Man uses the family in the service of his heightened instinctual needs. But the family also uses him, converting both his strength and his potency to its service—in time, perhaps, even triumphing a little over his individual anthropoid cantankerousness. Family life achieves the final domestication of the male too.

But it is a genital and not a philoprogenitive drive that does it. The human male has no instincts, no anatomy, and no physiology to teach him to love the child as such. If the male learn the pleasures of paternity as opposed to those of procreation, it is the result of the mother's teaching him, and through some identification of his with mother and child—and not because as a mere male he knew all about it beforehand, or got some organic satisfaction out of the little beast. Furthermore, the selfish, opinionated, irascible featherless biped that man is, would not by inveterate and universal habit live in mixed sexual and age aggregates—the ambiguous blessings of his bachelor freedom a memory of the past—were it not that, on the whole, he found it more fun to do so than otherwise. Males form sexual associations with females not out of a tiresome, dutiful, pious, half-unwilling obedience to the demands of the culture but in fulfilment of the biological nature of the beast. The family is not a creation of culture: without the family there would be no culture!

In thinking of the long human latency period in his last extended work, Freud asked a significant anthropological question:

[Consider] the hypothesis that man is descended from a mammal which reached sexual maturity at the age of five, but that some great external influence was brought to bear upon the species and interrupted the straight line of sexuality. This may also have been related to some other transformation in the sexual life of man as compared with that of animals.

Since all the anthropoids other than man reach a relatively early sexual maturity, this is a reasonable conjecture. On good primate and anthropoid evidence, we believe that this "external influence" upon latency was the increasingly familial association of hominids. For an increased dependency and slower growth in the infant are concurrent with the growth of the permanent non-seasonal sexuality of the adult and the increasing cohesion of the family. Indeed, we have seen that this infantilization of the child, in the long delay of sexual maturity, is related to the human "fetalization of the ape" and to those "infantilizations" or evolutionary fixations which constitute racial traits. Furthermore, the "transformation of the sexual life of man" certainly includes the setting-up of the universal human incest-taboo, as also does "familial symbiosis" in man and the manifold physical manifestations this has wrought. The change from seasonal estrus or "heat" to the year-round operation of the menstrual cycle in the female and the permanent sexual drive of the male are also clear "transformations in the sexual life of man" and his anthropoid relatives.

From a heightening of mammalian functions, both of dependency and of sexuality, the new symbiotic unit, the human family, necessarily posed problems. Of course other problems had to have been previously solved biologically, for new solutions to be built on this base. Indeed, the organs of the mother-child relationship, and the organs of male-female relationship and their heightened physiology, are peculiarly evident in the human animal. These are no problem. The problem arises with respect to the living-together of other members of the family.

For the anatomy of paternal love is missing, as it is also missing between males in general. In fact, the male in the old-style mammal was largely structured for aggressive competition with other males of its own species, as well as for fighting its natural wild enemies of other species. But if others than mere heterosexual mates are to live together in the human family—and if still larger social aggregates are to be formed—then some new adaptive mechanism is necessary among humans.

This adaptive mechanism is culture. Culture is the non-bodily and non-genetic contriving of bonds of agreement that enable this animal to function as human. Such relationships—of father and son, and of male and male—must be forged *morally*. They can operate only through the discipline of aggression, through identification with one another, through the contriving of communication and understandings, and through the discovery or invention of agreements and compromises. Women often wonder that men are so passionately concerned with generalizations and with principles, when from a female point of view all human relations seem so simple and uncomplex, being given in her anatomy. But the simple fact is that males do not have female bodies: human males need principles and agreements by very virtue of their being males and being the kind of animal that necessarily and still usefully embodies the old mammalian male aggressiveness. No amount of feminine example and persuasion can un-teach the honest masculine animal of this knowledge of his nature.

Moral bonds and cultural structures—styles of thinking—are an area of men's present and future evolution that are not yet and probably never will be made bodily organs and somatized. It may be true that some of the arts—probably pottery, agriculture, and weaving—are the inventions of women. But principle or generalization is a male artifact: the *logos* that is the endless preoccupation of male metaphysics. What connects father and son, male and male, is the mystery of *logos* and logos alone: logos as the literal "word" which conveys linguistic meaning and understanding; logos as laws, agreements, rules, and regularities of behavior; logos as the implicit means and substance of common understanding and communication, and of cultural joining in the same styles of thinking; and logos as shared pattern, within which father can identify with son and permit his infancy, within which son can identify with father and become a man, and within which a male can perceive and forgive the equal manhood of his fellow-man. This does not mean, of course, that women are biologically unable to become great philosophers, creators of literature, or indeed scientists—all of whom are concerned with generalization—but it does mean, as is historically manifest, that men are more characteristically and inescapably motivated to formulate principles and generalizations. For, biologically, women are closer to realistic particulars.

Primitive men know rightly that women can make children with their bodies. But it takes men to make men, that is, members of the tribe. Hence that universal preoccupation among men everywhere with initiation, that mysterious male re-birth of the youth into full membership in the society of men. Often in this the initiates are actually taught the tribal lore formally and the metaphysical "facts of life," forcibly and fearfully indoctrinated in the supernatural wisdom that holds the male group together. Often, as with the Arunta and their tribal lore of the *churinga* or bull-roarer, the cultural nature of this wisdom is pitifully evident. Often, as with the Zuñi, when the youth learns that the masked gods who have whipped him are only men of the tribe and that he must now wear the god-mask himself, the nature of man's cultural burden becomes poignantly evident. But no matter: these myths serve. The initiates may also be tested in the enduring of pain; and sometimes they are painfully marked with the male sign of tribal membership. (A woman can give proof of her femaleness in a very simple and irrefutable way, by having a baby—but a male must always *prove* something, his manhood within the group. What reason, indeed, would press women to create great poetry, music, or art—when they can do better than that and make real human beings!) Thus, very often the initiates must keep the secret of these male myths and mysteries from women and children, under pain of death. Perhaps primitive men are right: women don't understand these things.

The complexly mammalian human family has its characteristic rivalries and aggressions and satisfactions with each stage of physical growth and physiological maturity. There is a proper and necessary role with each stage of psychosexual development in its members, given their differential strengths and special needs. The family—with its necessary disciplines, segmental sharings, and culture-historically elaborated roles—is the font of all morality, law, and indeed of all human culture. Manifestly, seals do not have sin because they do not have human social organization biologically. Bees do not have culture because their bodies build something else, the meta-organism of the hive. The kangaroo-rat *Dipodomys* lacks morality because it lacks the biological dilemmas demanding morality. Culture is man's adaptation to his humanity. Man secretes mores partly because his humanity would otherwise not operate from friction, or would otherwise fall apart from centrifugal governorlessness, and partly because he could not otherwise survive as an animal species.

It is an error to attack Freud, who observed man's psychological predicament in the family, by thinking that he "reduced everything to sex." For this is not true. Freud was in fact pointing out that there are *other kinds* of pleasure and love than the genital. For if love is realistically defined as a tender concern for the source of one's organic pleasure, then it obviously applies to the love of a mother for her child and to a child's love for its mother, as well as to the love of a man and woman. It is of course oedipal guilt, clinging to the dependent love of the mother, which leads adults to this stubborn psychic blindness.

Children know better. For they love, and they love passionately and overwhelmingly, long before genitality.

There can be no doubt that the baby does love in a dependent infantile fashion the woman who mothers him well. It is only when sexual love supervenes that the categorical imperative—the human incest-taboo—emerges. There is no mystery at all in why men love women or in why women love themselves: as children they loved their mothers. The only psychological problem is how women come to love men. A man's love for females in general may explain his affection for his daughter; but this still leaves physiologically unexplained a daughter's love for her father and her emergent love for other men. Perhaps men should enjoy this double largesse of wifely and daughterly love, and cease pondering its theoretical improbability. But in any case, as far as a man is concerned, the mature sexual love of women is permitted only if the woman so loved is not the woman *first* loved in dependent infantile fashion. This is the universal incest-taboo in all human beings wherever they are found.

The profound and provocative nature of the Riddle of the Sphinx then becomes clearer. "Who may love, but not love the one whom he loves?" The answer is human beings: of whatever kind and condition, primitive or civilized, male or female, old or young. For the Riddle admits of various solutions, at least one of which is appropriate for each human situation, and some others of which are inappropriate, because they misidentify the love object or use a non-adaptive way of loving it. For the child the solution is this: "He may love (dependently), but not love (sexually) the one whom he loves (mother)." For the adult man there is a different solution: "He may love (women, sexually), but not love (sexually) the one whom he loves (dependently once, mother)." A man has the pride and privilege, with his maleness, of returning to a woman a shared pleasure, like but unlike that which another woman, with her breast, conferred upon him first as a baby. Cherished and nurtured to strength by his mother, he may then protect and cherish another woman in his turn. And of all the things in this world these two, maternal and conjugal love, are without any qualification wholly good.

All this is a process of growth, psychological and physical, and of phatic communication culturally. It is no easy, automatic process. For the male change of phase enjoins upon him that he change almost entirely from dependent to protective love of women; for the residues of his infantile self, when in excess, are disruptive of his adult male responsibility and power to create and to provide security, and not (as once) primarily to consume it. More than that, and purely for himself, any unconscious confusion of mate with mother tends to disfranchise him of enjoyment, because of the anxiety in violating incest-taboos. Women, because they must learn to change the sex of the early love object in loving men instead of mothers, may have a difficult time adjusting to the complexities of their femininity. But men, because of this reversal of dependency roles vis-à-vis women, perhaps have the harder time growing up. Conversely, men may have less problem being male and taking their maleness for granted, in their naïve and unchanging love of women. But women, perhaps, in dependency terms, are not so fiercely and desperately embattled in growing up as men are.

For the adult woman, the answer to the Riddle is still different: "She may love (men, both sexually and dependently), but not love the one whom she loves (neither mother, dependently, nor father, sexually)." Thus feminine psychology is more complex. Men have to change from the original love object, and from the child's way of loving her. But women, in addition, have to change the sex of the original love object in order to love men. Furthermore, adult women have several ways of loving, but men only one. To her child the woman must now give dependency-sustaining love, as her mother did to her, this maternal love being of her body which is adapted to the needs of the deeply infantilized human baby. But meanwhile, for the purposes of her maternity, she must often give up her own competence and security in dealing directly with the world, and accept the difficult role of a trusting and fairly complete dependence on another person, her wisely chosen husband. Small wonder that women in general are more psychological-minded than men, and more skilled in reading the minimal phatic indices of character or of emotional climate. They have to be, biologically.

What remains puzzling psychologically is how the woman, who as a child also first loved her mother, can make the mysterious change in the sex of her love object and come to love her father, and hence to be able later to love men. Some students of the problem suggest that women depend emotionally on men to a greater degree than adult men do on one another, and hence love dependently first the mother, then the father, and then the husband, with the accent on the dependency. Others believe that on the girl's identification with her mother, this love for the mother reappears as the greater "feminine narcissism," which is later large enough to encompass both herself and her child (which is herself) in mature maternal love. This explanation suggests that the woman loves the man because he alone can give her the baby that fulfils her femininity, as she understood femininity in childhood through her mother. These explanations are ingenious, if labored. But something of the mystery remains, because some women seem just arbitrarily to love men, and we can't understand why this should be so in terms of early childhood. Perhaps there is a touch of all-encompassing maternal love in all the love that women feel, whether for children or for men. We do not know. But we do strongly agree with our fellow-anthropologist Ashley Montagu, that women are biologically structured to know more about love than men do.

What we must not forget throughout is that the *psychological* sexual constitution of the human individual is not given at birth or soon thereafter. The human baby has no "instinctive" sexuality whatever. True, it has primary sexual characteristics even some time before birth. And it acquires secondary sexual characteristics at a much later puberty. But its "tertiary" sexual characteristics of psychological masculinity and femininity are quite wholly the learned experience of living in one or the other sex-defined kinds of body, and in any one of an infinity of family constellations shaped by the sexual constitutions of parental individuals. Masculinity and femininity are even shaped as roles by the expectancies of a given culture. This influence however—though Margaret Mead makes a strong case for it—is one we believe to be relatively minor, as compared with the more fundamental experience of living in a body of one specific human sex.

The fact that human sexual roles are partly learned means that human individuals, unlike wild animals, can sometimes learn wrong answers to the Riddle of the Sphinx. For example, the homosexual woman appears to have resolved the Riddle wrongly as: "She may love (women), but not love the one (father) whom she loves (and hence she cannot love men)." Or she may continue, as initially, to love women: "She may love (women sexually) but not love (dependently) the one whom she loves (mother)." For some males too, because of the child's inordinate fear of the father's categorical imperative, there come other biologically wrong answers to the Riddle. This may be either because the boy remains fixed in an outmoded dependency relationship with his dominating or over-protective mother and does not dare the rewards of a more dangerous manhood; or it may be because the permitted dependent love of the child for his mother becomes contaminated with sexualized love, and then the terror of the father forces the son to repress all love of women and to masquerade instead as a lover of men, whom he really destructively hates. The homosexual man believes that "He may love (men, in a variety of non-adaptive ways), but not love the one (mother) whom he loves (dependently and/or sexually)." He has, however, mistaken a mere object-taboo of a single specific person, his mother, for a generalized aim-taboo of a whole sex, i.e., the heterosexual love of women—which is a grievous denotative confusion. And he has also been confused about the modes and the means of love—which is a grievous connotative confusion, both symbolically and psychiatrically.

The perverse and the neurotic, therefore, contrive behavior that is in a sense "adaptive." But the behavior is adaptive not to the new biological roles of the adult in his new family-of-procreation, but adaptive rather to a childish misconception of roles, which is rooted in his old family-of-origin. For the homosexual, even in anthropoids, obviously "loves" out of fear and hatred and frustration; sporadic homosexual behavior in infra-primate animals we can only view as trial-and-error learning or *faute de mieux*. By a merely pseudo-effeminizing or meretricious infantilizing of himself, the homosexual also defrauds and unmans or effeminizes the other male. An examination of the various perverse methods of loving establishes this point clearly. The illogic of his answers to the Riddle is quite plain.

Now the biologist is quite prepared to accept any kind of organic behavior, however bizarre—if it is adaptive. For example, in *Ceratias holboelli,* a curious deep-sea fish in which it is difficult for the sexes to find each other, there is a vascular connection between the female and the parasitic male, the latter receiving bountiful nourishment for further growth and maturity—in order to fertilize the female. This extraordinary behavior is obviously adaptive biologically. But neurotic behavior is "adaptive" only psychologically, and adaptive only to a misconceived view of biological roles. For it is difficult to see how a "love" based on fear, destructive hatred, and frustration of one's own and others' essential biological nature can be adaptive. To rob someone of his or her love of the other sex, and hence to rob them also of paternity or maternity, is doubly to rob the individual of his full human potentiality. The biologist is therefore forced to conclude that behavior which is non-adaptive biologically, but only adaptive psychologically, is properly not his concern but the psychiatrist's; that homosexuality among humans is not a genuine variety of love but a dishonest and desperate neurotic game, arising from tragic unsuccess in escaping from the family-of-origin to a family-of-procreation. Neither biologist nor psychiatrist can accept the views of literary apologists from Plato to Gide that homosexuality is a "normal" abnormality. For the normal process is clear. A girl becomes a woman by an identification with her mother and through a mysterious change in the sex of her original love object. A boy must become a man by similarly admiring manliness—in a rival he may hate or envy—through the mysterious love of male *logos,* not of physical males. When he begins to discover this logos or pattern in himself, he gives up wishing to destroy the father, but instead identifies with him and wishes to become like the father, in admiration of things masculine that comes out later as a normal adult manly self-confidence.

The psychiatrists, no doubt rightly, tell us that there is no neurosis without some basic libidinal role-misidentification. In this lies the value of their explanations of psychopathy for a biologically oriented understanding of the human animal. Their findings also fit in exactly with those of the physical anthropologist. For the family is the factory of human sexuality. The process is very largely one of individual life-history, post-natal, and conditioned. Psychologists agree that man's very sexuality is not furnished with instinctive channelings. It is, in fact, the dependent human child's very lability, ductility, and eductability which make the socialization process possible. Man does not have completely structured sexual instincts which fit him soon to adult animal life. The only "instincts" he is born with, such as the grasping and the sucking reflexes, are minimally and specifically those that fit him to the condition of the human infant. And the cultural anthropologist agrees with them all: for he is aware that man either invents his own responses, or accepts those invented for him.

Man has "socialization." His significant speciation is not the racial, but his post-natal, moral, and superorganic *learning*. So far from being born full-panoplied with instincts adjusting it to an adult solitary state, the human child on the contrary is born in a very markedly plastic, neurologically immature, "neurobiotactical," and educable socializable state. His moral humanity is not a hereditary given, but an artifact of social stimuli. For the child is biologically dependent upon his parents, *vulnerable* to the social influences of adults, and hence a potential culture-bearer. This basic inter-individuality is biologically given in the nature of his species. But what is done with it, and through it, varies from society to society and from family to family. The child is the domesticate of the man.

"Human nature," therefore, in this sense is not automatically organic, not instinctually spontaneous, but necessarily disciplined and shaped by a long apprenticeship to childhood. A child perforce becomes a Right Thinker before he learns to think at all. His very language is an arbitrary given, which teaches him the canons wherewith he must apperceive reality; and it is doubtful whether, after this seduction, he can ever again peer around the veil of language and gaze on naked nature with pristine innocence. His language is at once an aspect of his culture and the major vehicle of his socialization to all the rest of the culture. Indeed, by looking at the human child and its predicaments, it is very easy to see how mere relative cultural fiats become emotional absolutes. It is clear enough how moral commands, introjected or taken in from hard necessity, seem in turn logically necessary and "hard" when re-projected again as institutions, value systems, religions, and cultures. He has been "taken in," so to speak, by what he has taken in.

For there is no gainsaying it: all[1] adaptive human institutions *including morality* relate to man's oedipal nature. For lawgivers, judges, and kings are but larger social images of the father. All law that has any social substance is mere codifying of prior social convictions. It is the socially objective re-externalizing of morality which was internalized in childhood from the commands of the real father, and ultimately of the cultural fathers before him. The State is our struggle to find both paternal power and brotherly justice in the governing of men. Human character and morality is a peace-making between family-born conscience (superego) and animal organism (id). Religion is a yearning for rapport with the divine father, a seeking for a homeostasis of self and the organism with Superego and the Logos. Art is rebellion against the real, a stubborn defiance of the authority of reality, an unbending animal wilfulness in humans, a usurpation of creativity, a controlled psychopathy, a playful As-If schizophrenia that is only by courtesy of culture not psychotic. Poetry is a revolt against prose, an insistence that semantics be enlarged to contain recreant desire. Literature is the fan-

1. Curiously, this seems even to apply to man's "symbiotic" domestication of other animals. That man himself took an active role in the domestication of such large animals as horses and cattle without doubt has some of its significant roots in the human oedipal constellation: man did not kill, but dominated them, in domestication. Indeed, the widespread totemic-oedipal symbolism of the bull remains into historic times in Mediterranean cultures—notably in absolutist Levantine states—and into modern times in India, Africa, and Spain.

It is also significant that man has never domesticated any animal—quadruped, insect, or bird—that was not already in its wild state a social animal. Possibly only those animals responsive to social stimuli are ever humanly domesticable.

The persistently patriarchal organization found almost universally in societies which have domesticated large and dangerous animals, and the possible relationship between the patriarchal and the pecking-order dominance of animals as substitute objects, are not to be ignored. One can scarcely fail to see this role of dominance even in a small boy's relationship to his dog.

Interestingly, the pig, like the bull, is a formidable animal in the wild state; and in the Near East centers of its early domestication it is also nearly universally a totemic animal—that is, an animal involved, through projection and transference, with attitudes (fear and reverence) and attributes (fertility or ancestorhood) appropriate, respectively, to children and to fathers. The Creator rain-bull of the sky is everywhere a totemic animal symbol in the ancient Near East, from Egypt, through Asia Minor, to northwest India (where he reappears as the Hinduist Shiva in modern times); and the Spanish bull-fight drama can be traced completely through its Punic, Minoan, and Dionysian sources to these ancient Near East centers. In *The Golden Bough* Frazer has literal volumes on the many instances in which Attis, Adonis, and the other youthful consorts of a mother-goddess were killed by a vengeful wild boar. Thus man's own active domestication of such animals as bulls and boars may have an ultimate relationship to man's biological nature as an oedipal, familially organized animal.

tasies and the records of men who have struggled to resolve the moral, the social, and the erotic problems of men. Speculative philosophy (a branch of lyric poetry) tells us how greatly feeling men think projectively about the Universe, and persuasively invites to feel as they do. Painting and sculpture re-see the world, imposing on created and conceptualized forms the artist's wish for the order and meaning he does not find in the world. Music, that abstractest art, is the pleasurable (since most largely self-chosen) apperception of that divine voice saying those things we most want to hear. All economic activity is a seeking of power over others and a means of demanding goods of them for the succorance of one's own. And Science itself is a disciplined, indefatigable, and largely masculine appetite to know the facts of life, despite the traditions and the untruths our cultural fathers have sometimes told us, and to find the true and only worthy father of man: the high, implacable, invincible, inseductable and unbeseechable that-which-is, the real.

No morality is an absolute, the safely proven, the caught bird with salt on its tail. It is the chosen and the hoped-for, a loyalty that is man's burden, his glory, and his cross. For in the last analysis every culture is a moral geometry—a system *not* inalternatively imbedded in the physical world, but a contingent means of triangulating one's course through reality. But culture is also the immortality of dead men, a way in which their judgments and choices manage to coerce the living. Still, all men, including dead men, can be wrong.

This startling vision of possibility is not given to the man protectively domesticated by a currently successful culture. It is not vouchsafed the man safely immersed in intellectual tribalism: he finds a comfortable consensus as to truth among all his fellows and does not know the tribes on the other side of the hill with other truths. It was not blind Hellenic Homer, singing of an almost mythic tribal past, but a weary and sophisticated Hellenistic man, burdened with moral responsibility in a foreign land, who said "What is Truth?" Indeed, science itself has arisen only out of the necessity of choosing amidst conflicting truths, conflicting tribalisms, and warring hypotheses. So long as tradition is deified Truth it is mere tribalism, naïvely bound by ignorance of alternatives. So long as culture and morality are seen as the Sacred Superego, unassailable by doubt, we are imprisoned in eternal childhood by the fathers of the past.

The Riddle of the Sphinx is that every man was once a child who felt adults were omnipotent—and so they were in his creation and shaping—yet the child must achieve an adulthood that is always quite sadly lacking in omnipotence. Ultimately, we are all Zuñis, who are forced to wear the mask of omnipotence in order to do the world's cultural work. Men are potent, especially when they join together into groups. But men are never omnipotent, either alone or together. In the face of any presently insurmountable difficulty—for the Zuñi were not really able in their dances to bring rain to their crops—it is always a dangerous fallacy to pretend that they are. Larger power for humans always lies in the universe, like Promethean fire, and man must patiently learn and humbly know it in order to use it. Nor should he ever forget, in the midst of his problems, that there are large if circumscribed powers that lie within himself, singly or joined with his fellows.

Though man must always discover the limits of his power as an adult, yet he always thirsts after the omnipotence he thought he witnessed as a child. There are therefore, understandably, synthetic fathers in every age who promise to purvey The Truth—in return for a docile child-like faith, prayerful dependent obedience, and sometimes the surrender of goods and the abnegation of sexuality. The authoritarian paranoid prophet obtains his own reassurance and social reality only by destroying the independent manhood of other men. And others become his communicants, and worship him to omnipotence, only at the expense of a frightened retreat back into their own dependent childhood. For the prophet obtains real social power only by providing the supposed omnipotence of the father, as seen from a child's-eye point of view. In this, politically speaking, it matters little whether he is a charlatan or self-duped: his communicants are duped.

Most men ultimately, in achieving some power themselves, see through the supposed omnipotence of their fathers and no longer either worship or seek for themselves such a non-existent commodity. Most men settle for a real if finite potency, in return for a merely fantasied omnipotence. But the paranoiac is still trying to wrestle with—to bow down to, or to master—an omnipotence that was never there. As we become men, we are the better able to assess the mere manhood of our own fathers. Nor do we need to project the omnipotent father's image into the political world.

These extravagant absolutes of the child are not very useful concepts operationally. Nowhere can we discern—in nature, in life, or in man— the omnipotence, the omniscience, and the omnibenevolence a child requires of its father. Dead matter or physical reality is not "omnipotent"; for throughout evolution living matter has learned to coerce and to exploit matter to its ends. No existent life is "omniscient," certainly not man, in knowing all about the nature and the possibilities of matter. And every sound organism, by virtue of its being an organism, soon learns that its environing reality is not conspicuously "omnibenevolent," that is, bent exclusively upon the organism's purposes and ends.

No one ever really experiences in the universe any "omnipotence" save that of the human father. The hypothesis that man can have a good fate by wilful belief in and blind submission to an omnipotent father he neither knows nor understands, as imputed to the physical universe, is not in our historical experience a very adequate hypothesis either. The hypothesis is even less adequate when it is exploited, emotionally and economically, intellectually and socially, by paternalistic institutions. Whether political or religious or both, these falsely insist that they have the authoritative omniscience the morally infantilized communicant hungers for. Rather than making for a good morale, which is its only social excuse for being, this belief is in itself an index of poor morale.

We believe that good morals are even more important than good morale so defined. For morale is a product of sound morality. An alternative hypothesis to that of a projected cosmic Omnipotence is that all animals have adaptive techniques and that man's adaptive techniques are morality and culture. Man's intelligence and hands and peculiar togetherness with others of his own kind create the human adaptations. The only available friends for human beings are one another. In his biological battle in the universe, the human animal truly has need of all the allies he can find. If we seek this larger friendship, it is potentially there: our greatest conceptual ingroup can one day include all mankind. But this must be a brotherhood of brave men, and not of frightened dependent children. The adaptive behavior of the child to his father is not appropriate as the adaptive behavior of a man to his fellows, or of men to their universe. If we will nevertheless insist, beyond all our evidence, that somewhere there exists disembodied Will, gutless Spirit, brainless Mind, and organless Organism—then that is our self-chosen moral paedomorphy, and we must still take the consequences of it as men.

Such regressive peace of mind is easy and cheap emotionally, but very expensive politically and economically and, in the last analysis, morally. The ability to distinguish between physical and moral reality, to discover the boundary between wish and fact, and to discern the location of his own organic skin, is an ability which every mature thinker must strive to achieve and must ever thereafter strenuously cultivate and refine. The difficulties admittedly are inordinate: as a child one rarely meets reality unedited, as it is, and in ways through which *it* can teach us. We meet it largely via the pre-judgments, the superstitions, and sometimes the neuroses and psychoses of allegedly infallible adults and culture-ancestors. Man lives in a ready-made symbolic world, and as he learns and perfects the symbolisms the real world recedes. As man's symbolic systems more and more protectively house him, more and more is he indoors talking to himself—more and more the oyster spinning his pearl comfortably within a protective shell.

But we are not mistaken in our inexpugnable loyalty to moralities. The important point, however, is what the moralities consist in. Moralities do ultimately discover hard ecological truths: in this sense the family is a moral structure, a biologically validated "truth" now permanently imbedded in the physical and physiological nature of man. But inasmuch as the family is a universal human trait, our choices have already been made—and the significant speciation of man still remains the cultural and the moral, not the organic, the genetic, or the racial. The making of moralities is the spearhead of human evolution. Once human cultures are achieved and *Homo sapiens* becomes a series of cultural meta-organisms or societies, then not individual man but societies and ways of life are the ultimate units of survival. Still, as with all evolutionary choices, *a culture is our responsibility*—our salvation or the chance we take, as the case may be, and not a guaranteed haven of safety. We must choose at every moral parting of the ways and use our best wits and our soundest feeling in making these choices.

For example, one might choose culturally to believe with the totalitarians that man is not a polytypical anthropoid but a polymorphous arthropod—an insect species structured into many physical castes, each a proper slave to the codified instincts of the hive. Or one can recognize with the democracies that man in society is an almost infinitely complex aggregate of persnickety individual persons, partly inhabiting their own skins and partly slopping joyously all over into one another, inter-individual members of one another in the symbiotic family and symbolic brothers in their culture—difficult mammals admittedly, but somehow still able to get along without the aid of a self-appointed synthetic father.

In other words, one can choose to believe with totalitarians that the only appropriate political relations are those of obedient sons and divinely right autocratic fathers, or take a chance with the democracies and really implement the thesis—socially, economically, and politically— that all men are brothers. Surely, at this time of history, we should be able to see how the automatic insistence on who shall be father rather gives the whole oedipal game away! No: it is too easy for the single human being, however benevolent, to be fatally wrong, for autocracy to be safe as a political process. The best use of individual differences in persons within a society is to let them share in the manifold pressures on the tiller of the ship of state and not permit any paranoid pseudo-omniscience that comes along to play with it disastrously. The mystique of the charismatic supernaturally anointed Individual is far older than Napoleon or Hitler. The hallmark of the adult human being is *responsibility*, for himself and for others; and because this is rooted in anatomy itself, it may never be abdicated. We believe it is anthropologically and politically sounder to regard adult age-mates as brothers than to suppose that some are the mystic fathers of others. If such is not scientifically acceptable as self-evident, then it still remains the moral assertion of the democracies.

On historical retrospect, it appears there is undoubtedly some differential survival-value for the societies that hold these varying beliefs. It depends upon which society has made the more nearly accurate operational definition of the anthropological facts about man's nature. If man is not really an "arthropod," he cannot be made one by political decree: anthropoid realities will ultimately catch up with and punish that group which tries to manufacture biological truth politically. The locus of truth is in the external world, not in the fiats of any party or Politburo: the whole scientific temper rests on this implicit and unvarying respect for the impregnable and inexpugnable reality of the real, which is discrete from any organic will, individual or group. But if such an authoritarian society sets its face against man's basic nature as it is in fact constituted, then man's basic nature will eventually destroy it.

To be sure, culture is an adaptation; but it is sometimes adaptive not to outer realities but to inner tensions. That is, a culture is a defense mechanism—partly valid technologically, partly anxiety-allaying magic only—not cheaply so, but magnificently, for it is the work of many minds and hearts and hands. However, the same emotional necessities and libidinal economics cling to the *origins* of culture as they do to both our *taking on* of a culture and our later attempts at *assessing it*. Many people dare not see culture for what it is: a moral construct, a contingent non-physical set of human hypotheses. For if culture is so viewed (as the anthropologist must view his own among other cultures), it may then cease to do the emotional and psychological job these others require of it and which is for them its unconscious *raison d'être*. They dare not see culture as man's "radial evolution" and the cultural realm as potentially an infinite untried and unknown universe of moral choices for this would be to assail the epistemological divinity of the sacred superego, the supernaturally ordained culture. This would be psychological treason to one's tribe and the original sin against the cultural fathers. It would be arrogating to ourselves the divine prerogatives of self-creation, self-responsibility, and moral maturity. For we should be as gods, having knowledge of good and evil. Promethean man stole fire from nature as recently as the Old Stone Age—and with stupendous consequences, for by it he ceased being a simple animal and became human. Dare he appropriate, too, the moral thunderbolts of the All-Father?

Why not? Every animal is self-created by its own and its ancestors' biological discoveries and inventions; and this is equally the case with man in his own peculiar animal improvisation, culture. Man *is* self-created, ethnologically speaking. It is not that every generation creates its own culture whole-cloth; but some human generation in the past has created every ultimate thread of it, and we too may be doing a little embroidery on the fabric here and there, though we do not know it. Furthermore, in the historical rise and fall of cultures and of societies, man gives every evidence of being ultimately self-responsible for his fate. The viability of a society does seem to depend upon a maturity of moral decision and upon the sheer hard-boiled animal effectiveness, adaptability, and survival-value of the choices made.

Operationally viewed, history seems almost to provide us with a ready-made series of laboratory experiments in cultural viability. Thus we can see that every one of the Near Eastern absolutisms of ancient Asia Minor uniformly failed to give their societies adequate solutions to their *political* problems. The technical inventions of agriculture and animal domestication in the Neolithic for the first time in history permitted large aggregations of people into permanent villages, a situation that was not possible in the Paleolithic hunting economy. Our best modern archeological information seems to indicate that the "Neolithic Revolution" occurred in Asia Minor. And when, significantly in the same area, in the Bronze Age metallurgy (and hence better weapons) and writing (and hence better communication) increased still further the potentials of human contact, obviously some new political adaptation was necessary to supersede the probably kin-organized Paleolithic horde. This was the territorial state.

But our experience of history should lead us to infer that if the absolutist god-kings of Asia Minor and Egypt could not even hold these relatively small aggregates of people together, there is no good reason to suppose that charismatic rulers—Hitler, Stalin, and the Japanese divine Emperor—would achieve any greater stability and continuity for even larger empires. The evil of Russia is not the impulse to economic reform (so it was at least initially)—though this is of course what mainly exercises economic Bourbons on Main Street. The evil in the Russian experiment is its inhumane and historically inadequate political method, absolutism. Furthermore, inadequate political solutions tend to snowball in their consequences: Russian political absolutism currently fails to provide the moral atmosphere necessary for free intellectual enterprise—in a modern world where technological skill is critically important to the power-potential of *rival* societies. Russia borrows easily the West's technology—but does she the moral culture out of which true scientific innovation grows?

Similarly, Greece "fell" partly because Greek society failed to solve its intellectual (primarily epistemological) problems, but also because it failed to solve its political problems *in competition with* a better contemporary Roman solution. Indeed, an actual Platonic "Republic" would have fared no better, and for several reasons: the city-state of its implicit assumption is doomed to be weaker than the civic Roman state, just as the Renaissance city-states were weaker than modern nations; but also because, as Hanns Sachs has shown, although Greek intellectuals knew the principle of the steam turbine in "Hero's engine," the separation socially of hands and brains into different individuals in a helot society actually imposed a "delay of the machine age." The "rational" mind of the intellectual went free-wheeling along, un-clutched to a pragmatic experiential contact with the real physical world, and idling in its grammatical mechanisms; the hands of the unrewarded and hence unmotivated helot were cut off from the ener-gizing influences of educated, theorizing brains.

Rome fell partly because Roman society failed to solve its economic and moral problems, for all the brilliance and temporary success of its political and military solutions. The Chinese imperial system failed to solve its society's transportation and communication problems, de-spite (or perhaps because of) the diffusion of a uniform family-oriented Sinitic culture over vast regions. Its Confucian ethic may have been adequate in coping with inter-individual relationships within the Chinese society, though there can be some doubt of this, but certainly not politically and militarily in its international Asiatic setting: the otherwise primitive Mongols far surpassed the Chinese in military mobility and group-organization, and conquered half the world for a time. Nor did the Confucian-Taoist ethos evolve tech-nological solutions at all competent in a modern industrialist world.

Similarly, traditional capitalism has given us no great assurance that our society has solved its economic problems. Indeed, our highly developed technology may actually exacerbate these economic problems, though a partly adventitious Christianity sabotages and undercuts capitalism's worst excesses. Meanwhile, the contingent successes of a capitalist world may indeed be a function of its historical association with a sound and effective political method, democracy, the inner assumptions of which may be antagonistic to the inner assumptions of capitalism. The matter is thus not quite so simple: it is the algebraic sum of the pluses and minuses *in contemporaneous competing societies* that is the critical test. Which culture *as a whole* provides the most efficient *contemporary* solution to human societies' problems—economic, political, moral, military, and technological? For land insects had no great biological problems until amphibians arrived on land. It took reptiles to outdo amphibians, and it took mammals to surpass reptiles. If human societies are now the units of natural selection and competing societies one another's "natural" enemy, then moral and cultural speciation in man is the technique of the competition.

Some moralities *are* better than others, not as we *think* they are, but as in anthropological reality they *do* mobilize more physical energies and engender more effective social and political morale. We are the moral legislators, but reality is the Supreme Court of our rightness or wrongness. Our safety is still in the real world and not merely in our minds. But absolutists need their flight from freedom, and protect their emotional bondages jealously as defenses against anxiety—the anxiety attendant on the sin of being morally mature, self-responsible, and on our evolutionary own. Of what use is an ethical prop to the emotionally crippled if it is not an absolute they can psychologically "depend" upon?

The answer is that the use inheres in the relationship of the moral to the real. Values must from emotional necessity be viewed as absolute by those who use values as compulsive defenses against reality, rather than properly as tools for the exploration of reality. "Moral" choices are those we regard as having some realistic consequence, "aesthetic" as those which do not matter biologically. But is there ultimately any real difference? In the long run may not even aesthetic choices also have some contingent differential survival-value that we do not know about? Surely this must be true of taste in domesticated racial traits, for who else than man is responsible for them, and who else benefits from them? Psychologically, values are immortal only in the sense that they are believed to be immutable, that their life is believed to be coextensive with the existence of the world: viz., that such and such a value-geometry is "the soul of the universe," that moral laws have the "same" ineluctability as physical laws—that the universe and our tribal god are coextensive, reality is the body of this world-soul, and all reality would whisk away if this fortunately immortal soul were to die.

However, the descriptive historical fact is that values are "immortal" only with respect to the individual life. A given value-paradigm exists before, during, and after the existence of an individual human being in a given society. Quite literally, "a man's values do not die with him," for they were never exclusively his. "Spiritual" (moral and cultural) values do have this contingent immortality, they do indeed live beyond the span of the individual human life, but during the individual person's lifetime even changing values have an existence that is super-individual. Nevertheless, historically, every such cultural *anima mundi* may be ultimately mortal: the tribal spiritual values continue to exist only so long as the society remains, or until there are mutations of values during the culture-history of the society, or until contiguous societies borrow and change the values. The fact that values and cultures are "super-organic" and super-individual does not indicate, however, that they are either supra-human or super-human.

In an ingenious and ably argued paper, White has shown that even the "truths" of mathematics are not cosmic, but cultural. In mathematics, a historically continuous group of men agree on the assumptions that are to be made, and they agree on the rules which must be followed in tracing out the consequences of these assumptions. Consequently it is possible to have alternative assumptions, and hence alternative geometries or other mathematical systems. The locus of mathematical truth is therefore in the culture or sub-culture of a defined human group. The locus of values or moral postulates is identical with the locus of mathematical postulates: it is always in a definable human society. This locus is extra-individual in being inter-individual —but it is not, for all that, extra-human or discrete from any human society whatsoever! We can and do have moral Lobachevskians, moral Bolyaians, and moral Riemannians (all of which systems make different postulates), no less than we have the familiar and only spuriously inevitable Euclideans. It is only what we can operationally *do* with symbolic systems, differentially in relation to reality, that makes any difference. And if diverse "parallel postulates" in these different geometries seem equally to "work," then perhaps reality doesn't care about parallelism, which is a human irrelevance. Reality may be as little concerned about the Fifth Postulate as it is about how many angels can dance on a pinpoint!

Because of this psychological need for absolutes, man persists in puzzling himself. Men continue to discover and rediscover that their tribe's moral laws *do not* have the same ineluctability as physical laws: fire always burns, but crime sometimes pays. The just man ("just" in the terms of a given society's morality) continues unaccountably to suffer, and the wicked to flourish like the green bay tree. The microorganisms in Job's boils have nothing to do either with his monotheism or the way he treats his wife. The universe refuses to be committed to the picayune legal task of individual retribution. Reality is not a traffic cop: it blandly neglects to punish the individual sinner against tribal moralities. The moral red light is a human contrivance; only the impenetrability of matter when two trucks crash is a physical fact.

Nature's jurisdiction is natural law; it is domesticated man who culturally selects his individual fellow-man for survival. Reality's job, rather, is the larger one of selecting for survival those *societies* which have made the most apposite solutions of their social—that is, moral—problems. The selection of the moral *species* to survive is the properly ecological or biological process. Man proposes ethical theorems, reality disposes. We do not now know (though we would like to pretend we do know) what is ultimately best for us—and we may sometimes doubt that our ethical ancestors have judged any better, if as well. We can only put forth our propositions out of considered or unconsidered choice, much as a mollusk must choose between secreting a shell or a cuttlebone somewhere in the history of mollusk-hood.

The kind of animal association we shall have has long since been settled for us by our animal ancestors. We no longer have free moral choice as to whether or not we shall be the kind of dimorphously specialized hyper-mammals that we are: these things are literally in our blood and in our bones. It is also very likely our settled fate that we couldn't be arthropods, even if we wanted to be: the anthropoid die is irrevocably cast, and we must be content to enjoy the emoluments of primate success willed to us genetically. Nor can we join with those who uselessly deplore or deny the fact that we are mammals, that we have this fabulous patrimony thrust upon us willy-nilly. We are the slaves of evolutionary success, the helpless prisoners of our animal triumphs. But any cultural choice, made in pain and uncertainty by our merely human ancestors, is not irrevocable even now, for all its seeming so. Who shall be saved? The societies that create the humane conditions—socially, politically, and economically—within which human beings can most effectively be human. These choices are moral choices. And in the moral sense *we make the societies.*

13. And People Sometimes Sick

Men's symbolic systems, so long as they (1) make for communication among human individuals and (2) attempt to point to selected aspects of reality, are undeniably adaptive and necessary for the human animal. Certainly such systems (of one kind or another) are found quite universally in all groups of men, whether such groups embrace all the members of a society or only a sub-group like a congress of mathematicians. But when a symbolic system no longer *communicates* the views of one individual to others, then by common consent that individual is regarded as being mentally ill, that is, he has a psychosis— no matter how clear and logical the system may appear to himself. And when symbolic systems of a people no longer *point* to objective aspects of reality, then the probability is that we are dealing with superstitions and not science, with folklore and not with fact.

In their symbolic systems individual humans are in a sense mutually parasitic upon one another, like ants with social stomachs. And if a taint enter the social stomach of one, it may affect those of all the rest in the group. But the curious fact about the human animal is that individuals are not mentally sick so long as they are in step with the symbols of their fellows—no matter what preposterous things they believe. They are quite sane bearers of a culture or of a sub-culture. To our mathematical physicists, reality is a verb equal to a noun multiplied by a squared adverb. Indeed it is! For this curious language both communicates internationally among mathematical physicists as individuals and attempts with some success to point to the behavior of certain aspects of reality. Reality "is" also a cubed hawk divided by the square root of a handsaw, if for our purposes we can see it behaving in this manner. Reality is also (culturally speaking) a thing called *yang* plus a thing called *yin*, a dragon and a phoenix, respectively—and you can toot it on two properly tuned calliopes if you wish!

But this statement, since we are not Chinese, for all that it undeniably remains "culture," is sure to be regarded by us as superstition and not as science. It does not communicate to us, and we do not know what the Chinese are talking about—that is, it is folklore and not fact. For the sad situation is that *Homo sapiens*, the "knower," knows a great many things that are not so. The folklores of the world consist primarily in such things—indeed, perhaps the bulk of all human belief is in things that are not only not so but cannot possibly be so.

An instructive example of this may be taken from the folk belief of the Cassubians, a peasant group in Poland of Balto-Slavic speech. This is the belief in the mysterious flower of the fern, which blooms only at midnight on Midsummer Night. The uncanny blossom is a strange red in color and appears to be glaring at the onlooker with the unnerving glitter of a glass eye. If a person sees it, he must not stand still, or speak, or look around—even if fearful voices or howls are heard behind him—lest he die by the hand of a witch. The flaming fern flower may be picked with a red silk cloth, but this is very difficult, since access to it is barred by thorns, or by the Evil One in the form of a monkey, bull, or wolf; or a late wanderer may ask the way, and the flower vanishes in an instant if one replies to him. If a man does succeed in plucking the fern flower, however, he will be able to understand the language of animals and to see great hoards of hidden treasure in the ground, and he will live hale and hearty to a great age. But no one has ever seen it. This fact will not surprise botanists—since all ferns are non-flowering plants. The botanist may, however, be puzzled as to how the legend of a fern flower ever could have arisen, since it has no possible referents in the objective plant world; but the psychiatrist would not be, since he recognizes the legend as a characteristic oedipal fantasy arising from the subjective inner world of human beings. What is surprising to the non-anthropologist is that the Cassubians have so much detailed and circumstantial knowledge about the fern flower—when no man has ever seen it!

The ability to know things that are not so is an extraordinary and unique peculiarity of man among animals and arises out of the profoundly inter-individual nature of his being. In all their symbolic systems men are members of one another in a society: their symbols are projected and introjected like the crop-contents of a commonwealth of ants. But what is biologically nourishing, so to speak, and what is merely the emotional coloring of the food, they do not always know. Beyond any question, this fern legend spread among the Cassubians because it communicated phatically with the unconscious of each, structured similarly by their common learned culture. Indeed, the non-Cassubian psychiatrist is even able to understand it too, since he happens to be a human being also.

The protozoans that improvised sexual conjugation (the exchange of germ plasm) had invented genetic heredity. But when man became the quintessentially social animal that he is, he had invented social heredity (culture). In seeds, eggs, spores, and social stomachs organisms pass around genes and pass around food. But man alone passes around symbols. The human organism's worst barrier to knowledge, however, is the imputation of its own and other humans' purposes and wishes to reality—the not knowing of "inside" from "outside" and the intellectual inability to discriminate "ego boundaries." The Cassubians all think the fern flower exists in botanical reality; the botanist and the psychiatrist agree that it can exist only in their minds.

The treacherous nature of symbols is that, like the two-faced Roman god Janus, they point two ways: both inside and outside. Symbols arise from our own organic interests; but to have any effective meaning or value as such, they must point to outside realities as well. It is also the nature of symbols to be "invented" and not "discovered." That is, a symbol is a human artifact or tool, a willed putting-together of things chosen to be "like" each other for given purposes. Suitable aspects of reality can then be exploited for the organisms' purposes. But a symbol-equation is not something imbedded in the nature of reality that all men are everywhere bound to discover and re-discover. All individuals who use the symbol to communicate have not individually discovered it in nature but have learned to use it in common with others to point to something that they all think they see: the critical matter, however, is whether this is mainly outside them or mainly inside them.

We must remember that the symbol never *is* the thing: it *represents* the thing. Thus if an hysterical woman dreams of a phallus as a snake, this allegation may infuriate common-sensical men in the street, who know (quite rightly) that the two are not the same thing; and they will be sure the psychiatrist is crazy who merely reports the symbolism or neurotic libel of his patient. And yet the anthropologist could easily map the areas in Christian Europe, the ancient Near East, nearly the whole of Africa, and much of Asia (India, Indonesia, perhaps China, but not Japan) in which this same symbolic equation is made by millions of people—all of whom, admittedly, are quite thoroughly wrong in natural science terms. And it would be just as easy to show that in the whole Hindu area the elephant is symbolically equated with the male and the phallus, and the lotus with the female and the womb. These are not the crazy inventions of the psychiatrically oriented anthropologist, but merely his discovery of an ethnographic reality insisted upon by millions of people over an enormous area and through two dozen centuries, and which can be demonstrated in literally hundreds of folk tales in the huge body of Indic literature from Buddhist times to the present day.

The anthropologist is no more crazy than the maligned psychiatrist is. They are both merely reporting humanistic data—the psychiatrist from his patient, the anthropologist from the society he studies—without either of them, sophisticated fellows as they both are, necessarily believing these things themselves. And if other people's symbols (like the *yin-yang* hypothesis) do not communicate to us and do not point out aspects of the real world to us, we certainly cannot call the billion or so Chinese who have believed this all "crazy" either. They are not: they are a canny, ancient, and lovable people. We are forced to accord their beliefs the courtesy of being a culture, though we are not forced to share the use of their symbolic system. $E = mc^2$, similarly, is not actually the whole physical universe—but it certainly most conveniently and usefully stands for it in a defined context of meaning! After all, this is merely saying that *events* are the peculiar *how* of *things*. And meanwhile there is nothing to prevent us from letting the same signs E and mc stand for Edward and the master-of-ceremonies in a night club, if we wish it. You can't call *us* crazy!

No man is human who does not share large symbolic systems with his fellows. The price of his being socially sane, however, is to share the bulk of his fellows' semantic group-insanities, so to speak. The remarkable biological fact is that his "fellows" in this context include potentially any human being, living or dead, related or unrelated to him—for it is the nature of social heredity not to be bound by any physical genetic mechanism whatever. Thus, cultural sharing may be not merely with one's contemporaries in a society, and not merely with ancestors long dead, but also with men of other racial stocks relatively remote genetically. In this manner a Mongoloid Tibetan scholar may read Indic Sanskrit, or a West African Negro in the medieval University of Timbuktu learn Hellenistic and Arabic science. In this manner a Viennese (of heaven knows what racial origins) may drink chocolate, though he has in any case no American Indian blood in his veins; or a Canadian may drink tea, though he does not trace his ancestry to southwest China. And in this manner an English gentleman may wear a tailored suit—though the art of tailoring was invented by Siberian tribes not quartered on his arms.

The very essence of human nature, then, is its promiscuous and fantastic inter-individuality. This is initially rooted in the biological nature of the human family. But culture and language, as the symbolic symbiosis of individuals, are already spread to the larger society, in which even the most ancient human family, by its very definition, must from the beginning have been imbedded. Such culture traits, of course, spread over varying numbers of individual humans. Some of them, for example, virtually cover the human race in their scope: the diffusion of the use of fire, the spear, the bow, and the domestication of dogs has spread over all the continents of the world, and into otherwise unrelated cultures. On the other hand, the belief that God is a praying mantis is found, so far as we know, only among the Hottentots. Man's is the newest and strangest animal symbiosis, in which symbol-systems and culture traits unite people into a kind of reticulated meta-organism—in size all the way from a small society to mankind at large (feebly, and in a few traits only), in a manner similar to his net-like genetic relationships discussed earlier.

Any culture is a great pyramid of symbolic understandings. But as such it rests on the treachery inherent in each of its component symbols. And as Sapir has remarked, in the symbolic pyramid of a culture very few bricks touch the ground. To use Stefansson's phrase, culture can be a "standardization of error"—instead of being a means of ecological adaptation. Culture can be a bane as well as a boon. The solitary wild animal has no way of perpetuating mistaken solutions to problems: if a mutation is anti-adaptive, the animal dies. And if the environment changes, a one-time adaptation may become a lethal trait. When the animal dies, all his possible progeny die with him. But culture has its own peculiar progeny and social descent, and quite ignores biological heredity. Human culture is a technique for transcending space, time, and genetic race in the sharing of merely socially inherited traits.

Thus cultures may include traits that are non-adaptive, but "immortal" over long periods of time; and several cultures may embody these lethal traits. How can cultures embody "lethal traits" not immediately fatal to the society? As well ask how lethal genes are not immediately eliminated from the stream of germ plasm! It is only in the specific context of fusing germ cells or gametes, and of the organic configuration of the individual resulting from this, that the fatal latency emerges. For the total culture of a society may give it a strength to be able to afford a great deal of nonsense. A culture is the algebraic sum of the traits that are technological "pluses" (behavior that effectively exploit reality) and traits that are superstitious "minuses" (emotional self-deceptions that give a merely psychic "peace of mind").

For example, a definition of individual human excellence which mistakenly follows racist lines robs our society of the use of the real abilities of some Americans who happen to be Negro. For the ability to shoot a rifle is plainly a function of hands and eyes, and not of skin color; and the ability to assemble a tank depends more on trained fingers than on thick lips or frizzly hair. On the other hand, in the absence of such faith in a falsehood, the Russian factories of Magnitogorsk can avail themselves of the real abilities of individuals only a generation from tribalism in Siberia. The relative lack of racism in Russia (so long as this remains the case) therefore results in a technological "plus" for Russian society. But the Russian political process is a technological "minus" which (on historical grounds) we believe will ultimately prove literally lethal to the Soviet society and culture —though not necessarily to all people who are genetically Russians. Similarly, the large "plus" which the democratic political method gives to Western society would be reinforced by an enormous additional "plus" were the racist fallacy discarded. But we freely admit that these are only speculations on faith. Only in the laboratory of history can the mixture of symbols and hypotheses in a culture be tested out. Only historical circumstance and context can test the viability of a society that is given it by its total culture, that is, its defense mechanisms and adaptations. When an emergency like the conflict with another powerful society and its culture occurs, only a favorable balance in its cultural bank will keep a society solvent. And only when an impossible summation of absurd symbolic equations mounts up, does the hypothetical house of cards collapse.

Culture is this super-metazoan's way of defeating individual metazoan death. But a culture does not always succeed in obtaining immortality for its society. For man has the peculiar ability among animals to be spectacularly wrong, and wrong over long spans of space and time. True, all culture arises from an attempt to solve human problems. But the end so earnestly sought is by no means the end actually achieved. Sometimes the discovery or the invention that results from the pressure of a human problem or wish may have a technical appositeness and may genuinely adapt the animal to its environment. Man's playing with introjected symbol-substitutes for reality may give him the atomic bomb; or he may achieve a tolerably relevant hypothesis for the understanding of some social reality. Thus it might well be argued that honesty and integrity, tolerance and non-exploitativeness in human relationships, are all adaptations with a positive biological value, if we are right about the kind of interdependent animal we think man is—and such behavior may secure for societies of such individuals an increased survival potential. Thus we might be right in supposing that the psychopathic chicanery that seems to be developing in the Russian elite and the almost paranoid fear that understandably came to ravage all ranks of Nazi society can both be as "lethal" a trait politically to their societies as unchecked endo-cannibalism within a primitive tribe might be.

All culture traits evidently carry psychological conviction as to their effectiveness and desirability (even cannibalism), else they would not be adopted as behavior patterns. But only *some* culture traits do secure real adaptation of the societies in the ultimate biological sense. Quite as often as genuine solutions occur—or oftener, perhaps, given man's intolerance of anxiety—the continuing pressure of the unsolved problem drives the society (as it drives the individual when realities are unfaceable) to a precipitate and spurious defense mechanism: to a merely autistic "solution," a merely fantasied answer, a facile and fallacious psychological homeostasis and "peace of mind" that is unsafe and biologically fraudulent.

Consider, for example, the problem of sparganosis, an infection by an embryonic worm not uncommon in Indo-China. The worm is normally a parasite of frogs, and is acquired by humans through the native practice of applying split frog poultices or compresses of frog tissue to inflamed spots, especially to the eyes. The custom derives historically from the immensely prestigeful culture of China in this area. The rationale of Chinese medicine is double: inflammation produces heat, frogs are cold-blooded, therefore frog tissue will remove inflammation (since cold moist *yin* counterbalances hot dry *yang*); but also, inflammation of the eye is often owing to worms, and frogs eat worms, therefore frogs applied to the eye will remove the inflammation. Now one may well agree with the Indo-Chinese that sparganosis is an undesirable affliction. One must also admit that the Indo-Chinese, with genuine motivation and sincere intent, adopt a remedy thoroughly well-intentioned and logical in Chinese terms. But it is nevertheless impossible to grant that a technique for infecting human beings with sparganosis is an effective technique for curing sparganosis. It may give "peace of mind" to an Indo-Chinese with a sore eye, but it will surely give him sparganosis if he didn't already have it. And if he already did have sparganosis, it is hard to see how a re-infection with it can help matters much.

Consider also another characteristic example. The Dinka believe that members of the totemic Crocodile clan can swim the upper Nile rivers without being harmed by crocodiles, since crocodiles are thought to be their blood relatives. However, it may well be doubted whether culturally unindoctrinated crocodiles know the difference between Crocodile clan members and other Dinka—or, even knowing, care. Nevertheless, a man of this clan will not hesitate to swim a river, even at night, enjoying as he does complete peace of mind. Since, however, this belief and peace of mind may induce Crocodile clan members to swim rivers oftener than other Dinka dare, then in cold statistical fact the belief undoubtedly accounts for a higher mortality from this cause in the Crocodile clan than in any other clan. What you don't know *will* hurt you.

On the other hand, the Dinka of the Lion clan do not believe themselves of the same totem as man-killing lions, understandably, but only of ordinary animal-killing lions. Blind as cultural speciation may be, this distinction probably has some survival-value for members of the Lion clan. Now perhaps Dinka can sometimes swim rivers on occasion and not be eaten by crocodiles. But they misidentify the reason: there was no crocodile there at the right time, or, if there was, he may not have been hungry for Dinka at the moment. On the other hand, you can ordinarily see a lion, and if in doubt as to whether it is a man-eating lion or a blood brother, take to your long Dinka legs just to be on the safe side. Now, you cannot see a crocodile in the water, especially at night, and so the protective Crocodile clan belief is more needed, and therefore psychologically more appetizing.

But the appetite of lions and crocodiles for Dinkas may not necessarily vary accordingly.

Or take as an example the tall vertical tail vane of the Marquesan and Maori canoes in the Pacific. Such a fin would be technologically more useful under the keel of the boat as a centerboard, to facilitate tacking in the wind and thus give a wider choice of sailing direction than mere awkward yawing before the wind. That's all right: we can't blame the islanders for not having invented the keel, even though their having the sail might seem to us logically to suggest a keel or centerboard also. But actually (as an aerial stern fin) this vane seriously robs the yawing canoe of efficiency—making it both harder to maneuver and easier to capsize in a heavy wind. Having here manufactured their problems themselves, the Polynesians attempt to solve them by using as protective magic on the poop fin the feathers of a species of sea bird. Now psychiatrists and anthropologists can see why, symbolically, the feathers of a sea bird that never founders (and not the feathers of a land bird) might provide a sufficient though somewhat schizoid "peace of mind" for Polynesian sailors—but you could never get a marine engineer to agree that, actually, either poop fin or feathers solve the nautical problems technically involved.

Or, for another example, consider the Koryak of Siberia. Their religion enjoins upon them the yearly sacrifice of their dogs—out of the belief that otherwise the gods who "own" the various species of wild animals would not send them as food for the Koryak. In hard ecological fact, however, in this subarctic environment dogs are an important adaptive culture-trait insuring the human hunter's survival. Thus, in the pursuit of a factitious security, the Koryak actually narrow still further the already narrow margin of their survival. Were it not that they can get new dogs from near-by tribes (who impiously lack Koryak dog-killing but manage to survive nevertheless), the Koryak would probably long since have ceased to exist. Nor, strangely, has the spectacle of their irreligious but well-fed neighbors ever taught the Koryak to modify their own dangerous and destructive behavior. Meanwhile, the dog-breeding neighbors have adapted to Koryak anxiety-behavior and make a good thing out of trading their dogs comfortably for Koryak meat and furs, and everybody is happy. Thus if any crazy Koryak reformer ever arose to point out that they might give up the privilege of hunting for everybody (if only they also gave up killing dogs), then this subversive radical might also be sacrificed to the supernatural "owners" (who would surely be angry at the drying-up of the supply of dog-souls). The neighbors might really be angered too, at the sharp downtrend in international trade in live dogs.

All cultures are full of fraudulent sparganosis cures, deluded Dinka Crocodile clans, Polynesian poop fins, and irrational religious behaviors: all cultures are loaded with useless (even dangerous) baggage, just as languages are. Ethnology is full of examples of economic systems like Kwakiutl potlaching (the prestige-enhancing destruction of property) that impoverish rather than enrich; social organizations like Hindu castes that minutely separate rather than unite man and man in society; political systems (every absolutism in the world, primitive or civilized, ancient or modern, is an example of these) that destroy rather than give a voice to the natural power and dignity of the individual man; and religions (perhaps the reader can think of his own examples) that hamper rather than enhance our seeking for truth.

The reason for this may be that the inventors of new culture are most likely to come from the ranks of those individuals who most acutely feel in themselves the pressure of contemporary problems. Quite seriously, we must expect to find that our greatest artists and thinkers and scientists were often very unhappy men personally, men with some central core of discontent with the *status quo*, or current fashions in ideas, or the way the world has used them. They are great because they somewhat mastered their problems (not because they had problems)—by turning their energies outward to the real world "alloplastically," not inwardly into themselves "autoplastically" as a neurosis or a psychosis. Great men seek for communication with their fellows, and in their distress seek for new cues from the real world. But the psychotic loses his communication with his fellows, and seeks desperately for what supports he can find in the magic of his own mind. Thus mature people learn to judge others not on the basis of the personal problems they may have or may have had, but on the basis of what they do about their problems. Lincoln's depressions, for example, were at times almost psychotic—but he successfully led a nation in one of its times of worst travail. Darwin was at times acutely neurasthenic —but he nevertheless produced *The Origin of Species*. And the Russian chemist Kekulé once had a possibly dubious dream—which happened to solve the problem of the odd behavior of carbon in organic compounds.

But primitive people (primarily for lack of writing) lack sufficient "communication" with their own intellectual history to be able to have much perspective on or moral sophistication about their problems—just as a child lacks the experience of a long life-history, which might help him to get bearings on himself and his predicaments. Psychotics in a sense are still imprisoned in their childhood: they are still using now-inadequate old ways of solving new problems, and they are relatively cut off from the other humans and a current clear experience of the real world, both of which might help them with their problems. Now "primitive" men (those who lack writing) are not children. Nor are they psychotics either. Each of these—primitive, child, and psychotic—is in a different human situation or predicament and may not immediately be compared with any other. But all of them share three things in their predicaments:

1. They do not have (or have not yet achieved) an adequate communication with their fellows—other tribes, intellectual predecessors, and contemporary age-mates, respectively.

2. They have too small a stock of technological solutions and ego-controls relative to their unresolved life-problems.

3. And they have insufficient critically-assessed large knowledge of the real world as it is, relative to the great amount of special edited "knowledge" of "reality" they have got from the few immediate humans who have shaped them.

This means that in each case, when feeble ego-controls fail, they must fall back on magical control of reality—the sacred cult, the day-dream, and the psychosis—though in other ways primitives, children, and psychotics are vastly different. In their relative inexperience of the variety of humans and of human beliefs, they all tend to turn inward upon their own limited resources: the primitive to his sacred tribalism, the child to his narcissistic self and body, and the psychotic to the inward resources of his autistic thinking. Thus the primitive's culture, the child's unstable personality, and the psychotic's mental illness all partake of the nature of a defense-mechanism against anxiety in the face of unresolved problems—and in this there is danger of losing touch with reality. But also tribalism, narcissism, and psychosis all separate humans from their potential fellows. Nevertheless, even primitive tribalism is the result of mutually threatened men's joining together, though their cultural "solution" may be partly or wholly magical; the child's emergent personality is an increasing awareness of the reality of other human personalities and of his increasing emotional integration with them; and even the symbolizing activity of the psychotic is something initially learned from his human fellows—and in all of these there is some good, because they contain some aspect of present or potential communication. All of us (did we but remember it) have passed through a period of magical thinking, when we hesitated between the gratification of the Pleasure Principle of the organism and a necessary allegiance to the Reality Principle of the environment—and we are all human together.

Every human growth is an integration. Thus culture is in part a means that people have of sharing one another's emotional burdens. A sound personality is an insistence upon the dignity of the self and its needs and an equal respect for the reality of other people and of the outside world. Only the psychotic is lost—unless through another person's love he can learn to respect both his human self and the real world of other people and of things. Each integration, whether in a culture or in a personality, is the result of a favorable balance between respect for the self (narcissism) and respect for the other (object-love)—and each is the result of largely inarticulate phatic communication with others. And each disintegration into a psychosis is the result of self-hatred and fear of the self, and hatred and fear of others and of reality. The worst illness that a human being can know is not to know that he belongs.

Anthropologists have a technical term for the successful culture-innovator, the "culture hero." It is he (often become mythical and often built up from a number of actual human beings) who is credited with having first invented all the tribe's useful arts and with having given them their economic, marital, and other social institutions. Now it is conceivable that the psychotic in many cases is a potential culture hero who has not succeeded in communicating with his fellows—an individual sorely pressed by current and common problems to make fantastic solutions for which his fellows have no appetite. And certainly, judged on their products, there are plenty of culture heroes (Hitler is an example) whom we in other cultures find it hard to assess as other than plainly psychotic. For the distinction between the "culture hero" and the "psychotic" lies, in any absolute sense, not within themselves but only in their social context: Hitler might have been locked up permanently in England or America as a certified paranoiac—instead of only temporarily, as he was under the Weimar Republic, and as a political prisoner. Nor does the distinction lie qualitatively in their products: "paranoid" it may have been, but Naziism was a genuine culture—though hardly lasting the thousand years predicted of it. Qualitatively there is no discernible difference in content between a culture and a psychosis. The only objective or operational criterion is quantitative: the number of their respective communicants. This is no doubt an alarming statement, thus to equate cultures with psychoses. And do not all cultures allege their own categorical rightness—anyway *ours* must be right! But cultures and psychoses are identical in these ways: qualitatively, in being symbol-systems; functionally, in being anxiety-allaying; and also operationally, in being mere human hypotheses to be tested by reference to the real world.

Indeed, psychotics and the bearers of a culture are further alike in refusing to put belief to the test, or in not being aware of why reality-testing of belief is necessary. The psychotic rests his case on a blindly defended emotional need to believe; the tribalist supports his belief in finding the same emotional will to believe in his fellows. The tribalist uses his *society* for purposes which can only properly be served by the real world: that is, as a source of infallible knowledge and as a test for truth. Both psychotic and tribalist alike mistake their needed beliefs for Nature.

Part of every culture is thus "defense-mechanism." The function of culture and psychosis alike is to be "homeostatic," to maintain preferred equilibriums. And the same anxiety arises in both psychotic and tribalist alike when these beliefs are questioned. The psychotic refuses to have his system tampered with; the tribalist is aroused by any out-rage to received tradition. The psychotic is the individual who makes up his own private "culture" to contain his personal anxieties. The culture hero is the individual who provides the most desirable and ac-ceptable solution for a *society* of individuals under the pressure of much the same problems. His success in this is a function of successful phatic communication, not necessarily of semantically proper state-ments about reality. The psychotic, however, has somewhat atypical pressures; does not succeed in phatic communication; or does not suc-ceed in making solutions that are consoling to others. Rather, he in-creases our anxiety. Therefore, whatever phatic communication does occur succeeds only in separating the psychotic from his fellows. He thus has a "culture" borne only by a "society" of one person—and neither is therefore truly a society or a culture.

Thus the quantitative is the only criterion of the cultural. A sect of one member defines the religious paranoiac; but a paranoid system with adherents is a cult. Indeed, we have cases that are ambiguously in-between being a culture and a psychosis. A *folie-à-deux* (in which two individuals in a mental hospital come to share the same psychosis by a kind of "cultural diffusion") is already an incipient culture. When two or three are gathered together in symbolism's name, there abides culture—or where else numerically are you going to draw the line! But we do not ordinarily recognize the *cultural* nature of this phenomenon, because of the small social weight of a society of only two persons—particularly two persons already defined institutionally as psychotics. Likewise, we hesitate to see the *psychiatric* nature of the phenomenon when it involves whole societies (Hitlerism) or parts of them (mc-carthyism)—precisely because we are accustomed to using a quanti-tative criterion in distinguishing psychoses from cultures. But even a culture of the most grandiose proportions may for all that (in a world society of mankind) be no more, operationally, than a "folie à nth degree"—n being the number of individuals in the society adhering to that culture.

Now, the anthropologist is entirely proper and modest in refusing *as* an anthropologist to make judgments on other cultural beliefs with respect to their epistemological truth. For he knows no better than

anybody else what cultural hypotheses reality will select for ultimat
survival. Besides, what special tools does he have for the purpose any
way? A large knowledge of the alternative beliefs of peoples? Som
statistical sense of which beliefs are most widespread? But these are o
no value. A physicist might know a great number of alternative theorie
and still not know, on these grounds alone, which theory was bes
And if the anthropologist is going to go around counting noses in orde
to establish the truth of a belief, then he is no better off than the triba
ist. As a scientist checking on what the members of a society believe
the anthropologist is concerned only with ethnographic fact, not wit
epistemological truth. The anthropologist is really in the same positio
as the psychiatrist here. Would a sane psychiatrist build up his own per
sonal world-view on the basis of what his patients told him?

Indeed, the cross-cultural sophistication of his own profession ma
lead the anthropologist to be even more wary than most people are o
making such judgments on cultures. But, if he has his wits about him
he will also refrain from making the positive judgment that "all cul
tures are equally good"—as have, unfortunately, even some professiona
anthropologists. In the face of his own knowledge, how can he mak
such a statement! For if culture is the adaptive technique of the huma
animal, how shall he view the virtual disappearance of many contem
porary Stone Age cultures before the onslaught of European Iron Ag
cultures? And if some of man's cultural adaptations had not been bet
ter than others, he would still be an ape. What can "better" mean, ex
cept in biological terms of the purposes of culture, and of the surviva
value to societies?

The anthropologist's most extreme intellectual tolerance can neve
lead him to give weak assent to the positive (and really arrogant!
assertion that all cultural propositions are equally true. They are no
as we know from history, though we do not always know at the tim
which is which: we too are only human, our knowledge is limited, an
we certainly have no knowledge of the evolutionary future. The an
thropologist must know that he too is not the arbiter of cultural truth
but that nature is. He must also accept a belief in a real world beyon
himself, which shall do this job of natural selection. Otherwise, w
collapse into a shapeless solipsism and a feckless relativism which ar

the death of science, anthropological science included. And meanwhile, as a citizen, even the anthropologist is forced in some situations to make moral postulates that rest less on his scientific knowledge than on his simple manhood.

Still, it is part of his job as a scientist to recognize clearly the limitations of his manhood. In many (no doubt most) cases we plainly do not have enough scientific knowledge to make sound judgments. But does that mean that we should decry science? Not at all: it is still the best knowledge-technique that we know. For example, we do know something scientifically about frogs and their parasites. Operationally, we must insist that in terms of the discoverable realities the Indo-Chinese sparganosis "cure" is woefully unrealistic ("psychotic") behavior. The only difference between this and a similarly self-perpetuating genuine psychosis in an individual is in the number of people involved and in the fact that many persons share the "psychosis." We know what we know. It is only a lurking awareness of our equal predicament as bearers of culture that leads us to such caution and cross-cultural courtesy as to distinguish cultures from psychoses. But it is also our sophistication as civilized or intellectually aware men (in communication with a long history behind us) and as emotionally aware men (in communication with our own life-histories and disposed to give up all infantile claim to paranoid omniscience) that lead us to the knowledge that whole societies, too, can be mistaken, even our own.

Minorities may be right, and majorities wrong. The culture hero may be the psychotic who gets the cultural vote, and the "psychotic" may be the sane man of the future, out-voted by his contemporaries and imprisoned (in his time at least) within his own private culture. Not cosmic but only cultural truth can change thus in so brief a time as human history! We are forced to the disenchanting conclusion that the only objective yardstick mere men have in measuring the difference between a culture and a psychosis is the quantitative one of counting noses. Not only is it the only one to use, it is also actually the only one we do use—unless we have the benefit of historical hindsight and can make inferences from this. Cultural truth can never be what "I" make it, but only what "we" make it. The quantitative difference between culture and psychosis in the number of their respective adherents is a matter of inter-individual or social communication, and arises almost entirely from the skill in phatic communication of the usual culture hero—versus the characteristic failure of most psychotics in achieving such phatic rapport with others.

The social dimension of mental illness is even more clearly evident in the mechanisms of the "functional psychoses" (that is, mental illnesses for which, try as we may, we can find no organic basis). Schizophrenia, for example, could not be solely diagnosed in terms of its belief content or its symbolisms. In several mid-Southern states individuals have been admitted to mental hospitals with manifest delusional systems, including the belief that they could handle live rattlesnakes and drink quantities of poison with impunity—only for it to be discovered later that these "delusions" are standard beliefs of a snake-handling cult, dogmas for which they could cite scriptural support. Now it is quite improper for the town Presbyterians and Episcopalians to say of these snake cultists, "They all ought to be thrown into jail"—at least if they are mindful of the Constitutional guarantees of religious freedom which protect them all impartially, if they are mindful of the minority origins of their own Protestant sects, and if they remember the low-class origins of the cult of Christianity itself. It is no news historically that comfortable people are often made uncomfortable by the fantasies of their uncomfortable kin. The rural poor whites of the Snake Cult are (in part) wrestling with the paradox of their divinely superior white skins—a dogma, incidentally, in which many of the townspeople would support them—and their nevertheless Negroid economic status, which is a puzzler indeed. But they are reassured that God loves poor whites too, if in this extreme test of their faith they are not struck down. When (as occasionally has happened) a worshiper rather promptly dies in discomfort from the effects of poison, then this demonstrates for the other communicants that this one did not "have faith." And, meanwhile, police action can always drive the cultists into another county or another state.

Actually, of course, in every clinical diagnosis the psychiatrist is measuring off his patient against a social norm (often the psychiatrist's own). But the patient's illness is not a function of the discrepancy between the psychiatrist's Episcopalianism and the patient's Snake-

Cultism: it is a function of the patient's delusions that go beyond the Snake-Cultism of his own immediate cultural background. Since the psychiatrist is already, often unconsciously, measuring his patient against some cultural background—the psychiatrist's own—he could make his diagnosis more acutely and exactly if he knew what he was doing, and did it properly: by seeing the patient against the *patient's* background of social expectancies and sub-culture.

For "maladjustment" is meaningful only as over against the base line of an identifiable culture or sub-culture. Maladjustment is never to thin air. We would call this a possible contribution of the "anthropologist" to the "psychiatrist's" thinking, were it not that they both are really pretty much the same thing: the psychiatrist studies individuals, some of whose beliefs are crazy; the anthropologist studies societies, some of whose beliefs are untrue. The difference is that the psychiatrist studies the abnormal symbolisms of an individual patient in order to reform the patient, the anthropologist the symbolisms normal for whole societies. But even this difference may partly disappear if one of the anthropologist's unacknowledged motives is the reform of his own society. And if one of his unknown purposes actually is such social reform, then his "purpose" need not even be in him as a motive psychologically, for it still to be there in his social context operationally.

Objectivists may protest that they do what they are doing quite innocent of any practical motive. But such protest is suspect in the social sciences. It is even possible that this is a belief which serves the social scientist in maintaining an illusion about himself. True, the uses to which either physical or social knowledge can be put are best not kept in the foreground, lest they blind our vision of objective data—but do they not lurk in the background? True, sheer curiosity can carry the scientist a long way—but what are the personal motives behind his curiosity? Furthermore, pure science has a stubborn way of plunging even motiveless animals like us into practicalities. If this is the case, and if this is the inescapable result of the anthropologist's activities, then perhaps there is something to be said for consciousness of motive and knowledge of purpose. And, meanwhile, is there anything immoral in either the psychiatrist or the anthropologist if they just don't like to see people acting irrationally?

The fact is that schizophrenics make us anxious—and anxious precisely to the extent to which we would like to suppose that we are different from them. They do things that all of us at one time or another would very much like to do; and they think things that every one of us does at night in our dreaming. Moreover, they use psychic mechanisms that all of us knew as children or, as hard-pressed adults, we use in our individual and group retreats from reality. We have all passed this same way many times before.

Nor can schizophrenia, we repeat, be diagnosed in terms of its symbolic content alone. For if the anthropologist were to describe, say, religious belief and behavior in a society as if it were that of an individual (tacitly to be measured in terms of our own cultural norms) and neglected to identify it as group behavior (e.g., of the Koryak), then the psychiatrist would quite promptly and quite properly identify the beliefs and the behaviors as psychotic. Moreover, if just any Siberian hunter, and not a pious Koryak, were to kill the dogs on which he depended to subsist and did it for self-invented symbolic reasons, then the psychiatrist would be quite right if he suspected that this particular hunter was schizophrenic too.

For the schizophrenic, in any society, is feeble precisely in the phatic rapport that achieves such cultural consensuses: for good reasons he has not adequately taken on his society's symbolic systems, and for much the same reasons he is not able to induce the society to take on his. Schizophrenia is, literally, a social disease. Decades and decades have been spent in painstaking physiological and anatomical research on schizophrenia. It is safe to say that every single part of the human body, its every juice and function, have now been exhaustively compared in the normal and in the schizophrenic. But to what avail? In the words of the child's song, we've been to the woodpile and stayed there a good while, we've been to the clover, looked all the field over—but nowhere can kitty be found. Is there a characteristic body-build in schizophrenics? Most practicing clinicians and most physical anthropologists do not think so, though it still makes a colorful and popular case for the layman. Is there some specific vascular abnormality among schizophrenics? Most psychiatrists and most physiologists do not think so, though a few do. Perhaps the exclusively biological orientation of most medical men has made for the "fallacy of misplaced concreteness" in the bulk of research on schizophrenia: kitty has been behind the kitchen stove, dreaming, the whole time.

Meanwhile, the clinical psychologists and the cultural anthropologists are increasingly certain where schizophrenia is likely to be found: in the social animal, and not in the State Hospital cadaver. They believe—and most modern psychiatrists join them in this—that schizophrenia is a disease of the mind, and not of the brain. It is easy to see, however, why doctors and laymen alike would prefer to believe that it is in the brain or the body: for this we are not morally responsible, and for this the techniques of the older biological medicine could find a remedy. If it is in the mind, then we (or some other persons!) could be accounted responsible. Psychologists and anthropologists believe that this mental disease is primarily mental: all the few and dubious physical changes in the body that have been unearthed by physical-science–oriented research over industrious decades are the results and not the cause of the disease. Blood or bone anomalies, if they exist, do not cause schizophrenia: the schizophrenic's psychic habitus, on the other hand, if lifelong, could well enough account for these. Nor is there anything to be gained by diagnosis-after-prognosis, the semantic dodge of splitting the disease into two entities, just because we happen historically to have two names for the same thing: Kraepelin's "dementia praecox" (chronic, somehow physical, and now to be called incurable) versus Bleuler's "schizophrenia" (?more acute, ?more psychological in origin, ?curable). This is mere word magic.

One clue to the social nature of schizophrenia, of course, lies in just this feeling of anxiety and distrust, socially and psychologically, that people feel toward schizophrenics. Another reason for our belief in the social and psychological origins of schizophrenia lies in the "linguistically" and semantically unfair way in which we treat schizophrenic beliefs. On the one hand, it is customary to say that the schizophrenic is "poor in conceptual thinking," that his ability to make generalizations is feeble, while on the other hand we accuse his *systems of thought* of being "bizarre." Thus, when confronted in the psychiatrist's office with his successful and dominating father and asked "Who is this?", the schizophrenic boy may ignore the answer "My father" either as self-evident or too painful to be admitted. And his answer will be a "concretist" one ("He's tailored and I'm ready-made"), which is accounted "bizarre"—because it does not make generalizations on the denotative-connotative level preferred and expected by normal people, who can more easily accept the paternity of fathers. However, the boy *is* making generalizations, though on a different and private "bizarre" level. From one point of view schizophrenics have a "superior" human ability to make generalizations, since they make them all on their own without cultural help.

If the doctor would turn linguist and cultural anthropologist for a while, he might in time learn the schizophrenic's individual "language" and "culture." It might then become apparent that what the young man is saying is "This man you see here belongs to a class of powerful self-made (custom-made) men with whom I could never compete or identify, because I am only a weak little boy (now confronted by two powerful men) on whom hand-me-down decisions have been thrust ready-made, so that I have been systematically robbed of a man's right to self-decision." True, the boy's private clichés may hide his situation from him also by making a protective invidious comparison—and that is partly their purpose, for symbols can also be used to *hide* the things they stand for. But they also embody the means of communication and insight, if the doctor can only learn to listen and understand the new lingo—and this is also partly its purpose, since symbols are a means of handling and mastering reality, as well as of communicating about it. Instead, the semantically rigid attitudes of aggressively sane people can punish the schizophrenic again, and we are surprised that the next time he has learned not to bother talking at all. Withdrawn? No, phatically he is only more exquisitely sensitive to rejection than most people are.

We believe that schizophrenia as a social disease is primarily the product of interference with the deeply rooted and immensely ancient mammalian ties between mother and infant, extravagantly heightened as they are in humans. It is the wrecking of that dependency bond among humans which is necessary to the child's humanity. With a mother whose femininity has been functionally mutilated in a male-centered society, the infant is abandoned by those ancient mammalian (and especially human) mechanisms, precisely at the time of its greatest physiological need and psychological vulnerability. Infantilized to an extreme dependency, how is he to exchange his endoparasitism within the mother's body if an adequate ecto-parasitism is not ready for his support in place of it? We will not enter into the literalist controversy over the breast versus the bottle. For phatic "tone of voice" is far more important than mere nutritive fact. Synthetic makeshifts may keep him alive, even gratify his physiological appetites—if he can succeed in adjusting the rhythm of his appetite to what wise men know is best for him, and not have to depend upon his body's cry of frustration and an ignorant loving mother.

But he misses the emotionally rooted warmth of organic inter-individuality in humans. How, then, can he learn symbolic cultural language, when he has not learned the phatic language of love, as he is currently fitted to understand it physiologically? He has not learned that the sating of human appetite is best done in inter-individual love. How, then, is he motivated to bear the conditioning of his behavior thrust upon him by adult members of his family? Why should his organic wish be submitted to the shibboleths of his society's semantic insistences? He knows that his own magical thinking soothes his frustrations and his anxieties more willingly than others do. Why, unrewarded phatically, should he take on the burden of his fellows' semantic understandings culturally, if he has not learned to feel that it is good to do so, and that being human consists in being with other people?

Precisely at this point we can see, once again, that the difference between culture and psychosis is *social*. Man can build upon his humanity in any prosthetic direction he chooses. But he cannot with impunity substitute prosthetic devices for the very animal foundations of that humanity. Here, however, a mere infant is involved, an individual who is in a poor position to protest, and his protest may be delayed until decades later, when the additional inter-individual problems of adolescence and sexuality convince him that the game is not worth the candle. One can only speculate at the results of suggesting to the adult male prosthetic contraptions as substitutes for his own segmental equity in women.

Schizophrenia is therefore not only a difference in symbolic content of thought from that "normal" in the society. It is also an illness of the social animal. Hence as a process or a psychic mechanism it is more or less visible in any society—depending only on the amount and kind of recourse to autistic thinking characteristic of that society. The schizophrenic is the emotionally poorly-mothered individual, assaulted and frustrated in the area of his earliest human inter-dependency: he never *learns* how to be human. He lacks, or knows only feebly, blood-lessly, the robust erotisms that stir deeply in the very autonomic nervous system of the normal individual. For all his own busy private symbol-making, the schizophrenic's allegiance to the symbol-shibbo-leths of his outside "objective" human society is neither primary nor profound. What organism can be bought into the hard acceptance of the arbitrary psychic foot-bindings of any culture, unless there is some-how accompanying it pleasurable gratification of its basic physiolog-ical and psychological needs? On the other hand (to paraphrase Lewis Carroll), humans can evidently, with practice, believe as many as a dozen impossible things *after* breakfast.

Nevertheless, in a curiously mutilated way, the schizophrenic re-mains inescapably a symbol-making animal, and certainly to this ex-tent human. His symbolic equations, however, are untypical, dictated by his towering unsatisfied emotional needs, and undomesticated by his acceptance of others' group-elaborated symbolic systems. Thus the content of the schizophrenic system is bizarre and *outré*, for his "cul-ture" is confined to the "society" of his own feeble Ego and imperious Id. Still, his psychosis may appear no more bizarre than the culture of the society into which he is born—at least to members of other societies!

But for all the threat which the fact of schizophrenia presents epistemologically to comfortably socialized men, one currently favored remedy, lobotomy, is often clearly further punitive: this consists in amputating the association centers of the schizophrenic's forebrain, severing it from his autonomic animal brain—and removing his hu-manity along with his untypical "culture." Lobotomy is at best a management technique, or a last-ditch measure to assuage intolerable psychic pain or anxiety, and should never parade as a therapy. The same surgical-minded rationale suggests the brilliant possibilities of blinding schizophrenics to cure their visual hallucinations, or cutting off their hands to prevent their crawling on all fours. (Evidently, also, it requires a cultural insanity to manufacture this kind of psychotic in such large numbers in Christendom: viz., the superstition that man is not a mammal and hence is forgiven the necessity of mammalian behavior—or the other superstition of our society, that males can do everything, even suckling, better than females.)

Not only schizophrenia but also other functional mental illnesses can be usefully viewed in social terms. The manic-depressive is the individual who reflects (in his wild and savage ambivalences toward himself) the corresponding fluctuations in attitude of the human sources of his learning who he is and how he should regard himself. The paranoiac has never abdicated the omnipotence of childhood and become a mere adult man—or he is one who imagines (from a terror-binding child's-eye view) that the supposed omnipotence of his parents is now his. The psychopath knows the values of his society intellectually (as a visiting anthropologist might)—even astutely and exploitatively—but he cares not a whit about these values himself emotionally. These values are only handles to manipulate the people who are the dupes of the values, and he makes them dance, as masterfully and guiltlessly as the impresario of a puppet-show handles the strings of his puppets. The psychopath hates the parental source of his learning, and as a natural result hates his whole society. Similarly, neuroses can be seen as a confused psychological drama full of semantic miscues and role-misidentifications, with considerable anatomical mix-up as to who should do what to whom and with what. Or (to change the figure) mental illness in the oedipal animal is like an orchestra in which the wrong persons play the wrong tunes on the wrong instruments at the wrong times.

Man is the only animal that knows how to make mental illness. No wild animal can have a psychosis arising from a confusion of cues and symbolisms and appropriate reaction patterns. The external reality which conditions the animal, and to which its genetically provided instincts are adapted, is too consistent to lead it into such error. Reality must be consistent, otherwise no animal could ever discover and know it: if we cannot know a reality conceived of anthropomorphically, and hence vitiated by human inconsistencies, then conceivably such an anthropomorphic definition may be wrong. For if we do know anything, it is that reality is consistent. All organisms, including man at his best, have discovered statistical probabilities of 1, for they all live by and upon them: the leaf soundly knows that light will always behave like light, and a root that water is wet. If the "environment" (a local pattern of such consistencies) should change massively, then the species adapted to the old environment either adjusts to the new objective set of conditions, or it becomes extinct.

It is true that some animals can be made "neurotic." But the interesting fact is that it takes human beings to do it. Reality is too holistically honest, too non-seductive, and too serenely ever the same to confuse the wild animal with antic contradictions. It takes the human psychologist to manipulate the laboratory situation even to make neurotics of experimental animals, as has been done with pigs, sheep, and dogs. But because of the great difference of ability between humans and infra-human animals in symbolic thinking, we believe those psychologists are right who say that only humans can become psychotic—so deeply and pervasively deranged in their symbolic systems as to be unable to cope with reality. Other animals can at most be made only neurotic— taught to be confused about cues concerning food and punishment in a given laboratory situation and reduced in that context to the quivering immobility of indecision.

It takes parents, genetic and cultural, to make human beings psychotic—that is, to make them confusedly-conditioned psychological "domesticates" and responsive to human cues and choices rather than to nature's. The possibility of psychosis is another result of man's fetalization and domestication. Wild animals have a genetically-set-up instinctual system adjusting them to their environment, with only a modicum of free thinking or insight into unaccounted-for contingencies. Not so the big-brained human infant; and the effective "environment" of the baby is people, not raw nature. The infantilism of the human infant is shown in the fact of his few organically prepared instincts and in the brain that has "swallowed" his spinal chord and its reflexes. This brain either invents its own responses (psychotics and culture heroes) or, more commonly, borrows the responses from the baby's social forebears (culture). The human has a minimum of guiding instincts and a maximum of learning and insight-thinking. By contrast with the wild animal, the human has the maximum of tuition from other individuals of his species—and most especially in his dependent formative infancy he meets reality very largely via the not disinterested individuals that make up his immediate family and society. He adjusts perforce to their mistakes, to their cultural superstitions and misconceptions about man and about nature, and not to nature itself. The infant's "instincts," such as they are, specifically adapt him to dependent human infancy—and as a man he will be whatever outlandish domesticate his parents unconsciously prefer or unwittingly shape.

The human infant can no more exist normally as a value-ingesting social animal without both its parents (or their substitutes) than it can exist nutritionally without its special dependent relationship to a mother. But the other side of the coin, obviously, is just this possibility of mis-growth in aberrant human environments, most especially of the limited nuclear family. Error can thus become domesticated and self-cumulative. But the individual can be doubly damned: he can suffer not only from his own individual past but also from the past of his whole society, his free ego-response and spontaneity thus doubly imprisoned in outmoded and inappropriate molds.

Thus, if learning is a "feed-back" mechanism through which experience communicates cues for the correction of an organism's future action, this mechanism can be doubly interfered with in humans. In the individual, neuroses and psychoses are past-experience-structured mislearnings and misbehaviors of the organism, which prevent the tuition or feed-back of current data from influencing present and future behavior. (In schizophrenia, perhaps the thermostat or "teleceptor" is anomalously inside the autistic organism and not outside in cold reality or in the inter-individual weather, as it should be.) But, additionally, a culture itself may cause a "phylogenetic" failure of feed-back in man, since it structures individuals to respond inappropriately, through learning culture-historically established falsehoods.

But all this seems (and no doubt is) alarmingly critical of culture as "the wisdom of the ages"—and most suspiciously friendly to schizophrenics! Schizophrenics are human beings? (Well, so far as we can discover, schizophrenics are perfectly normal people physically, or were initially; they are schizophrenic primarily in terms of maladjustment to a particular society and its culture; and only people can have made them schizophrenic.) Cultures can be "crazy"? (Well, what is the scientist and the intellectual but just this kind of critic of traditional belief and culture?) Our alarm in each case derives from the same anxieties and the same group-narcissism. Each must be discussed in turn.

It may seem odd to suggest that schizophrenics are in a sense only exaggeratedly "human" individuals. For they make us uneasy, and we are motivated to emphasize our differences from them. True, their symbolic innovations fail of a wider social currency than, at best, a *folie à deux*. Certainly they largely fail in communication and in the "cultural diffusion" of their beliefs—no doubt because their constructs contain more fantasy and less fact than we are usually comfortable in permitting ourselves. But we have already ample reason to question whether some of the group-fantasies of culture are any more reality-oriented than is the schizophrenic's individual fantasy: cosmic truth lies no more in popular consensus than in private conviction. And groups of people show as much "will to believe" as single individuals do—with the further danger that they insulate one another from unpleasant fact, because of their inter-dependent and reciprocal strengthening of belief. Perhaps it is safer to say that we do not know how to turn the creative innovations of schizophrenics to possible social usefulness—at least so far as incarcerated culture heroes are concerned—than to state flatly, as we might sometimes wish to, that schizophrenics are somehow "inhuman." For schizophrenics have real problems they are assiduously trying to solve—human problems that are very like our own. Perhaps we are the ones who have too easily given up the battle and too soon accepted the protective masks and the "solutions" provided by our culture. Perhaps they only lack somewhat the kinds of inter-individual help (or meddling) that most of us have enjoyed in growing up.

We mean it quite seriously when we say that schizophrenic, poet, and scientist are all part of a human continuum. The schizophrenic is systematizing and symbolizing some part of his real experience, no less than are the poet and the scientist. A large humanity permits no invidious distinctions among them on the basis of their common human nature. We need only be clear about the primary locus of their respective subject-matters. Indeed, if we want to learn about human psychology, there are no better teachers than schizophrenics, once we learn to listen to them and to learn the symbolic language of their private cultural cosmos. For the difference between schizophrenic and scientist is primarily one of human communication and reality-orientation. The schizophrenic is oriented relatively to the "inside," the scientist to the "outside" of his organism. Because of mutilation during development of his human social nature, the schizophrenic has peculiar difficulty also in communication. He ends in frightening us about ourselves, rather than successfully informing us about himself, which is his primary subject-matter.

By contrast, the poet—and all other creative artists—at least succeeds in establishing phatic communication with his fellows. In Joyce's *Ulysses* some will say that the artist ranges close to the border of compulsion neurosis. And some might say that *Finnegans Wake* similarly skirts psychosis—were it not that this magnificently articulate writer successfully manages to communicate with a sufficient number of thoroughly sane people. With essentially the same oedipal problems as Joyce, Melville wrote the greatest of American novels, *Moby Dick*, as *Ulysses* is perhaps the greatest novel in any language. There can be no doubt that the artist does make valuable and useful statements, primarily of course about a human being and predicaments of feeling in his own life and times. Thus creative artists in general are one of the very best sources for an understanding of the subtler points of psychology and of culture history.

Nor do scientists escape the changing climates of culture history either. For world-views change with the times—and are related to them, as the "sociology of knowledge" has amply demonstrated. The main difference in the scientist is that he is still further out along the "inside-outside" subjective-objective continuum: he conscientiously tries to purify his beliefs and his hypotheses of subjective elements. He struggles for a closer and closer understanding of reality, and no one would dare suggest for a minute that an Einstein, with even the most abstruse of equations, is not awesomely close to the reality of the atomic bomb. The scientist's theory more and more approaches or parallels reality, but—because of the inherent nature of symbolic systems—never quite touches the co-ordinates of reality. Thus all human beings are part of the same symbolic continuum. The schizophrenic's autism is literally and primarily a subjective concern for the mutilated dependent human self. The poet and the artist are concerned primarily with oedipal and human problems of subject and object. And the scientist is trying, with at least some relative success, to rule out the subjective and to look at the world as it is. But he never totally succeeds in this, for he must communicate with his fellows in culture-elaborated symbolisms.

Each of them—schizophrenic, poet, and scientist—has his meaning, moreover, only in terms of a society. No wild animal can become schizophrenic, but only man in society. The poet must have an audience to fulfil his nature. And the scientist must achieve some inter-subjective agreement and consensus with a society of fellow-experts. Furthermore, the schizophrenic would probably not survive outside a human society, so poorly oriented to reality may he become. Only a society with a comfortable margin of survival can afford the poet and the dreamer. And certainly the scientist has his primary meaning as one kind of culture hero in a modern society.

For it is evident that human intelligence is to a large degree in the service of societies, and not of individuals. While the benefits to all members of a society of the scientific activity of some of them in adjusting man to reality is clear, it is equally clear that the social and economic rewards for such scientific activities do not primarily accrue to the scientist or to the intellectual. Still, that has perhaps been his own moral speciation, a choice of one properly humane activity: to have knowledge of things, not to have things. If he loves and has knowledge, all is well. However, Plato's fantasy of the ideal state, in his *Republic*—in which the state exists mainly by and of the philosopher-king—we believe to be a characteristic Greek narcissism and arrogance of the intellectual.

Indeed, Greek society did give mankind the beginnings of a new rational and humane way of looking at the world, and of looking critically at man and his past—and all this is the precious heritage of modern man. But if the intellectual is a critic of his society and of history, his society and history are also critiques of the intellectual. For in the Peloponnesian civil wars, the Greeks failed intellectually and politically to transcend Hellenic tribalism in a Hellenistic international world, and fell victim to the Macedonian imperialism of Alexander the Great. Perhaps, for good reasons, Greek society was not yet strong enough technologically for this moral and epistemological confidence. But part of the failure, we believe, was for this very reason a fault of the narcissism of the intellectual in Greek society: the over-valuing of the rational intellectual self. And part of it was a failure of the Greek social and political system, of human attitudes toward internal helots and toward the "external proletariat" of the barbarians.

For Plato (and Greek rationalism in general) over-valued the rational mind. The Greeks relied too much on the mind's logic, too little on experience. Greek rationalism paid far more respect to the human mind as an organ for secreting truth than Freud has taught us the mind, in fact, really deserves. Greek rationalism also insufficiently understood or took account of irrational feeling in human affairs. As a consequence —though Roman political skill stayed the collapse of classical culture for half a millennium—the ancient world was nevertheless overwhelmed by a culture of non-rational and anti-rational feeling for a full millennium more.

Our society, perhaps reasonably, rewards far more highly the entrepreneurs or cultural "middle-men," who mediate scientific knowledge into social action and use, and in economic terms communicate the scientist's findings to the whole society. Possibly our society, in turn, even over-estimates the social value of the entrepreneur. Still, intellectuals as such can never be economic and political Platonic kings—for that is not their function as intellectuals. True, their relatively schizoid failure in communication is not wholly their own exclusive "fault"; for the bulk of men in our society, for some curious reason, cannot see the satisfaction and the security that come from the scientist's disciplining himself to a knowledge of the world, and to a vocabulary to discuss it! But if the scientist will not or cannot bring himself to proletarianize his world, and to feed reality to others in "easy" predigested and sugar-coated form, as do aphids and termites (for it is evident that most human beings can bear only a little or a highly edited reality), then the scientist must not protest if other social species of men reap the benefits that accrue to any animal that learns to know reality better. For this will only have demonstrated again that man is a social organism.

Once again, as minorities, the schizophrenic and the poet and the intellectual are all in the same boat, culturally. The schizophrenic gains no consensus; the poet may similarly not communicate, or not be attended to; the intellectual may attain communication and the consensus of his coterie or "school," and yet fail of a wider communication and usefulness to the whole society. It is true that the intellectual, as in the case of Socrates, may on occasion be a sacrifice to his own society's tribalism (if by "tribalism" we may mean the culture of a society of individuals, of whatever technological advancement, who may intellectually know of alternatives to their own cultural dispensation, but who are not emotionally convinced that these can be morally respectable and genuine alternatives). However, the intellectual is *in essence* the critic of tribalism. If he is punished for over-stepping the bounds of his society's tolerance, then this is a failure in his phatic understanding of the society's problems and of the anxieties of its members. Or it is a failure in his phatic communication with the society, and he is then an "insane" or unclean reject, quite like the psychotic. In this case, the intellectual, too, has intensified rather than allayed anxieties: very possibly Freud, who repeated the injunction to "Know thyself," is another Socrates. Indeed, a very minor Irish poet, Oliver Gogarty (the "stately, plump Buck Mulligan" of Joyce's great novel) has not only generously stated that Joyce was crazy, but has further taken it upon himself to inform us that Freud is "the enemy of the human race"! Of course it is but a short step from calling the student of human nature this to calling the physical scientists of the atomic bomb "enemies of the human race"—and, in shirking our moral responsibility to be men, to arrive back again at anti-rationalism and blind feeling.

On the whole, however, the social problem of the intellectual that Plato and Socrates pose is not really the primary one. The intellectual is merely one specialized (though doubtless valuable) part of the whole society. To function as scientist, the intellectual needs merely the scientific means of experimenting and a minimal protection, politically and economically, though neither of these can properly be had at the price of his social and scientific integrity. For the rest, his major problem is that of social and economic "communication" of his new symbolizings of the world. And others are more than glad to feed upon him and to do this job of communication for him, where he fails or does not choose to do this. This communication requires for him his own peculiar kind of intellectual apartness and social schizophrenia, that of theorizing and of new symbolizing. For all his conscientious reality-orientation, he must retain enough of the organism's subjective wishing in order to motivate and to enable him to make new hypotheses about the world. But lèt no one be misled: the scientist is only a more practical poet.

For all human symbolic systems are hypothetical systems, the fiats of organic wills, and have no status whatever in non-human reality. In geometries and in hypotheses, in languages and cultures, and in art and moralities alike, at best "you pays your money and you takes your choice"—though, indeed, human beings do not always reach this level of intellectual emancipation from tribalism. But the intellectual and the scientist have as their basic job the cultivation of awareness that there are in fact conceptual alternatives to the culturally inherited anatomy of thought and of desire. In this, the intellectual and the scientist are identical with the schizophrenic and the poet.

While one stubbornly hopes that it is more difficult for many persons to be wrong over long periods of time than for the lone individual to be mistaken, ethnography suggests that this remains more a hope than a reality. It is entirely possible, we believe, that the majority of human beings have been consistently wrong on some points throughout history. The "wisdom of the culture" is often enough mere senile dementia. Unfortunately, this assertion places the present writer potentially in the uncomfortable position of a drastic minority, imprisoned in a private psychosis. Only successful communication and a lot of impolite pointing to reality will get us out of this corner—which is what we will try to do in the next chapter!

A psychotic's truth is what "I" make it, and cultural truth is what by unwitting vote "we" make it; but ultimate truth still remains in that outside world of that which is. Thus, much as a psychotic's "truth" may be out of step with his own culture's "truth," so too may his culture's "truth" miss the cosmic mark. The human being is thus vulnerable not only to the dead hand of his own ontogenetic individual past, but also (to the extent of his human inter-individuality and successful communication) to the miasmas of the "phylogenetic" cultural past.

As bygone species of animals seized too precipitately upon organic specializations and perished, so also men of the past have sometimes sought the facile and too immediate homeostasis of false cultural solutions to problems. Their false formulations are our civilized sicknesses. Only the doubters can save us. For these other men did not doubt, they did not question the fathers' fiats, they worshiped their flimsy hypotheses into Truths. They did not hesitate enough to wrestle with potentialities and with alternatives, they could not bear the anxiety of a continuing moral self-responsibility, they could not stay to learn from nature, they could not wait. They got immediately an autistic "peace of mind" and, ultimately, death. This punishment awaits all worshipers of the Pleasure Principle, who turn their faces from the sterner and more demanding Reality Principle. For the price of all regression and all fixation—individual or cultural or evolutionary—is death.

14. Superstition and the Soul

The durability of a belief and its dignity as "culture" (as opposed to "psychosis") have to do with the number of its cultural adherents, geographically and historically. Its viability is largely related to its emotional attractiveness and efficiency in providing a current equilibrium and peace of mind; its persistence in time has nothing to do with the cosmic truth of the belief. There is no "natural selection" among beliefs in cultural time—for ideas also are man's creations. The absolute length of time some fragment of "the wisdom of the ages" has lasted is in itself no measure of objective truth: a paranoiac's beliefs do not become true for having become chronic. Historical time is no doubt a severe critic of cultural truth, but it is not the critique of cosmic truth. Cosmic truth requires eternity to be true in, not mere historical time. But to be a human belief, obviously, an idea has only to be believed in by some human being. And for it to be a culture trait, it need only be a trait in the culture of a society.

"But it would not continue to find believers if it were not true!

Fifty million Frenchmen can't be wrong!" On the contrary, fifty million Frenchmen can be just as wrong as fifty thousand Fijians. And with the possession of writing, they may even be wrong for a longer time. To continue to be believed, an idea need only achieve a currency among people in space and time, and their number is merely a criterion for distinguishing a culture from a psychosis and not a criterion of objective truth. Cosmic truth, unfortunately, cannot be established by even the most democratic vote of mankind—any more than it can be imposed by an autocrat or promulgated by an oligarchy, even of scientists.

For reasons that we have discussed previously, one of the characteristics of man in society, uniquely among animals, is his practiced ability to know things that are not so. As individuals, only humans (and their laboratory animals) can be psychotic or neurotic. And in societies, only *Homo sapiens* can be superstitious. Further, since culture is a system of postulates, it is also cumulative and erects new symbolic structures on the old agreements of now taken-for-granted unconscious or covert culture. For these reasons, of all man's superstitions, the most useful to study—both theoretically and practically, didactically and therapeutically—would be those that are the most "archaic" culturally, the most ancient and widespread.

It is worth while to discuss here in the beginning the senses in which the term "superstition" has been used in the past. The classic meaning of *superstitio* in Latin is a witnessing, or "standing over" in amazement and awe—whence by natural derivation of usage it comes to mean the chronically awe-filled attitude, an excessive fear of the gods, and an ignorant or irrational fear of the unknown, the mysterious, or the spiritual. Superstition suggests in its very word-history something involved with an emotional state, something deriving from ignorance, helplessness, and fear. Superstition is consequently something toward which we refuse to apply the criteria of secular truth, ego strength, and reality-testing and, instead, in our anxiety, cling stubbornly to emotional defenses and rationalizations. As applied to gods, the roots of this propensity in specifically human nature are clear. For of whom in the universal human experience do we stand in awe but the father—the inveterately and the irrationally feared, the irascible and ambivalent human being who cannot be rationally known as consistent reality is known? It is he in respect to whom we must contrive to believe fanatically what we would not of ourselves necessarily choose to believe—the unpredictable arbiter whom we may learn to fear in a way that indifferent and unchanging neutral reality does not teach us to fear.

A second, rather rare and literary, sense of the term "superstition" is a modern false etymology, with an imputed meaning that is entirely foreign to Roman thought. Lowell states it thus: "A superstition, as its name imports, is something that has been left to stand over, like unfinished business, from one session of the world's witenagemot to the next." Though historically incorrect, this sense of the term is nevertheless useful. For one thing, superstition has to deal with the unknown, the uncontrolled, the unmastered, and the unsettled—with the moot, a problem on which men must work as a group. A superstition is the best that a "moot of wits" could do in an emergency (for the Anglo-Saxon witenagemot met only in crisis situations). For another thing, this sense expresses the perverse historicity and durability of a superstition, tabled from further consideration and action, but embodied in our writ and precedent nevertheless. Both science and common sense often tell us that a superstition is not so; and yet such is the cultural compulsive that a hoary untruth continues to influence our actions, much in the manner of the compulsive neurotic who "knows better" but still "can't help himself." The figure of a legislative body enacting the ignorant fiats of the elders or a judicial body establishing misguided precedents for the future is also an illuminating one.

More commonly, nowadays, the term "superstition" is used in the derogatory sense of "our tribe's beliefs are religious truths, but their tribal beliefs are superstitious nonsense." This easy ethnocentrism is of course rejected by the sophisticated mind, which knows that ultimate truth is not a function of the race or the cultural affiliation of the believer. But there is a related invidious sense of the term that is difficult to avoid. This is the judgmental use of "superstition" in discriminating between better beliefs and worse beliefs. Still, functionally and historically, this is exactly what superstitions are: beliefs based on the false premises of the ignorant past, outmoded cultural hand-me-downs that do not really fit the framework of modern man. It is a traditional folk-religion which better science has made intellectually *declassé,* a vestigial survival from the past, a dying god. What we are clearly alleging in this usage is that we have at hand better hypotheses to explain the phenomena involved.

What, then, is the most ancient and pervasive of human beliefs? Is it not the belief in the ghostly authority and power of the human father that persists mysteriously after he is gone? Stated in more generalized terms, this most inveterate and generic of all human beliefs is *the belief in a soul which is separable from the body.* From an ethnological point of view it is difficult to emphasize sufficiently the magnitude and the importance of this notion of a soul entity. The great British anthropologist, Sir Edward Tylor, has even stated the minimal definition of religion (as found everywhere in the world) as "a belief in spiritual beings"; and later anthropologists expert in this field have concurred in his definition. No other single belief has so profoundly influenced so many human beings for so unimaginably long a time. Possibly because of the universality of the family, it is perhaps even the most widely present of all human purely cultural traits as well. Indeed, if truth were merely a *consensus gentium,* with all mankind voting, then this would unquestionably be the most firmly established truth in man's whole armamentarium. The difficulty, however, is that ultimate cosmic truth is not located in the minds of men, however numerous, but in the body of the universe. It is in all the senses discussed that the belief in an ec-static or separable soul is here designated a "superstition." It is culturally outmoded; we now have better understandings at hand; and the false premises and postulates behind this belief are not sufficiently known or conscious to the present-day believer—exactly as a neurotic does not know the origin of his symptoms (a failure, in each case, in communication with the past).

A word must be added here concerning the anthropologist in his varying roles as scientist and as citizen. As scientist, the anthropologist must merely report accurately and objectively the descriptive ethnographic facts concerning the beliefs of the human beings he studies. He may analyze the historical sources and the intellectual rationale of the beliefs, he may describe their context and function in the culture, and he may even expose the hidden postulates of the system in the covert culture of the group—much as a linguist derives rules of grammar from the actual speech behavior of a group. But when the anthropologist judges concerning the "truth" of the beliefs, or chooses to accept or to reject the postulates on which the beliefs are based, then he becomes a moral citizen like everyone else. It is this indiscrimination of roles which has so confused some anthropologists, and their audiences as well.

In the description and analysis of animism (or spirit belief) which follows we continue to aim at the meticulous accuracy and objectivity of the anthropologist in reporting ethnographic facts. These facts are all open to verification by experts, and, indeed, the general reader can check them against his knowledge of folklore and of philosophy. But when we choose to accept the postulates of explanatory systems alternative to animism, then we go beyond this merely reportorial role of the anthropologist. We then become scientific biologists, linguists, psychiatrists, and whatever else—but no longer anthropologists as such.

We are therefore, self-consciously and with a positive awareness of the issues, reasserting our loyalty to our own society's scientific culture. For even the choice of an over-all scientific (as opposed to an animistic) view of phenomena is, after all, a choice. It is also ultimately non-rational and, if you like, emotional in its motivation: the scientist *feels* differently toward the universe than does the practitioner of magic or the religionist. The choice of scientific postulates or hypotheses—indeed the choice of the scientific stance itself—has nothing to do with the subsequent "if-then" procedure and discipline of scientific activity. Postulates are not proven facts but the hypothetical chosen. They are, strictly speaking, the grammar of science; and no one can usefully argue over the "rightness" or the "wrongness" of any linguistic system but only attempt to communicate about reality in using it.

In what follows, then, the reader disciplined to scientific method will clearly see when the role of anthropologist as descriptive and analytic scientist is exchanged for the role of biologist and the like. Clarity in this procedure is necessary, if we are to demonstrate the scientific usefulness of anthropological analysis. It is the peculiar dilemma of the social scientist that he remains such only so long as he describes and analyzes societies and cultures and the human animal. But as a member of a society, a moral citizen, and an exponent of even a consciously and wittingly chosen sub-culture of the scientist, he then reverts from student to subject-matter. That such a choice is made hereinafter we have neither the ability nor the wish to deny, since our wish is to be consistently scientific. If the logical inferences from this scientific reasoning are emotionally distasteful, then the reader has every human right to choose postulates other than those of the various sciences. Many people do. We do not.

A comparative examination of various tribal beliefs concerning the soul makes it clear that at one time these were rationalized and even plausible conclusions, deriving from genuine and identifiable experience—but based on premises which we would now regard as unsatisfactory if we examined them. The simplest formulation of the concept of the separable soul may even have the dignity of crude folk science. It is only when the concept is intellectually outgrown (but economically and politically exploited and institutionally defended) that it becomes the cultural property of vested religious interests and of the mystic fathers deriving their authority from the cultural past, who infantilize modern man. The experiences from which animistic belief derives are, in fact, universal human experiences: the phenomena of *birth, death, dreams, seeing, memory,* and *thought,* of *conscience, language,* and *culture.* But for every one of the unacceptable analyses of these phenomena made with the soul-hypothesis, we have in modern times more adequate hypotheses and explanations—though the whole body of beliefs constituting "animism" still retains an unsuspected and formidable entrenchment in our thinking nevertheless.

Probably the most important basis for a belief in animism is the fact of life itself. The materiality of a baby is easily seen: it grows in the mother from the food she eats. But what *initiates* this mysterious process of conception and creation that ends in birth? Old Stone Age drawings of phallic cults show that even ancient man was able to infer that this is somehow a contribution from the male—since it is observable that he is always needed for the process to begin. (True, some modern primitives like the Australians officially deny male paternity, which they impute to the *churinga* or "bull-roarer." Nevertheless, a study of its symbolism makes it plain they must know the facts of life in order to project these so fully into the *churinga*-stick—whatever oedipal reasons may have led them to this displacement and denial. Furthermore, the firmest believers in the "bull-roarer theory" still have patrilineal descent.) Since the father obviously is needed for the forming of matter into a human being, Form, therefore, is the *male principle,* and the soul or life is a male entity. The root of animistic belief is then the Mystery of Life itself: conception, creation, and birth. All other derivatives of animistic theory flow easily from this initial postulate as to the nature of life. The apostolic succession of life from father to son is thus the divine mystery of creation. Animism rests on human *fatherhood.*

All metazoans die, and all men sometime learn of *death.* What is the mysterious difference between a living man and a dead man? Naïve observation readily reports several facts: the phenomena of warmth, breath, movement, and volition appear to have been "subtracted" from the living body to make the dead one. The sum of these may then be taken to be the man's "life" which has "departed" his body. The soul is therefore the algebraic difference between the living man and the dead one, the mystery of life, the unknown X. The soul-hypothesis, therefore, again explains the fact of life.

As *warmth,* this life or "soul" possesses by analogy the attributes of fire, heat, or light. For example (one among many), the Indo-European root word for spirit or deity is *di-,* "the shining, the heavenly"—the deity being the fire-soul of a dead man or an ancestor and still constituting the essence of his volition, consciousness, and power: a spirit is the ghost of human power that still has to be reckoned with. Man must often have speculated about fire, since it was one of his earliest cultural possessions. Fire mysteriously consumes, giving off heat and light; is dangerous and punishes with pain; and unaccountably changes one substance into another—and then is gone. Man has a little warmth within him and feeds this central flame with food, which it consumes —and this is the same fire that leaves him at death. Surely fire is spirit and deity in nature, for it reappears in larger guise beyond man. It comes again as lightning in the storm, and it is the sun, moon, planets, and the stars.

Small wonder, then, that the All-Father Jupiter and his Indo-European cognates (Zeus-Pāter, Dyaush Pitar, and the like) is literally the "Shining Father," appearing in various guises in myth. Sometimes he is the Sun, the paternal source of all fertility, the giver of all increase in nature. (Indeed, earthly life, if it would worship anything, can with reason worship the sun as the source of all terrestrial energies—that is, if worship is a proper phatic stance to take in the face of the atomic conflagration of this star.) Sometimes he appears as the figure of Time, in whom all things are born and all things perish. Sometimes he is the shining benevolent heavens, the personified Sky over us all; or Day, which contemplates all human acts with all-seeing omniscience; or the Light of the cosmic eye that is the compeller of conscience. But also, sometimes, he is the lightning-hurling, angry, fearsome storm-god—Jove, Indra, Thor, Varuna—who simultaneously sends the fructifying rains upon the mother-earth, grumbles and roars with his great welkin-shuddering voice, and ragingly hurls the destruction of his divine fire as a weapon against guilty man. As Jehovah he is the burning mountain, the volcanic god of the iron-smith Kenites who spoke to Moses in the burning bush. In India, as Shiva, he is Fire, Time, the trident Phallus, the god of the Bull, and Destruction. Animistic personification of nature here "explains" the whims and moods of the weather, the great powers of nature, and paternal creation and destruction.

The Spirit of spirits, like the paramount patriarch of the group in life, is therefore very like a father, and the Sky is well suited to be his symbol: exalted, remote, all-encompassing, over all beings, benevolent, creative, angry, punitive—and, above all, changeable. The cyclic Moon, a lesser luminary of night (and mysteriously related to the tides of life in women) is almost as commonly seen as the presiding female deity and wife of the paramount shining soul. Stars are widely believed to be the fire-souls of departed men and heroes. And the major planets (which have, in addition, an errant movement bespeaking a larger volition than the fixed stars') are similarly equated with the lesser gods who rule reality and the affairs of men. This notion is still inherent in the paranoid "science" of astrology, which projects onto outside wills an omnipotent control over the wills and lives of men—the Voice of the cosmos men must listen to in order to know their destiny. As astrology, then, animism purports to explain Fate, or why history happens as it does; but non-believers in astrology continue naïvely to believe that men make history happen, not planets.

Moreover, fire itself is a powerful and dangerous thing, mysteriously hidden in some objects. Primitive man often assimilates his fire-stick or fire-plow to the phallus, evoking this "life" and fire by friction on its female hearth. And burning is apparently the "death" and certainly the transfiguration of many things in nature. Fever, especially with delirium, is the dangerous possession of a body by too much fire, or by too many souls—and sometime this "consumption" or faster burning ends in earlier death. All in all, the soul is not unreasonably thought of as the mysterious fire of the human body: as fire leaves the body, warmth leaves it too; therefore, life is warmth. In this way of viewing life *additively* as an insubstantial substance, the soul-concept is understandable. We must remember that the "phlogiston" of the early chemists was also so conceived as something additive. But though interpretations may err, honest observations cannot be denied: the living man *is* warm, the dead one cold, and, when seen as *process,* the metabolic "burning" (or heat-producting oxidation of living tissues) is part of the complex truth about life. Furthermore, many men have thought of the sun as burning, though quick calculation of time and fuels would prove them wrong, until men knew the secret of atomic power —in which energy is seen not additively but as transfigured mass.

But primitive man, a naïve materialist, sees life and the soul as a thing, and not, as we do, as a process or pattern. He also thinks (since he believes in word magic) that if an entity can be named, then it must necessarily exist as a thing. From these errors was derived the immemorial nonsense that has since bedeviled the human mind—the concept of the thing that by necessity must be a non-thing, the nothing that is somehow a something, the material that is non-material, and the substance that is insubstantial. What an abuse of symbols! the symbolic-logician cries. And no wonder this Mystery mystifies, says common sense. Of this disease of symbolism is born the dubious dualism of mind and body, matter and spirit, *materia* and *logos,* particulars and Forms, things and Ideas—and perhaps even the Mass and Energy of modern physics.

The extraordinary thing is not, perhaps, that we should be guilty of this simple anthropomorphism, but that we should have gone so far with such a symbolic system. For in all of these (when Materia is the maternal, and Pattern the paternal principle) we are falsely imputing human sexual dimorphism to nature! It is therefore likewise not strange that mankind has continued to suffer confusion from this analysis, burdened as it is with false gender as some languages are. For belief in ghosts is a stubbornly wilful belief and has emotional dividends, as we shall see; it is schizoid and is a largely autistic system with minimal relevance to reality; and it is also a superstition, a hand-me-down and much outmoded intellectually. Animism is a fallacy with many progeny, many of them misshapen.

This separable soul of man is also like the insubstantial and invisible, but tangible *breath* of the body—and breath (like warmth) leaves the body at death. Thus the soul is seen as the *pneuma* of the Greeks, the *atman* of the Hindus, or the "breath of life" in the breath-soul concepts of many other societies. The various "breaths" of the body—upward, downward, and sidewise—are particularly conspicuous in the endless maunderings (one almost said the "hot air") of the Upanishads and subsequent Hindu metaphysics. The faintly embarrassing theories of the bean-forswearing Pythagoreans also come to mind; indeed, a case has even been made for the proposition that the bean was a totem or soul-source of the most ancient Indo-Europeans! In these ways, animism "explains" the conspicuously important physiological function of breathing.

Movement as an attribute of living things is also a plausible component of the soul or "anima"—the moving organism being "animate," the motionless thing "inanimate." The fetus first "lives" when it stirs in the womb: what was once mere matter (*mater*-ial substance) is now infused with the divine afflatus of the male soul or logos from the father. Animism, therefore, here explains "the facts of life." With respect to movement, it is for their motion as well as for their "fire" that the planets are regarded as animate beings. And it is because of their motion that winds and waters and other natural phenomena are personified. The views on motion of modern biology and astronomy, however, are more discriminating: we know that all living things do not necessarily show gross and visible movement, nor do all moving things necessarily have life. Modern atomic physics has penetrated even more deeply into the secret: nature is itself, and is neither she nor he—but a self-identity which we dichotomize as motion or Energy (male) and substance or Mass (female). After millennia of thinking in terms of dualistic animism, man now knows that E quite demonstrably and indubitably equals mc^2; that is, matter and energy are the same thing under a different guise, or the same fundamental reality in a different phase or state of being.

The soul as an *initiator* of motion in matter was further suggested to primitive man by an awareness of his own psychic and neuromuscular processes. Hence *volition* was early seen to be an attribute of life—an observation, incidentally, which later science has seen no reason to deny. But as projected from persons to planets, this unjustified extrapolation of volition once again gives rise to the persecution mania and "ideas of reference" of astrology: outside animate planetary forces are thought to be inexorably and omnipotently pushing helpless humans around, much as the discrete and disembodied demiurge Culture of the "culturologists" omnipotently coerces hapless human beings in their every act, or as some schizophrenics think an "influencing machine" controls them. We will return to this point later.

Astrology is of course a false projection of volition into planets that move and that burn. But the believer in astrology sees what he has to see. To the extent that he himself cannot control events or feels he cannot, he sees everywhere the relentless coercer. After such projection, it is not surprising that to the animist the most compelling and most powerful forces *in the universe as in the family* are further conceived of as personal, parental, or paternal. A society's projective "ideas of reference" may even take the form of religious belief in a Prime Mover. For to the extent that we do not know the objective world and how to deal with it, our notions are colored by the subjective and the human. And the projective system will necessarily reflect our unresolved anxieties, our impotence, our libidinal needs, and our social structures: in this sense part of every culture is a projective paranoia.

Pure motion without body seems to occur in *dreams* and gives further impetus to a belief in the soul. The dreamer apparently moves

277

about at will in the past, as well as in the present—and many even think (with unwarranted hope) that in the dream the soul can move about now in the "future." In dreams the self makes journeys not only in time but also in space, journeys which both seem to the waking self and are for the waking self manifestly impossible. Obviously, then, the mysterious "spiritual" self has transcendent mobility in space and time and has left behind the gross frustrating physical realities of the body and the waking world. (Actually, of course, we now know that *memory* and *volition* perform these miracles, not a separable soul.) The dreamer sees incredible movements of the "self" on the dream screen. He sees the distant land and the long-dead person. He "travels" in known and in unknown places. Dreaming, with the critical sense-oriented and reality-oriented ego in abeyance, is in its very essence a belief-seducing experience: it releases enormous psychic energies arising from the primitive organic will. Dreaming is an indiscipline of the mind, a temporary psychosis that unfetters the organism from reality, social and cultural as well as physical.

It is therefore entirely plain why the apparent omnipotence of the dream and its reality-resolving powers should further invest the "spiritual" with a superiority over the mundane physical workaday world. For during his dreaming the dreamer is the omnipotent creator of any "reality" he desires. The great emotive potential of such a state makes it understandable how the very direction of one's entire life may come from this explosion of the id (or organic wish) in the vision quest of the Plains Indians, or in the mystic experience of our own visionaries. It is also understandable how the self-chosen world-creating of the dream can come to be *preferred* to the vexations and the frustrations of the organism in the real social and physical world. (For this reason, too, tender-minded philosophers invariably prefer a subjective idealism in which Self or Spirit is in the driver's seat: they give their allegiance to the seductive Pleasure Principle of organic wish. But the tough-minded are disenchanted of this illusion of omnipotence and know that the organic will constantly stubs its toes on obdurate reality: they have gained a chastened respect for the Reality Principle, the world in which all organisms are immersed.) The "deeper wisdom" of the dream is merely deeper in the psyche.

As with all artistic and autistic artifacts, the dream is more comfortable and more desirable to the organism, more facilely and more immediately equilibrium-preserving. We *want* to believe, though we are here compelled by internal (not external) necessities.

Any explanation which would take account of the presence of animism among peoples almost everywhere must of course be founded upon facts which have a universal human relevance. Curiously, there is a universally human *physiological* phenomenon which remains to be mentioned and which may partly account for "seeing ghosts"—particularly when joined by other motives we shall mention in a moment. This involves the anatomy and physiology of the human eye. Now the eye has almost fantastic powers of accommodation and can see objects illuminated with a brightness all the way from that of a noon-day coral beach to that of a jungle path on a moonless night—a ratio of a billion to one. However—and understandably perhaps—this physical gamut of light-intensity is not apprehended by means of a single physiological continuum in the human eye. That is, daytime and night-time vision are quite different functionally.

In daytime vision the greatest sensitivity is found in the region of the *fovea* or "yellow spot" on the retina, and our habit therefore is to turn this part of the eye on the object we wish to see more clearly. At night, however (or in conditions of very dim lighting), the fovea is no longer the point of greatest visual acuity. The *rod cells* alone respond to light of low intensity, and these are concentrated in a ring-shaped zone about 20° off-center on the retina. Thus we may see at night, with this zone of rod cells, something which (when we follow our daytime reflexes and "look" at it with the fovea) may then completely disappear. In other words we may *see* something at night that disappears when we *look* at it—an "uncanny" experience indeed!

What part of his retina can a man believe? The incalculable number of times this physiological phenomenon has been experienced by human beings may well have aided them in believing that they can at times (viz., at night, or in dimly lit places) see "ghosts" with a "second sight," as it were, wholly different from workaday vision. Since extrafoveal vision is also more sensitive to movement, the very movement of the head and eyes may compound the confusion—and the sly spirits appear only when we are not actually looking at them. Understandably, then, we can honestly assert we saw things that to foveal vision are "not there." To explain this, we do not need to postulate any extra-sensory perception: we have only to understand sensory perception physiologically. But the "now you see it now you don't" phenomenon fits fatally well the definition of a "spiritual" entity, which *is* a thing that *isn't*.

The eye at night also cannot distinguish color, though it responds best to light having a wave length of 510 mμ, which would become bluish-green if the intensity of the illumination were increased in this same wave length alone. Because of this fact it is hardly surprising, therefore, that in conditions of dim threshold vision pixies and elves should so commonly appear to be bluish-green.

But even daytime seeing, under conditions of more than adequate illumination, also has its idiosyncrasies. Sometimes in looking at the bright sky one sees semi-transparent *muscae volitantes* or "curlicues," which are the shadows of substances contained in the vitreous humor of the eyeball, projected upon the retina or visual screen of the eye. But if one moves the eye, the better to see a curlicue near the edge of vision, then this, in wilful and antic fashion, moves too—which is scarcely surprising when it is realized that it is within the eye that moves. (How many *muscae volitantes* do we not see in the universe when we fail to examine the human instrument that does the seeing!) The curlicue lazes provocatively by, only to dart swiftly when the eye turns to see it. This, however, is no vision of some external entity with a perverse volition of its own. It is, rather, the inertia of a substance with weight and with, moreover, the high viscosity of a semi-colloid or watery jelly. Once again the "spiritual" thing is in ourselves, and not in the outside world. And once again it behooves us to examine the human organism that does the perceiving. Still, for these several reasons, the physiological behavior of the human eye may be interpreted as further "evidence" for an animistic belief in mysterious "spiritual" entities. Animism, therefore, helps to explain some of these curious phenomena of seeing; and these in turn appear to support a belief in animism.

The physiology of sight as it relates to "seeing ghosts" and pixies by no means exhausts the facts which may be relevant to animistic belief in man. The "unseen" is almost literally identical with the uncanny and the unknown, and hence with the "spiritual." The biological and libidinal importance of seeing has surely further bearing on animistic belief. For the unseen (but the otherwise psychologically present phenomenon) may be that which is to be feared; and in the absence of sight, which is man's chief reality-testing sense, the fear of the unknown may be compounded. It is interesting that the *small* lemurs are nocturnal and live in pairs or single families, while the *large* lemurs are diurnal and live in small groups containing members of at least another family. From this, several conclusions can be drawn. First, the small arboreal primates can evidently survive better by being active at night, defenseless as they are, most effectively in solitude, in pairs, or in small family groups—and through the use of their enormous eyes as a special nocturnal adaptation. Second, the increase in body size may have been an important factor in releasing the early primates from their nightly or twilight feeding habits, by allowing them better to hold their own against aggressors—and this, together with the potentialities of day-time life, led to the growth of wider social relationships with other members of their own species, with all the securities (and the possibility of mass delusions) inherent in social life.

As a large primate, man is evidently to be regarded initially as a diurnal animal, and with day-adapted senses. But with the cultural acquisition of fire, this biological restriction no longer necessarily holds. We must therefore return to a discussion of fire in a second context. In one of his most interesting papers, Devereux has suggested that the day-time animal man's inadequate night-time vision may be related to his social gregariousness and to man's mastery over fire. The first seems probable even for primates in general, for they lack the physical defenses many other mammals have; and protective gregariousness may be even more important in a primate like man that has come down from the trees, for the partly terrestrial anthropoids retreat to the trees at night. As for fire, this is one of the absolutely undisputed traits that differentiate man from the other animals. The biological value of fire both for man's seeing and as a protection against night-hunting animals with better night-adapted vision than man, is clear:

for the physiological reaction of these animals' eyes to a bright light would destroy any visual advantage they otherwise had over man at night. (One might even venture the suggestion that the recreational gregariousness of man at night is related to his artificial and controlled power over light, that removes the situation psychologically from that of the day world of work and puts it in the area of fantasy, recreation, and the Pleasure Principle: some economic classes, indeed, and some individuals are "night-owls," conspicuously and exclusively devoted to gregarious play.) Devereux is also supported by the monkey and ape evidence in asserting that the eye is physiologically and psychologically the most significant sense in all primates (though the nocturnal lemur with its huge eyes is a still more special case). In man, he thinks, the depriving of visual contact with reality ("shut-eye") is significantly related to sleep, to coitus at night, to a child's frightened conception of it, and to the projected terrors of the nightmare. Certainly it is the mind as deprived primarily of visual reality-contact (for one can hear in the dark) that creates dream-fantasy equilibriums. Furthermore, we dream largely in visual terms. Similarly, the delusions of psychotics are very commonly visual hallucinations; but, because of the social nature of man and the social nature of some patients' illnesses, delusions are also very commonly auditory. But in any case, spiritual "voices," as well as "seen" spirits, are paranoid projections of fragments of the individual's own fearful psyche—which thinks it hears and sees outside what is truly only inside.

Another source of animistic belief, though one not commonly attended to, is the phenomenon of *conscience*. In one sense, the feeling of disparate wrangling voices, in a mind confronted with moral decision, suggests that the individual is inhabited by multiple wills, persons, or spirits. On occasion the human being—so accustomed to the compelling of his will by other persons both as child and as culture-bearer—may even conveniently claim to be "possessed" by *alien* spirits whenever he does wrong, and hence *he* is not to blame. In psychiatric fact, however, it is the originally alien "spirit" of his conscience that is trying to make him behave, and it is his own organic will that makes him misbehave! The conflict is between the organic "person" and the social "person" (the conscience laboriously learned under cultural pressure), and the arbiter is the hard-bitten but reality-taught conscious mind. Thus the animist easily and dishonestly rids himself of blame by making a demon (a "bad" spirit, an initiator of "bad" action) out of his own disclaimed or unrecognized wish. This naughty thing he psychically excretes or places projectively outside "himself"—much as the hysteric fears to find under the bed the burglar she wishes were in it (it is not she who has the reprehensible wish, it is the lustful burglar).

Similarly, the animist fortifies his wavering will with the god, a "good" spirit—a value reprojected before it was entirely introjected, and hence retaining still the shadowy lineaments of another person external to the self. People with immature consciences actually believe men would not be good without gods! It is as if a man convinced that a "good" was *good* did not *really* believe that it was a good. He needs to be told what is good and coerced to seek the desirable by an external Will! The morally integrated person, however, has no need of these fractionings of his mind into devils and gods and learns to be responsible for his own psyche. Animism is here a belief that is very much in the service of moral alibi-ing. The belief in animism is a moral and intellectual infantilism of man—a dependent clinging to what is archaic in the individual as well as ancient in the race.

In another way animism receives an additional powerful impetus from our experience of the working of conscience. One is often aware of the overpowering and mysteriously compelling quality of conscience, or socially derived moral sense, and his physical organism is seen constantly to bow to this "spiritual" power not wholly himself. The "spiritual" (superego) imperiously wills what the physical "flesh" (the id) but weakly accepts. Thus spirit is seen again as initiator of movement in inert matter, and as a soul predominating over and directing a thing. In this manner animism serves to rationalize subjective psychological facts.

Animism is deeply linked with the biological nature of the human species. Animism—there is no doubt of it—is an inevitable way of thinking about the physical world that an animal will fall into when its effective "environment" is so significantly and predominantly made up of *persons*—persons animated, so often vexatiously, with alien wills.

For the domesticated infantile animal in the human family is shaped more by other humans than by unedited nature. Scratch any child and find an animist. Surrounded by wills in the family all through his period of learning to become human, it is not surprising that he often feels surrounded by wills in the natural world.

Animism is therefore to be expected in an animal influenced more by persons than by physical reality, for that has been his own peculiar and limited experience of life. But the grown person who remains an animist is one who has not sufficiently discerned the serene and predictable real world beyond the screen of crotchety persons surrounding him—and heaven help him if his Reality is then anthropomorphic too! It is interesting to notice in this connection that domesticated animals like dogs or horses sometimes seem to dream and to "see ghosts." But it is more economical of theory to see these things as being related to their domestication by man, rather than to postulate for them some special extra-sensory perception of further postulated spirits or ghosts. Like children, domesticated animals are plainly dominated by and beholden to adult human beings, whom they may fear and projectively dream about in "paranoid" or persecutory fashion when these persons are not actually present.

With still greater justification, probably, than in the case of conscience, the soul may be seen as prepotent over mere things in another way. For the mind (the "spiritual") *is* a maker and a fashioner of quite formidable proportions. It is impossible to deny, when a human will and purpose have fabricated a tool, that then and thereby something entirely new has been created in the universe. The human mind also does undeniably create symbols—and here even more impressively and whole-cloth than in the case of material tools. For as symbol systems neither inhere in Nature nor are even themselves material, they are unquestionably the product of concerted or individual human wills.

In explaining human psychoses it is remarkable how much of our thinking is animistic. The psychotic person is "alienated," and the law still calls in an "alienist" to decide whether he is criminally responsible or not. In hysteria the "hysteron" or womb is literally wandering about the body as a separate vagrant spirit and producing symptoms, now here and now there, in the body. In epilepsy (significantly the "sacred disease") the person is "seized upon" by some outside force. In paranoia, etymologically, we have a "mind beside itself." When an individual has multiple personalities—differing in temperament, character, knowledge and memory—the "dissociated" individual is alternately "taken possession of" by these separate souls. Hallucinations are evidently the seeing of (probably supernatural) things by some people and not by others. In sleep-walking we seem to have a dream walking about with a body, and the conscious person somewhere else. In the medieval "dancing mania" people did (amazingly!) just those things they would never do "in their right senses." In an erotic dream a demon incubus comes to "bed upon" one sex and a succubus to "bed beneath" the other. Naturally one has to exorcise ("curse out") such evil spirits. In delirium a man is "out of his mind," and in a concussion he is "knocked out of his senses." And a slightly queer feeble-minded person is said to be "a bit touched."

Animistic concepts are rife in our everyday speech. We "can't imagine what possesses him" when a child slaps his brother or a man goes off with another man's wife—as if the little darling and the old rip were not doing it themselves. (Still, even respectable citizens like ourselves feel you should "let yourself go" once in a while.) A blameless invalid has a heart "seizure" or a gall-bladder "attack," as if these weakened organs were grabbing or hitting at him. If you run fast, you get "out of breath"; if you fall down heavily, you "lose your breath"; and if you hold your breath (in your hands?), you are very likely to "pass out." On a vacation, oddly enough, you spend a lot of good money in "getting away from yourself." If you are enthusiastic ("driven by a god inside") about some good work, this is regarded as "taking you out of yourself"—no doubt owing to the influence ("flowing in") of strong emotions ("moving out"). All of this shows a feeble sense of ego boundaries!

In ecstasy we "stand outside" ourselves at an inspired ("breathed into") actress who "really enters into her part"; but if there should be a panic in the theater, this is the goat-god Pan taking possession of people, and who invited him? But perhaps our companion is "not herself" (an alarming thought!), that is, she "has the vapors," so we go home to sit before the fire bemused—which means that the spirit of one of those plump Greek ladies wearing cheesecloth, the Muses, has laid hold on us. Really, "a man can't call his mind his own"! If this goes on, perhaps tomorrow we'd better see a "medium" (for the voice of a spirit), and her "control" will tell us what is best to do. Tormented "soul"!

Primitive people are, if anything, even more animistic in their thinking. A hiccough is plainly a dis-ease of the breath spirit in us— and beware of sneezing ("God bless you"), lest you lose your soul. Many plants, primitives know, have powerful spirits in them. Teonanacatl, the Aztec narcotic mushroom, is the "flesh of the gods." The Hindu assassins used hashish as devotees of the goddess Thuggee. The southern Plains Indian "red bean" (*Sophora secundiflora*) is full of "power" (indeed it is, since it contains the powerful narcotic sopho-rine) and hence is good to put in a medicine bundle or to wear on the moccasin fringe to protect a man from stepping on dangerous things. Eating Jimson weed enables a Southwestern Indian shaman to see things far off and to find lost articles. But the button of the cactus *Lophophora williamsii*, eaten in the widespread modern Plains Indian "peyote cult," has the greatest "power" of all: it contains no less than nine narcotic alkaloids. Peyote gives visual hallucinations in technicolor, which the Indians know are spirits talking to them. Because their cultural background leads them to value abnormal psychic states, these Indians are particularly vulnerable to "spirits" of alcohol. (For the Greeks, wine was the god Dionysus himself—for look what he makes a man do!) In fact, even tobacco was never used secularly by Indians but only in sacred contexts, because of the "power" in it. The primitive belief in possession by spirits would take a long book even to list its many occurrences all over the world. In the Marquesas, for example, certain priests are possessed by gods who tell them when to go on a cannibal raid. Indeed, primitives characteristically listen to and obey the injunctions of psychotics, either as culture heroes in their own right or as the human medium for the voice of the gods.

From an anthropological point of view, it would be naïve to attack animism with the weapons of science if it were only the world-view of primitive men. On the contrary, however, it is part and parcel of our own frequently primitivistic thinking. Human narcissism makes of the real world an opaque surface, and then we are surprised to see our own faces mirrored in it everywhere we look! And once the concept of the separable soul has been originated on primitive "scientific" grounds, there are other non-theoretical and purely psychic dividends which unite to compel and to seduce our continuing belief. First of all, the notion of a separable soul enables man (fruitlessly) to combat the fact of metazoan death. It is a homeostatic device of purely psychiatric relevance: it comforts the psyche without changing the biological fact. For with only a little additional effort, the separable soul (that something which is a nothing) can be regarded as a non-existent—which by the fact of not-being therefore exists indestructibly forever! Like the grin on the Cheshire cat, the soul remains when the cat is gone.

The death of another person is consequently not a threat to the animist. On the one hand, the loving soul will meet loved souls again in eternity—now that they have left merely existential reality. (But since the bond of any kind of love is always an organismic bond, is the lover really comforted by the bloodless sop of the soul?) On the other hand, the hostile person is not really guilty in any permanent sense of the now accomplished death wish against an enemy. (But is he in any better position to escape the revenge of a ghost now defined as categorically indestructible?) Plato's pun (on $\sigma\hat{\omega}\mu\alpha$-$\sigma\hat{\eta}\mu\alpha$) has it that the body is a tomb in which the psyche or soul lies dead, awaiting resurrection into true life, which is life without the body. Aristophanes hooted at this idea (and so did Euripides) as the height of absurdity—for did not all the Greeks know that the psyche is life itself? One is reminded of another much later philosophical pun, "No matter, never mind"!

Equipped with the hypothesis of the separable soul, the animist may likewise find that the death of the self ceases to be an unbearable threat. The guilty person who excessively fears death, anticipating it as a punishment and unconsciously acknowledging the justice of such a doom, can now be reassured. It is only a game; he will be forgiven any infraction of the rules; and it isn't played "for keeps" anyway. The moral responsibility for what one is and for what one does can thus be turned over to a parentalized universe; and one can then remain the naughty and irresponsible child, seducing and cajoling forgiveness from fate. Fate will be "merciful," give in, and let the individual have his own way. Sin then becomes completely satisfying, since you can eat your cake and have it too. The person knows beforehand (though his be allegedly a "mortal" sin) that his immortal soul will be ultimately saved just the same, once he knows the right mediators to cozen the right gods. Such cut-rate and packaged forgiveness will always find a ready market with a public infantilized by parentalized institutions. Such service constitutes the commodity dispensed by the soundest and (understandably) best-thought-of business institutions—though the genuine trade-marked article has now lost its monopoly, in a freely competitive market with many brand names.

As Erich Fromm has clearly shown for Naziism, all that a supposed total human helplessness needs for "peace of mind" is for a correspondingly omnipotent paranoid messiah (Hitler) to offer himself: total power is the answer to total lack of power. The Leader's own fantasied omnipotence is willingly offered to all who will buy it culturally, and it finds a ready market: if the others join his paranoid cult, this confirms his fantasy. The paranoid culture hero thus achieves a synthetic institutionalized fatherhood and potency which he grievously failed to achieve in his own psychosexual maturation. He does not father children as do ordinary men, but he becomes the mystic father of other men—but only at the price of infantilizing all the communicants of his cult. The mechanisms are particularly clear in the cult of Father Divine: the communicants may hear and read only his Word, they must turn over all their property to the messiah, and they must give up their adult sexual intercourse and love only Father. More literal infantilization would be hard to imagine.

A belief in animism is similarly to the advantage of the narcissistic person. He has not been properly loved, so he has to contrive to love himself. But not having been loved, he knows that he is not lovable. The narcissistic person, therefore, cannot really love himself but must hate himself for being unlovable—and hence his pretended "love" for himself is unsatisfying and insatiable. Thus he is doubly vulnerable to the notion that his essence is indestructible. If he supposes himself precious and irreplaceable, or if he hatefully fears his own destruction, he will in either case be reassured of his indestructibility. Death is not destruction of the self, for animism assures him that his soul goes marching on.

The more vulnerable, too, are the culturally weary and heavy-laden, and those who have not loved this life and this body. Only those who cannot live are insatiable of life: the "comfort" of immortality can appeal only to those who have not had enough genuine experience of mortality. For the maintenance of the complex equilibriums and integrations that in their totality constitute human life is an energy-consuming task that must be viewed with horror if it is also to be endless. Mortality may just as well be viewed as the fitting and desirable reward of the weary metazoan, after a gallant and brave game against insurmountable odds, his life a distinguished human artifact with a dignity and an aesthetic satisfaction all its own. And if the metazoan animal has passed on the germ plasm's immortality to his offspring, then his death is biologically irreproachable and he can lay his burden down. Better the more probable belief that our sons will do better than we, than the belief that our errors and our sins will be preserved in perpetuity!

Furthermore, biological death is a logical and inevitable part of a larger process. Life is a functioning integration of parts, an organismic and shifting but equilibrated pattern. But the patterns of life itself change with evolution. Metazoan death is a necessary biological technique for allowing new genes an opportunity to experiment with an organism's erstwhile body materials. Orchids (the most highly evolved plants) could never have appeared if all plants had been ferns or fungi. Any "immortality" that is involved in life is the universal differentiated germ plasm's. It is true that the germ plasm, from which all earthly life has arisen, has evidently existed for roughly one billion years—a period which by human standards is a reasonable facsimile of immortality. But let narcissistic man take another look: without the successive death of all individual metazoans (and the destruction of most of the body of protozoans), the universal germ plasm would never have had the material wherewithal to have evolved this elegant creature, man. *Gigantopithecus* must step aside for *Pithecanthropus*, and *Heidelbergensis* for *Homo sapiens*. And Dante's medieval world-view must die for Melville to hurl his New World defiance at fate. Without the death of Caesar, we could not have had Lincoln.

The individual animal in all metazoan species is a temporary organization of contingencies, a germ-self-created environment to insulate germ plasm and to preserve its immortality. It does violence to hen-centered sensibilities, but from a biological standpoint a hen is only the immortal egg's devious strategem of making other eggs. It is Ferenczi's "perigenetic" view that the body in all the metazoan species is merely the monumentally stubborn germ plasm's successive ways of surrounding itself with an ever more secure environment, in which the germ plasm itself remains forever the same. The body is a safer sea for the germ cell to swim in until it makes itself still another home.

So far as even the "immortality" of the germ plasm is concerned, the most we can believe on the evidence is that perhaps life is one of the natural states or phases of matter, just as originless and endless as matter itself. We do not know. But if life is thus regarded as triumphantly co-equal with death, then the biologist must further comfortlessly assert that the aged or the ill organism must therefore quietly wish to die, for in any case (supposing it has a choice about the matter) this is precisely what every metazoan without exception ultimately does. But even so, the wish for the remoter immortality of the germ plasm may press the facts too far. Perhaps the living organization of matter at one time did not exist, and perhaps at one time it again may not exist. Meanwhile, not even the germ plasm is changelessly "immortal"—for the organic pattern of a given species is never in any final sense permanent and immutable. And even the most archaic living form did not always exist as the present species in its present form; were this not so, we would see life arising continuously about us anew and spontaneously, no doubt much as in its original form—or if chemicals still do arrange themselves spontaneously into quasi-organic compounds, these are no doubt quickly and gratefully appropriated by the lower organisms they so closely resemble, before we get a chance to see them. The biological facts cannot be twisted around in any way for the solace of the precious, narcissistic, somatic self. For it is the pattern of life that goes on, and not the individual "spiritual" self. And this pattern is always and invariably *embodied*.

The greatest service of all that the concept of the separable soul renders to humans is as a *rationalizer of human morality*. When, inevitably, the moral world of humans does not behave with the same rigor and inexorability as the physical world in its dealings with individual human beings, it is very convenient to be able to suppose that the retribution—manifestly absent in this life!—will nevertheless be visited upon the soul of the person in a postulated "after" life. Now only a properly immortal soul is available for the punishments somehow missed in secular life. Thus we must believe that the indestructibility of soul-stuff is the same as the indestructibility of matter. (Unfortunately for this concept, however, soul stuff gave up its indestructibility when it gave up its materiality, since its first act was not to exist!) Animistic belief therefore comfortably takes up the slack between moral and physical reality, and makes Fate the guardian of our tribal morality against individual offenders.

The truth is that no man is ever wholly satisfied with his culture. Each of us has his psychopathic streak of self-will and rebellion against society. A Rousseauist lurks under the skin of every human being. Thus we are often not quite satisfied with the fact that not alone is "Virtue its own reward," but worse, Virtue is its *only* reward. The business of a value is, of course, to be valuable. But when we are somewhat doubtful of the real value of a proffered "value"—from not feeling or experiencing or enjoying it ourselves—then, like bribed children, we human beings demand additional payments in eternity for virtuous behavior in life. (We want candy for eating our ice cream!) If the capital investment in virtue is dubious, we at least want dividends on it in perpetuity.

This is felt to be all the more equitable, since some of our contemporaries permit themselves gratifications (the so-and-so's eat their cake too!) which we virtuous ones forego. But our abstention from a consumable good really ought to trans-substantiate it for us into an interest-producing capital virtue. These other rascals, meanwhile, ate their cake instead of banking it as a virtue, and nevertheless seem to do reasonably well in life. This is grossly unfair: such persons, naturally, must be punished eternally (for our eternal abstention) in order to balance the scales. This is of course in order that the improvident wicked may learn their moral lesson so well (after all, they have all eternity to learn it in) that when eternity ends they will "know better" when eternity begins again.

The wisdom of Solomon will not help us out of the semantic snarl these scrappy children get us into! If, as its definition seems to indicate, eternity never begins—much less begins again—when, then, can the wicked apply the hard-learned lesson of eternity; and if they can't apply it, then what's the moral of their learning it so thoroughly? And if eternity never ends, then it seems pointless to punish them eternally except as gratification and reward for the virtuous—which tends to make the virtuous in turn into highly immoral monsters, having purchased the right to the eternal wickedness of enjoying others' suffering, through a limited secular investment in virtue. There is something wrong with this hypothesis somewhere! It must be that physical reality does not always care about individual sins against tribal morality. For the rain continues to fall on the just and on the unjust, and a church steeple must have its lightning rod as well as the road-house.

Of course it is absurd to expect that the organism's essential work, value-making, has already been done for it by the non-organic world. But an emotionally defended hypothesis is safe from attack. With accretions of further rationalization, the fantasy of a separable soul still permits the initial rationalization that the tribal mores are every bit as rigorous and ineluctable as the Second Law of Thermodynamics —every bit as infallible as fate in the physical world. Now every human being suspects, at some time, that such and such a tribal shibboleth doesn't really make much sense. Everyone has the secret conviction, at moments, that the cultural parents do *not* know what is best. But he is the more likely to stay obediently in line, if he can be brought to believe in a non-physical "moral" world that nevertheless behaves exactly like the physical world—to believe in the mystery of the thing that is not a thing, and in the mystery of a life that is lived after life is in fact ended.

Thus the belief in the separable immortal soul preserves the tribal mores and ethical hypotheses from ever being seen as such—from ever being examined, criticized operationally, or in any other manner dealt with rationally and realistically. Animism is a morally infantile inability to see the real world that exists beyond the ghosts of all the human fathers surrounding us. Animism is a product of the familial social organization of human beings and of the biosocial infantilization of man. The soul-concept is the homeostatic guardian and defender of the culture from change—the dubious "wisdom of the ages" with the dead hand of the past still on the throttle of the present. A mistaken hypothesis is not necessarily innocent of evil consequences, however. (It is easy to pass over the critique of our own culture, to see more clearly the beam in the eye of another. For example, when the doctrine of Karma is used to rationalize and to preserve the miseries of caste, then the potential iniquity of the separable soul-hypothesis is realized. Operationally, and in this world, the concept of Karma looks a good deal like the moral sparganosis-cure of Hindu society.)

But the hoary hypothesis of animism is not downed so easily. There is one last-ditch argument to be marshaled forth: the fact of *culture*. Surely, no one will deny that man, as opposed to the other animals, is a "spiritual" being? Do we not know that man everywhere lives immersed in things "above and beyond himself"? Is he not intimately and daily aware of values in and of himself that "live on after his death"? Of course! But these are not the attributes of a hypothecated animistic soul: they are the derivatives of his nature as an animal species! There is no question that symbol-systems and tools are the product of his "spirit" as *mind*—a commodity man is conspicuously endowed with organically. There is no doubt that his basically inter-individual social nature facilitates language and other symbol-systems of culture—indeed, these are meaningless except as they are hyper-metazoan bonds "above and beyond himself" as an individual. And it is the very essence and nature of any human culture to embody values and patterns that "live on after his death." Man is in some ways different from other animals. But these differences inhere in his possession of culture, not of a separable soul.

It is interesting that traditional Christian culture should have been so much exercised to discover differences between man and the animals. These differences are by no means so evident to (or so sought for by) a majority of peoples of non-European origin. Most non-Europeans in their philosophy and folklore have easily assumed a kinship of man with other animals—which Darwinian evolution has been able to demonstrate to Europeans only against their strongest emotional and institutional resistances. Buddhism, for example, is both more generous and more logical; for, after all, on purely "scientific" grounds, all warm-blooded animals like birds and mammals must have souls too, since they also become cold when they die.

The fact is that the attempt to discover such differences from the animals as man's exclusively possessed "soul" is very much in the service of the human oedipal conflict. The pose that man is a "spiritual" being "above" the gross (sexual) animals is obvious nonsense—if it is the pretense that he is not a mammal, which he certainly is, and in generous measure to boot! It is a preposterous protective coloration psychologically—which deceives no one with open eyes who can see that, with shocking conspicuousness, the Emperor is wearing no clothes at all. As a process, the individual human life-history makes man guilty about his sexuality. For it is admittedly an intricate and difficult thing to transform childlike dependent love of others into grown-up sexual love, and to change oedipal dependency into independence of the oedipal. What man is actually saying, in his assertion that he is "above" the other animals, is that he does manage to contrive familial life through the imposition of taboos, and that he is not a potentially incestuous animal as all infra-human animals are. But if his cultural behavior earns him the right to say this, it is still his buried but life-history-disciplined wish that gives him the need to insist on saying it.

The place of animism in this oedipal picture is clear. To have an immortal soul is to be accessible to punishment; but to be a moral animal is to be able to avoid it. The "original sin" against the father is not so much loving the mother dependently as it is the compounding of this later with the wish to be like the father and partake of his potency. Jehovah can permit Adam and Eve an oral paradise, but when they seize the parental prerogative of genital knowledge and carnal creation, then they must be cast out of the infantile familial Eden. As parents they must foster their own family by the sweat of their brows, and forge their own morality by the agony of their own creative choices in a morally self-responsible world, having knowledge now that human good and evil are mere parental fiats. This great legend sums up the whole story of oedipal man.

The original phenomena which the soul-hypothesis attempted to explain still remain. *Homo sapiens* does have some differences from other animal species. But when his biological distinctions and their consequences are clearly described, man's "morality," his "soul," and his "immortality" all become accessible to a purely naturalistic formulation and understanding. These are necessary consequences of man's peculiar humanity in the anatomical and physiological sense and can be viewed in their place as part of the continuous process of evolution, as part of the total web of life.

Man's morality is not an absolute physical given, but consists in the relative choices of his radial speciation: in the ethnological house of this world there are many cultural mansions. In the final analysis, man's "soul" is no more than his heat-producing metabolism and warm blood, lung respiration and breath, his inordinately large brain and questing mind, the creativity of his hands, his memory, dreams, and volition, his familial social organization, conscience, and culture. And man's "immortality" (in so far as it differs from the immortality of the germ plasm of any other animal species) consists in his time-transcending inter-individually shared values, symbol-systems, languages, and cultures—and in nothing else.

We repeat, a scientific analysis of animism would be a waste of time if it were only the superstition of a few primitive peoples without writing. But the fact is that metaphysical animism is literally the Great Tradition of occidental philosophy and religion, as it is almost the whole of Indian thought. Nevertheless, animism and the philosophies to which it has given rise can be plainly seen as a purely human extrapolation the origins of which are easily understandable. *In animism reality is persistently viewed in human and familial terms.* Metaphysical animism asserts that the Macrocosm (or universe) is created, as is the microcosm (or self), and that the whole is ruled by a celestial father.

Let us state these propositions in the language of the tradition itself. The visible world is the product or offspring of a cosmic father and mother. The Male Principle is the Soul or Spirit, the Logos or Lord. In Nature or the Macrocosm, he is manifest as the Sun, Fire, Lightning, and the Sky (which sends the inseminating moisture and warmth of the light and rain of the heavens upon the Mother-Earth). In the human microcosm, he is manifest as the breath of life, consciousness, and conscience; and, as a fragment of the Divinity resides in each body as the individual soul, all men are in this sense the sons of God and shaped after his image. But the souls of sons are separated from the divine spiritual substance of the Father and must ever struggle to reunite with and be with God and be God. This separation is the result of their reification or being made things: a fragment of the paternal Form, the Divine Idea, or Cosmic Mind has given shape to (but is imprisoned in) the particulars, or objects, in the phenomenal ("seen") world of appearances. Thus the Ideal or male principle is made impure by its various existences in reality. The world is a dreary "life-sentence" for each individual being.

Greek and Judeo-Christian philosophy make no bones about their contempt and condemnation and fear of the Female Principle. The maternal principle is Materia, the Body, Substance, and the Flesh. Only the Noumenal (mind-like) world of the Male is "real" and permanent and everlasting. The Phenomenal world (of appearances) is unreal, Maya the Illusion, and the Female Principle or Void (on which the male Word wrought the miracles of creation). "Particulars" or objects, therefore, are the reified offspring of the Word made Flesh—which is the befouling mirror of the divine, the reifying principle, the separator of the ideal One into the imperfect Many—the female divider of the Son from the Father, the fleshly prison of the spirit. The spirit must struggle to free itself from the bonds of matter, the child and the male flee the mother and the female, who is the origin of their strife. For the Son *is* mystically the Father, though temporarily laboring under the gross difficulty of being particulated in mater-ial. As we are men, only the spiritual (the male) is good and ultimately real: matter is a hateful illusion from which the self must struggle to find purification, as of dross and sin. Only in Death can the Son rejoin the Father, and the self blissfully blend with the Self, which is its proper home. We must contemn the seductive[1] material world of the flesh as we must flee the maternal; we must lust after the spiritual world of uranian (literally "heavenly," that is Greek paiderastic male-worshiping) love. On our lips must be constantly the oedipal submission, "not my will but Thine be done," the worshipful sons eternally praising the Father.

The continual praise of the Father by the Son, however (if they are of one "homoöusian" Substance), is inordinately narcissistic and self-worshipful; and if they are of separate ("homoiousian") substances, the praise is either highly dubious psychiatrically (viz., homoerotic) or hollow and spurious in tone. It is interesting that all the great heresies and controversies in Christianity have been specifically concerned with the relationship of the Son to the Father; and this is perhaps as it should be, for our solution to the familial problem will color everything, from our theory of the state downward.

There is little mystery in the perennial appeal of Greek animistic metaphysics to men of certain character-types—the mildly paranoid, systematizing, autistic individual with an introverted and tender-minded trend. For no paranoiac ever asks more than that the self become the Self and ruler of the universe. And as a system, animism "explains" everything that it takes a whole congress of sciences to work out piecemeal in modern times, and none too surely at that. As for autism, the very essence of the autistic is preoccupation with the self.

1. Hinduism quite parallels the Greek tradition. In all Indian thought since Buddhism, the original sin has been Desire, which ensnares the spirit in material incarnation, alienating the self from the Self, and contaminating the perfect maleness of the spirit with fleshly particularizations. It is Desire (Kama, the Hindu Eros in later thought) who despoils the Ideal with materialization, projecting Maya the Illusion or the phenomenal seen world from the meditations of the Noumenal One (Thought, Brahma)—imprisoning the magical omnipotence of thought in the fetters of actuality. The evil one is Kama, the God of Love, who disturbs the Lord Shiva's ascetic meditations on his divine Maleness as the Lingam—enticing Him to mundane preoccupations by sending *apsaras* or celestial demon-maidens to seduce him. Thus is shattered the schizoid oneness of the One. The fearful demon is Eros (the binding or synthetic principle) whose evil contrivances in the dreadful world of the flesh only Thanatos or Death (the dissolving principle) can repair. The Hindu Kama or Eros resembles somewhat in this the Christian Devil (plus some traits of the Greek goat-god Pan). The Evil One—goat-horned, goat-hoofed, arrow-tailed, and trident-bearing Demon—beckons us to (sexual) sin, which would alienate us from our perfect submission to the will of the Father and seduce us to the World, the Flesh, and the Devil.

And if the introverted look too persistently within, we should not be surprized that they see only themselves and not the outside world. The tender-minded, too, are made happy to know that something autistically Mind-like is divinely behind the scenes. And the narcissistic self-worshiping male is reassured to know that the essence of the Macrocosm is also male.

For in animistic metaphysics, as in Platonic idealism, the Divine Pattern is unquestionably and exclusively male. Delicate ghostly paradigms or Patterns are laid up in mothballs in a celestial Bureau of Standards—which no man ever sees—hidden as the Word is hidden in the mind or as Fire is hidden in the flesh. Absolute Values or Norms are on deposit in the Bank of the Universe—deep in the vaults of some Platonic Fort Knox, whose location no one knows. The genetic jewels of the World Father are hidden. But the animist mystifies himself semantically because he has forgotten what he was talking about: the Mystery of the Creator, the Fire-hurling Triune One, is the mystery of the phallic trident and of fatherhood. Yes, moral law is paternal and male, and the super-ego primarily a male introject; we must bow down and submit ourselves—but within limits, please—to the Paternal, the Spiritual, and the Divine and open the moral ear and heart to the entrance of His Spirit. But we must have a little energy left over to enjoy the material world—defined as the female, the flesh, or however you like. Greek Platonism and the Hebraic patriarchal tradition alike mistakenly over-value the male principle. It is fine up to a point to be well-pleased with one's own manhood and self. But the Not-Self—the female or the real world, if you like—is really by no means so nasty as the animistic tradition would claim, nor yet so dangerous. And Eros isn't a bad chap either. We suspect that the metaphysical "solutions" to our common familial problems have been occasionally formulated (as is to be expected) by those to whom it was most an insoluble problem. Adolescents of later generations have repeatedly chewed on the regurgitated cud of philosophy's undigested "problems": but meanwhile linguistics, biology, and the other sciences have pretty clear ideas about them all. And the scientist, happy in his work, doesn't feel metaphysical tonight; he guesses he'll have a simple Dagwood sandwich and a glass of milk and go on to bed.

For these, one submits, are not really the Facts of Life, even with respect to the microcosm. The origin of the individual is *not* from the union of the substanceless male logos-soul with the attributeless pure substance of the female void. The spermatozoön and its chromosomes are every whit as material as the maternal egg; and the egg and its chromosomes show quite as much formal Gestalt and organization as does the sperm. As embryological theory concerning what actually happens in family-generation, philosophical animism is simply not so. Childhood theories about sex misapprehend the facts: animism, as knowledge of the total facts of life, belongs to the scientific childhood of man. Unless we are confusedly motivated to cling to these childish untruths, we ought to be able to give them up for the clearer vision of intellectual maturity. But animistic thinking remains seductive because it is a comfortable regression to the historic and the individual past.

What is untrue of the microcosm (the supposed history of which gave the pattern for the larger metaphysical paradigm) is certainly less true projectively of the Macrocosm. Indeed, the Macrocosm does not necessarily projectively parallel in its structures the structures of the microcosm. As man is not a mixture of paternal phlogiston and maternal mud, so, too, the Sky is not his father. "Sky" (as troposphere and ionosphere, and their respective meteorological phenomena) has more to do with adiabatic lapse rate than with Jupiter Pluvius. And "sky" (as the solar system and the galactic universe) is not really the charming if reprehensible personages of Greek myth.

With respect to the rest of the natural world we have the same confirmed doubts. A lion, for example, is not the result of the impingement of ideal *Lion* upon a certain amount of Nothing, descending like a ghostly mold on a gob of metaphysical butter, or like a spirit insinuating itself into a lion-size quantum of pure Quantity. Not quite. It is a little more complicated. But linguistic science will tell us, if we want to know:

"Lion" is merely a symbolic tag—a Gestalt of intricate and arbitrary neuro-muscular disciplinings of some human larynxes, mouths, and noses. These are associated, arbitrarily again, with semantic contexts through arduously learned conditioned reflexes in human beings.

299

In another sense, "lion" is a disturbance of the mixed gases of the troposphere by an anthropoid organism—a vocal and auditory event built up of our habitual phonemes, arbitrary in English too but long since agreed upon (save for unreconstructed regionalisms) by the unwitting, unassembled witenagemots of our cultural ancestors.

Or, alternatively, "lion" is, as written word, a visual stimulus and response, based on an assemblage of phonetic symbols (owed to the Aramaeans) and impressed in black on thin slivers of felted cellulose (a Chinese invention). In either spoken or written form "lion" must behave in context in obedience to ultimately Indo-European grammatical habits—a set of curious traditional customs employed when people in this society concertedly choose to pay selective attention to the specifically leonine aspects of their total zoölogical environment.

Otherwise, as a phenomenal event, a lion is a furry, clawed, carnivorous quadruped, with an embryological history not so unlike our own—though phyletically it is hardly even a "speaking cousin," being quite as distant a mammalian connection as are pigs, or dogs, or cows.

There you have it! And for the rest, lions give no evidence whatever of appealing to a Noumenal Lion for their existence.

The *logos*, seed of the metaphysics of all Christendom, is merely the linguistic *word*. Plato unwittingly discovered (via Greek) that Indo-European languages are in part noun-languages structurally. His system, incidentally, never got very far in medieval Arabic scholarship, since Semitic languages like Arabic have "triliteral roots"—three consonants with a variable vowel filling—that do not remain respectable nouns but slide around into all manner of parts of speech: now noun, now verb, and now adjective. Platonism simply doesn't make sense in terms of Arabic grammar. Thus what pretends to be metaphysics is literally only bad grammar.

As Socrates was an unwitting ethnographer when he sought truth in the minds of men by questioning his fellow-Greeks, so Plato was merely an unwitting and not really very good linguist. The fatal mistake came from not correctly locating human ego-boundaries and mistaking "inside" language for "outside" fact. In the Eskimo language, in which the protean word is exploded by qualifying affixes into a whole sentence, grammatical habit obviously would automatically reject Platonism as preposterous—though, incidentally, Eskimo is grammatically well fitted in some ways for dealing with the world as modern atomic physics sees it. Nor is there much prospect of philosophical indoctrination with Platonism of the American Indians who speak polysynthetic languages.

It is to be expected that Socrates' unwitting Greek ethnography and Plato's unwitting Greek grammar were not (as it turned out) adequate techniques for gaining knowledge about the real objective world. The epistemological despair, arising from discovery of other peoples with other languages and cultures, was the famous Greek "loss of nerve," when the happy absolutes of rationalistic Hellenism collapsed into Hellenistic relativism and mysticism. For ethnography and linguistics tell us nothing about the physical world. But when traditional speculative philosophy deals only with Indo-European words, it can at best expect to discover the Indo-European parts of speech—though Platonists are not even aware they have done that!

But before we too comfortably congratulate ourselves on our semantic sophistication, it is well to look at Aristotle too—the father of Western science as Plato is the father of Western philosophy. For Aristotelian Substance and Attribute look remarkably like Indo-European nouns and predicate adjectives. Still, history has made the choice: Aristotle did not have the linguistic gift of Plato, but he was certainly more disposed to look about him in the real world, and therein lies the difference. Meanwhile, more modern science may well raise the question whether Kant's Forms, or twin "spectacles" of Time and Space (without which we can perceive nothing) are not on the one hand mere Indo-European verbal tense, and on the other hand human stereoscopy and kinaesthesis and life-process—which might be more economically expressed in terms of the c, or light-constant, of Einstein's formula. But we must remember all the time that $E = mc^2$ is also only a grammatical conception of reality in terms of Indo-European morphological categories of speech. A Hopi, Chinese, or Eskimo Einstein might discover via his grammatical habits wholly different mathematical conceptualizations with which to apperceive reality. And meanwhile let us pay heed to our eldest scientific brothers and shrewdest symbolists, the mathematicians. They know that if you can say a thing, it isn't true; and if it is true, then you can't say it.

The animistic hypothesis of the "soul" is, then, in all its forms, a tender-minded misapprehension of the nature of human nature, of life, and of reality. And it is tainted with some of the historical sicknesses of Greek society and culture, through which the tradition has come to us. For just as the individual neurotic still clings to the false beliefs and symbol-identifications of his past that contradict his present experience, so too do societies of men hold to the out-moded beliefs of the past—which are more profoundly and inextricably entrenched in time, more comfortably integrated with the rest of the culture, and long since skilfully flavored for the emotional appetites of men— when other and better explanations are long since available. It is one thing to try to understand why sensible men believed as they did in the past; but it is another thing to make a cult of their beliefs. And science is not the hand-maiden of philosophy: philosophy waits or should wait on science. You can't keep pouring new wine into old bottles all the time. Once in a while you need new bottles.

For all its alterations and retailoring, the soul-hypothesis is nevertheless a garment ill fitting modern man. As physics, metaphysical animism is a poor explanation of the nature of things and of such energies as heat and light. As a statement of the facts of life, it is bad embryology. And as an explanation of the nature of life and death, it is bad biology. As a religion, it is a useless narcissistic protest against the fact (and the probable blessing) of metazoan death. In dealing with mind, memory, volition, and dreams, animism is a poor approximation of a useful psychology. As a comprehension of man's possession of hands, brains, culture, language, the family, and human interindividuality, it is a wholly inadequate anthropology. Psychiatrically it expresses the inveterate homoerotism of the Greek tradition in philosophy. And as philosophy, it is certainly very bad grammar.

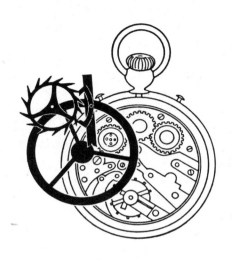

15. Three Minutes to Midnight

In Mexico there is a curious amphibian called the *axolotl,* which never goes through the normal amphibian metamorphosis, or change from water-born to land-living animal. It keeps its gills throughout life and even breeds in this larval state. A four-legged animal with a tail—but no fur, and obviously not a mammal—it looks more like a monstrous tadpole about to emerge from the water than anything else. When scientists discovered the axolotl, they thought for some time that it was a kind of "missing link" between fish and amphibians, which had not quite made it yet to the land. Comparative studies, however, now show clearly that several species of these axolotl-like creatures remain in a prolonged and sometimes even permanent stage of immaturity, much like the "mud puppy" or "water dog" found in rivers of the United States. The axolotls and their kin are simply a kind of salamander that never grew up. Indeed, appropriately, the axolotl even retains unchanged its ancient Aztec name!

Axolotls illustrate the principle in biology called *neoteny,* or "remaining young." Neoteny is an interesting curiosity found from time to time in a number of different animal groups. However, when we look back now over the odd and unique biology of man, it is clear that the process of neoteny is peculiarly significant in the case of *Homo sapiens*. For man "remains young" in a variety of ways. In general, of course, all the primates have stayed relatively unspecialized physically, in comparison with other mammalian groups. But we mean "neoteny" in a number of exact and specific senses in the case of man: his "fetalization" as a species; his differential "paedomorphy" racially; and, indeed, his "infantilization" both socially and individually on some occasions. Let us review and summarize these in turn.

As a species, all human beings in some respects retain for a long time or keep permanently throughout life certain features characteristic of fetal apes: the bulging brain and its continued post-natal growth in humans, the late-closing skull sutures, the retention of the ape baby's small jaws and feeble supra-orbital ridges, the retention of relative bodily hairlessness, and the like. This accounts for many of the major human traits that differ from those of adult apes; it is the basic human neoteny. This process, I believe, is related to the increasing cohesion of adults and young in the characteristic anthropoid family, which in man reaches a climax in the semi-permanent human family, a biological symbiosis that in fact leaves its physical mark on all members of the family. Since the family is universal in humans, and since mankind is a single inter-breeding species, these traits of "fetalization" are therefore universal in all groups of mankind.

Racially, groups smaller than the sum total of mankind further specialize to varying degrees in remaining physically infantile in some trait or other: the Mongoloid "button nose" and epicanthic eye-fold, Nordic light eyes and hair and skins, and the like. Man's physical "paedomorphy," seen in these breed differences among races, thus involves additional neoteny of traits. These I believe to be products of man's self-domestication, primarily; possibly other factors operate, or have operated, in the formation of races, but domestication is certainly one of these factors.

Similarly, "infantilization"—the extravagantly prolonged period of human dependency—is a still further kind of neoteny: one that is at the root of our peculiarly human nature. It means that matured animal instincts are replaced in man by learning and socialization. Animal adaptations ordinarily become genetic traits or hereditary instincts; but the human adaptation is culture. Through dependence upon other members of his kind, the individual accepts "adaptations" that have been shaped by his society, and these adaptations have a merely social heredity. The human being is the only animal that has a child-hood in the true sense. This prolonged biological dependency, first of all, shapes the innate inter-dependency which is characteristic of the human animal, and does it in several ways. As mammals, human infants depend extraordinarily on the mother, whether inside or outside her body; but they also, unlike other mammals, depend on the human father in a new familial and socializing sense to an extraordinary degree.

At one time in the past, moreover, as primates and as proto-hominids, members of the family depended on one another symbiotically to make human beings, viz., the physically differentiated and exaggerated human maleness, femaleness, and infantilism. Further, such inter-individual dependency is normal for whole societies of human beings. People in society invariably have languages and cultures; and both language and culture are non-existent and meaningless outside the biological framework of man's social organization. There is a real possibility, too, that whole races may in the last analysis depend on one another genetically for the ultimate survival of a polytypical species. Quite probably, the incest-taboo which is universal in the human family, and which enforces out-breeding, has been a factor in this polytypicality; for if sons were not forced to go afield for their women, then mankind might have undergone radial evolution into many separate species. The incest-taboo in the human family has doubtless also been a factor in the further shaping and diffusion of culture, as it surely has been of language. For, historically and ethnologically, it is not unreasonable to state that human societies have further profited from interdependent borrowing of one another's social heredity. Indeed, a full moral awareness of the contingent nature of culture might enhance this useful process to a much greater degree.

Even in the further individual sense, human dependency is significant. For it is misgrowths in emotional learning during dependent childhood that make for human neuroses and functional psychoses. The schizophrenic suffers emotional neoteny; for schizophrenics remain "fixated" at emotionally infantile levels that most individuals successfully pass through on the way to maturity. The social dependence of schizophrenics is likewise obvious in societies with mental hospitals and, perhaps, even in all societies. Mental hospitals (or even human societies at large) are in a sense protective environments in which there develop new and extreme intellectual domestication experiments and symbolisms. Of course the survival rate of schizophrenics is somewhat less than that of normal people; but societies do preserve alive many individuals who, unprotected, would otherwise not survive in a "wild" state, because of their poor adaptation to physical reality.

Similarly, it is the emotional dependency of people on one another, in the face of common unsolved problems and common anxieties, that makes for the intellectual infantilizations we call superstitions. Whole groups of people can retain a belief in animism, which represents a world-view archaic both in human history and in the individual life-history. A surprisingly large part of every culture is merely the phatic sharing of common emotional burdens, and has no relevance at all to the outside world. Thus societies themselves make up a mutually protective "environment" for the individuals constituting them.

This of course could hardly be indefinitely the case, for societies can survive (at least for a time) only if the culture embodies in addition a sufficient number of real technological adaptations to the real world, in competition with other contemporary societies. We have mentioned the obvious social neoteny of the schizophrenic; it is perhaps not so obvious that all the real technological triumphs of scientists at large provide a wide social and economic margin for the moral and intellectual neoteny of perhaps the greater mass of other individuals within the society. For just as the body of an idiot girl, relying on the past genetic triumphs of the species, can with clever chemistry produce a normal baby—so, too, idiot boys, relying similarly on the technological achievements of the society, can and do drive intricate motorcars they have not and could not have made with their own minds and hands.

But more than this, within the protections of the larger "family"—society—many individuals can with apparent impunity remain essentially infants forever, intellectually. The mill-hand can safely and easily hold notions that are ultimately contrary to the Second Law of Thermodynamics; the bishop can believe in spirits as much as he likes. It is not necessary for the poet to understand the symbolism of $E = mc^2$—for inter-dependent sub-cultures within a civilization contribute variously to one another like individual cells in a metazoan animal. And the scientist's sub-culture is only one among these, human intelligence being, as we have seen, primarily in the service of societies and not of individuals. But if we are to suppose that reality-assessing intelligence is a normal moral estate of the adult man, then we must surely admit that, like axolotls, many human beings never metamorphose into full moral manhood.

The individual metazoan animal among humans, whether an intellectual or not, we may still protect and cherish. For there are many kinds of "culture heroes" and the scientist is only one among them. Indeed, we must somehow provide the highest possible order of freedom, if the individual is (as we believe) the ultimate source of all our cultural speciations. But *blind* symbolic human ideation does seem so wasteful! Possibly the *kinds* of culture heroes a society has may have something to do with differential survival of that society among others; but for all our cherishing of the individual, reality may attend only to a hyper-metazoan unit for survival, the society. Biologically, the individual metazoan is merely a local organic environment for a fragment of the germ plasm of his species. His life means as little or as much to the society as does the death of a cell to an organism. His social value is purely a question of his individual gerontomorphic intellectual and moral growth. But the ultimate criterion is a *social* one. We must therefore, in the present chapter, examine some of the further consequences of intellectual and moral paedomorphy in human beings, both within societies and among societies, this time in the specifically social and political senses.

Societies have done much to refashion the old mammalian bull into human male *persons* going about their common tribal business of being human. But the largely unresolved problem is that of the impingement of tribe upon tribe. As every tribe has achieved within itself the means of forging its own hyper-metazoan bonds in social heredity, so too do societies themselves need to achieve a still larger human integration. Such integration would provide a learning of one society from another by means of an intelligently selective cultural diffusion, a kind of inter-cultural exchange of social heredity—indeed, it is only the predicament of tribalism against traditional tribalism that has historically given rise to science itself as a new conflict-resolving and reality-testing technique. If this learning from other cultures is a worth-while goal (and it obviously has been, historically), then to obtain it we should seek the highest possible order of freedom for variation among cultures, an idea which to many men of good will seems to mean the world-elimination of war. These men say with some cogency, that our maximum conceptual in-group must sometime include, socially and culturally, the whole species *Homo sapiens*—as has already been the case biologically for perhaps a million years or more.

Concerning war as an international process in the human species we have tried to maintain a respectful tentativeness which is commensurate with our real ignorance of its possible biological meaning for man's moral future. Here, as always, we must attempt to discriminate human wish from biological fact. But perhaps some biological considerations that are available may help us to narrow down the problem. The disposition to war or to peace in human societies seems to be a matter of the economic, political, social, and psychological structurings of the society itself. Thus human inter-societal war may not be the biologically inevitable matter that intra-species wars are for some of the social insects like harvester ants.

In ants, for example, the "soldiers" are the non-reproducing offspring of a single breeding queen, who also reproduces all the other ant castes. The life or death of the individual ant-soldier is therefore reproductively meaningless, except as it secures the survival of the rest of the nest-organism, most especially of the queen. Conceivably a given queen might obtain a better chance of surviving by a greater production of soldiers, even though most or all of the individual soldiers were killed. But since ant-soldiers must be fed, in some cases by the labor of other ant castes, there is evidently an "economic" limit to ant militarism.

In human beings, however, there is no such queenly monopoly on reproduction, since human soldiers may also reproduce and their life or death have genetic significance. Further, the "altruism" of soldier-ants is no more than the "altruism" of any specialized cell in a metazoan organism, so far as reproduction is concerned—viz., no altruism at all. The moral altruism of human soldiers, however, is a more complex affair, and more fraught with genetic meaning. On the one hand, this altruism appears to be part of the adult male's sexual dimorphism, which is protective of females and young—a specialization, so to speak, in the incipient meta-organism, the family. On the other hand, it is significant that functional "infants" make the best infantry: unmarried, late-adolescent males with no great stake in functional adulthood. Such youths are also closer to the habits of parent-dominated obedience and have a sufficient residue of oedipal aggression to be displaced, channelized, and exploited for the larger society's ends—the ends of older post-mature males as much as those of females and young.

The "altruistic instinct" given the soldier-ant in his caste-structured body is thus useful to the whole ant-nest meta-organism, of which the queen is the only reproductively significant group of cells, even though these instincts shorten the life and the functioning of individual soldier-ants. That such soldierly altruism in humans may be similarly useful to the whole society usually goes unquestioned. But it is necessary to indicate that in the human species this is not based on instinct, but on conditioning and on social neoteny. And as this has genetic consequences, we may question the desirability of holding a large number of individuals in the semi-permanent immaturity of military life. The loss of genes to the home society may be counter-balanced in the long run by the gift of genes to the quondam enemy society, so mankind at large has suffered none at all in the encounter. But the major evil of such military neoteny, if massive and consistent, is the psychological one done to the individual: it is much of a piece with the other moral infantilisms that adult humans sometimes force upon their young and against which we have for good reason protested. In the technical sense of man's humanity, militarism may in fact be anti-human.

Thus, unless we altered entirely our mode of reproduction, which seems hardly possible or even desirable, there seems little chance that any society could make warlike activities instinctual, even if it chose. The specific manhood of men prevents this. Furthermore, if the instincts of some human beings were specifically bellicose, then the higher self-selection of such individuals for death in war (while those less endowed with the instinct stayed at home and reproduced) would tend in time to rid the society of such a putative "bellicose instinct" in its members. The fact is, however, that warlike behavior is not immediately instinctual but oedipally conditioned. And whatever is thus humanly conditioned into social groups can therefore be conditioned out of them.

There remains, however, the possibility that war is the last area in which natural selection operates upon humans: in the selection of which competing society is to survive, as measured in physical power and psychological morale. Who can say whether this is so? But even if it is, this blind natural process may operate only so long as man permits it to operate, through his passivity and his ignorance. Man by self-domestication, has already removed his physical traits from the immediate operation of natural selection. It is an open question whether he is actually free to choose to remove his social heredity from such natural selection in war, and to manipulate it himself in what he may regard as a more satisfactory and efficient manner. Again we ask, out of ignorance of our moral future, who can say? But if human males can form successful multi-individual in-groups like families and like societies, why then can they not successfully form still larger in-groups? It would be tender-minded to assert, before the event, that man can do so. But it is only tough-minded to try.

To arrive at this cultural communication among societies is evidently a political task. Now, the inveterate political error of the past is the concept of forced empire. It might for want of a better term be called "the Roman idea," except that it is far older and far more re cent than Rome. This is the attempt to diffuse a tribalism by means of political, economic, or military force. Earlier, Alexander too had dreamed the splendid dream of a single united mankind. But uncriticized tribalism, even if it is Greek, is inadequate as a knowledge-technique—as the Socratic method of self-ethnography shows us, or the unwitting Platonic grammar—so what is the ultimate value of forcing its spread? Like the Australian Bushmen with the cult *churinga* or bull-roarer, tribalists gather gravely round, each group admiring its own tribal Dingus, but with insufficient wit to look to other societies for an aping of this cultural gesture, the understanding of which would help all men to see the common culture-predicament of all men everywhere.

The federation of neighboring towns and villages around the nucleus of early Rome was a sound political procedure. For it was made on the basis of self-choice and was founded on many common cultural agreements. This larger political unit, we can have no doubt from subsequent history, was certainly competitively superior to the usual autonomous and separate city-states of the Greeks. Indeed, it was not the least among the excellences of the Athenians that they did temporarily manage to unite peacefully all the towns of Attica into a single polity. For with it the Athenians successfully led the defensive league of other Greek city-states against two onslaughts of the powerful and autocratic Persian Empire.

In the first of these, the Athenians largely by themselves, aided only by a thousand men from Plataea, won the battle against Darius at Marathon in 490 B.C. And in the second, against Xerxes in 480 B.C., after the brave episode of Thermopylae, their famous city sacked and burned and all Attica over-run and abandoned, the Athenians fought their way, with some grudging Corinthian and Spartan aid and with a citizen-bought navy, back from an island retreat to the shattering naval victory at Salamis. We must believe from this that a federation of even imperfect democracies is superior in morale, and indeed in ultimate power, to even the most powerful of autocracies.

For the Greek naval strategy at Salamis was based almost solely on morale. The Greeks had only *aretē*, manliness and decision, on their side. But it conquered Persian *hubris*, the over-weening arrogance and fatal pride in great power. And after these events, with understandably secure morale, the Athenians went back to the ruins of their city to create in the next decades the most civilized society of men that has ever existed. They built the Parthenon, only a modest two hundred and twenty feet long, but the most subtle and intellectual edifice ever made by man. And among them arose the great tragic poets, whose dramas remain the most profound ever written.

Perhaps the spread of Athenian culture and the largely voluntary joining of other city-states into the Athenian League might have seemed in time to provide a solid basis for Greek federation. Once before, Spartan militarism, based on an enslaved helot population with which the Aryan conquerors never mixed their blood, had tried unification by conquest, failed, and remained a second-rate garrison state for the rest of its existence—and was later to destroy Greek genius in the Peloponnesian civil wars. All hope of any ultimate federation was dashed by the *hubris* of a deified man, by the purely military conquests of Alexander the Macedonian, by force, beyond the limits of diffused Greek culture (far off in Mesoptamia, in northwest India, and on the Danube), and following the old and faulty pattern of countless imperial despotisms in Asia Minor before him. And when, after 390 B.C., Rome took arms against successive Latin cities to force "federation" upon them, the Romans made the same mistake as Alexander's in human political technique. As conquest extended farther and farther beyond the area of Mediterranean cultural similarity, the political empire of Rome became more and more jerry-built. For federation and empire are two mutually opposed ideas.

Successful and permanent diffusion of political structure, as history seems to indicate, is not best accomplished in this manner by the use of military force. This is not to suppose that Romanism was not contingently a great success, or that classical civilization did not in fact become diffused under Roman law. (Ironically, the same Rome that early successfully overthrew the Tarquinian tyrants, in the process of autocratic conquest was in time ruled by its own deified Emperors.) But the sound political nucleus of early Rome was founded on prior and already consolidated cultural and economic contacts. Given time, numerous technical superiorities in Mediterranean culture might well of themselves have recruited Celtic and Germanic peoples into its orbit. In fact, with the later spread of Roman culture, it was human contacts that accomplished this, and militarism was only its accidental vehicle. This later diffusion occurred, in the main, because Roman soldiers and administrators often settled permanently in the border regions of their long-time service; and such diffusion ceased when border troops were increasingly recruited in the later Empire from barbarian tribes as mercenaries, an arrangement which in time was scarcely to be distinguished from Roman tribute to barbarians. *Limen* then became *limes:* the open "threshold" of spreading Roman culture then became its outermost fixed "line of defense." In time, Roman morale, degraded by militarism and the imperial state, was not even able to defend this.

True, militarism was the historic vehicle. But Phoenician mercantilism since ancient times in the Mediterranean had been doing the same job of cultural diffusion and doing it perhaps better; a good case might even be made that it was upon these achieved cultural unities that later political structures were built. For Phoenician influence in early mainland and island Greece, as well as in Etruscan Italy, North Africa, and even Spain, was considerable and deep. The Minoan sea traders of Crete, who were conceivably Phoenician as well, first brought Asia's culture massively to southern Europe, just as trade had probably first brought it to central Danubian Europe. Athens was in fact an amalgam (which Sparta was not) of the culture of the pre-Greek Mycenaeans with that of the invading Indo-European Greeks. This is forcibly shown in the fact that Athena herself is not an Indo-European but a pre-Greek goddess; nor is Hera of Argos, later wife of Zeus, Greek in origin either. And both the *Iliad* and the *Odyssey* are legends of pre-Greek maritime peoples, probably Mycenaean-Minoan, and possibly of Punic or Phoenician inspiration ultimately: the successive razings of Troy were not all due to one Helen, but to the repeated mercantile attempt to penetrate into the Black Sea region and gain access to the Danubian trade route into central Europe.

Thus both Greek and Roman culture were to an extent founded on prior cultural diffusions, part of them mercantile in origin; and the most civilized of the Greeks, the Athenians, were those who blended themselves relatively peacefully with the original natives of the land, and not the Spartans, who spent their energies in trying permanently to subdue them. To be sound and lasting, culture patterns must first seduce the belief of new communicants. This is no simple matter, since every culture is a resistant and emotion-laden network of symbolisms. But it is questionable whether any autocratic or planned military imperialism has ever been successful, which might not have been equally or far more successful through diffusion and non-military modes of acculturation. For war polarizes cultural differences, mobilizes resistances, and emotionally impedes diffusion by its very nature, whereas peaceful diffusion through trade and other contacts has no such problems.

Indeed, culture areas are characteristically larger than stable political areas. For example, the influence of Indic Buddhism and Hinduism (both in mainland Tibet, inner Asia, China, and Japan, and in island Indonesia as far as Bali) spread far beyond the dominion of any unified political state (whether Hindu, Moghul, or British) or of any Hinduist island empire in Indonesia. Nor was the extraordinary spread of Buddhism due principally, or even importantly, to militarism at any point. Similarly, the culture of the Chinese, in inner Asia, in Japan, Indo-China, and Malaysia, has always spread farther than the Chinese imperial grasp. Likewise, the Roman Church has had a far greater domain and longevity than the Roman Empire. Indeed, the Church's present pre-eminence in Europe goes as far as the area of consolidated Roman cultural influence, and no farther. (In fact, all political empires of conquest that have been erected upon the base of the Church itself have everywhere failed in the subsequent history of Europe, though the Church is the ghost of a state forever seeking resurrection.) And in the eye of anthropological history it may yet be that the influence of GI chewing gum, Singer sewing machines, the kerosene can, Coca-Cola, and the Hollywood movie will far outweigh all the Clives and Napoleons and Moltkes of military history.

The "idea of Rome," of cultural absolutism and forced diffusion, always ultimately over-reaches itself and achieves its own destruction: the Hellenic becomes the Hellenistic world, and the Church conquers Constantine. This is because such military imperialism characteristically lacks an appreciation of the contingent nature of any culture, and of the areas of inexpugnable autonomy of human beings, alone or in groups. No state or empire can long operate without the cultural consent and acquiescence of its communicants. As Hume was one of the first to point out, no state—whatever its own theory of power—has ever in actual fact long existed without the ultimate consent of the individuals composing the society. Even the "divine right of kings" operates as a political fiction only so long as the governed believe in the divine right of kings. The natural democracy of human societies is always present, even if it is hidden from men's eyes, and even when subverted in autocracy.

This latter fact is forcibly demonstrated even in the historic strongholds of Asiatic absolutism. Through all the procession of autocratic empires, whether rajahdoms or sultanates, on the village level the ancient Indian *panchayat* or "council of five" has continued to operate to the present day; essential political power remains locally in the village, and the empire is mainly an alien taxing body. In China, indeed, the inward orientation of the local clan-ruled village has always weakened Chinese political nationalism; and once again in Asia this empire was chiefly an external bureaucracy. With far greater centralization of the state in Japan than in China, political power in the ordering of men's daily lives still remains potently and significantly on the Japanese village level. In fact, modern scholarship repeatedly discovers traces of local democracy even in the area of the most intense absolutisms of ancient Mesopotamia.

Still clearer is the historical evidence, from ancient Asiatic times to the present, that any federation of states depends for its effectiveness and continuity upon a continuously contrived consent and upon the painstaking discovery of areas of consensus among constituent states. Federation is the antithesis of Caesarism and Napoleonism, of Hitlerism and Stalinism alike. The process of larger federation is best facilitated by seeking the greatest possible cultural inter-communication, economic inter-dependence, and culturally shared values. It is possible that military imperialism in the service of tribalism, therefore, is even more pernicious than it is useless. Since the real conquests are the conquests of ideas, and the real revolutions the cultural ones, war not merely fails of its own aim but also in this view impedes the movement of ideas and the bridging of cultural differences by communication and diffusion—and this is war's further and greater crime. But precisely because of the greater range and effectiveness of economic and cultural communication in modern times, autocratic upstart imperialisms have had a harder and harder time to establish themselves in the last five hundred years of European history; likewise, our understanding of current European cultural history is that Russian culture is evidently failing of diffusion in the long run, because the resistance based on prior cultural commitments of subject peoples has been underestimated in strength. And meanwhile the grasp of Soviet political imperialism (as in every such case in history) is far feebler than its ambitions, precisely because it is a conquest state.

I think, therefore, that in contemporary times men are in danger of mistaking their real problem, which is political rather than economic. The content of controversy is not quite so important as is the process, either in science or in politics. At best the problem of preference for one economic myth over another—"Capitalism" versus "Communism," for example—is only a tactical one; the strategic problem is that of the political structure within which inevitable economic changes will occur and be directed. The relationships and communications of people, in other words, are more important than their separate beliefs; for the former control the latter. In this sense, the oedipal problem of power today transcends any problem of economic dependency-needs. Of the two major human jobs—getting a living and getting along with others—the second is now far more critical. For the problem of technological production is amply solved, or at least we have the knowledge to go about solving future technical problems of production. The modern problem in technically advanced states is that of distribution and consumption, which are social and, I believe, ultimately political problems.

Scientific technology produces more goods in America than our present economy can successfully distribute. This is as true of industry as it is of agriculture. The machinery of competitive selling and advertising is forced by surplus, not by scarcity; the consumer is limited in his buying power, not in his desire for consumption of goods!

Agriculture must be subsidized in a price-economy, and huge unused surpluses pile up beyond the reach of consumers, or production must be controlled and surpluses destroyed; but subsidies are a way of taxing potential consumers in order to bail out presumptive over-producers. Meanwhile the subsidized goods must be withheld from the market, lest these publicly owned goods compete with those goods which the consumer must buy privately from producers. But the "surpluses" themselves are factitious except in terms of the implicit assumptions of a maximum-profit economy; for it is absurd to suppose that consumers, in America and in the rest of the world, would not willingly increase their consumption if a better distribution were possible under a different economic myth.

Therefore, since I believe that the human organism is probably at least as intelligent as other organisms, man will of necessity contrive new and better economic techniques of distribution. For the goods are there. It is only the economic misuse and manipulation of political power by some, and the ignorance of their own economic self-interest and political power by others, that permit the situation to continue. For is not the state properly the instrument of power of the whole society? The conservatives who pretend otherwise—that the state is the power-arm of a class—play directly into the hands of Marxists who proclaim this identical doctrine. And if the state belongs to the whole society, should it not use this power for its own social ends? Otherwise the anarchists are right in maintaining that the state is a categorical evil; and meanwhile the economic class that resists the social control of the state makes a strange bedfellow for anarchists. For if the state is not a "welfare state," then what else is it to be?

It is evident that traditional capitalism is historically obsolescent, simply because it is not good enough for our scientific technology. We are Koryaks who must somehow give up killing our dogs, if we are to survive. But witch-hunts and a search for scapegoats have never helped a society to solve its problems before, and probably will work no better now. There is no reason to attempt to punish those who would point out our predicament to us; nor, on the other hand, is there much sense in a "dictatorship of the proletariat," since this attempts to punish still other people as having been guilty of history-by-plot. This is scapegoat thinking too; we are all "guilty" of cultural belief, for that matter. Besides, the capitalist is as well-meaning, and as confused, as anybody else—that is, unless we persist in seeing him as an all-powerful oedipal ogre before whom both labor and consumer are totally helpless. And this is hardly the case in a democracy.

While capitalism does not deserve credit for the triumphs of technology in any simple sense, for all its present defects there is no doubt that historically it has managed a better distribution of goods than earlier economic systems, and has been by chance or otherwise closely associated with the scientific technology which can produce abundance. But it is more important to notice that free enterprise, in economics as in science, owes much to the accompanying political technique, democracy. The democratic method has some real consistencies with the scientific temper and is the method which alone seems capable of modifying our economic system soundly and securely. And thus it appears again that our current problems are political and social, not technological or, in the broad sense, economic.

Revolution has point and substance only when men appear to be faced by an immovable tyranny. This is certainly not the situation in the Atlantic world; it is far more the case in the revolutionary Russian state itself. Given the complex of capitalist economics, scientific techniques, and political democracy, which have historically been intertwined throughout their development, can one part be ruthlessly and summarily removed? Very likely not, and random violence may destroy what we wish to preserve. The culture traits of any human society are far too closely integrated functionally for such surgery to be either safe or successful. This is another argument against revolution as a political process, and in favor of the democratic method already at hand. Why trust a Soviet absolutism —a political technique proved inadequate over and over again in history? What is the alleged advantage in a change of "class dictators"?—which, in itself, is a failure in class communication, a genuine breakdown in "civilization" technically defined, at which we are not prepared to say the democratic method has failed. Is there any discernible "fading away" of the State in Russia, when a powerful oligarchy exploits economic myth for clear political purposes? Is this group itself under any illusions about its aim: sheer political power, enforced by any terrorism it can command?

But absolutists, both in Europe and in America, whether of the right or of the left, would seize political power precisely for the purpose of "freezing" the situation, thus preventing our orderly search for social and economic change. Hence we cannot trust our own home-grown absolutists, who promise us salvation if only we will submit to the dictatorship of their version of purified tribalism. If a Senator has successively tried to usurp the functions of the Presidency, the State Department, the Department of Justice, the United States Army, the FBI, and the Attorney-Generalship, are not such acts plainly subversive of the form of government which they tend to destroy? And since mccarthyism is also terroristic, dictatorial, and absolutist, there is little accuracy in calling it "anti-Communist," when it is in fact anti-democratic and identical in tactics with Communism.

On what can be considered good grounds in anthropology, human biology, and psychology, most of us believe that democracy is the natural political relationship of adult human beings. And on what can be considered good cultural and historical grounds, we believe, quite simply and correctly, that we—the people of the United States and the Atlantic world—are already in charge of our own political and social destiny. There is no mysterious omnipotent "they," paranoid complotters against our political and social destiny. No, our enemies are perfectly identifiable: absolutists, of whatever kind. At worst, it is only observable that those in a minority do not agree with a perfectly identifiable majority of the people. And meanwhile, if anyone feels persecuted enough, he can always run for Mayor—or even Senator.

Since democracy as a process was unknown to Marx, it is evident that he was still confused about the oedipal problem of power that Western democracies have in fact already largely solved. When the son achieves successful phatic communication and identification with the father, he can become a man himself, and as powerful as the father. There is then no need to replace the supposed dictatorship of the oppressor with an omnipotent dictatorship of the oppressed. If the son fails in his identification with the father, his failure is his psychiatric immaturity. A man can never be socially or psychiatrically ill, in the measure to which he achieves an adult use of his powers among his peers and in the measure to which he takes both the burdens and the blessings of his shared culture—for such is the nature of mental illness and of culture. It is only by virtue of having been (and remaining!) children that people can be mentally or socially ill.

But man is politically an axolotl at times. Like axolotls, many humans never metamorphose into moral manhood; if they cannot take the step from moral dependency onto the dry land of political maturity, democracy, then they are in an infantile predicament indeed. For dependency will always find a political father to exploit it, as the history of absolutism sufficiently shows. And if a man does not become his own small part in the state, then the state must always seem to him an omnipotent external power. I think that something like this happened in the case of the state-worshiper Hegel and his philosophical heir, the state-hater Marx—both of whose world-views were essentially shaped by the Prussian absolutist state.

It is therefore possible to be critical of the Hegelian metaphysical system. One hesitates a little before suggesting that the philosopher Hegel did not know what he was talking about; and yet this is literally and embarrassingly the case. Hegel supposed that he was talking about the facts of history; but without knowing it, unfortunately, he was really talking about "the facts of life." Indeed, we can trace his historical origins in German Romanticism, which borrowed directly from Hindu metaphysical animism. Hegel's notion of the facts of life is that the male Self or "Thesis" breeds historically with the female Not-Self "Antithesis," which the Self has "posited" (like Sakti from Shiva's mind, or Eve from Adam's rib?). Whatever this hitherto unknown biological process of "positing" may be, Thesis and Antithesis together produce the saviour Synthesis. Now this is plainly just another metaphysical trinity, obviously but unwittingly borrowed from the holy trinity of the human family. It is a false extension of thinking from the microcosmic process of individual generation to the macrocosmic process of history. I seriously think that

Hegel was just one more characteristic example of a familiar figure: the speculative philosopher who did not sufficiently locate his subject-matter, who literally did not know what he was talking about, individual microcosm or social macrocosm, "inside" or "outside." As we speculate and generalize more and more in isolation from the events outside us, we regress more and more to our infantile ignorance of things and of differences. For History is not the same thing as a life-history.

Derivatively from Hegel, Marx takes several tacks in turn. To continue in a vein of disrespect, it must be said that at times he suggests the infantile "paranoid" pattern: the persecuted proletarian son must first murder and destroy the father, the exploitative bourgeoisie, in order that the son may sit in the seat of omnipotence as a "dictatorship of the proletariat." At other times Marx seems to deify History as the messiah who will bring about the new dispensation on earth. The demiurge History is fighting man's battles for him, a mystic "good father" as opposed to the "bad father" or exploitative classes. But when Marx does this, he is surely mistaking the Recording Angel of history for the Avenging Angel! For the obvious fact is that men make history happen—living men, as influenced by men of the past.

There is an influential school in American social science, "Culturology," that has found an alternative father to enthrone in the intellectual cosmos. The Culturologists' major premise concerns the omnipotence of Culture, which they believe shapes everything human—not only our beliefs but even the form and content of our protests against belief. Culture is all. Indeed, they state in so many words that the study of culture should proceed as if human beings had never existed, since apparently their humanity has nothing at all to do with their culture. This is a position with which a holistic view of the human animal obviously cannot agree.

Of course all students of man will acknowledge the powerful and often unwitting influence of culture on human beings But this seems to be throwing out the baby with the bath. The Culturologists are naturally quite critical of the "culture and personality" school, which sees the process as a kind of perpetual dialogue between the individual and his culture (which is merely the values of other individual human beings), and which insists upon examining the facts of individual life-history as a relevant part of the process (since all culture is individually learned from other individuals). But with their view, how can the Culturologists account for the origins of culture?—except as the product of human animal need and desire! And how can they account for the manifest facts of cultural change? —except as protest or bias based on individual life-history!

If our present analysis of human nature is at all correct, neither Culture nor man is omnipotent: the symbolic father is not omnipotent, nor is the son. Culture is the residue, as embodied in living men's behavior, of historically and socially ancestral men's wills. But the morally mature man has the *same* potencies in his consciously willed choices. Of course cultural institutions are powerful in the shaping of individual men. But the end and aim of maturity in individuals is to reduce such institutional "fathers" to their actual mere human stature; and science as an institutionalized activity is concerned precisely with this endless task of criticizing one traditional authority after another, fearlessly following new facts and one's own best judgment about them.

"Culture" never exists except in and of individuals in a society. All cultural influences are always ultimately the influence of individuals on other human individuals. As a falsely reified entity, Culture is only as "omnipotent" as a morally child-like bearer of the culture believes it (or the tribal ancestors) to be; and man is only as potent as his creative dealing with the objective world can prove him to be. The products of a technically adequate adjustment to reality constitute these many proofs of human potency; indeed, we would insist that the Culturologists are probably right in their evolutionism: there has in fact been a real increase in man's control of power, in the size of his social organisms, and in his technological adjustment to reality. But it is a real mystery, who makes the machines and the institutions, if it isn't our old friend *Homo sapiens*.

Paradoxically it was Durkheim, another source of the Culturologists, who so strongly maintained that culture is a *social* product: the religious or totemic or tribal cult is a kind of ritual celebration of the in-group's own "in-groupness." With this we can agree. Part of culture is shared attitude-stances that are merely autistic, in individuals who share the same pressure of unsolved problems. There is a group "will to believe." Any in-group is formed by a tacit sharing and forgiving of one's fellows' partial inadequacies and anxieties. But we must also agree with the cultural evolutionists that another part of any society's culture is shared technological triumphs. It is these protections, in fact, which technological triumph afford a group, that permit some of its members the indulgence of an infantilized and historically regressive clinging to the falsehoods of the sacred past. Society insulates them from reality and its teaching, as parents shield children. But paternalized institutions committed to the defense of an archaic folklore will inevitably infantilize their communicants, for mature intelligence must be surrendered as the price of emotional security. However, neither Synthesis, nor History, nor Culture, nor the Holy Family is going to take care of man. No one will save man but himself.

But why not accept some concept of cosmic fatherhood as a "harmless" symbol for the social organization of men? For many reasons: because we know as men that fathers are never omnipotent, omniscient, or omnibenevolent, but only as children think them so; because we also know and recognize the motherhood of women (who in some respects have more to teach men about love than they know as fathers and the sons of fathers) and hence no longer permit ourselves this exclusive male arrogance of belief that only men shape men; and because we have learned from history that the mystique of the autocratic father has always infantilized men politically, just as in arimistic religion it has always infantilized them morally.

The societies and the sects which follow the paternalized mystique are harmless only with respect to their small size, confusion, and impotence. It matters not their kind or rationale, but only their size. We see no difference in effect on men and on reality between the promulgation of Lysenkoism in Soviet biology by the Politburo and the promulgation by a holy hierarchy of the recently voted-in dogmatic truth of the Assumption. In both, authoritarian oligarchies are handing out canned and processed truths for the consumer, which he must buy on pain of excommunication. This is an artificial monopoly of truth and allows no free competition scientifically among various brands of ideas or better-tailored styles of thinking. We see no real difference in the torture and murder of men for the glory of God in the Holy Inquisition, or for the glory of the Aryan race and Der Führer in Germany, or for the glory of the proletarian state in Russia. If the Millennium were to come at 10:00 A.M. tomorrow, that still would not justify the sacrifice of one single human individual to procure this hoped-for miracle. And we are, with some evidence, historically suspicious of any institution which uses these as its necessary means.

Our grounds for this stand are those of the scientist. No one knows better than he the conditional nature of his beliefs and the elusiveness of truth. In his self-criticism he has to be constantly aware of the nature of his hypothetical statements about nature. No one is more anxious than he to preserve free commerce in ideas. Yesterday's hypothesis is never good enough to state today's new knowledge. He must be emotionally free from commitment to any merely traditional belief. He knows that cultural speciation comes from the individual successfully and freely communicating with his fellows. Scientists may form schools of thought, but these can never become cults because there is always some impolite maverick pointing to some new unassimilated fact.

We have suggested that in inter-society controversy the disposition to war or to peace is a function of the society's own internal structures. If this is true, then democracies enjoy a further advantage. The historian Tannenbaum has advanced the interesting thesis that American foreign policy is derived from our internal political comity, that of federation. The House of Representatives declares a respect for the numerical democracy of individual men; but if Americans have also repeatedly insisted on the right of self-determination of even the smallest nation, this is related to a respect for the equal sovereignty and representation of both Rhode Island and Texas in the Senate. Much of our foreign policy can be interpreted in this light: the Monroe Doctrine, the "Open Door" policy in China, the Philippines, and the like. Belgium, Poland, Abyssinia, and Korea are none of them large places on the map, yet we have fought wars when their sovereignty was impugned; that Poland, Czechoslovakia, and the eastern Baltic states are now "occupied" sticks in the back of our minds as somehow historically unfinished business.

In themselves, from the Revolution onward, Americans have shown *aretē*, which is both the source and the result of democracy. *Aretē* is a curious Greek word, difficult to translate. It means the inner virtue or essence or excellence of any thing. It is related to the name of Ares, god of War, and thus implies unsubduable courage and willingness to fight for a principle; but it does not mean simple street-corner belligerence. It connotes manliness, wholeness, integrity, purpose, moral clarity, decision, and self-responsibility. Perhaps our nearest word to it is simple "spunk"—which is sometimes lacking in our contemporary public life. Toward other nations our foreign policy has maintained, on the whole, the same respect for *aretē* and sovereign self-determination. But actual power and leadership must be disciplined in any federation like the United Nations, lest we ourselves fall into becoming an autocracy the like of which has been our historic enemy from the Revolution onward, and against which (mainly) we have fought our subsequent wars. We must avoid contamination by *hubris*—a sometimes arrogant pride in our great but limited power. Like all men, we need *aretē* and knowledge of our strengths, but without *hubris*, which is an ignorance of our limitations.

These words might well apply to the social scientist. As scientist he may state social facts; as citizen he must hold opinions that are in the last analysis moral. Both physical and social scientists are becoming increasingly aware that they have a moral if not a scientific responsibility to communicate more of their insights than they have done heretofore. For their scientific activities are not innocent of moral consequences. The scientist may never presume upon his role, and he should be quite candid and self-conscious about this on any occasion when he speaks merely as a moral citizen. Nevertheless, we believe that our present knowledge of man, of his history and his culture, enables us, without sacrificing either modesty or conviction, to attempt an expression of what we view as the implications of our knowledge, and expect to find some consensus in it.

We believe that a "world-culture" need not necessarily be entirely ours or anyone else's. Perhaps we need in cultural evolution the same variety of differentiation into species that we have seen in organic evolution. A world-culture need only transcend tribalism to become what may be technically called a "civilization"—that is, a federated group of co-existing, symbiotic, mutually adjusted, and inter-dependent sub-cultures. These need to share only a portion of their total of beliefs or culture traits: the conflicts between bishops and intellectuals, employees and entrepreneurs, businessmen and politicians, and the like, are often dramatic and acute; yet all these nevertheless permit and need each other's continued existence in one civilization. We have merely to agree on the usefulness of human variability. The uniformity and limited physical adaptiveness of a wild animal species is clearly poorer in its survival value than the vast safety of the complex strands of human heredity and the many racial traits of human domestication. Perhaps social heredity obeys the same realistic laws, ultimately, as does physical heredity. If so, then tribal insistence on individual conformity and group uniformity also contrasts greatly in survival value with the opportunities for sub-cultural variation permitted within a civilization.

International co-operation by no means demands a monolithic cultural uniformity all over the world. For it is highly doubtful that we know surely which is the best social, economic, or other cultural dispensation for human beings—notwithstanding the fact that each society alleges its monopoly of the best. Our insight into more "primitive" societies should teach us that possibly all cultures, *including our own,* are a mixture of wishful and of realistic responses to nature. Since cultural differences do in fact exist and science has grown out of them, we can believe that they are themselves valuable and necessary for the survival of the species. Thus we need to cultivate systematically the utmost tolerance of differences, both in individuals and in groups, forsaking the tribe-centered *hubris* of supposing that a human selection among them is possible when this selection is ultimately nature's, but still maintaining the *aretē* of making our own conscious moral choices. Very possibly there is no one "best" cultural geometry; the tribal absolutism of the Roman idea can be safely rejected.

Organic evolution seems to have proceeded on the basis of multiplicities and divergencies, and the development of human cultures and personalities may require this too. We need the best possible conditions to aid our search and our experimentation in cultural forms. Minorities must always be regarded as positively valuable and hence zealously to be protected. Would Europe ever have been Europe without that precious minority, the Jews? Other peoples have offered mankind their own tribal pasts; but who save the Jews have taught us to think in terms of the future, a future to be bought by man's own moral reform? Likewise, in the ancient world, Greek society was a pitiful minority, a mere handful of men by modern standards; but the Greeks taught men democracy.

The one battle every civilized society must fight is the continuous one against powerful emergent tribalisms. The democratic law of brothers must continually protect itself against another and still another new autocratic paternalism. The family is not the state; but the propensity to confuse the two is in a sense imbedded in our human nature, and waits ever to threaten us when we forget or do not use our strengths as mature men. Civilized men must somehow preserve their chastened awareness of the nature of their scientific and moral and cultural experimenting as a human process and a human responsibility; they must not slide backward, like moral amphibians, to blind dependency on ignorant and unsophisticated tribal absolutism and "right-thinking" or political authoritarianism.

Historically, any civilization is a cumulative borrowing from a long past and from many tribes and cultures. American civilization has perhaps enjoyed as much cultural borrowing as any yet known. But no thoughtful American could imagine for a minute a more dreadful thing than that the world should become in all cultural ways uniformly American. We are appalled at the complexity of our culture. But American culture is not complex enough. In the technical sense our civilization needs to become far more "civilized" in conceptual alternatives. For example, a majority of Americans, for good historical reasons, are aesthetic illiterates compared with almost any of the great oriental peoples. In our contriving of functional intricacies of form in social organization, most experts would agree that we lag far behind the complex cultures of the Guinea Coast of west Africa.

Even in our marked ability for social experimentation and cultural change, we are probably inferior to many Micronesian island peoples. And in subtleties of communication in inter-individual relationships, any cultivated Chinese could far out-do his occidental counterpart. The wider one's ethnographic knowledge spreads, the more he becomes aware that the many cultures in the world are a veritable treasure-trove of social heredity.

We know this best and most recently from the most valuable export that European tyrannies could have sent us, their scientists. In our frontier-nurtured worship of the practical, Americans have forgotten or have never sufficiently learned that there is nothing quite so practical as a theory. America is strong in technologists, in Edisons, Burbanks, and Fords. But where are our native Clerk Maxwells, our Mendels, and our Darwins? Meanwhile the worst epithet that we can hurl is that a position is "theoretical," forgetting that *it is the business of the scientist to be theoretical.* Have we so much appetite for fashionable thinking that we do no thinking at all? Must we so hasten to clothe differences in the sack-suit of American conformity? Surely any tendency toward "right-thinking" is a peril to all scientists, American and European alike: it is certainly not the best moral atmosphere for the nurture of creative scientists. The same democracy that is conducive to the best individual growth, political freedom, and economic experiment, is also the best atmosphere for scientific activity. If there are differences in opinion, and if these are themselves valuable because they force us to seek new evidence to support them, then why cannot we have more of them?

This respect for difference is equally necessary, I think, on the inter-societal level as well. Do the peoples of the world have the power and the right to require that no one society's experiments shall jeopardize the existence of other societies and their cultural experiments? Should the most intense cultural evangelism and world-sectionalism stop short of international war? Is the nation that breaks the world's peace an aggressor against all mankind and the future? If narcissism of one's own society is more or less characteristic of all societies, is intensity of belief equivalent to possession of the truth? Does not any tribalism assert its blindness in its fanaticism?

In this matter of war we have to proceed on the basis of faith in the correctness of our understanding of man and of society. We believe that the social and cultural factors, in any case, are all open to scientific study and modification, whatever the biological limits of the situation may be. These, at least, are all within man's potential if not actual control; and, if so, then they are within his human moral jurisdiction whether he chooses to recognize this fact or not. If we do have this area of human freedom, it follows that we should make all our structurings of society in the interest of international peace—so long as all rival societies maintain the same consistent respect and humanistic regard for all other members of our species. We will allow all men *aretē*, but none of them *hubris*.

The protection of individual and group freedoms is no easy task. But one principle is sufficiently clear: the genuine fulfilment of individual or group needs can never be purchased at the expense of other individuals or groups, for then the inhuman means negate the human ends of our seeking. If the very basis of human nature, the family, was founded on a live-and-let-live polity in the midst of great biological differences, and if the best flowering of human individuality is in an atmosphere of freedom from the annihilating aggression of individual upon individual in societies, then it would seem that the basic right and need of societies of civilized men is to be freed from the consequences of inter-group aggression. In any totalitarianism, even an international one, fanaticism covers a weakness of moral position that cannot stand on its own merits in a forum of mankind. International organization itself makes a case only in so far as it is the self-chosen instrument of federation by its many members. Even freedom cannot be compelled, for then it is not freedom. But to secure the largest agreements and the soundest ones, we must constantly discipline our demands down to the smallest and the most essential ones.

But because of the biological nature of the human animal, we can never afford to lose sight of the individual. We must be sensitive to the fact that all moral and intellectual advance depends on individuals who have developed their individuality to a marked degree. Thus the manner in which we bring up our children is of central importance.

This is an area in which we can use the best thinking of psychiatry, sociology, anthropology, and all the other social sciences including economics and government; indeed, it is impinged on by all the discoveries of the physical and biological sciences and the art of medicine. If adult personality is even partly shaped by the environing conditions of childhood that we are able to modify, then our greatest rewards will lie in our effort to see that all children have the greatest freedom for individual growth. It takes good individuals to make good societies. One condition, therefore, of any good society is that it somehow nurture individuals who are mature, self-reliant, reality-assessing, non-paranoid, and secure—both permitted to achieve and able to achieve real gratification of their real needs. This is the real business of all societies, however they may proceed about it, as it is the real business of all governments. "Freedom of enterprise" is not the private property of economic man, for there is freedom of intellectual enterprise to be considered, and other kinds as well.

The human problem remains, as ever, a problem of how we can love other people. But there are many patterns for loving that are available in our human nature. If it be a dependent love by the mother, we see no mother in nature to nurture human beings. If it be the precarious love of the son for the totemic tribal father, perhaps we have already had enough of the intellectual infantilization of human beings by tribalism. If it be the allegedly all-good and all-wise paternal love for the son, we have had enough of that too: we reject the Rome-descended institution which has given the very pattern of fascism and absolutism to Europe, complete with thought-control, terrorism, and the intellectual and cultural isolation of its communicants from the outside world. The mystique of political and religious paternity has already been sufficiently explored in European absolutisms, and more than sufficiently in Asiatic paternalized states. It is the less justified in a Europe which pretends to have founded its comity upon brotherhood, a dispensation from which its institutions have surely far wandered.

We still believe that the bond of brotherhood is the difficult but the only proper pattern for the state. For this form alone permits and fosters mature manhood in all its members. Its form and process is democracy, a statement of faith on which we are prepared to stake the whole future of our society and its culture. But let us not be deceived: this is a moral postulate we must assert and defend and give political body to—not an established situation which is yet safely inherent in any of the structures, organic or inorganic or super-organic, human or extra-human, in the universe.

Probably most political communication is in purely phatic terms. But can we be sure that the phatic stance of most electors is emotionally sound and grown-up? This is the crisis of modern times. But all history is crisis, and all decision is made in uncertainty and anxiety. The problem we speak of is timeless. Shall we choose as leader the Great White Father, the "man on horseback," dripping with charisma, who promises all kinds of miracles in his person—and delivers perishingly few of them? Or can we appreciate the honest man who says in effect: "Look, fellows! Things are tough everywhere. I don't know all the answers—I put my pants on only one leg at a time—but we can't dodge this issue, and this one, and this. What are we going to do about them?"

Our danger, as I see it, is one of political neoteny. Men breed, indeed, but shall they continue to breed while otherwise still in a morally larval state? Is the complexity of the modern world, socially and morally and politically, just too much for the manhood of modern men? Or are we grown up enough to take on the tremendous moral burden of democracy? Do we seek anxiously for a mystic father, or for a brother to implement our self-choices? For the only help mature men can get is from one another. And let the future take courage from life's past triumphs in co-operation.

The other problem—no less important than our definition of the nature of man—is our definition of the nature of reality. But whatever central Eurasiatic man may succeed in believing about the political origins of truth (a fantastic fiction of a father-child mystique of political relations, half exploitative psychopathy, half paranoid megalomania), Western man is forced to a faith in a real outside world, whose truth is beyond the coercions even of the vote of all mankind. This is admittedly a phatic stance, non-rational, and based only on moral feeling; but it has admittedly been the fundamental postulate in our scientific thinking since science began. This belief of science in an orderly outside world, as Whitehead rightly observes, the belief in *ananke*, is one we owe to the Greek tragic poets, not to the philosophers. But in the last analysis such a non-rational moral tonus is as much a shaper of societies as it is of individual men.

We feel we know now at least what the universe is not, as we have come to discover the boundaries of the human ego. An easy, arrogant, unselfquestioned paranoid assumption of world-rulership and domination-by-right, that never dares to examine into the nature and effectiveness of its techniques, characterizes the practitioner and believer in magic. A dread-ridden, helpless panic fear of reality—that is not sure what is its own ambivalent will, and what the external world—makes up the primitive superstition of animism. Reverence and fear of gray-haired cultural truth and traditional authority constitute oedipal religion.

But *arete* without *hubris* gives us another possible stance. A self-confident but disciplined and self-responsible assertion of respect for both organic self and inorganic universe—which accepts the differences and tries tirelessly and honestly to discriminate the boundaries of each—makes up the emotional stance of science. This, truly, is a matter of morale, and we must somehow owe it to our parents, physical and spiritual, and to those whom we love. All such attitudes, without question, are non-rational postulates of feeling and are beyond all argument; but their fruits in dealing with reality are geometrically different. The differences constitute the most fundamental and large-scale aspects of all cultural and intellectual history.

In attempting to know the world, it is evidently an error to fall into such easy self-centered, tribe-centered, race-centered, even human-centered, views as man has done historically. The seed of macrocosmic reality is not the Logos, the conceptualized seed of the father. The God-Father as patriarch of the tribe must rest in the grave of history, having devolved his potency upon men, if his sons are to become men. Man must somehow cure himself of whatever cultural neuroses this animistic childhood of the past entails upon him. For the great "mystery" of religion and the main "problem" of philosophy is in essence the mystery of life, of creation, of generation, and parenthood; but how the universe works is more important to understand than anthropomorphic speculation about how eternity began. These problems and these mysteries are understood already or are potentially understandable in biological, anthropological, linguistic, physical, and psychiatric terms. Logos lies within life, and within men as the heirs of life.

Nor is the world my autonomous body, as the believer in magic unconsciously assumes, with omnipotent verbal strings attached to and compelling the world-body, as nerves are attached to muscles, and as my mind and will compel my body. Nature is not my nurse, on whom I can passively depend. Nor is the world my father, that I should cringe guiltily before his patriarchal fiats, or that I should feel naughty for prying into the secrets of matter and of manhood. Nor are the world's limits those of my own tribal society, that I should accept docilely everything that tradition tells me. The world is in some manner a not-self, whose nature is both like and unlike my own, a nature which in either case inspires not fear but a deep respect.

For if man merely fears the Promethean fire "stolen" from heaven, he remains the cringing ritualist and worshiper. Man need not worship Fire, or any other aspect of the physical universe. If he learns to respect the nature of fire as a behavior independent of his own will, but one which can be used by him without guilt or fear, then in time he may become the scientist and the civilized man. In the same manner, if we only fear what we are, we will never know ourselves as men. We must come to be disenchanted of the seemingly magical nature of culture, language, and symbolism, and learn to assess these instruments of man's humanity for what they are: his creatures. What is demanded of us is an awareness without alarm of our nature and its predicaments. The nature of human nature needs only to be respected.

In our new knowledge and power over the atom we wait, it would seem, some new morning for mankind. But at this instant in human history it is already three minutes to midnight. That all our world-views are colored by our human problems and needs, we must all finally admit. But that we struggle manfully with these problems and needs is at least an animal dignity we might all strive to achieve. A billion other worlds may turn, without end and without meaning, in the cold cosmic night. But on this one earth, at least, now live animals able to become even a little like gods, having knowledge of good and evil.

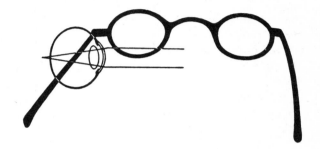

References and Reading

The intention of the present section is to give my sources and to direct the reader to further investigation of questions that especially interest him. Both books and periodicals are chosen for their usefulness and accessibility to the non-specialist.

Walter Taylor, an archeologist, and James Spuhler, a physical anthropologist, also criticized in 1954 the lack of genuine holism in anthropology (in their reviews, respectively, of "Archeology," *American Anthropologist*, LVI [1954], 480–83, and of "Physical Anthropology," *ibid.*, pp. 472–75, in A. L. Kroeber [ed.], *Anthropology Today* [Chicago: University of Chicago Press, 1953], and Sol Tax *et al.* [eds.], *An Appraisal of Anthropology Today* [Chicago: University of Chicago Press, 1953]). But, increasingly since that date, a number of fine holistic studies have been published. See, e.g., Frederick S. Hulse, "Linguistic Barriers to Gene Flow," *American Journal of Physical Anthropology*, XV (1957), 235–46; *idem*, "Some Factors Influencing the Relative Proportions of Human Racial Stocks," *Cold Spring Harbor Symposia on Quantitative Biology*, XXII (1957), 33–45; *idem*, "Exogamie et hétérosis," *Archives suisses d'anthropologie générale*, XXII (1957), 103–25; and J. N. Spuhler (ed.), *The Evolution of Man's Capacity for Culture* (Detroit: Wayne State University Press, 1959).

CHAPTER 1

FROM AMOEBAS TO MAMMALS (PP. 1–21)

There are a number of good basic texts in biology. I am partial to L. L. Woodruff and G. A. Baitsell, *Foundations of Biology* (7th ed.; New York: Macmillan Co., 1951), because it was the one I read in college. For the reader who wants a fact-filled comprehensive view of the whole field of biology, H. G. Wells, J. S. Huxley, and G. P. Wells, *The Science of Life* (New York: Doubleday, Doran & Co., 1931) seems to me the most successful popularization of any science that I have yet encountered. E. G. Conklin's *Heredity and Environment* (Princeton, N.J.: Princeton University Press, 1930) is a very readable book by a distinguished scientist; avoid, on Dr. Conklin's own advice, the Russian editions of his book, which leave in the environment but take out the heredity! J. S. Huxley's *Man in the Modern World* (New York: Mentor Books, 1948) and *Evolution: The Modern Synthesis* (London: Allen & Unwin, 1943) are collections of stimulating essays to which I owe much. Those who know Willy Ley's books, *The Lungfish and the Unicorn* (New York: Modern Age, 1941) and *Dragons in Amber* (New York: Viking Press, 1951), will understand why I recommend them for others to read just for the fun of it. The same goes for Hans Zinsser's *Rats, Lice, and History* (Boston: Little, Brown & Co., 1935).

For a geological background a good shorter book is W. B. Scott's *An Introduction to Geology* (3d ed.; New York: Macmillan Co., 1932). Those who want a bigger serving will be rewarded by reading C. R. Longwell, A. Knopf, R. F. Flint, C. Schuchert, and C. O. Dunbar, *A Textbook of Geology* (2 vols.; 2d ed.; New York: John Wiley & Sons, 1941)—a book notable throughout for the beautiful spareness and clarity of its scientific prose.

In paleontology, A. S. Romer's *Man and the Vertebrates* (Chicago: University of Chicago Press, 1933) is excellent for the general reader, and so also is P. E. Raymond's *Prehistoric Life* (Cambridge: Harvard University Press, 1947).

The reader who wishes no unexaminable mysticism in his biology may be disturbed to find "knowing" suggested even for organisms that are granted purposes. But if we permit ourselves an inclusive operational definition of "knowing"—viz., when an organism has made an effective adaptation to reality, then we may say it "knows what to do with reality" in achieving its purposes—it is clearly necessary to forego a man-centered view of knowing and to be generous to non-human organisms. In this sense, of course, other organisms may know things that *Homo sapiens* does not. For example, many organisms know more about certain aspects of chemistry than man does: they know how to synthesize certain complex chemical compounds that man cannot. Again, we know that homing pigeons know how to fly home, but we do not know *what* it is that they know in so doing: terrestrial magnetism? the Coriolis force? or something else? More baffling examples are afforded by the behavior of some very highly evolved plants. In Algeria there is a wasp-like burrowing insect, *Scolia ciliata*, with indifferent eyesight, the male of which emerges from its burrow, usually in March, a month earlier than the females. An orchid, *Ophrys speculum*, which frequents the same sandbanks, has learned to make its flower resemble the body of the female of this insect species; and the orchid achieves its pollination through the pseudo-copulation of the male insect with the flower—the symbiotic association of two entirely different sexual systems, those of wasps and of orchids. But since intermediary evolutionary types are lacking and the adaptation is already perfect, the grave question arises: How could the orchids, without blind random preliminary investigation, *know about* these undiscriminating, myopic, month-long insect bachelors? And what was the *process* of the orchids' evolutionary adaptation to this? At present biologists have no idea how this could have been done; the orchids must have, because they did it. And how did the orchid *Cryptostylis leptochila* learn to seduce the male ichneumonid wasp, *Lissopimpla semipunctata*, by smelling like the female insect? The world's leading orchidologist considered these carryings-on as deplorable as they are inexplicable (Oakes Ames, "Pollination of Orchids through Pseudocopulation," *Harvard University Botanical Museum Leaflets*, V, No. 1 [1937], 1–29). If we do not agree that the plants know how to make adaptations in making them, then we are in a corner indeed—the more especially since this adaptive knowledge is somehow passed on genetically. Shall we postulate the operation of "Ophrydean-Frustration" and a hitherto unexplored "Lissopimplan Complex"?

G. E. Hutchinson (*The Itinerant Ivory Tower* [New Haven, Conn.: Yale University Press, 1953], p. 20) has also pointed out that "until an organism is so big that random thermal agitation is not significant in its physiology, no constant behavior patterns can be developed, still less can an exact knowledge of the environment be built up from sensory data. Liberation from the Brownian [Movement] world is essential to sensory, neural, and intellectual progress." Many insects, further, are not large enough to escape the surface tension of water, and, should they accidentally touch it, they are imprisoned until they die or are eaten. On the question of optimal size for an organism, it is interesting that man's body is about midway between atoms and stars in mass.

For *Trichonympha* see L. R. Cleveland, "An Ideal Partnership," *Scientific Monthly*, LXVII (1948), 173–77. And does cytoplasm "eat" viruses, or do these invade it like a spermatozoon with new genes? On the *chemical* level this distinction is meaningless, though not on the biological. Indeed, genes themselves can be "transducted" from one bacterium to another by an infective virus (Morton D. Zinder, " 'Transduction' in Bacteria," *Scientific American*, CXCIX [1958], 38–43).

An interesting description of *Paramecium aurelia* that is not overly technical is by T. M. Sonneborn, "Genes, Cytoplasm, and Environment in Paramecium," *Scientific Monthly*, LXVII (1948), 154–60.

On man as a metazoan, it is estimated that a man weighing 155 pounds contains 26,500,000,000,000 cells, not counting the red blood cells, of which there are 10,240,000,000,000 in each of his 12 pints of blood—a total of 149,380,000,000,000 cells in his body. This is not the largest number of cells in any metazoan (for reptilian dinosaurs and mammalian whales far surpass it), but it is evidently enough to afford the large and complex nervous system in man. The estimate is from Homer W. Smith, *From Fish to Philosopher* (Boston: Little, Brown & Co., 1953), p. 175.

On crinoids and trilobites see P. E. Raymond, *Prehistoric Life*, pp. 69 and 47–48.

CHAPTER 2

The Primates Take to the Trees (pp. 22–54)

Some students consider that the very early mammals were all tree-livers for a while, in which case we must say that the primates not so much "took to the trees" as, by and large, remained in them; while most other mammals took to the ground again. However, in view of the evidence that mammals are arctic in origin, the position we take would appear to be the conservative one. In neither case are the major points obscured: *primates in particular* are arboreal, and man's giant-ape or hominid ancestors came down from the trees relatively late in evolution.

The literature on primates is large and is scattered in technical monographs. The revised edition of E. A. Hooton's witty (though sometimes crotchety) book, *Up from the Ape* (New York: Macmillan Co., 1946), is longer and more technical than the original edition, but it is still probably the most authoritative summary in popular form.

For subjects included under the general topic of "physical anthropology," William Howells' *Mankind So Far* (New York: Doubleday & Co., 1947) is without an equal for the general reader—a charming book by a genuine authority.

A readable statement on biological "laws" may be found in G. G. Simpson, "Evolutionary Determinism and the Fossil Record," *Scientific Monthly*, LXXI (1950), 262–67.

Orthogenesis was once plausibly argued in the case of the extinct giant European elk whose antlers grew to enormous and seemingly disadvantageous size. But, if *fast-growing* antlers advantaged younger breeding males, the *continued* growth in displaced older males takes on a new perspective adaptively.

In addition to the *anatomical* argument that birds lost by abandoning forelimbs for flight what they had gained by warm blood, there is another *physiological* climatic argument. Mammals were earthbound, to be sure, but to their ultimate advantage. Warm blood brings a hunger much enhanced and constantly sustained by the demands of body-temperature regulation. In winter, warm-blooded birds with flight can *migrate* to a warmer climate and thus largely escape the problem; even so, some birds like hummingbirds have such a tremendous metabolic rate that they must slow it down to survive overnight when they cannot feed constantly. But earthbound mammals had to "stick it out" in cold climates. Many fish can live frozen in winter ice, reptiles and amphibians can become dormant, and some mammals hibernate in winter. But, like arctic birds, primate man had to stay active in cold climates to get food to sustain warm blood. However, instead of a bodily change to hibernation, man adapted non-bodily means (fire, furs, and flints) to solve his metabolic problem—and human *culture* had now begun. The climatic argument is H. W. Smith's (*op. cit.*, pp. 133–34).

The data on bird instincts with respect to waste disposal may be found in J. S. Huxley, *Evolution: The Modern Synthesis*, p. 424. For a discussion of the significance of these facts in man, there is an excellent article by Lawrence K. Frank, "Cultural Control and Physiological Autonomy," in Clyde Kluckhohn and Henry A. Murray (eds.), *Personality in Nature, Society, and Culture* (rev. ed.; New York: Alfred A. Knopf, 1953), pp. 119–22. The classical psychiatric sources are, of course, Sigmund Freud, *Collected Papers* (5 vols.; London: Hogarth Press, 1924–50), II, 45–50, and V, 88–91; Ernest Jones, *Papers on Psycho-Analysis* (5th ed.; Baltimore: Williams & Wilkins Co., 1948), pp. 413–37; and Karl Abraham, *Selected Papers* (London: Hogarth Press, 1927), pp. 370–92.

Facts concerning the effects of tree life on the primates are summarized in the brilliant and sometimes controversial book of F. Wood Jones, *Arboreal Man* (New York: Arnold, 1926). A most severe criticism of Jones is by Hooton in *Apes, Men, and Morons* (New York: G. P. Putnam's Sons, 1937), pp. 66–67. But most experts would take the more moderate position of Howells (in *Mankind So Far*, p. 93); indeed, Hooton himself has considerably modified his position in the revised edition of *Up from the Ape*.

Recent experiments with artificial wire and cloth monkey mothers have underlined the significance of infant-monkey prehensility and the need for body contact: baby monkeys preferred the texture and reassurance of cloth "mothers" even when wire mothers had nursing bottles attached (Harry F. Harlow, "Love in Infant Monkeys," *Scientific American*, CC [1959], 68–74). Does this mean any more than that the grasping reflex in baby primates must be more constantly in use than the sucking reflex? "Of course this does not mean that nursing has no psychological importance. No act so effectively guarantees intimate bodily contact between mother and child. Furthermore, the mother who finds nursing a pleasant experience will probably be temperamentally inclined to give her baby plenty of handling and fondling" (p. 70).

Human attitudes toward sexuality have also doubtless been affected by an ancient evolutionary anatomical accident. With the evolution of the glomerular kidney, a battle began between the genital and the urinary functions for an opening to the outside world that lasted for three hundred and fifty million years. Not until the reptiles was a truce accomplished. As Homer Smith says:

> To sum up this confusion as succinctly as possible, the archinephritic duct sometimes retains a pure urinary function (hagfish and lampreys); or it may carry both sperm and eggs through nearly all its length (Australian lungfish, sturgeon, garpike, common frog and mudpuppy); or the gonads may take over the anterior part of the duct, leaving the kidney only the posterior part or forcing it to develop a separate duct wholly independent of the archinephritic duct—the pattern in the female even within the same species not necessarily conforming with that in the male (sharks and some salamanders); or the kidney may abandon the fight in favor of the testis, when the archinephritic duct becomes the spermatic duct, which carries the sperm from the testis to the seminal vesicles for storage; and in the last case the kidney has to build a new duct entirely of its own—the true ureter as it appears in the reptiles, birds, and mammals [*op. cit.*, p. 39].

The anatomical intimacy of the reproductive and excretory functions undoubtedly confuses some people into thinking "sex is dirty." However, the theologian who railed that *Inter faeces et urinas nascimur* was not quite accurate either structurally or functionally—at least in all animals since the reptiles—and undoubtedly drew the wrong moral conclusion for man.

At least a half dozen bird species, for whatever reasons, have retained a serviceable sense of smell. But high-flying hawk-sighted predators have not.

Comparison of the sense of smell in dogs and in men is made by Fritz Kahn, *Man in Structure and Function* (2 vols.; New York: Alfred A. Knopf, 1946), II, 605-7. This book is thoroughly delightful and is very highly recommended for the general reader; Kahn has what amounts to genius for schematic illustration in drawings, of which his book is generously full.

The work of Hecht on rhodopsin and Einstein's "law of photo-chemical equivalence" are reported by Lorus J. and Marjory J. Milne in "The Quantum and Life," *Scientific Monthly*, LXXII (1951), 139–47.

H. J. Muller ("Genetic Principles in Human Populations," *Scientific Monthly*, LXXXIII [1956], 283) writes that "it has long been a pet contention of mine . . . independently espoused by the distinguished ophthalmologist, Riddell, of Glasgow, that myopia, although certainly a detrimental condition for most individuals, was advantageous in primitive communities for those possessing it so long as they remained a small minority, by giving them the relatively privileged, safer jobs of doing precision work such as shaping fine arrow points." If so, this is a good example of "balanced polymorphism" in man, comparable to the sickle-shape blood cells aiding man against malaria.

Color vision is also found among some birds, reptiles, fishes, and perhaps even some amphibia and insects—but among placental mammals only in primates (E. N. Willmer, "Colour Vision and Its Evolution in the Vertebrates," in J. Huxley, A. C. Hardy, and E. B. Ford [eds.], *Evolution as a Process* [London: Allen & Unwin, 1954], p. 264).

Since eye color is to some degree a racial trait, one must examine carefully the possible racial differences in vision:

The senses of vision and hearing appear more acute in primitive people, but this may be due to early training in observation, so vital to their mode of life. On the other hand, hereditary influences appear to be more important than environmental in determining some skills. It is found, for example, that the Chinese and the Japanese are more commonly short-sighted than the Anglo-Saxons, while optical errors are as frequent among Arabs living in the desert as among the members of industrial communities in Europe. Dark-eyed people have higher resolving power under intense glare than those whose eyes are lightly pigmented. The pigmentation of the retina is partly an antiglare mechanism. The survival of hunters depends so much on ability to distinguish game at great distances that in the hunting stage dark-eyed people have always been at a considerable advantage in deserts. However, in moonlight and twilight the resolving power of unpigmented eyes is equally good [Kenneth P. Oakley, "Skill as a Human Possession," in C. Singer, E. J. Holmyard, and A. R. Hall (eds.), *A History of Technology* (5 vols.; Oxford: Oxford University Press, 1958), I, 35–36].

Has the anatomical fact of the *fovea* been an unconscious psychological substrate in the development of "figure-and-ground" Gestalt psychology?

On the reduction of the arboreal primate family, see Wood Jones, *Arboreal Man*, p. 138; on what he thinks keeps the primate family together, see p. 187. Edward Clodd ("Evolution [Moral]," in *Hastings Encyclopedia of Religion and Ethics*, V, 624) also argues that "the condition of helplessness and dependence strengthens the self-sacrificing instinct of the parent," which is very implausible evolutionary biology. But evidently this tender-minded notion is very old, for Clodd traces it through John Fiske as far back as Anaximander.

The ecology of *Dipodomys* is discussed in Wells, Huxley, and Wells, *The Science of Life*, p. 901; the feeding instincts of bees, on pp. 1125, 1129, and 1187; of ants, on pp. 1166–67; of termites and of wasps, on p. 1167. An accessible summary of the "dance language" of bees may be found in Émile Benveniste, "Animal Communication and Human Language," *Diogenes: An International Review of Philosophy and Humanistic Studies*, No. 1 (1953), pp. 1–7. The original work of Karl von Frisch in Munich is reported in his book on *Bees, Their Vision, Chemical Senses, and Language* (Ithaca, N.Y.: Cornell University Press, 1950).

The table on primate development is considerably added to and modified from one in R. M. and A. W. Yerkes, *The Great Apes* (New Haven, Conn.: Yale University Press, 1929), p. 568; the additional sources are Weidenreich, Hooton, and Gesell.

CHAPTER 3

THE ANTHROPOIDS CLIMB HALFWAY DOWN (PP. 55–68)

The best comprehensive summary on the anthropoid apes still remains the careful and scholarly summary of the Yerkeses, cited immediately above, though specialists have added to our knowledge since it was written. One such special study that can be recommended to the general reader is C. R. Carpenter, *A Field Study in Siam of the Behavior and Social Relations of the Gibbon (Hylobates Lar)* ("Comparative Psychology Monographs," Vol. XVI, No. 5 [1940], 1–212). The chapters on the great apes in Howells' *Mankind So Far* are, if anything, the wittiest in his very witty book.

Gibbon vocalizations are reported in Louis Boutan, "Le pseudo-langage:

observations effectuées sur un anthropoïde, le gibbon (*Hylobates Leucogenys* Ogilby*)," *Actes, Société Linnéenne de Bordeaux*, LXVII (1913), 5–80, esp. 31–33; but these observations are more accessibly summarized in Yerkes and Yerkes, *The Great Apes*, p. 77.

In addition to phatic communication with their own kind, some chimpanzees can develop "iconic signs" for use with humans. The Hayeses' chimp Viki, reared like a human baby, would bring a "Kleenex" to her "parents" as a sign of her wanting to take a walk, perhaps equating it with the diapers that were always taken with them on an airing (K. J. and C. Hayes, "The Cultural Capacity of Chimpanzee," *Human Biology*, XXVI [1954], 299).

Sokolowsky's observations on chimpanzee sexuality are contained in Alexander Sokolowsky, "The Sexual Life of the Anthropoid Apes," *Urologic and Cutaneous Review*, XXVII (1923), 612–15, at 614; descriptions of primate genitalia may be found in W. C. Osman Hill's papers in the *Proceedings of the Zoölogical Society of London*.

In their study of "The Cultural Capacity of Chimpanzee" (*op. cit.*, pp. 300–301) the Hayeses espouse the hypothesis that chimpanzees lack culture because they are adequately adapted to their environment without it (Nissen), and point out that their mortality is due primarily to infectious disease (Schultz) which would not be reduced by the techniques of a primitive culture. Food shortages, predators, or a rigorous climate might be combatted by simple cultural means. but these are not important factors in chimpanzee survival. Man, by contrast, was forced to evolve because of his food-getting problems.

Jasper von Oertzen's threnody on the gorilla is from p. 7 of *In Wildnis und Gefangenschaft: Kameruner Tierstudien* (Berlin, 1913), pp. 3–21, as quoted in Yerkes and Yerkes, *The Great Apes*, p. 525.

Since the present book has been completed, I have learned at secondhand of a study by Arnold Gehlen, *Der Mensch: Seine Natur und seine Stellung in der Welt* (Bonn: Athenäum-Verlag, 1950), through a review by Ernest Manheim in the *American Journal of Sociology*, LIX (1953), 289–90. Gehlen, a philosopher, rejects on dogmatic grounds the conception of human behavior in a zoölogical continuum and seeks to differentiate rather than to trace continuities between man and the anthropoids. He considers man an archaic type, a consequence of endocrine fetalization, the other anthropoids specialized; and attempts to see how human thought and language derive from man's biological situation. I regret that Gehlen's book was not familiar to me, but it is encouraging to learn that, however widely divergent our approach and method, we have apparently come in some cases to similar conclusions.

CHAPTER 4

MAN STANDS ALONE (PP. 69–84)

I believe that it was Julian Huxley who first disturbed my faith in angels by remarking somewhere in his writings that an animal of this particular model would require a six-foot breastbone; the rest of my excursion into un-natural history is not to be blamed upon this distinguished biologist. And it is certainly to Huxley that all of us owe the most perceptive insights into man's verticality since Anaxagoras, in the title essay of *Man Stands Alone* (New York: Harper & Bros., 1941), also reprinted in *Man in the Modern World* (New York: Mentor Books, 1948). With regard to the mechanics of human verticality, most physical anthropologists will agree that the knowledge and understanding of the late Franz Weidenreich were unmatched; S. L. Washburn and Davida Wolffson have edited the *Anthropological Papers of Franz Weidenreich* (New York: Viking Fund, Inc., 1949), and, as often the case with the leading scientists of all, Weidenreich's papers are so clear and succinct that they may be read with profit by the non-specialist.

With respect to angel ancestors I must here confess that, some years after writing the text, I have encountered in Alexander von Humboldt, an authority I am bound to respect, a mention of flying scorpions with air bladders in the rivers of Japan (in A. C. Spectorsky [ed.], *Book of the Sea* [New York: Appleton-Century-Crofts, 1954], p. 267). Eight-legged scorpions with wings even have an excess of limbs to be ancestral to angels. The question of angels must be regarded herewith as now reopened—a sometimes vexing but always edifying happenstance in scientific reasoning. Open, that is, until physicists and physiologists raise the old problem of chitin again.

Brain weights are graphically shown in Kahn, *Man in Structure and Function,* II, 544–45. Of course, everyone agrees that absolute brain weights do not mean much of anything; but proportions and trends do.

On man's increasing roundheadedness see Franz Weidenreich, "The Brachycephalization of Recent Mankind," *Southwestern Journal of Anthropology,* I (1945), 45–98, reprinted in his *Anthropological Papers,* pp. 45–98. Mechanical measuring of the skull as a fetish was of course dealt a deathblow by the famous paper of Franz Boas on "Changes in Bodily Form of Descendants of Immigrants," available in his book, *Race, Language and Culture* (New York: Macmillan Co., 1940), pp. 60–75. As Macalister puts it: "When we, in our sesquipedalian jargon, describe an Australian skull as microcephalic, phaenozygous, tapeino-dolichocephalic, prognathic, platyrrhine, hypselopalatine, leptostaphyline, dolichuranic, chamaeprosopic, and microseme, we are no nearer to the formulation of any philosophic concept of the general principles which have led to the assumption of these characters by the cranium in question, and we are forced to echo the apostrophe of Von Török 'Vanity, thy name is craniology.' " Nowadays physical anthropologists take the larger holistic view of human biologists in the matter, for the skull is the most often preserved of fossil parts and, properly viewed, can tell us a great deal about genetic relationships, posture, and the like. In studying any animal, we must ask ourselves which systems are to be weighted in phyletic classification. "In the case of man," says Weidenreich (*Anthropological Papers*, p. 40), "the answer does not seem to be too difficult. His phylogenetic evolution went in the direction of the special development of the brain. Therefore, characters of the brain or the braincase should have priority over other parts of the body." Both because of their relative indestructibility and because of the importance of food adaptations to animals, teeth, similarly, are useful in tracing descent (see, for example, the important paper by W. K. Gregory, "The Dentition of *Dryopithecus* and the Origin of Man," *Anthropological Papers, American Museum of Natural History*, Vol. XXVIII [1926], Part I).

In the years since writing the above paragraph I have sunk more deeply into an older Anaxagorean position (that man has brains because he had *hands*), instead of the Aristotelian one (that man has hands because he had *brains*). But with a wry twist: I now believe that the important feature about earliest man was not so much his brains as his feet. For *small-brained* Australopithecines of South Africa were undoubtedly bipedal, hunted large animals, and made weapons; and at least *Australopithecus Prometheus* of Makapansgat seems to have possessed fire. If we are to hold to the functional (cultural) criterion for the change of phase from ape to man (and not arbitrary morphological taxonomizing), then sadly oligophrenic *Australopithecus* was nevertheless undoubtedly "human." Of course all the arguments remain on which my respect for the brain was based—the phylogenetic increase in brains from mammals onward, the qualitative improvements in nervous tissue throughout evolution, relative body-brain ratios in animals, the human baby's enormous brain weight at birth, the swelling forebrain in neotenous man, the rise in cranial capacity from fossil hominids to modern man, and so forth. But there are new facts to be considered, only hinted at on page 81, and the old facts can now be seen in a new light.

In recent years the question has been argued as to who hunted whom in South Africa (S. L. Washburn, "Australopithecines: The Hunters or the

Hunted?" *American Anthropologist,* LIX [1957], 612–14; R. A. Dart, "The Myth of the Bone-accumulating Hyaena," *American Anthropologist,* LVIII [1956], 40–62; Alun R. Hughes, "Hyaenas versus Australopithecines as Agents of Bone Accumulation," *American Journal of Physical Anthropology,* XII [1954], 467–86; R. A. Dart, "Bone Tools and Porcupine Gnawing," *American Anthropologist,* LX [1958], 715–24; and *idem,* "The Minimal Bone-Breccia Content of Makapansgat and the Australopithecine Predatory Habit," *ibid.,* pp. 923–31). But most authorities would agree with F. Clark Howell ("Australopithecines: Threshold of Humanity?" [paper read at the Fifty-seventh Annual Meeting of the American Anthropological Association, Washington, D.C., November 20, 1958]) that in the lower Pleistocene at Sterkfontaine small-brained, small (75-pound male) Australopithecines, using the "Villa-franchian" type of pebble tools, killed small antelopes and baboons. Since swift South African antelopes could probably be hunted by relatively sluggish bipedal man only if he co-operated with his fellows and since the formidable South African baboons live in large bands, these Australopithecine hunters must also have lived in bands to have made baboons a significant item in their diet. "A single australopithecine, even armed with a club, would not be a serious threat to a band of baboons" (G. A. Bartholomew, Jr., and J. B. Birdsell, "Ecology and the Protohominids," *American Anthropologist,* LV [1953], 491).

It is an attractive theory to suppose that the moral necessities of living together, as necessitated by their food ecology, put a premium on the further evolution of the forebrain, for inhibition of thalamic spontaneity seems to be a major function of the forebrain. But another function of the forebrain is psychological association; and any necessary symbolizing and co-operative culture-making among these band-hunting Australopithecines would put a further premium on brains. That is, an animal *way of life* fomented brains in the first instance; and, chronologically, early Pleistocene limbs of human *type* preceded brains of human *size.* As Le Gros Clark puts it, "In the process of human evolution the expansion and elaboration of the brain followed, and were perhaps conditioned by, the perfection of the limbs for an erect mode of progression" (*History of the Primates* [Chicago: Phoenix Books, 1957], p. 117; see also S. Zuckerman, "Correlation of Change in the Evolution of Higher Primates," in Huxley, Hardy, and Ford [eds.], *op. cit.,* pp. 300–352).

Let us continue this organismic thinking and take another feature of the Australopithecines, their teeth. In three fossils the canines are small and nearly level with the other teeth, even in males and even in the earliest stages of wear. Would not this reduction have taken place in these early hominids only after the functions of the canines had been taken over by *hands* and *tools* which they are known to have had? And with *fire* in cooking the meat of animals they undoubtedly hunted, would not canines for tearing raw flesh be less important? As for weapons, a bipedal hominid, hunting in hordes, could far more easily kill cornered animals (and one another) with clubs and rocks thrown with their hands than with canine teeth, which anthropoids mostly use for stripping fruit rinds anyway. Furthermore, life in the open puts a premium on cunning and co-operation; and, if the animals' furs were used as well, then sharp stones are far better than canines for skinning animals. Thus tool-making, like weapon-making, also arose from early man's carnivorousness (Oakley, *loc. cit.*, p. 20).

Another point: it has been shown experimentally that "a more generous diet, notably of meat, increases the average stature and physical efficiency of human bodies" (V. G. Childe, "Early Forms of Society," in Singer, Holmyard, and Hall [eds.], *op. cit.*, pp. 38–39). Again: "It may be that finer diet leads to refinement in thinking" (*ibid.*, p. 39). But hunting may have been selective for larger and stronger males in the species at the same time that meat-eating made it possible in individuals. Thus meat-eating may have benefited both man's brain and body.

Still another point. "The fact that, in most individuals, language-associations are built up in the part of the cortex which controls the right hand is probably connected with their being right-handed—another indication of the close connection between manual activity and speech. Both may be considered as forms of tool-making" (Oakley, *loc. cit.*, p. 19). Thus language, like tools, may derive in part from bipedal man's handedness, as it may derive, also in part, from the societality inherent in his food-ecology. Incidentally, for whatever bearing it may have on language, Mousterian Neanderthals were already right-handed (M. Boule and H. V. Vallois, *Fossil Men* [New York: Dryden Press, 1957], p. 233).

A question arises. If chimpanzees have nearly as big brains as do Australopithecines, then why do not chimpanzees have culture? The Hayeses, who raised a chimp in their family, have reasoned thus:

Such processes as forming or retaining an association, perceiving a relationship, drawing an inference, or generalizing a principle, should be relatively independent of sheer mass of tissue. We consider it likely that the quantity of brain is primarily related to a quantitative aspect of its function—specifically to its information handling capacity. One of the most distinctive tasks imposed upon the human brain by man's cultural way of life is the assimilation and storage of a tremendous amount of information. On the other hand, the chimpanzee's 400 gram brain seems to be fully capable of handling all the useful information likely to be encountered directly by the individual. From this point of view, an increase in the size of the anthropoid brain would be of no advantage to its possessor, so long as he continued to lead a non-cultural existence. We suggest the possibility that most of the fourfold increase in cranial capacity, from anthropoid to man, took place after the appearance of culture and language, and therefore after primate behavior had become essentially human [Hayes and Hayes, *op. cit.*, p. 294].

Therefore (p. 296), they believe that "the 'higher mental functions' observed in man are more nearly results of culture than causes of it" and (p. 297) that "the most important step in the evolution of modern man from an anthropoid ancestor was an increase in the experience-producing drives relevant to the skills of communication."

This gives us an important clue. Their carnivorous life in the open surely put a premium on societality and semantic communication (hence symbol-using, and hence culture) among the Australopithecine hominids, which was selectively far greater than the merely phatic communication in the merely defensive hordes of merely fruit-eating tool-less apes in the trees. Animal play ("experience-producing drives"), as in bear cubs and in kittens, seems mainly to be *practice for adulthood,* i.e., for fighting and for hunting; but primate play seems to be supererrogatory, a restless "monkeying" with things that proceeds from an overplus of cortical energy and interest in one another and in their environment (from food-erotized hands?). But this is not enough. Truly human *experiments* with the environment are impossible without *hypotheses,* and hypotheses are impossible without *language* (linguistic structure *is* built-in hypotheses about the world)—and language, we may suppose, first arose from the necessities of bipedal horde-Australopithecines hunting other, quadrupedal, primates, baboons.

The reasoning is intricate and long, but cumulative to this conclusion: phylogenetically, feet and hands fomented brains in the last analysis (as Anaxagoras thought)—and not brains, hands (as Aristotle thought). Meanwhile, though causal explanations change, the same facts remain: the oldest skulls that can be called human had room for only 20 ounces of brains; later, Stone Age men had more than two pounds; today most men have about three pounds of brain. In each such human brain there are a hundred times as many nerve lines as are contained in the world's entire telephone system. This is surely the *physical* substrate of man's genius. An ant brain has only about 250 cells; a bee's, nearly 900; a human brain contains some 13,000,-000,000 cells, about five times as many pink and gray neurones as there are people in the world (George R. Harrison, "How the Brain Works," *Atlantic Monthly,* CXCVIII [1956], 58–63). This obviously makes for the contrast of insect with human societies—but evidently also we need the more brain cells the more numerous we become as people, i.e., as the social symbiosis of men becomes increased by culture and the *coagulation* of our human communications, and hence the same selection pressures that began with the Australopithecines still operate today in modern men. Biologically, the trunk lines of the communications system must increase because of the ecological demands made upon them. Can our brains continue to keep up with our ecology?

On the ontogenesis of the lumbar curve in man see F. P. Thieme, *Lumbar Breakdown Caused by the Erect Posture in Man* ("Anthropological Papers, Museum of Anthropology, University of Michigan," No. 4 [Ann Arbor, 1950]).

A three-dimensional diagram of man's family tree is found in A. H. Schultz, "Characters Common to Higher Primates and Characters Specific for Man," *Quarterly Review of Biology*, XI (1936), 259–83 and 425–55, reprinted also in Carpenter, *A Field Study in Siam of the Behavior and Social Relations of the Gibbon.*

The healthy lampoon of nationalism in physical anthropology is E. A. Hooton's in *Apes, Men, and Morons*, pp. 107–12.

Regarding the genetic unity of *Homo sapiens*, an authoritative statement is that of Franz Weidenreich, "Generic, Specific, and Subspecific Characters in Human Evolution," *Anthropological Papers*, pp. 25–43.

Bartholomew and Birdsell (*op. cit.,* p. 495) have reasoned that in the Pliocene the evolving protohominids lived only in the tropics, subtropics, and perhaps the fringes of the temperate zones and that "the only place in which human populations could have expanded into a vacuum was at the margins of the then habitable areas." But, with a new ecology, why could not neo-carnivorous men have competed with other primates in their own territories? Certainly the very earliest fire and pebble tools are found among the baboon-hunting Australopithecines. As for the Neanderthals, Weckler and others favor the "caught-short" theory:

Some of these pre-Neanderthal men wandered inland into Asia north of 40° during a period of warm climate. Part of this population may subsequently have been trapped north of the barrier in the general vicinity of Inner Mongolia or Sinkiang at the outset of the next glacial period. Primitive man caught in this area would have been unable to retreat directly southward because the great mountain mass that lay in that direction became frigid sooner than the lower lands to the north [J. E. Weckler, "Relation between Neanderthal Man and Homo Sapiens," *American Anthropologist*, LVI (1955), 1010].

Howell thinks that some of the physical characteristics of Neanderthal man may actually represent adaptation to a glacial climate, and Coon has long thought this also (Weckler, *op. cit.*). However, the time and place of origin of the modern type of man, *Homo sapiens* in the strictly morphological sense, still remain a dark mystery.

CHAPTER 5

Man Hands Himself a New Kind of Evolution (pp. 85–97)

Paleontologically, elephants once looked like a good bet biologically, with their prehensile trunks and good brains. But they have been in retreat throughout the time of man even into historic times. Elephants were found in predynastic Egypt, but in early dynastic times they had retreated to the First Cataract, where the city of Elephantine was named for them. In Eritrea elephants are now extinct but were common until Roman times (Pliny *Natural History* v. i. 15; Loeb ed., 2:228 [1942]). The Eighteenth Dynasty naval expedition about 1500 b.c. to Punt (?Somaliland) brought back elephant ivory, and elephants were then abundant in Libya and Mauretania, and at least available in North Africa in Hannibal's time (R. D. Barnett, "Fine Ivory Work," in Singer, Holmyard, and Hall [eds.], *op. cit.*, I, 663).

Neuroanatomists have thoroughly explored the brain cortex by electric stimulation and other means, seeking to find which parts are sensory, which motor, and which are functionally related to specific parts of the body. This localization, however, contrary to the phrenologists, is more a matter of functional *pattern* than of anatomical *place*, since the same areas change their function and since the functional areas change their locale and size during the growth of the individual. Thus, if one were to outline on the head of a baby the areas concerned with parts of the body, the homunculus resulting would consist in an enormous mouth and tongue and big nose, almost entirely surrounded by two hands. This is surely the neurological substrate of the "oral" psychological phase of Freud, though these facts may justify the additional stress I have laid on libidinized hands. Sucking and grasping are primate-baby necessities *at birth*. Only after some months do the mouth and hand areas shrink as the eyes, ears, and feet come to get attention; and only later do the shoulders, toes, arms, thighs, and, finally, the back acquire significance. A speculation: Do the phatic tonuses of the individual oral experience still reside in the now-taken-over areas of his brain? Is this one part of the persistence of personality?

The popular version of Norbert Wiener's work on cybernetics is *The Human Use of Human Beings* (Boston: Houghton Mifflin Co., 1950), whence the concept of "feed-back" is taken.

The concept of alloplastic and autoplastic changes is from Sandor Fe-
renczi, *Further Contributions to the Theory and Practice of Psychoanalysis*
(London: Hogarth Press, 1926), pp. 97 and 164; I use the term here in
Huxley's derived biological sense.

The estimate of the population of Old Stone Age man is that of S. L.
Washburn, "Thinking about Race," in Earl W. Count (ed.), *This Is Race*
(New York: Henry Schuman, 1950), pp. 691–702.

On the environmental origin of racial traits, the best modern source I know
is Carleton Coon, Stanley M. Garn, and Joseph B. Birdsell, *Races: A Study
of the Problems of Race Formation* (Springfield, Ill.: Charles C Thomas,
1950). But it is only fair to state that theirs is the minority position.

A great many anthropologists join me in my admiration for J. N. Spuhler's
paper, "On the Number of Genes in Man," *Science*, CVIII (1948), 279–80.
It is an elegant example of scientific ingenuity and careful reasoning.

The Hayeses (*op. cit.*, p. 293) argue that, since evolution operates by
selection and not by foresight, tool-using came before bipedality, for "only
then could the intrinsically inefficient bipedal mode of locomotion be favored
in selection." Besides, "most of man's tool using occurs in a sitting position,
or a stationary, standing position—neither of which is difficult for chimpanzees." With respect to *tools,* perhaps so; but *weapons* in hunting would seem
to enjoin bipedality on Australopithecines, and ecologically this latter is possibly the more important.

CHAPTER 6

FATHER COMES HOME TO STAY (PP. 98–109)

This chapter rests on the insights of Sigmund Freud in his *Three Contributions to the Theory of Sex* ("Nervous and Mental Disease Monograph
Series," No. 7 [1930], but available also in the "Modern Library" ed. of *The
Basic Writings of Sigmund Freud,* pp. 553–629). These less than a hundred
pages are widely regarded as the most important in the history of psychiatry.
Freud's *Totem and Taboo* (New York: Modern Library, 1938), pp. 807–
930, is still a useful study. This book has some defects in theory, since it
was based on a now-inadequate early anthropology. But if, by assessing a
book in its proper scientific setting and time, one is able to read what a man
means and not merely what he says, then this remains one of the most insightful books we have in anthropology. J. C. Flugel's *The Psychoanalytic Study of
the Family* (London: Hogarth Press, 1931) is a fine summary of the analytic
position concerning the critical importance of the family in personality forma-

tion. The best general introduction in one volume to analytic thinking is, in my opinion, Karin Stephen, *Psychoanalysis and Medicine* (Cambridge: Cambridge University Press, 1939).

The earliest suggestion I can find in anthropological literature on the relationship of the permanent human breast to non-seasonal sexuality is that of Hermann Klaatsch, *The Evolution and Progress of Mankind* (Philadelphia: Frederick A. Stokes Co., 1923), p. 156. Some students have stated that something like incipient permanent breasts are visible even in some of the quasi-familial anthropoids—in which circumstance the case for the exclusiveness of the human breast is weakened, but the causal argument is strengthened. That udders occur in herding animals also strengthens the causal association.

On the longevity of Old and New Stone Age man see Franz Weidenreich, "The Duration of Life of Fossil Man in China and the Pathological Lesions Found in His Skeleton," *Chinese Medical Journal*, LV (1939), 34–44, but available also in *Anthropological Papers*, pp. 194–204. Additional figures, from Todd, are in Hooton, *Up from the Ape.*

The permanency of the sex drive in primates is discussed in Yerkes and Yerkes, *The Great Apes*, p. 512.

My use of primate social life as edifying "parallels" in the probable origins of the family in primal man would at least obtain support from Hooton. "I shall no doubt evoke the indignant disagreement of social anthropologists when I suggest that more is to be learned about the genesis of the human family and the beginning of social organization and community life in early man by the study of contemporary infra-human primates living under natural conditions than by the studies of retarded human groups living today under conditions variously described as 'primitive,' 'uncivilized' or 'savage'" (E. A. Hooton, "The Importance of Primate Studies in Anthropology," *Human Biology*, XXVI [1954], 185)—an opinion echoed by William Straus (*Human Biology*, XXVI [1954], 310).

The social function of sexuality in the anthropoids is quoted from Wolfgang Köhler, *The Mentality of Apes*, trans. from 2d rev. ed. (1925) by Ella Winter (New York: Harcourt, Brace & Co., 1931), p. 303.

On homosexuality as indicating biological inferiority see E. J. Kempf, "The Social and Sexual Behavior of Infrahuman Primates with Some Comparable Facts in Human Behavior," *Psychoanalytic Review*, IV (1917), 127–54, esp. 153.

Infantile dependency as the cause of the human family—a position with which I disagree—is stated in Kluckhohn and Murray, *Personality in Nature,*

Society, and Culture, p. 64, the authors evidently following Wood Jones. But Kluckhohn is a leader of an important trend in contemporary anthropology: the recognition of the central significance of the family to human nature. See, for example, Clyde Kluckhohn, "Universal Categories of Culture," in A. L. Kroeber (ed.), *Anthropology Today* (Chicago: University of Chicago Press, 1953); see also G. P. Murdock, "The Common Denominator of Cultures," in Ralph Linton (ed.), *The Science of Man in the World Crisis* (New York: Columbia University Press, 1945), pp. 123–42. Perhaps I might cite my own paper, "Family and Symbol," in George B. Wilbur and Warner Muensterberger (eds.), *Psychoanalysis and Culture: Essays in Honor of Géza Róheim* (New York: International Universities Press, 1951), pp. 156–67.

CHAPTER 7

AND MAKES IT LEGAL (PP. 110–31)

Although anthropologists today do not accept Edward Westermarck's main thesis, that of "natural" human monogamy, his great work still remains the best compendium of the ethnological facts: *The History of Human Marriage* (3 vols.; New York: Macmillan Co., 1925). Similarly criticized for his method, the work of Sir James George Frazer nevertheless remains monumental. This "last of the scholastics" actually wrote the twelve volumes of *The Golden Bough* as an extended footnote to a line in Virgil he felt he did not understand clearly! The influence of *The Golden Bough* on scholarship and literature is enormous and incalculable.

Probably the best text on social organization and kinship is that of George Peter Murdock, *Social Structure* (New York: Macmillan Co., 1949), though specialists criticize some aspects of it. The comparative data on the sexual access of a man's brothers to his wife are cited from Murdock, p. 25.

Undoubtedly the best anthology of ethnographic readings on marriage and the family is that of Bernhard J. Stern (ed.), *The Family Past and Present* (New York: Appleton-Century Co., 1935).

A good cross-cultural study of sexuality is C. S. Ford and F. A. Beach, *Patterns of Sexual Behavior* (New York: Harper & Bros., 1951).

In case anyone has any doubt of Captain Cook's veracity on Polynesian youth groups, I cite (for the Marquesas) the original sources in whaling voyages which I read years ago for a student paper: C. P. Claret Fleurieu, *Voyage autour du monde par Étienne Marchand, An VI* [1797] (6 vols.; Paris: Imprimerie de la République, An VI–VIII [1798–1800]), 1, 52–53, 70, 171–74; G. H. von Langsdorff, *Voyages and Travels in Various Parts of* the World (Carlisle, 1817), pp. 91–92; Captain David Porter, *Journal of a Cruise Made to the Pacific* (2 vols.; 2d ed.; New York, 1822), II, 59–61; C. S. Stewart, *A Visit to the South Seas* (2 vols.; New York, 1831), I, 213, 216; F. D. Bennett, *Narrative of a Whaling Voyage round the Globe from the Year 1833 to 1836* (2 vols.; London, 1840), I, 315; Capitaine Abel du Petit-Thouars, *Voyage autour du monde sur le Frégate "La Venus"* (2 vols.; Paris, 1841), II, 341, 361, 369.

In my opinion, too much has been made of Bronislaw Malinowski's discovery in *Sex and Repression in Savage Society* (New York: Harcourt, Brace & Co., 1927) that the Trobriand Islanders have a differently configurated Oedipus complex than do the Central Europeans described by Freud. Of course they do. Indeed, they must; for family structures differ. But Trobrianders still have family life and oedipal problems just the same. For a more moderate statement, in which psychiatrists and all analytically informed anthropologists would agree, see Heinz Hartmann, Ernst Kris, and Rudolph M. Lowenstein, "Some Psychoanalytic Comments on Culture and Personality," in George B. Wilbur and Warner Muensterberger (eds.), *Psychoanalysis and Culture: Essays in Honor of Géza Róheim,* pp. 13–14.

The alleged exception to the father-daughter incest taboo is discussed in J. S. Slotkin, "On a Possible Lack of Incest Regulations in Old Iran," *American Anthropologist,* XLIX (1947), 612–17; Ward H. Goodenough, "Comments on the Question of Incestuous Marriages in Old Iran," *American Anthropologist,* LI (1949), 326–28; and J. S. Slotkin, "Reply to Goodenough," *American Anthropologist,* LI (1949), 331–32. The Azande and Thonga cases are from G. P. Murdock, "The Social Regulation of Sexual Behavior" in P. H. Hoch and J. Zubin (eds.), *Psychosexual Development in Health and Disease* (New York: Grune & Stratton, 1949), pp. 256–66.

Lactation-taboo data are summarized from N. Miller, *The Child in Primitive Society* (New York: Brentano's, 1928), pp. 41–42. The primate material is from Yerkes and Yerkes, *The Great Apes,* p. 263.

The Arunta information is from Sir Baldwin Spencer and F. J. Gillen, *The Arunta: A Study of a Stone Age People* (2 vols.; London: Macmillan & Co., 1927) and, by the same authors, *Native Tribes of Central Australia* (London: Macmillan & Co., 1899). This latter book, by the way, contains a classic typographical error: in discussing the only clothing that the men in this sexually complex tribe wear, there is reference (on p. 570, ninth line from the bottom) to a "public tassel"! This, of course, is a libel—as may be seen by referring to our diagram from G. P. Murdock, *Our Primitive Con-*

temporaries (New York: Macmillan Co., 1938), p. 28. The natural reference here is to Freud's *Psychopathology of Everyday Life* (New York: Modern Library, 1938), pp. 35–178.

CHAPTER 8

PEOPLE ARE DIFFERENT (PP. 132–48)

Good general discussions of race are found in a number of introductory textbooks in anthropology. I recommend the following: A. L. Kroeber, *Anthropology* (New York: Harcourt, Brace & Co., 1948), pp. 124–205; Ralph Linton, *The Study of Man* (New York: D. Appleton–Century Co. 1936), pp. 22–59; Melville J. Herskovits, *Man and His Works* (New York: Alfred A. Knopf, 1948), pp. 133–52; John Gillin, *The Ways of Men* (New York: D. Appleton–Century Co., 1948), pp. 97–143; and E. Adamson Hoebel, *Man in the Primitive World* (New York: McGraw-Hill Book Co., 1949), pp. 69–93. The treatment of race in Franz Boas, *The Mind of Primitive Man* (New York: Macmillan Co., 1938), while excellent and stimulating, is not so systematic and comprehensive as are the above texts; his chapter on race in Franz Boas (ed.), *General Anthropology* (New York: D. C. Heath & Co., 1938), pp. 95–123, is one of the best.

For more advanced readers, Earl W. Count (ed.), *This Is Race,* is the book. This is an anthology of the great classic studies of race in man, selected from the large international literature on the subject and translated into English; a better book of its kind could hardly be made.

A very careful and succinct summary of the anthropological position of the Jews—indeed, it is the best that I know anywhere—may be found in Carl C. Seltzer, "The Jew: His Racial Status," in Count, *This Is Race,* pp. 608–18.

That man was a domesticated animal has been known since the end of the eighteenth century. The classic paper is that of Johann Friedrich Blumenbach, *Beyträge zur Naturgeschichte,* republished in *The Anthropological Treatises of Johann Friedrich Blumenbach* (3d ed.; London, 1795). Blumenbach was also one of the first to note that *Homo sapiens* was a single species. Another important paper is by Eugen Fischer, "Racial Traits of Man as Phenomena of Domestication," in Count, *This Is Race,* pp. 281–92.

Although I do not consider man's major racial differences to be simple adaptations to local environments, there does exist some evidence that the general body size and shape (i.e., proportions) may involve an ecological element. The contrast of "linear" Nilotics and compact Eskimos is at least suggestive; studies in stature and sitting heights in American Indians, and in body size in the American puma, *Felis concolor,* both show latitudinal variations according to Bergmann's and Allen's rules. See Marshall T. Newman, "The Application of Ecological Rules to the Racial Anthropology of the Aboriginal New World," *American Anthropologist,* LV (1953), 311–27. But, as Newman himself very carefully points out, these differences may be non-genic; and many other factors than temperature and humidity may be involved.

The quotation on page 143 is from J. von Uexkull, *Theoretical Biology* (New York: Harcourt, Brace & Co., 1926), p. 243, a stimulating book but not recommended for the non-specialist.

On family symbiosis as a factor tending to remove the individual from the full effects of natural selection in the wild, it is interesting that Raymond Dart has unearthed a number of scoops or spoons made of animal bones at Makapansgat half a million years ago which were used, he thinks, as scoopers of flesh, fat, and other soft or fluid pulps to put food into the mouths of the very young and very old toothless Australopithecines.

I have not the slightest doubt that *selection* continues to occur in human beings, but this is by no means the same as *natural* selection at all. For example, there is no reason to suppose that blonds were more numerous than Bushmen ten thousand years ago; in fact, Old Stone Age art found in much of Africa and depicting Bushman racial types suggests that the contrary might have been true. The biological fact that there are now 100,000 blonds for every living Bushman is no sign of superior biological equipment among blonds. In the first place, the population of England in the last four centuries of the Industrial Revolution has increased eight times as fast as the rest of the world *for cultural reasons* (economic-technological), and the area of blondness in North and West Europe some four times the average. For quite accidental geographic reasons, it has been from the area where genes for blondness are commonest that overseas migration has been most easy; and it was in this same area that industrialization and the high population increase had proceeded the furthest and produced the highest population pressure. Again, a large number of migrants to British colonies were minority religious groups who felt themselves oppressed at home—and by surely a fortuitous circumstance these groups were commonest in East Anglia and Ulster, where blonds are more numerous than elsewhere. The Industrial Revolution, geographic ease of migration, and religious minority-group membership—all these can hardly be claimed as factors in any *natural* selection of blonds. At the same time, the world population of Bushmen has declined no doubt because the pastoral *cultures* of the Hamites invading Africa and the agriculture of the Negroes simply had a higher adaptive potential than the hunting culture of the Bushmen. I see no way to argue a racial superiority of Negroes over African Bushmen; any superiority they have had is not in biological equipment but in cultural. Such facts, perhaps, may justify our argument that culture is man's ecology. Again, the entire Eskimo population of Southampton Island starved to death in the winter of 1902 because they had earlier lost knowledge of how to make kayaks and had no way of leaving after they had hunted down all available land game—an admittedly biological event, but resulting from cultural causes. As Theodozius Dobzhansky says:

The history of the human species has been brought about by interactions of biological and cultural variables; it is just as futile to attempt to understand human biology if one disregards cultural influences as it is to understand the origin and rise of culture if one disregards human biological nature. Human biology and culture are parts of a single system, unique and unprecedented in the history of the living world ["Human Diversity and Adaptation," *Cold Spring Harbor Symposia on Quantitative Biology*, XV (1951), 385].

Gigantopithecus blacki and *Meganthropus palaeojavanicus* now seem to be no problem, as apparent exceptions to "Depéret's law" of phylogenetically *increasing* size (up to man). Since we know only their teeth, "the simplest and most economical explanation is that the big-toothed forms were simply big-toothed forms" (S. M. Garn and A. B. Lewis, "Tooth-Size, Body-Size and 'Giant' Fossil Man," *American Anthropologist*, LX [1958], 879).

CHAPTER 9

Man Climbs Back up His Evolutionary Tree (pp. 149–62)

W. Garstang, in a paper read to the Linnaean Society in 1922, first used the term "paedomorphosis." In this he clearly crystallized the idea that neoteny—the adaptations to larval or young life—might have a profound influence not only on adults of the race but on the whole future evolution of the stock. "Ontogeny," he boldly says, "does not recapitulate Phylogeny: it creates it" (A. C. Hardy, "Escape from Specialization," in Huxley, Hardy, and Ford [eds.], *op. cit.*, p. 125).

On man as a fetalized ape, the important paper is L. Bolk, "On the Origin of the Human Races," in Count, *This Is Race*, pp. 419–25, in accessible excerpt. The reinterpretation of Bolk's original insight into endocrine terms is that of Sir Arthur Keith. A brief expression of this view is in Sir Arthur's "Evolution of the Human Races," excerpted in Count, *This Is Race*, pp. 426–35. The brashness and extremism of his pupil irritated many conservative physical anthropologists; yet a sympathetic reading can still extract much of value from J. R. de la H. Marett's *Race, Sex and Environment* (London: Hutchinson & Co., 1936). The quotation is from Sir Arthur Keith, *A New Theory of Human Evolution* (New York: Philosophical Library, 1949), p. 195.

Domesticated traits in animals are paedomorphic phenomena also at times. The plain red or reddish-brown common among cattle is a retention of juvenile coloration; but other colors like black, white, and piebald seem due to mutations. Dewlaps and skin folds, normally characteristic of young animals only, are retained in the adult in some breeds of dogs and cattle. "Many characters of domestication are in reality juvenile characters persisting to the adult stage" (F. E. Zeuner, "Domestication of Animals," in Singer, Holmyard, and Hall [eds.], *op. cit.*, I, 327–52).

A justly famous book is Lawrence J. Henderson's *Fitness of the Environment* (New York: Macmillan Co., 1913), which first pointed out in detail the peculiar physical and chemical nature of conditions which fit the earth for life as we know it.

I have said that earth is a rare place. But Harlow Shapley, the astronomer, has for many years argued on statistical grounds that in the visible universe there may be millions of suns with satellites like our own. However, the question is not a simple quantitative, astronomical one. There are qualitative aspects, too, like those advanced by the biologist Henderson, and doubtless many other aspects that we do not know. For example, there is the matter of earth's own satellite, the moon. Most geologists agree that our moon was probably flung off from the area of the Pacific Ocean. Had it not been for the moon, and hence no Pacific depths to drain off the earth ocean, and had the earth cooled off with no other catastrophic occurrences, the earth today would be almost entirely covered by ocean, with only a few granitic islands of low relief. Life might perhaps have evolved in such a universal sea. But would vertebrates? For their evolution was conditioned by the rich amounts of salts leached out of 95 vertical miles of strata in the earth's dry crust; and, furthermore, the first ancestral chordates, with their spindle-shaped bodies and symmetrically placed muscles for rhythmic contraction, were adapted (as T. C. Chamberlin showed in 1900) in response to rivers constantly flowing in one direction and not to a random local ebb and flow in the sea—even added to by moon-made tides. Brackish estuaries of *rivers* thus gave a necessary environment for the first dynamic chordate ancestors of the vertebrates, whose fossils are found in the Old Red beds of freshwater origin but are suspiciously absent from deep marine "Neptunian" strata. Meanwhile, both for leaching of salts and for rivers to flow, there must be *both* land and ocean, as well as cataclysms to turn up successive masses of land. H. W. Smith has assembled much of the argument (*op. cit.*, pp. 11, 29, 33, and 218–20). But Dr. Smith has contributed the clinching argument himself, in showing that the glomerular kidney characteristic of vertebrates was an evolutionary response to fresh water rather than to salt. The gravamen of all these arguments is that an almost endless set of "accidents" was biologically required for earth life and that it is no simple matter of a (revolving!) satellite (of optimal size and constitution!) optimally distant from its sun. That an identical assemblage of all such accidents producing *Homo sapiens* has occurred elsewhere compounds statistical improbability; that a functionally equivalent assemblage *producing organic intelligence* has occurred elsewhere, perhaps equally so. Earth is a rare place.

The triumph of man as an animal within these physical necessities and the complex prior contingencies necessary for man's evolution are brilliantly summarized in Julian S. Huxley, *Evolution: The Modern Synthesis*, pp. 569–71. Some misanthropes cavil at Huxley's rich and unashamed enthusiasm for *Homo sapiens*—but who better has a right to such opinion than this deeply learned biologist?

CHAPTER 10

Man Starts Talking (pp. 163–86)

In the unanimous judgment of professional linguists, the best comprehensive text in their field is L. Bloomfield, *Language* (New York: Henry Holt & Co., 1933). It is indeed a superb book; but it is difficult for the unaided beginner. Another brilliant but somewhat less technical book is by Edward Sapir, *Language: An Introduction to the Study of Speech* (New York: Harcourt, Brace & Co., 1921). Of more restricted range are two fine books: Otto Jespersen, *Growth and Structure of the English Language* (New York: D. Appleton & Co., 1923), and Henry Bradley, *The Making of English* (New York: Macmillan Co., 1928). D. Diringer on *The Alphabet* (New York: Philosophical Library, 1948) is a justly popular account of an interesting subject.

The emotional significance of the oral zone has, I believe, been best pointed out by Karl Abraham, in chaps. xii and xxiv of his *Selected Papers* (London: Hogarth Press, 1927).

The predominance in apes of sight over hearing in their communication is an observation quoted from Yerkes and Yerkes, *The Great Apes*, p. 546. See also C. R. Carpenter and N. M. Locke, "Notes on the Symbolic Behavior of a Cebus Monkey," *Journal of Genetic Psychology*, LI (1937), 267–78.

The quotation on the origin of speech is from Edward Sapir's article on "Symbolism" in the *Encyclopaedia of the Social Sciences* (New York: Macmillan Co., 1937), XIV, 492–95, used with the permission of the Macmillan Company; reprinted in *Selected Writings of Edward Sapir* (Berkeley: University of California Press, 1949), p. 565. Parts II and III of this selection contain some of the most brilliant anthropological writing that has ever been done. It is difficult for me to restrain my enthusiasm for Sapir because I was his student. Kluckhohn, another of his students, has written that "for sheer brilliance Edward Sapir is unsurpassed by any American anthropologist or linguist, living or dead." Perhaps his friend, Dr. Harry Stack Sullivan, put it best: "He was one of the most articulate of men, a poet, a musician, an intellect that evoked reverence, a personality unendingly charming, a genius largely wasted on a world not yet awake to the value of the very great." Sapir had in speech a veritably Santayanesque suppleness and articulatedness of style, a wholeness of utterance that is aesthetically enchanting; it is one of the signs that we are in the presence of a fine mind. His was surely one of the great intelligences of our time in the Western world.

On human symbolizing see Martin Grotjahn, "Georg Groddeck and His Teachings about Man's Innate Need for Symbolization," *Psychoanalytic Review*, XXXII (1945), 9–24. For those equipped with some technical knowledge of analytic theory, an extraordinarily insightful article is that by G. B. Wilbur, "Some Problems Presented by Freud's Life-Death Instinct Theory," *American Imago*, II (1941), 134–96, 208–65.

The thoroughly researched study of the calamitous mistranslation of the Japanese word *mokusatsu* which ushered in a new era in world history is by William J. Coughlin, "The Great *mokusatsu* Mistake," *Harper's Magazine*, CCVI (March, 1953), 31–40. See also Robert J. C. Butow, *Japan's Decision To Surrender* (Stanford, Calif.: Stanford University Press, 1954) pp. 142–49, 171.

An excellent example of how linguistic study enables us to reconstruct prehistory is the very readable little book by H. H. Bender, *The Home of the Indo-Europeans* (Princeton, N.J.: Princeton University Press, 1922). A man of surpassing scholarship, Bender wrote all the etymologies for the new second edition of the Merriam-Webster *International Dictionary*.

The connotations of the German word *Herr* are discussed in Isidor Thorner, "German Words, German Personality and Protestantism," *Psychiatry*, VIII (1945), 403–17.

The Hopi illustrations are taken from Benjamin Lee Whorf, "Science and Linguistics," *Technology Review*, XLII (1940), 229–31 and 247–48; reprinted also in his *Four Articles on Metalinguistics* (Washington, D.C.: Foreign Service Institute, Department of State, 1949). Whorf was a remarkable scholar, an insurance man who took up linguistics as a hobby and became expert even to the point of trying to crack the hard nut of Maya hieroglyphics.

The availability of intonation in English for complex semantic innuendo (since frequency is not much used in it either lexically or grammatically) is brilliantly shown in a naughty popular song of some years ago. In this the mere words "John" and "Marcia," inflected intonationally, produced the whole phatic drama of "the way of a man with a maid."

The Aymara examples are from my own field notes for *The Aymara Indians of the Lake Titicaca Plateau, Bolivia* ("Memoirs of the American Anthropological Association," No. 68 [1948]).

CHAPTER 11

AND GETS ALL BALLED UP IN HIS GRAMMAR (PP. 187–207)

This chapter owes much to B. L. Whorf's paper on "The Relation of Habitual Thought and Behavior to Language," in Leslie Spier, A. Irving Hallowell, and Stanley S. Newman (eds.), *Language, Culture, and Personality: Essays in Memory of Edward Sapir* (Menasha, Wis.: Sapir Memorial Publication Fund, 1941), pp. 75–93; also reprinted in Whorf's *Four Articles on Metalinguistics*. Another important paper is by Charles Hockett, "Biophysics, Linguistics, and the Unity of the Universe," *American Scientist*, XXXVI (1948), 558–72. Herskovits, in *Man and His Works*, p. 27, also has some interesting remarks, based on Cassirer.

The term "phatic" I borrow from Malinowski—his Supplement I to C. K. Ogden and I. A. Richards, *The Meaning of Meaning* (2d rev. ed.; New York: Harcourt, Brace & Co., 1927), pp. 296–336, esp. 315. I wish particularly to acknowledge the source of my term because I regard the evolutionist naïveté of the remainder of Malinowski's essay as mostly nonsense, linguistically, psychologically, psychiatrically, and anthropologically. My understanding of the matter derives from putting the primatological facts adduced by Boutan and others side by side with the linguistic insights of Edward Sapir. But, before these, both Rousseau and Vico had the concept of human speech as arising from animal sounds of a merely emotional character. These men, however, got the notion from Lucretius and Epicurus, and they in turn from Democritus. I do not know where Democritus got the idea.

Kalispel, an Indian language of Washington state, differentiates between a verb and a noun as far as form is concerned. But many ["]things["] we apperceive as nouns they insist grammatically are verbs processing, eventing [themselves]. The Kalispel noun designates persons, animals, and man-made objects only; but things in nature, such as island, lake, creek, mountain, or tree, are verbs: "Treeing here, there the path creeked and laked; beyond, it mountained" (H. Vogt, *The Kalispel Language* [Oslo: Norske Videnskaps Akademi, 1940], p. 30).

Karlgren's various scholarly works are largely responsible for the traditional notion in Western linguistics that Chinese is a rigorously isolating and monosyllabic language. His case has perhaps been overstated, as is shown by John de Francis, *Nationalism and Language Reform in China* (Princeton, N.J.: Princeton University Press, 1950), chaps. vii and viii.

On mathematics as a cultural construct see Leslie A. White, "The Locus of Mathematical Reality," *Philosophy of Science*, XIV (1947), 289–303; reprinted also in his book *The Science of Culture: A Study of Man and Civilization* (New York: Farrar, Strauss & Co., 1949).

The Hopi and Shawnee examples are from Whorf's *Four Essays in Metalinguistics;* see also C. F. Voegelin, *Shawnee Stems,* and the Jacob P. Dunn, *Miami Dictionary* ("Prehistory Research Series, Indiana Historical Society," Vol. I, Nos. 3, 5, 8, 9, 10 [January, 1938–August, 1940]). Joe Blow, the GI linguist, is a figment of my imagination: the real fellow was too busy using his rifle to discuss it semantically. The Navaho materials come from my own, I believe accurate, notes taken in Sapir's graduate course in Navaho.

Indo-European originally had a rich system of verbal aspects and three modes, in addition to the categories of active and medium voice, i.e., action undertaken in the interest of the subject, viz., quasi-reflexives (A. Meillet, *Introduction à l'étude comparative des langues indo-européens* [7th ed.; Paris: Hachette, 1934]). Greek verbs like the aorist are more aspects than tenses. In one daughter dialect, English, these are all lost entirely, save for the ghost of a subjunctive in old fashionedly literate speech and writing. And, yet, in the "vulgar" Southern Piedmont dialect a new set of modal auxiliaries is appearing. I have recorded a kind of double optative ("The train *should ought* to be here soon"), future-potentive ("You can ask him; he *might could* do it"); potential-future ("It *might will* rain"), inceptive ("I was *just fixing to* tell you"), obligative ("She didn't *had to* say that!"), and the almost-but-not-quite auxiliary in several tenses ("I *like to die* laughing. Law, was she mad! She *like to killed* us all messing with that old gun"). Southern Piedmont also retains the old Indo-European "ethical dative"—"I get time, I'm gonna fish *me* a mess of bass."

CHAPTER 12

WHY MAN IS HUMAN (PP. 208–32)

The quotation is from Sigmund Freud, *An Outline of Psychoanalysis* (New York: W. W. Norton & Co., 1949), p. 27, n. 6—but this very condensed book is not the best introduction to his ideas. After reading his basic work on dreams and his earlier introduction to psychoanalysis, the reader is invited to go on to *The Ego and the Id* (1942), *Group Psychology and the Analysis of the Ego* (1940), *Civilization and Its Discontents* (1939), and *Beyond the Pleasure Principle* (1922). This last, which I first read in wartime Calcutta, I find a particularly enchanting book. In these non-clinical works, Freud is an especially lucid writer: on their basis, Thomas Mann, who ought to know, said that Freud was a stylist of European stature. The best single comprehensive work on the whole field, of course, is by Otto Fenichel, *The Psychoanalytic Theory of Neurosis* (New York: W. W. Norton & Co., 1945), but this fine work requires extensive preparatory reading for the greatest profit from it. Fenichel had an incomparable knowledge of a vast literature; in years of use and reference I have found no major paper left uncited in his magnificent bibliography. The interested reader will find of much value the excellent annotated bibliography in P. M. Symonds, *The Dynamics of Human Adjustment* (New York: D. Appleton–Century Co., 1946).

The basic insights of this chapter come from an anthropologist's re-reading of *Totem and Taboo*. I owe most of my understanding in this area to Edward Sapir and John Dollard, of Yale, and to George Ham, of the University of North Carolina. But I am also indebted to my colleague, M. J. Herskovits (*Man and His Works*, pp. 234 and 268), and to my teacher, Clark Wissler (*Man and Culture* [New York: Thomas Y. Crowell Co., 1923], pp. 260 and 265), for stimulating incidental passages in their books that I have been turning over in my mind for years. My emphasis on the nuclear family is also shared by G. P. Murdock, Clyde Kluckhohn, and others, in recently published papers.

Margaret Mead's argument about the cultural origins of tertiary sexual characteristics is best shown in her book *Sex and Temperament in Three Primitive Societies* (New York: William Morrow & Co., 1935). A good summary of relevant ethnographic variants is Georgene Seward's *Sex and the Social Order* (New York: Mc-Graw-Hill Book Co., 1946). The best anthology of essays in culture-and-personality is Douglas Haring (ed.), *Personal Character and Cultural Milieu* (3d ed.; Syracuse, N.Y.: University of Syracuse Press).

On *Ceratias holboelli,* see E. Bertelsen, *The Ceratioid Fishes: Ontogeny, Taxonomy, Distribution and Biology* ("Dana Reports," No. 39 [Copenhagen, 1941]).

I am understandably proud of my former graduate student, Dr. Jack Randolph Conrad, who took a few sentences in the last paragraph of the footnote on page 220 and developed them into a doctoral dissertation which, moreover, achieved commercial publication: *The Horn and the Sword: The History of the Bull as Symbol of Power and Fertility* (New York: E. P. Dutton & Co., 1957).

"The Relation of the Poet to Day-Dreaming" is an interesting essay by Freud (*Collected Papers,* IV, 173–83).

H. Vaihinger's *The Philosophy of "As If"* (New York: Harcourt, Brace & Co., 1925) is a nourishing book for the general reader.

I admire the paper of Leslie White on "The Locus of Mathematical Reality." But I am in fundamental disagreement with Dr. White in his vehement and repeated rejection of the importance of psychology and psychiatry to an understanding of man and of culture. A clear résumé of the geometries of Bolyai, Riemann, and Lobachevski may be found in J. W. Young, *Fundamental Concepts of Algebra and Geometry* (New York: Macmillan Co., 1930).

The "culture and personality" school in present-day American anthropology stems from Sapir, who early influenced both Mead and Benedict and who personally taught most of the leaders in the field. A good historical résumé is Clyde Kluckhohn's paper on "The Influence of Psychiatry on Anthropology in America during the Past One Hundred Years," in *One Hundred Years of American Psychiatry,* ed. J. K. Hall, G. Zilboorg, and H. A. Bunker (New York: Columbia University Press, 1944). The existing literature is now enormous. The general reader is referred to the useful anthologies of Clyde Kluckhohn and Henry A. Murray (cited above, in the notes to chap. 2) and of Douglas G. Haring (ed.), *Personal Character and Cultural Milieu* (Syracuse, N.Y.: Syracuse University Press, 1949). In Kluckhohn and Murray, the articles in particular of Frank, Ruesch, Erikson, Parsons, Alexander, Fromm, Benedict, Dollard, and Mead are widely recognized as classics.

It may be that "civilization" itself, technically considered, is related ultimately to the lengthening of human infancy: the disciplining of adult maleness and femaleness to the biological needs of children not only develops skills and foresights and providences that are the seed of the material arts on which human life depends but also constitutes the origin of human morality. If so, then love and parenthood are the most potent civilizing influences of all; for though the moralities and the interdependencies thus developed do finally extend beyond the family, they had their origin in the family. The bending of adult strengths to the service first of immature individuals and then of other adults is evidently an adaptation that enhances survival. A "civilization" (defined as subcultures specialized within a larger society) may consequently have still greater survival value than a single uniform tribal culture. But even here the pattern of functional co-operation of diversities is *initially rooted in the human family,* which already, characteristically, has economic specialization of labor by sex.

CHAPTER 13

AND PEOPLE SOMETIMES SICK (PP. 233–66)

My major debt here is to the remarkable and almost unknown book of Géza Róheim, *The Origin and Function of Culture* (New York: Nervous & Mental Disease Publishing Co., 1943), esp. pp. 77–82 and 93. It is a gratification to me that my essay on "Family and Symbol," a summary of the present book, was included in his *Festschrift* as homage before he died. Both Róheim and I owe much to Sandor Ferenczi, *Thalassa: A Theory of Genitality* (New York: Psychoanalytic Quarterly, Inc., 1938), which I find an intoxicating book. My ideas on schizophrenia obviously owe something also to the early work of Jung. But my most conscious source of thinking on schizophrenia is clear to me: years of sitting on doctoral dissertation committees in psychology, as a representative of the candidate's minor department, and being repeatedly near "blowing a gasket" at their not seeing the plain and beautiful implications of their often fine experimental work. Gentlemen, wherever you are, I salute you!

My caution in excluding Japan from the large Asiatic area in which the snake is a culture-wide phallic symbol is dictated by a paper by M. E. Opler, "Japanese Folk Belief concerning the Snake," in the *Southwestern Journal of Anthropology,* I (1945), 249–59, in which the snake seems to symbolize the jealous or envious woman. But I am not wholly convinced. Women with snakes for hair (p. 252) are no problem at all symbolically (see Ferenczi, "On the Symbolism of the Head of the Medusa" in *Further Contributions,* p. 360; see also Freud, *Collected Papers,* II, 287). Also, people with a pit (as from smallpox) behind the ear or with a depression in the lobe of the ear are believed to have power over snakes, which turn limp at their touch (Opler, p. 256). And a tale told to girls, to prevent the unladylike behavior of taking a nap in the fields, is that there are certain snakes that go easily into women's genitalia, but cannot be pulled out because of their scales (pp. 255–56). These seem to me just possibly phallic symbolisms.

My sole acquaintance with the fern flower is in Friedrich Lorentz, Adam Fischer, and Tadeusz Lehr-Spławiński, *The Cassubian Civilization* (New York: Faber & Faber, 1935), pp. 97 and 265–66.

The Standardization of Error is a wry and edifying essay by Vilhjalmur Stefansson (New York: W. W. Norton & Co., 1927).

The data on sparganosis come from a British Admiralty handbook on *Indo-China* ("Geographical Handbook Series," B.R. No. 510 [Naval Intelligence Division, 1943]), pp. 119–20, which I hope is not now classified information.

The Dinka data are from C. G. and B. Z. Seligman, *Pagan Tribes of the Nilotic Sudan* (New York: Humanities Press, 1950), p. 144.

Polynesian poop fins are discussed in Linton's *Study of Man*, pp. 272–73.

Koryak dog-sacrifice is described in W. Jochelson, *The Koryak* ("Papers of the Jesup North Pacific Expedition," Vol. VI [1908]).

Incidentally, a great many intelligent readers would find general ethnography exhilarating reading, if they only knew where to get good books. Here is a random sheaf of them as a lagniappe:

G. P. Murdock. *Our Primitive Contemporaries*. New York: Macmillan Co., 1938.

R. Kennedy. *The Ageless Indies*. New York: John Day Co., 1942.

K. S. LaTourette. *The Chinese, Their History and Culture*. New York: Macmillan Co., 1943.

C. Osgood. *The Koreans and Their Culture*. New York: Ronald Press Co., 1951.

A. B. Lewis. *The Melanesians: The People of the South Pacific*. Chicago: Museum of Natural History, 1945.

R. Linton. *Ethnology of Polynesia and Micronesia*. ("Chicago Museum of Natural History Guide Series," No. 6). Chicago, 1926.

E. E. Sikes. *The Anthropology of the Greeks*. London: David Nutt, 1941.

P. K. Hitti. *The Arabs: A Short History*. Princeton, N.J.: Princeton University Press, 1944.

C. Wissler's *The American Indian* (New York: Oxford University Press, 1922) is good on North American Indians but out of date on South America because of the voluminous work of younger ethnographers. Ralph Linton (ed.), *Most of the World* (New York: Columbia University Press, 1949), covers Africa, Latin America, and the East. *Primitive Heritage*, edited by Margaret Mead and Nicolas Calas (New York: Random House, 1953), is a colorful collection of firsthand accounts which recapture the naïveté and wonder of early contact with "unspoiled" peoples, but it should not be read uncritically. An excellent general book is Clyde Kluckhohn, *Mirror for Man* (New York: Whittlesey House, 1949). On anthropological theory, I still find R. H. Lowie's *The History of Ethnological Theory* (New York: Farrar & Rinehart, 1937) sound, though stuffy on modern psychiatrically oriented anthropology. Of course, the best dissection of our own society still remains Thorstein Veblen's *Theory of the Leisure Class* (New York: Modern Library, 1934). In the same fine old Veblenian tradition of scholarly rowdiness—and influence on practical government—we have T. W. Arnold, *The Folklore of Capitalism* (New Haven, Conn.: Yale University Press, 1937) and *The Symbols of Government* (New Haven, Conn.: Yale University Press, 1935).

Kekulé von Stradonitz's dream and its circumstances are described in E. J. Holmyard, "Dyestuffs in the Nineteenth Century," in Singer, Holmyard, and Hall (eds.), *op. cit.*, Vol. V, p. 275.

CHAPTER 14

Superstition and the Soul (pp. 267–302)

It is evidently impossible to cite all the sources on metaphysical animism and ghost belief that have been gathered in a quarter-century of reading of speculative philosophy and other tribal folklore. But some general background might be suggested. First of all, read Plato. For he is, beyond doubt, the major source of metaphysical animism in the Great Tradition of Western philosophy. I am free to state also that Plato is my favorite enemy: it seems to me that he has managed to be more consistently wrong on all questions from physical science to politics and from ethics to education than almost any other philosopher. That is why he is so indispensable. Everyone should get a good attack of Plato in his youth and then recover from it as experience of the world gradually confers a life-immunity.

As a mine of information, nothing touches *The Golden Bough*, even if only the one-volume edition (New York: Macmillan Co., 1930) is available to the reader. No one is ever seriously harmed by the faults of Frazer's ethnological method, and his work has added permanently to our insights into magic and religion. Equally basic is Freud's essay on *The Future of an Illusion* (London: Hogarth Press, 1949). This is a shocking book, and only the tough-minded can take it, but it is an intellectual emancipation. Erich Fromm's *Escape from Freedom* (New York: Farrar & Rinehart, 1941) is in the same hard-bitten tradition.

If the student has a serious interest in the study of religion, there is no doubt that his best ethnographic source is India, which has the longest continuous development of a well-documented religious tradition, always changing and always the same. The four *Vedas* give a view of the beginnings of the markedly compulsive strain in Indic religion and a glimpse of the Aryan sources of a caste society. The *Jatakas* are folk tales of the Buddha's incarnations; the *Puranas*, folk cosmology and myths of heroes and gods (especially of the Hinduist Shiva and Vishnu), are equally important to know thoroughly. Only the most resolute scholar ever plows through the *Brahmanas* or priestly commentaries; and five or six dozen of the principal *Upanishads,* the windy source of yogin metaphysics, is about all most people are able to take. The *Mahabharata,* legendary tales of dynastic struggles plus much interpolated material, is too long for anyone but the specialist to read. More important is the *Ramayana,* the great epic poem which is the basic oedipal drama of the whole Indic culture-area. It is hard to convey a proper impression to Westerners of the significance of the hero Rama, his faithful wife Sita, the demon-king Ravana, and the monkey-god savior Hanuman: every peasant in the immense triangle from Kashmir to Cambodia to Ceylon knows its episodes by heart. Perhaps only Homer's epics in fifth-century Greece approached it in everyday reference in all walks of life. Contained in the *Mahabharata* is the short *Bhagavat-Gita,* which most readers decide is either the most sublime or the most asinine poem ever written.

For an early, firsthand ethnographic account I like the Abbé Dubois's *Hindu Manners, Customs and Ceremonies,* ed. Beauchamp (3d ed.; London: Oxford University Press, 1943), which gives us India as a by no means unsympathetic man saw it, and before the genteelism of European-educated Indians explained it all away. H. G. Rawlinson's *A Concise History of the Indian People* (London: Oxford University Press, 1940) is still, I think, the best in its area. For a solid cultural background, *The Cambridge History of India,* Vol. I, edited by E. J. Rapson, is quite without a peer in usefulness. *The Cultural Heritage of India* (3 vols.; Calcutta: Sri Ramakrishna Centenary Committee, n.d.) is extraordinarily uneven in its hundred contributors, but among them are some good articles. A. Barth, *The Religions of India,* trans. J. Wood (6th ed.; London: Kegan Paul, Trench, Trubner & Co., 1932), is a little dated in some respects but still the best short summary I know.

Lowell's false etymology of "superstition" is to be found in James Russell Lowell, *Among My Books, First Series* (Boston: Houghton Mifflin Co., 1870), p. 92.

Sir Edward Tylor's "minimum definition" of religion is in his *Primitive Culture* (2 vols.; 1st American from 2d English ed.; New York: Henry Holt

& Co., 1874), I, 424–27. Now also in New York: Harper Torchbooks, #34, 1958.

A very interesting paper is Alfred C. Andrews on "The Bean and Indo-European Totemism," *American Anthropologist,* LI (1949), 274–92. Because the insight is so new and unusual, Dr. Andrews has perhaps been a little overmodest about his striking evidence. I believe that his case is even better than he thinks.

The classic examination by a psychologist of the mystic experience is William James, *The Varieties of Religious Experience* (New York: Longmans, Green & Co., 1952). His views are now standard opinion on the matter.

On lemur size and sociability see M. F. Ashley Montagu, "On the Relation between Body Size, Waking Activity, and the Origin of Social Life in the Primates," *American Anthropologist,* XLVI (1944), 141–45. On the cathexis of vision see George Devereux, "A Note on Nyctophobia and Peripheral Vision," *Bulletin of the Menninger Clinic,* XIII (1949), 83–93. Both of these are papers of great originality and insight.

On childhood animism the best documentation is Jean Piaget, *The Child's Conception of the World* (New York: Harcourt, Brace & Co., 1929). His observations and conclusions, so far as he goes, are identical with those of child analysts.

Since peyote is such an interesting subject and since peyotism is the major religious cult of contemporary American Indians, perhaps I may be allowed to refer to my monograph on the subject, *The Peyote Cult* ("Yale University Publications in Anthropology," No. 19 [New Haven, Conn.: Yale University Press, 1938]), reprint New Haven, Conn.: Shoe String Press, 1960.

CHAPTER 15

THREE MINUTES TO MIDNIGHT (PP. 303–34)

My text for this chapter is the *Congressional Record* and any good daily newspaper.

My view of the importance of multiple neoteny in the human animal derives from a putting-together of Bolk's anthropological interpretations and Huxley's biological understandings along with the astonishing psychiatric insights of Sandor Ferenczi in *Thalassa,* which to me is a book of almost breath-taking brilliance.

The fatal step of Rome was taken in 390 B.C.

At one crisis—the sacking of Rome by roving Gauls in 390 B.C.—the Latin cities failed to aid her; they suggested federation, and Rome made up her mind that safety lay only in their conquest. At great self-sacrifice she reduced them to obedience, and then went forward as tribe after tribe appealed to her for aid, and eventually for alliance and the extension of her *"rights"* to their cities [R. H. Barrow, *The Romans* (Baltimore: Pelican Books, 1949), p. 33].

Some readers have asked why a man who admires "new styles of architecture" could admire so positively the Parthenon as "the most subtle and intellectual edifice ever made by man." It will take me two more books to explain this fully. Meanwhile, those interested may study the discoveries summarized in good old Banister Fletcher, *A History of Architecture on the Comparative Method* (8th ed.; New York: Scribner's, 1928), which I quote without his cross-references.

Many refinements were practised in the great period of Greek art, in order to correct optical illusions. The long horizontal lines of such features as stylobates, architraves, and cornices, which, if straight in reality, would appear to sag or drop in the middle of their length, were formed with slightly convex outlines. Mr. Penrose discovered that, in the Parthenon, the stylobate has an upward curvature towards its centre of 2.61 ins. on the east and west façades, and of 4.39 ins. on the lateral façades. Vertical features were also inclined inwards towards the top to correct the appearance of falling outwards; thus, in the Parthenon, the axes of the angle columns lean inwards 2.65 ins., and the axes of all the columns, if produced, would meet at a distance of a mile above the ground. The shafts of the Parthenon columns have an entasis of about ¾ in. in a height of 34 feet, and columns of other temples are similarly treated. Angle columns were not only set closer to the adjacent columns, but were also stouter, as it was found that they appeared thinner against the open sky than those seen against the solid background of the "naos" wall. Pennethorne points out a further correction in use in an inscription from the Temple of Priene, where, according to Vitruvius, Bk. VI, chap. ii, the letters at the top of the inscription were increased in size, and the letters at the lower part decreased, so that they might all appear of one size from the point of sight below [p. 71].

Great artifice in the temple of The Goddess! And, yet, this correcting of the rigid literalness of straight lines with subtle curves to delight the eye of man, this editing of nature for man's sake, expresses (so I think) both the essence of art and the essential *ethos* of Greek humanism—quite as well as does that seductive phrase of the philosopher Protagoras, "Man is the measure of all things." Or consider the breath-catching frieze of the Parthenon, lumbering off with slow carts and oxen; quickening then to swifter pace around the sides with walking men; now reaching great excitement, grace, and movement, with young men on prancing horses—and then, suddenly, around the corner to the tympanum, to the serene grandeur of the static, seated majesty of the Olympians! In this, Phidias tells the whole theology of the Greeks and their *aretē* and *hubris,* and no classic tragedy expresses better both the sameness and the vast differences between the immortal gods and mortal man, in this counterpoint of stasis and crescendoed movement. This is music, in Pentelic marble.

Marx himself, in his *Eighteenth Brumaire,* states quite clearly that "men make their own history, but not spontaneously in conditions chosen by them, but on the contrary, in conditions which they have ready to hand transmitted and given." This is an unexceptionable statement on the face of it; but when "conditions" verge upon being the Hegelian reification and deification of History, then it becomes metaphysical nonsense.

The Society of Atomic Scientists will not mind, I am sure, my borrowing as a title for this chapter the striking metaphor on the cover of their *Bulletin.*

Two books all well-read Americans should know: R. H. Barrow, *The Romans* (Baltimore: Pelican Books, 1951), gives us a comprehensive view of the contribution this great people made to European culture; and, as befits all civilized men, Professor H. D. F. Kitto is an enthusiastic partisan of *The Greeks* (Baltimore: Pelican Books, 1951). The only other people whose formative influence on us has been as great as theirs is the Jews, and they are best known from the greatest human textbook of them all, the Old Testament.

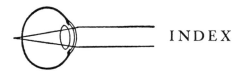 INDEX

Dart, R. A., 346, 356
Darwin, C., 244, 294
Daughter-in-law, 118
Deafness, 166
Death, 9, 273, 287–91, 297 n., 302, 307
Defense mechanism, 240, 246
Deformation of body, 157, 256
de Francis, J., 362
"Delay of the machine age," 228
Democracy, 147, 225, 229, 239, 311, 315, 318–20, 327–28, 331
Democritus, 361
Dependency, 21, 41, 45, 49–54, 101–2, 104–8, 124–25, 155–56, 161, 163, 209, 214–15, 219, 222, 255, 259, 294, 305–6, 316, 320, 352–53
Depéret's law, 84, 357
Descent, 113; see also Matrilineal descent; Patrilineal descent
Descent of man, 69–84
Devereux, G., xvi, 281–82, 369
Devil, 297 n.
Devolution, 134; see also Fetalization; Infantilization; Neoteny; Paedomorphy
Diet
    of chimpanzee, 64, 84
    of gibbon, 57
    of gorilla, 67–68, 84
    of man, 32, 83, 147–48, 160, 346–49; see also Food
Diffusion, 238, 247, 260, 314, 316
Dimorphism
    in birds, 106–7
    in chimpanzee, 59, 63
    in gibbon, 56, 75
    in man, 75–76, 102, 107, 209, 276; see also Female; Male
    in orang, 59
Dinka (Africa), 241–43, 366
Dinosaurs, 19, 22–25, 31, 71–73, 86, 89, 338
Diogenes, 58
Diplomacy, 58, 311–14, 324–26
Dipodomys, 45, 89, 213, 342
Diringer, D., 359
Disciplines by males in chimpanzees, 63–64
"Divine right of kings," 315
Doberman pinscher, 143–44
Dobzhansky, T., 82, 357
Dog, 26, 31, 36, 38–39, 48, 75, 100, 124, 145–46, 156, 158, 220 n., 238, 242–43, 252, 258, 284, 300, 317, 358
Dollard, J., 363, 364
Domestication

in animals, 31, 39, 48, 99–100, 143–46, 158, 220 n., 238, 258, 284, 358
in insects, 47–49
in man, 99, 107, 131, 134, 145–47, 149, 155–58, 162, 167, 229–31, 258–59, 284, 304, 306, 310, 326, 355
Dominance in chimpanzees, 60–61
Dragon, 205, 234, 336
Dream, 170, 244, 272, 277–79, 282, 284, 295, 302
Dryopithecus, 42, 82–83, 341
Dual number, 194–95
Dubois, Abbé, 368
Dunbar, C. O., 336
Dunn, J. P., 362
Durkheim, É., 322–23

Eagles, 35
Earth, 159
Eating, 163–64; see also Diet; Food
Echidna, 20, 50
Ecology, xiv, 42–45, 147–48, 238, 346, 349, 351, 353–57
Economics, 117–19, 221, 225, 227–29, 232, 316–19, 330
Ectoparasitism, 21, 51–52, 255
Edentata, 25
Eggs, 18–19, 27, 32, 50–51, 148, 290, 299
Ego boundaries, 235, 285, 300, 332
Egyptians, 125
Einstein, A., xii, 205, 262, 301
Einstein's equation, 205, 237, 262, 277, 302, 307
Einstein's law of photo-chemical equivalence, 341
Elephant, 24–27, 30–32, 52, 76, 81, 84, 86, 236, 350
Embryology, 8–9
Empire, 314–16
Empty word, 189–91, 202
Endoparasitism, 21, 51, 255
Endoskeleton, 159–60
Eng, 185–86
English language, 175–86, 188–90, 192–204, 359, 361, 362
Englishmen, 54, 176–77, 237, 356
Environment, xiv, 3–4, 7, 9, 13, 19, 23, 28, 31, 38, 41–45, 130, 139, 147–49, 159, 166–67, 171, 223, 238, 242, 245, 258–59, 283–84, 290, 306–7, 336, 358
Environmentalism, 139–40, 351, 355
Epicanthic fold, 153, 304

Hottentot (Africa), 146, 153, 182, 238
Howell, F. C., 346, 349
Howells, W., 339, 340
Hubris, 311–12, 325–26, 329, 332
Hughes, A. R., 346
Hulse, F. S., 335
Human biology, x, xvi, 134, 349, 357
Human nature, xiii–xiv, 219, 237
Hume, D., 206, 315
Hunting, 42–43, 48, 93, 123, 144, 157, 227, 243, 341, 345–49, 351, 357
Huron Indians (N.A.), 123 n.
Hutchinson, G. E., 337
Huxley, J,, xvi, 38, 159, 336, 341, 344, 346, 351, 357, 359, 369
Hyaena, 346
Hydra, 8, 10, 12, 17, 32, 46
Hysteria, 283–85

Icelandic, 176
Iconic signs, 343
Id, 220, 283
Iliad, 313
Immortality, 70, 230, 287–92, 295
Inca Indians (S.A.), 125
Incest taboo, 121–30, 207, 211, 214, 294, 305, 351, 354
Incisors, 137–38, 148
India, 220 n., 367–68
Indians, American; *see* American Indians
Individual, 329–30
Indo-Chinese, 240–41, 249
Indo-European, 172, 175–76, 188, 192–94, 198, 206, 273–74, 276, 300–301, 313, 360, 362
Industrial Revolution, 356
Infantilization, xv, 29, 52, 105, 150–56, 160, 166–67, 209, 272, 283, 288, 293, 304–7, 309–10, 323; *see also* Fetalization; Neoteny; Paedomorphy
Influencing machine, 277
Initiation, 212–13
Insectivora, 20, 26, 73
Insects, 14, 16–18, 20–21, 23, 26, 46–50, 69–70, 104, 147, 220 n., 229, 308–9, 337, 348
"Inside," 2–4, 171, 235–36, 261–62, 300, 321
Instinct, 32–34, 44, 46–47, 77, 124–28, 160, 167, 209–10, 216, 219, 258–59, 308–10
"Institutionalized unmarriage," 119–21
Institutions, 220–21
Intellectual, 228, 260–65

Intelligence
  in chimpanzees, 64
  in gorilla, 64
  in man, 260–65; *see also* Brain; Mind
Inter-breeding; *see* Cross-breeding
Invention, 4, 20, 50, 219, 236, 239–40, 245
Iranians; *see* Persians
Italian, 174, 194
Italians, 138, 192

Jabbo, 180
James, W., 369
Janus, 235
Japanese, 171, 341, 360, 365
Jaw, 14–15, 39, 65–66, 68, 72, 76–80, 136, 150–51, 154, 304
Jealousy, 111
Jehovah, 274, 294
Jerboa, 72–73
Jespersen, O., 347
Jews, 137, 182, 327, 355
Jochelson, W., 366
Joe Blow, 200–202, 362
Joe Blow-Snake, 202–3
Jones, E., xvi, 339
Jones, F. Wood, 340, 352–53
Joyce, J., 261, 264
Jung, C. G., 365
Jus primae noctis, 112–13

Kahioi, 120–21
Kahn, F., 341, 344
Kaingang Indians (S.A.), 111
Kalahari Bushmen (Africa), 130
Kalispel, 362
Kandyans (Singhalese), 156
Kangaroo, 27, 72–73
Kangaroo rat, 45, 89, 213, 342
Kant, I., 206, 301
Karlgren, B., 362
Kava, 120
Keith, A., 82, 152, 154, 357
Kekulé von Stradonitz, F. A., 244, 367
Kempf, E. J., 103–4, 352
Kennedy, R., 366
Kidney, 12, 32, 160, 340, 359
Kinsey, A., 111
Kinship, 109, 122, 125–26, 129–30, 353
Kiowa Indians (N.A.), 156, 181
Kitto, H. D. F., 371
Klaatsch, H., 82, 104, 352
Kluckhohn, C., 339, 352–53, 360, 363, 367
Knee, 74
Knopf, A., 336

Mathematicians, 233–34, 301
Matrilineal descent, 113, 126, 129
Matter, 3–4, 275–76, 296; see also *Materia*
Maya Indians (Mexico), 361
Mead, M., 216, 363, 364
Meganthropus paleojavanicus, 147, 357
Meillet, A., 362
Melanesians, 139–40, 158, 195, 366
Melville, H., 261, 290
Memory, 272, 295, 302
Menstruation, 61, 102–3
Mental illness, xv, 233–66, *see also* Hysteria; Manic-depression; Paranoia; Psychopath; Schizophrenia
Mentawei (Indonesia), 117
Metazoan, 8–14, 52, 70, 156, 158–60, 273, 289–90, 338
Microcosm, 296, 299, 320–21
Micronesians, 328, 336
Middle Ages, 140–41
Migrations, 93–95, 356
Militarism, 309–10, 312–15; *see also* War
Miller, N., 354
Milne, L. J., 341
Milne, M. J., 341
Mind, 295, 298, 302; *see also* Brain; Intelligence
Missing link, 83
Moa, 69, 72
Moby Dick, 261
Mokusatsu, 171, 360
Mollusks, 13–17, 19, 24, 231
Moltke, H. von, 314
Mongoloids, 93–94, 136–39, 148, 151, 153–57, 304
Mongols, 228
Monkeys, 29, 31, 34, 52–54, 57, 60–63, 66, 81, 86–87, 92, 100–101, 111, 152–53, 340, 343, 346, 347, 351, 360
Monogamy, 56, 67, 109–11, 117, 119, 207
Morality, 134, 188, 213, 221–24, 229–32, 291, 295, 346, 365
Morgan, L., 129
Morphophonemes, 185–86
Moslems, 112, 114–15
Mother, 29, 33, 40, 45–46, 56–57, 62–63, 99, 101, 104–9, 118, 122–25, 129, 167, 209–11, 213–17, 254–56, 259, 305, 330, 340
Motherhood, xv, 44–46, 54, 62–63, 101
Mother's brother, 113, 116
Mount Carmel finds, 96
Mouse, 25–26, 75–76

Mouth, 10, 12, 14–15, 17, 39, 87–88, 163–64, 169, 207, 299, 350
Mucous membranes, 105
Mueller, H. J., 341
Muensterberger, W., 353, 354
Murdock, G. P., 112, 353, 354, 363, 366
Murray, H. A., 339, 352–53, 364
Muscae volitantes, 280
Music, 221
Mycenaeans, 313
Myopia, 341

Nambutiri Brahmans (India), 113, 120
Napoleon, 225, 314–15
Nationalism in anthropology, 81–82
Natural selection, 144–45, 149, 231, 248, 267, 310, 347–48, 351, 356
Navaho Indians (N.A.), 175, 181–82, 195, 198–99, 201, 362
Nayars (India), 112–13
Naziism, 240, 288
Neanderthal man, 54, 81–82, 101, 135–36, 347, 349
Neck, 65–66, 80
Negroes, 102, 112, 237, 239, 250, 357
Negroids, 136–40, 146–47, 153–57
Neolithic; *see* New Stone Age
Neoteny, 303–34, 357; *see also* Fetalization; Infantilization; Paedomorphy
Nerves, 12, 24, 88, 95–96, 160
Nesting
  in birds, 32–33, 90, 99
  in primates, 32–34, 56, 59–60, 67
Neuroses, 269; *see also* Mental illness
New Guinea, 123 n.
New Stone Age., 48, 227, 352
Newman, M. T., 356
Newton, I., 204
Nickel, 172–73
Nilotics, 43–44, 74, 147, 355–56
Nissen, H. W., 343
Nordics, 137–39, 146, 154, 158, 304
Nose, 137–38, 153, 299, 350
Notochord, 11, 17
Noun, 188–90, 196, 199, 205, 234, 301
Number, 188–89, 192, 194–96, 199, 201, 203
Nutrition, 160; *see also* Diet; Food
Nyabonga, Prince Hosea Akiki, 117

Oakley, K. P., 342, 347
Octopus, 13–14
Odyssey, 313
Oedipal phenomena, 157–58, 161, 213, 220–21, 225, 235, 257, 261–62,

294–95, 310, 316, 318–19, 332, 354, 368
Oedipus, 208
Oedipus complex, 122, 354
Oertzen, J. von, 68, 343
Oestrus, 61, 102–3
Ogden, C. K., 174, 361
Old Stone Age, 48, 54, 93, 101, 147, 227, 272, 351, 356
Olivier, L., 181
Omnipotence, 222–23, 257, 277–78, 319–23
Omniscience, 223, 225
Omnivorousness, 30, 32, 147–48
Opler, M. E., 365
Opossum, 27–28, 41
Oral zone, 88, 350, 359; see also Lips; Mouth
Orang-utan, 54–55, 58–61, 64, 66–67, 75, 82, 102, 164
Orchids, 289, 337
Original sin, 69–71, 294
Orthogenesis, 28, 79, 339
Osgood, C., 366
Ostracoderms, 13–15
Ostrich, 69, 72, 75, 91
Out-breeding, 82, 95, 97, 132, 143–44
"Outside," 2–4, 235–36, 256, 259, 261–62, 300, 321
Owls, 35–36
Oxygen, 159
Oysters, 13, 224

Paedomorphy, 151–56, 158, 224, 304, 307, 357, 358; see also Fetalization; Infantilization; Neoteny
Painting, 221
Palate, 78
Paleolithic; see Old Stone Age
Paleontology, x, 42, 336, 347, 350
Pan, 285, 297 n.
Panda, 147
Parallel cousins, 126
Paramecium, 6, 12, 17, 143, 338
Paranoia, 222–23, 225, 246–47, 249, 257, 267, 277, 282, 284, 288, 297, 319, 321, 330–32, see also Hubris
Parenthood, 63; see also Fatherhood; Motherhood
Parrot, 35
Parsons, T., 364
Parthenon, 312, 370
Parts of speech, 188–92, 196
Patagonians, 136, 147
Paternity, legal, 112–17, 210; see also Fatherhood; Patrilineal descent

Patrilineal descent, 113–14, 118, 126–29
"Peace of mind," 164, 239–42, 266, 288
Pecking order, 63, 220
Pecos Indians (N.A.), 102
Pediatricians, 63
Pekin man, 147
Pekinese dog, 39
Pelvis, 60, 71, 74–75, 77, 79–81, 87, 106–7
Peppercorn hair, 139, 146
Perigenesis, 290
Persians, 114, 122, 172, 176, 311, 354
Person, 188–89, 191, 194–96, 199, 201, 203
Personality, 115, 245, 330, 350, 351, 360, 363
Petit-Thouars, Captain Abel du, 354
Peyote, 286, 369
Phallic symbolism, 236, 274, 297 n., 298, 311, 265–66; see also Logos
Phatic communication, 57–58, 165–68, 187, 215, 235, 245, 247, 250, 252, 254–55, 261, 264, 306, 319, 331, 343, 348, 350, 361
Phidias, 371
Philosophers, 77, 174, 205, 262–63
Philosophy, 58, 194, 205–6, 221, 295–302, 332–33
Phlogiston, 275, 299
Phoenicians, 313
Phoenix, 205, 234
Phonemes, 180, 182–87, 300
Photosynthesis, 4–7
Physical anthropology, viii, x–xii, xiv, 142, 218, 252, 335, 337–38, 345, 358
Piaget, J., 356
Pidgin English, 189–90
Pigeon, homing, 337
Pigs, 26, 31, 100, 146, 177, 220 n., 258, 300
Pitch, 179, 181–82
Pithecanthropus erectus, 82, 141, 290
Placenta, 20–22, 25, 27, 51, 62, 73, 163
Plains Indians, 118, 130, 278, 286
Plants, 4–7, 30, 337
Plato, 104, 190, 202, 206, 218, 228, 262, 265, 287, 298–301, 311, 367
Platypus, 20, 50–51
Pleasure principle, 171, 245, 266, 278, 282, 363
Pleistocene Ice Age, 19, 30, 42–43, 83, 94, 97, 147–48
Pliny, 350
Plurals, 188–89, 194–95

Poet, 261–62, 264–65, 307, 312, 332, 364
Poetry, 58, 220–21
Politics, 58, 134, 166, 223–29, 232, 243, 310–34
Polyandry (plural husbands), 111
Polygamy (plural spouses), 100, 111, 117–18, 129, 189
Polygyny (plural wives), 112, 117–18, 129, 189
Polynesia, 111, 119–20, 185, 242–43, 366
Polytypicality, 132, 134–35, 142–44, 149
Pondo (Africa), 118
Poop fin, 242–43, 366
Population,
    of gibbons, 56
    of gorillas, 67–68
    of Paleolithic times, 54, 93
Porter, Captain David, 354
Potlach, 243
Pottery, 212
Pregnancy, 54, 75, 103, 153
Prehensility, 31, 33, 85–88, 340, 350
Preposition, 188, 202
Priest-kings, 119–20
Primates, xv, 22–68, 89, 101–3, 135–36, 147, 150, 156, 160–61, 165–66, 281–82, 338, 340, 342, 352
Prime minister, 120
"Primitive" traits, 135–38, 150, 155
Primogeniture, 113–14, 119–20
Prognathism, 135–36, 138, 150–51, 155
Prometheus, 222, 226, 333
Pronoun, 188, 190, 193, 200
Property-monogamy, 119
Prosthetic evolution, 133, 255–56; *see also* Alloplastic evolution
Protagoras, 370
Protozoans, 5–10, 17, 52, 70, 159, 161, 235, 289
Pseudo-copulation, 337
Psychiatrist, x–xi, xiv, 218, 235–36, 242, 248, 250–53, 354
Psychiatry, x–xi, 330, 333
Psychoanalysis, xii–xiii, 338, 351, 354, 363
Psychokinesis, 36–37
Psychologists, 218–19, 253, 258
Psychology, x–xii, xiv–xv, 111, 261, 342
Psychopath, 257
Psychosis, 170, 233, 243–47, 249–52, 255–62, 266, 278, 282, 284–86, 306
Pterodactyl, 31, 85, 177
Pueblo Indians (N.A.), 112
Puma, 355–56

Purpose, 1–4, 13, 28–29, 79, 161–62, 170, 174, 178, 223, 234–35, 251
Pygmies, 146–47
Pythagoreans, 276

Quakers, 193–94
Quantum, 36, 341
Quaternary, 83

Rabbits, 35, 100, 123, 146, 205
Race, vii, xii–xiii, xv, 82, 93–97, 132–62, 229–30, 239, 304, 351, 355–58
Radial evolution, 21–23, 26–27, 92, 132–34, 148–49, 305
Radio, 37–38
Rapson, E. J., 368
Rationalism, 263
Rationalization, 28, 157
Rats, 26, 336
Rawlinson, H. G., 368
Raymond, P. E., 336, 338
Reality, 29, 133, 171, 187–88, 200, 207, 220–21, 226, 229, 231, 233–36, 243–46, 248, 254, 258, 262, 265–66, 278, 283–84, 323
Reality principle, 171, 245, 266, 278
Regression, 266
Reindeer, 48, 114, 119
Religion, 220, 223, 242–43, 302, 323, 332–33, 356
Reproduction, 19–21, 46, 69–70, 99, 109
Reptile, 18–19, 22–27, 32, 36, 71–73, 86, 89, 99, 160, 229, 340–41
Respiration, 16–18, 70, 159; *see also* Lungs
Reticulation, 142–43, 149; *see also* Polytypicality
Rhea, 69, 72
Rhesus monkey, 54, 63, 152–53
Rhinoceros, 25–27, 146
Rhodopsin (visual purple), 36, 341
Richards, I. A., 174, 361
Riddell, W. J. B., 341
Riddle of the Sphinx, 208–9, 214–17, 222
Riemann, B., 231, 364
Rodentia, 26
Róheim, G., xvi, 343–44, 365
"Roman idea," 310–16, 326
Romans, 228, 263, 350, 369–70, 371
Rome, 311–14, 330, 369–70
Romer, A. S., 336
Round-headedness, 139, 344
Roundworms, 10–12, 17
Rousseau, J. J., 291, 361
Royalty, European, 125, 141–42

PHOENIX BOOKS
in Anthropology

PHOENIX BOOKS
in Archeology

PHOENIX BOOKS
in Sociology